D1760524

LIVERPOOL JMU LIBRARY

3 1111 01483 9086

TERRORISM BEFORE THE LETTER

Terrorism Before the Letter

Mythography and Political Violence in England, Scotland, and France 1559–1642

ROBERT APPELBAUM

OXFORD
UNIVERSITY PRESS

OXFORD
UNIVERSITY PRESS

Great Clarendon Street, Oxford, OX2 6DP,
United Kingdom

Oxford University Press is a department of the University of Oxford.
It furthers the University's objective of excellence in research, scholarship,
and education by publishing worldwide. Oxford is a registered trade mark of
Oxford University Press in the UK and in certain other countries

© Robert Appelbaum 2015

The moral rights of the author have been asserted

First Edition published in 2015

Impression: 1

All rights reserved. No part of this publication may be reproduced, stored in
a retrieval system, or transmitted, in any form or by any means, without the
prior permission in writing of Oxford University Press, or as expressly permitted
by law, by licence or under terms agreed with the appropriate reprographics
rights organization. Enquiries concerning reproduction outside the scope of the
above should be sent to the Rights Department, Oxford University Press, at the
address above

You must not circulate this work in any other form
and you must impose this same condition on any acquirer

Published in the United States of America by Oxford University Press
198 Madison Avenue, New York, NY 10016, United States of America

British Library Cataloguing in Publication Data
Data available

Library of Congress Control Number: 2015938234

ISBN 978–0–19–874576–1

Printed in Great Britain by
Clays Ltd, St Ives plc

Links to third party websites are provided by Oxford in good faith and
for information only. Oxford disclaims any responsibility for the materials
contained in any third party website referenced in this work.

To Marion

Acknowledgements

My first thanks must go to the British Academy, which provided a seed grant for my research into literature and terrorism, and especially to the Leverhulme Foundation, which provided me with 15 months' funding for research expenses and a research leave from teaching. The Wallenberg Foundation provided support as well, allowing me to spend several months at the Stellenbosch Institute for Advanced Studies, South Africa, where I completed the last draft but one of the manuscript.

The bulk of the original research for this book was conducted at the Bibliothèque Nationale de France, at the François Mitterand and Arsenal facilities in Paris. I am grateful for the assistance from the librarians at both facilities. Other research was conducted at the Bodleian Library at the University of Oxford, the British Library in London, and Kungliga Biblioteket in Stockholm, Sweden. Again, I thank the helpful staffs at the different facilities.

Among the people who were there to help me formulate ideas and develop drafts for my work were Peter C. Herman, Alex Paknadel, Richard Wilson, Maurizio Porcellini-Slawinski, Hillary Hinds, Arthur Bradley, Bulent Diken, and Abir Hamdar. A special cheer also goes to Joseba Zulaika. I am grateful to all of them for their support. I also wish to thank three separate, anonymous readers from Oxford University Press for their invaluable comments. Because of them this book is much better than it would otherwise have been, although probably not as good as they hoped.

Contents

A Note on the Text

I have modernized English spelling throughout, except in cases where the early spelling seemed essential to the meaning, or when citing a title. French texts I have left as I found them, since there seem to be more important differences in them from the modern. But usually, in any case, I cite the French texts in translation. I have freely used the efforts of translators before me, but I have always checked the French original against them for accuracy. Unless otherwise indicated, however, the translations are my own.

Except for a few recent journalistic accounts, government reports, and databases retrievable from the Internet, I have assembled all the works used and cited in this book in the Bibliography. Only abbreviated versions of citations of works in the Bibliography will be found in the footnotes.

Introduction

1. FELTON AND BUCKINGHAM BEFORE THE LETTER

> The duke is dead, and we are rid of strife,
> By Felton's hand, that took away his life.
> Whether that fact were lawful or unjust...[1]

So begins a short poem, written in 1628, on the occasion of the murder of George Villiers the Duke of Buckingham at the hands of the demobilized soldier John Felton, the last major incident of terrorist violence in England in the time period being studied in this book, 1559 to 1642.[2] I call it a terrorist incident above all because the murder was political, intended to change the balance of power in England: I call it a 'major' one because it attracted considerable national attention. In his own words, the perpetrator thought that he was justified on behalf of objective political principles, and because he believed that his act would safeguard the welfare of his nation. The Parliament had already issued a Remonstrance against the Duke, accusing him of having betrayed the country's trust in order to enrich himself and his friends; and Felton had 'read some books, which he said defended that it was lawful to kill an enemy to the Republic'.[3] Whether it was actually lawful to kill a man such as the Duke, whose detractors could at once accuse him of being a 'tyrant', since they believed he abused his powers, and a 'traitor', since he had signed a humiliating peace treaty with the French after suffering defeat in a war fought on behalf of the Huguenots at La Rochelle, was an issue that the poem deliberates over. The poem concludes that it was unlawful: although Buckingham was a 'grievance to the state', Buckingham was a subject with legal rights, and Felton, a private individual, had no warrant to kill him. Other observers at the time, however, disagreed. Says another poet, asking the same question:

> What shall we say? was it God's will or no,
> That one sinner should kill another so?
> I dare not judge; yet it appears sometime
> God makes one sinner 'venge another's crime.

---

[1] *Poems and Songs Relating to George Villiers*: 52.

[2] For background on the assassination and its repercussions, see Holstun '"God Bless Thee!"' and its update in Holstun, *Ehud's Dagger*: 143–91. Holstun's treatment of the event is more comprehensive than mine, but Holstun does not analyse it as an act of terrorism. Also see Lockyer, *Buckingham*: 419:75; and Gardiner, *History of England*: 6.91–121 and 6.339–60. A new website, 'Early Student Libels', also contains the material discussed here, and includes valuable commentary: <http://www.earlystuartlibels.net/htdocs/buckingham_assassination_section/P0.html> (12/5/2015).

[3] Rushworth, *Historical Collections* 1:638.

Though Buckingham's murder was unlawful, a higher law seemed to be at stake, a divine law, placed into Felton's hands by divine will. 'But howso're it is', the poet concludes,

> the case is plain,
> God's hand was in it, and the duke striv'd in vain:
> For what the parliament did fail to do,
> God did both purpose and perform it too.[4]

The murder was surely controversial. But that too shows it to have been a case of what we now call terrorist violence. For terrorist violence operates not only by destroying or harming, but also by communicating; it therefore almost inevitably stirs controversy. John Felton intended to send a message. It was not a terribly coherent message. It seemed to be a violent expression of the prerogative of the Parliament; and it seemed to stem from monarchomach theory, which justified tyrannicide under certain circumstances. But it also expressed frustration with Buckingham's conduct in France, and the defeat of the Protestants at the hands of the French military led by Cardinal Richelieu and King Louis XIII. Buckingham, among other things, needed to be made into a scapegoat on behalf of the English. Nor was that all. Felton was known to be personally aggrieved at the failure of the English army at France, at his own maiming while in battle (he lost the use of a hand), and at the 'horrific slaughter of English troops during both the attack and the ignominious retreat that ensued'.[5] He was in addition said to be disappointed at his lack of advancement, and his failure to receive back pay the government owed him, the considerable amount of eighty pounds. Not only a scapegoating, but also a sort of 'vengeance' was supposed to be exacted with Buckingham's death. And there was still more. For Felton also thought of himself as a martyr. In fact, after mortally wounding Buckingham at the latter's residence, instead of absconding, Felton selflessly gave himself up. 'I am the Man that hath done the deed', he said, stepping forward: 'let no man suffer that is innocent'.[6]

Felton's message was as much the expression of a daydream of conflict resolution as it was a statement of ideological purpose. The Remonstrance, asserting the powers of the Parliament (to some extent in defiance of the king, who was Buckingham's patron), was connected in Felton's mind, apparently, with monarchomach theory, with divine vengeance over the defeat of the army and the Huguenot cause, and, finally, with the heroism of martyrdom. Felton's admirers compared him, in fact, to a number of biblical heroes: the young David; the zealous avenger and warrior Phineas; Jael, the woman who killed the Canaanite general Sisera by driving a tent peg into his head while he slept; Ehud, the killer of Eglon, king of the Moabites; and Judas Maccabeus: none of them martyrs, except perhaps the latter, but all of them people who risked their lives for the sake of their faith.

Coming in 1628, as I have said, this murder would be the last major episode of terrorist violence to occur for some years. It would be the last major episode not

---

[4] *Poems and Songs*: 53.
[5] 'John Felton', *Oxford Dictionary of National Biography*.
[6] Rushworth, *Historical Collections*: 1.635.

only in England but also in France and Scotland, the other two countries with which this study is primarily concerned. There would be a good deal of political violence to come, to be sure, some of it terrorist in nature, beginning in the 1640s, and some of that violence would answer to the same daydreaming and ideological positioning as Felton's. But the goal here is to point to the period up to the early 1640s, beginning about 1559. What Felton's audacious and murderous self-sacrifice expresses is, if not a culmination, at least a late resurgence of a complex of ideas, attitudes, mythical musings, and violent struggles that made the late sixteenth and early seventeenth centuries an especially active period for what I call 'terrorism before the letter'.

This is a book not so much about the violent struggles themselves as those ideas and mythical musings that intersected with them. It is about the literature of terrorism before the letter, fiction and non-fiction, legendary and contemporary, proactive and reflective, amusing or didactic, in favour or against the violence, or somewhere in between. The thesis is that there existed a 'mythography' of terrorist violence in the sixteenth and seventeenth centuries in England, Scotland, and France, a body of what Joseba Zulaika and William Douglass, who introduced the term to terrorism studies, identified as 'enabling fictions': fictions that make it possible to *think* terrorism, even if the word did not yet exist. If you can think terrorism, with or without a word to identify it, then you can think about and with it and at the same time support, revile, or defy it; you can do it or defend against it or stand aghast at what it has done; you can speculate about it and morally respond to its intrusions into the political life of a society.[7] A mythography is what enables you to do any of this, and such a mythography arose out of ancient and medieval storytelling and political theory in this period such that a man like Felton might feel justified in taking the law into his own hands and bystanders might be able to attach ancient legends and considered political opinions to what he did.

The mythography of terrorism before the letter was complex rather than simple. It was far more multifaceted and problematic than accounts of any discourse of terrorism usually take it to be. To understand the mythography of terrorism means coming to terms with some of the most vexing questions of literature and life. For the existence of terrorism, with or without a name, implies what is at once a vulnerability and a hope: a vulnerability to violence that disturbs the fundamental conditions of peace; a hope, by the same token, that violence, against all odds, might renew even as it destroys, and save even as it brutalizes. The existence of terrorism before the letter indicated the existence of a problem at the heart of civil society, a precariousness of its own making, where violence could be both destructive and creative. The problem was both in the nature of civil society and the discourse that it required. Discourse is a condition of peace and discourse is a condition of violence, and political discourse, in a civil society such as the one that developed in the sixteenth and seventeenth centuries, is a condition both of cooperation and disruption.

---

[7] Zulaika and Douglass, *Terror and Taboo*.

A strain of thought in the work of Jacques Derrida argues that language itself comes as the original violence, an 'arché-violence', which necessarily precedes any case of 'empirical violence'.[8] This is not to say that language directly causes violence, or always acts in a violent way. A corollary of the idea of 'arché-violence' is the idea that language makes possible the exercise of non-violence too. And as it goes for the 'arché' condition, a kind of transcendental condition preceding experience, so it goes for the phenomenal world of experience. Certain kinds of conditions of peaceful political life provide opportunities for certain kinds of disruption; and certain forms of disruption can provide opportunities for the creation or re-creation of conditions of peaceful political life. Hence, in a tradition that goes from Walter Benjamin to Jacques Derrida and Michel Maffesoli—and, in fact, that already had its advocates in the early modern period—it makes sense to speak not only of defensive and destructive violence but also of 'foundational violence', a violence that establishes the legal and social basis of political society, a violence that, having broken up one foundation, may replace it with another.[9] 'For what the parliament did fail to do', we saw a poet in praise of Felton say, 'God did both purpose and perform it too'. If a legal system cannot correct for internal errors, even with all the violence at its disposal, something outside the system, in the exercise of another gesture of foundational violence, may come along and change the terms of the problem, perhaps even transcend them by starting the political process anew.

In associating discourse with violence and civil society with terror, I refer to a kind of archetypal but unavoidable relation. To have terrorist violence, you need to have a political condition of non-terror, of peaceful political activity. Meanwhile, to have peaceful political activity, you have to be vulnerable to terror, and dreams of reconstituting society through eruptions of violence. At the centre of political life there would thus seem to be a kind of arché-terror, a structure of terror along with non-terror embedded in the pre-empirical life of the society, and always apparently ready to become empirical.

John Felton was an individual who was able to exploit the arché-terror, and make it empirical. That of course is not an excuse for the violence, or a suggestion that Felton had no other alternatives to air his grievances. But it is a description of how it was possible for Felton not only to ponder a violent solution to his dilemmas, but to act upon his idea and, by his own terms, succeed. He succeeded only temporarily, of course; for he was tried and hanged, and English society went on, largely unchanged. But then again, Felton's act called attention to tensions in English life that would lead not only to the 'personal rule' of Charles I, where Charles governed from 1629 to 1640 without benefit of Parliamentary consultation but also to that reaction against personal rule which ignited, by 1642, into the English Revolution.[10] The legacy of Felton lived on. Killing Buckingham

---

[8] Derrida, *Writing and Difference*. And see Marsh, 'Of Violence'.

[9] Benjamin, 'Critique of Violence'; Derrida, 'Force of Law'; Maffesoli, *Violence*.

[10] This is Holstun's thesis in *Ehud's Dagger*, that Felton's actions became a model of lower-class revolt during the English Revolution. Revolutionaries identified with Felton as well as Felton's own model, Ehud.

meant nothing; but it also meant a great deal, becoming absorbed into a current of life that eventually erupted into civil war.

In claiming that a discourse of terrorism, a 'mythography' of terrorism, is more complex than has been hitherto allowed, I am partly referring to matters such as these, in the case of Buckingham's assassination: miscommunications, unintended consequences, over-determined causes, uncontrollable legacies. The discourse of terrorism is more highly motivated than has been acknowledged before, in more ways, with more varieties of outcomes, and perhaps with deeper causes. The case of Felton and Buckingham is fairly simple, and yet it has been easy to note at least half a dozen nuances among Felton's motivations, from resentment at an injury to a desire for martyrdom; and there are even more, if one looks at them closely, from the time and place of Felton's violent behaviour to the battles between Parliament and the Crown that made Buckingham into a scapegoat for much of the populace and, for Felton, a marked man. I have not even begun to speak about the intentionality behind the poems written about him, the way the poems take an event and make it into a subject of literary form and ideological struggle. To come to terms with a complex motivation like this, which is evident in so many of the events and texts to be discussed, is a major challenge. So many things are *intended* when an act of terrorist violence occurs; so many things are *intended* when someone writes about an act of terrorist violence, even an imaginary or legendary one. So many things are *understood* or *misunderstood* in the case of both the act and the writing; so much *interpretation* is involved, and *misinterpretation* too, not to mention negligent incomprehension.

To meet the challenge I shall call upon what Kenneth Burke, the philosopher of rhetoric, called the 'grammar of motives': the many-sided syntax of ascribing motives to action. That may seem timid: to respond to a history of violence by looking at a 'grammar'. But it is by looking at the grammar of the violence that I shall be able to elucidate its mythic power. Grammar is inherent to its structure. Structure is inherent to its significance. Significance is what both the violence and the discourses about it struggle over, create and counter, destroy and remake, understand and misunderstand.

What is in question here are not only sensational events like the assassination of an unpopular Duke by an unhappy soldier, but also even more important events in France like the Massacre at Vassy and the Saint Bartholomew Day Massacre and the assassinations of Henry III and Henry IV; or in Scotland the murder of Henry Stewart Lord Darnley, the father of the man who would become James VI and I; or in England any number of assassination attempts against the life of Elizabeth I; and above all, again in England, the abortive Gunpowder Plot, one of the most infamous conspiracies to commit (terrorist) mass destruction in history. What is in question, moreover, are not only the doggerel verses and anecdotes put together on behalf of an unhappy assassin, but also some extremely impressive works of art: Pierre de Ronsard's *Discours sur les miseres de ce temps* (1562–7), Robert Garnier's *Cornélie* (1574), Guillaume du Bartas's *La Judit* (1574–9), Agrippa d'Aubigné's *Les Tragiques* (1616), Thomas Norton and Thomas Sackville's *Gorboduc* (1562), William Shakespeare's *Julius Caesar* (1599), Thomas Middleton's *The Revenger's*

Tragedy (1606). There are major works of political theory and polemics in question as well, among them George Buchanan's *De jure regni apud scotos* (1579) and the anonymous *Vindiciae Contra Tyrannos* (1579), and, in another vein, the collection of speeches, confessions, narratives, and court documents put together in what has come to be known as *The King's Book* (1605–6), though actually both a short and a long version exist of this 'book', and it came out in many editions.[11] 'Terrorism before the letter' is a phrase with two meanings: on the one hand, it refers to terrorism before the word and the concept of terrorism existed; on the other, it refers to terrorism so far as it was brought before the bar of literature, and became a subject of writing.

But many things still need to be explained. First of all, terrorism itself needs to be explained more thoroughly, both as a general idea and as a category of action that may be applied to a period in which the word terrorism did not yet exist. Second, what the study of early modern terrorism and its literature, of 'terrorism before the letter', may contribute to the historical and literary understanding of terrorist phenomena needs clarification. Third, the question of how and why a 'grammar of motives' might be a useful device in the study of terrorist discourse needs to be answered. In the following chapter, I will recount the terrorist contours of the sixteenth and seventeenth centuries and the political myths and theories behind them, and in subsequent chapters I will analyse the literature. But first I turn to the concept of terrorism; to the contribution to be made by early modern literary study; and to the relevance of the grammar of motives to the study.

2. DEFINITION

'To define is to kill', said the poet Mallarmé. Unfortunately, some kind of working definition is necessary for any discussion of terrorism. The problem is that terrorism may seem to be difficult, if not impossible to define. For terrorism seems to mean too many things to too many different people in too many different contexts for observers, however impartial, to settle on a single definition. An indiscriminate but coordinated mass murder in the streets and the Underground of London by British Islamists is terrorism.[12] The abduction of a Libyan citizen in Tripoli by American troops is terrorism.[13] The unsuccessful attempt against the life of a Czar in nineteenth-century Russia by a lone anarchist is terrorism.[14] Tree-spiking by environmentalists in California, meant to sabotage logging equipment and injure loggers, is terrorism.[15] The mass killing of civilians in war-torn Syria by foreign-financed

---

[11] The first main edition was *His Majesties Speach*; the second, *A True and Perfect Relation of the Whole Proceedings Against the Last Most Barbarous Traitors*.

[12] Rai, 7/7.

[13] 'US Killing': <http://www.presstv.ir/detail/2013/10/09/328509/us-kidnapping-of-allibi-act-of-terrorism> (11/10/2013).

[14] Verhoeven, *The Odd Man*.

[15] Judi Bari, 'Secret History of Tree Spiking': <http://www.iww.org/history/library/Bari/TreeSpiking1> (11/10/2013).

'militants' is terrorism.[16] The occupation of the Japanese Embassy in Lima, Peru by members of the communist political party Shining Path, in 1996, is terrorism.[17] The sabotage of power lines in South Africa by disgruntled utility employees is terrorism.[18] The massacre at Jamestown in 1622, where Powhatan warriors attacked and killed over 300 settlers, was, according to a highly respected historian, an act of terrorism.[19] The Zealots of Judea, in the first century AD, conspiring to overthrow the Roman government and destroy Hellenic culture, armed with daggers, formed an organization engaged in a campaign of terrorism.[20] The firebombing of Dresden in World War II by British and American pilots was terrorism.[21] The Stalin Purge of the 1930s was, if not terror*ism*, at least 'The Great Terror'.[22]

With so many different kinds of actions, undertaken in so many different ways for so many different reasons and in so many different contexts all characterized as acts of terrorism, it may be time to throw up one's hands, along with Walter Laqueur, a great expert on the subject, and renounce the effort to try to define terrorism once and for all.[23] A student of terrorism today needs to be ready for forms of terrorism as yet un-conceived, as well as to be able to negotiate the conflicting claims of the perpetrators and victims of acts of violence already committed (where 'terrorism' as a term usually vies with 'freedom-fighting'), and then do justice to the past. Terrorism, says Laqueur, is 'a very old phenomenon and it has changed its character and meaning over time and from country to country. It is most unlikely that any contemporary definition of terrorism would even come close to describing terrorism in 1850 or 1930.'[24] Those who study terrorism should be flexible in their approach, and have no need for a strict and comprehensive definition.

In fact, according to Laqueur and some other experts, the need for a rigorous definition is legal rather than scientific.[25] For in many countries, crimes suspected of being 'terrorist' in nature are subject to separate penal codes; they are investigated and prosecuted by agencies specifically charged with responsibility for them, and subjected to specially designated investigative procedures and penalties. In the United States, subsequent to the passage of the Patriot Act of 2001, the crime of terrorism, already a Federal rather than a local offence, is no longer protected under a statute of limitations; and persons convicted of participation in an act of terrorism are subject to mandatory lifelong judicial supervision, an unusual punishment. Even more of a radical departure from most penal codes, international terrorists suspected of conspiring or of having conspired against the United States

[16] 'Terrorists and Mercenaries': <http://syrianfreepress.wordpress.com/2013/10/11/terrorists-mercenaries-in-syria-financed-by-private-gulf-donors-carried-out-mass-killings> (11/10/2013).

[17] Council on Foreign Relations, 'Shining Path': <http://www.cfr.org/peru/shining-path-tupac-amaru-peru-leftists/p9276> (16/10/2013).

[18] Times Live, 'Johannesburg Power Sabotage': <http://www.timeslive.co.za/politics/2013/09/06/johannesburg-power-sabotage-terrorism-mec> (11/10/2013).

[19] J. Frederick Fausz, 'First Act of Terrorism', *History News Network*: <http://hnn.us/article/19085> (11/10/2013).

[20] Rapaport, 'Fear and Trembling'; Chaliand and Blin, *History of Terrorism*: 55–78.

[21] Sloterdijk, *Terror from the Air*: 56.   [22] Conquest, *The Great Terror*.

[23] Laqueur, *No End to War*: 232–8.   [24] Laqueur, *No End to* War: 232–3.

[25] In addition to Laqueur, see Crenshaw and Pimlott, *Encyclopedia*, volume 1; and Weinberg et al., 'The Challenges'.

were made subject to 'rendition', to being captured abroad and indefinitely detained by American military authorities.[26] In the United Kingdom, the Terrorism Act of 2006 permits the detention of persons suspected of terrorism for up to twenty-eight days without charge and makes it easier for investigators to obtain search warrants, intercept communications, and arrest suspects based on incomplete evidence.[27] Moreover, in both countries simply *being a terrorist* is a crime; that is, whether or not one engages in acts of terrorist violence, being a member of an organization that foments terrorist activity, or lending spiritual, material, or financial support to such an organization, is criminal, and subject to special legal treatment.[28] In the United Kingdom, simply *encouraging* terrorism, vocally, is a criminal act.[29] A young man was once arrested and convicted in Britain for a joke he made on Twitter about wanting to blow up an airport. He was only absolved in court after a third appeal.[30]

So on the one hand the phenomenon of terrorism may seem to have so many faces that it cannot, and should not, be too strictly defined; on the other, designating something as an act of terrorism has significant legal consequences, and clarity about the judicial nature of terrorism is essential. To call something an act of terrorism, or to identify someone as a terrorist, can be less a theoretical characterization than an accusation, and it opens a slew of law enforcement measures. An inquiry is set in motion. A set of procedures and rules, often extraordinary, are put into place. Special detention protocols and penalties have been established. And the accused, if found guilty, must therefore pay for a crime—even so vaguely framed an offence as the encouragement of a crime—based on the idea that for purposes of discovery and conviction the fundamental offence, 'terrorism', is perfectly clear and distinct. It is possibly because of the lack of clarity where one has been required that the American government held so many prisoners at Guantánamo Bay without trial for so many years. Those held in the compound stood accused; but the nature of the crimes they stood accused of lay outside the limits of conventional, domestic law.[31]

That international law also suffers from this dilemma, where great clarity is required about ambiguous circumstances, almost goes without saying.[32] The United Nations has never agreed on a definition of terrorism, although it has taken action

[26] 107th Congress Public Law 56. 'An Act To deter and punish terrorist acts in the United States and around the world, to enhance law enforcement investigatory tools, and for other purposes.' Oct. 26, 2001—H.R. 3162. <http://www.gpo.gov/fdsys/pkg/PLAW-107publ56/html/PLAW-107publ56.htm> (15/10/2013).
[27] Terrorism Act 2006: <http://www.legislation.gov.uk/ukpga/2006/11/contents> (14/10/2013).
[28] Executive Order 13224: <http://georgewbush-whitehouse.archives.gov/news/releases/2001/09/print/20010924-1.html>; 18 USC § 2339B.
[29] Terrorism Act 2006, Chapter 11: <http://www.legislation.gov.uk/ukpga/2006/11/pdfs/ukpga_20060011_en.pdf>.
[30] <http://en.wikipedia.org/wiki/Twitter_Joke_Trial> (20/10/2013).
[31] The United States government's own report on Guantánamo reflects the ongoing nature of such uncertainty. Guantánamo Review Task Force, *Final Report*, 22 January 2010: <http://www.justice.gov/ag/guantanamo-review-final-report.pdf>. Also see Worthington, *The Guantánamo Files*: 215–43.
[32] For a comprehensive treatment of this subject as of 2004, see the essays collected in Walter, *Terrorism as a Challenge*.

on behalf of reducing the threat of terrorism and has even 'reaffirmed' the imperative of all member states 'to combat terrorism in all its forms and manifestations by
all means'. At a pinch, the United Nations describes terrorism as 'criminal acts,
including against civilians, committed with the intent to cause death or serious
bodily injury, or taking of hostages, with the purpose to provoke a state of terror in
the general public or in a group of persons or particular persons, intimidate a
population or compel a government or an international organization to do or to
abstain from doing any act'.[33] But this definition, apart from the specification of
criminality, can apply to warfare between nations, armed national liberation movements conducting guerrilla warfare, and humanitarian military intervention in foreign countries as well as to the hijacking of airplanes and the detonating of suicide
bombs, and fails even to account for how criminality can be determined in the
context of international relations. In a word, as one reporter puts it, the United
Nations' definition is a 'political' rather than a legal declaration, even though it is
meant to provide legal guidance.[34]

Outside the world of penal law and international treaties, in the realm of political controversy and struggle, where the meanings of words are often ambiguous
and slippery, to call something terrorism is nevertheless a potent accusation. It is to
impose or attempt to impose an identity upon an activity; it is to try to make it
recognized as one thing rather than another. And today that usually means that it
is to try to make it recognized as a form of malicious malfeasance. Although there
have been times when the idea of terrorism has had a romantic cachet, and the
mantle of terrorism could be worn proudly, today the word is all but universally
pejorative. To call an activity terrorism is to denounce it. It is to discountenance
the claims of terrorists to be acting on behalf of a legitimate cause, or to be de-
ploying legitimate means on behalf of their cause, or even to be acting for any
purpose at all worthy of the name of reason. That is why, as Laqueur wryly notes,
those accused of terrorism today will often accuse their accusers of being terrorists.
That is one reason why the linguist and political analyst Noam Chomsky has often
responded to the American government's anti-terrorism fervour with the charge
that the American government itself is a terrorist organization, and extremely dangerous.[35] In a world where political and social conflict can at any time develop into
armed struggle, the name of that struggle becomes crucial. If it is called a protest,
an insurgency, a resistance, a revolution, a counter-revolution, or for that matter a
national security measure, a pre-emptive strike, a legally endorsed measure of
self-defence, or humanitarian intervention, an armed attack may be excused in the

---

[33] Security Council Resolution 1566 (2004) Concerning Threats to International Peace and Security Caused by Terrorism: <http://www.refworld.org/cgi-bin/texis/vtx/rwmain?docid=42c39b6d4>
(16/10/2013).

[34] Thalif Deen, 'U.N. Member States Struggle to Define Terrorism', *Inter Press Service News Agency*,
25 July 2005: <http://www.ipsnews.net/2005/07/politics-un-member-states-struggle-to-define-terrorism>
(17/10/2013). These issues have also been discussed in view of the Schmitt-Agamben theory of 'the
exception': sovereignty defining its lawfulness by being able to determine exceptions to lawfulness in
its own behaviour. See Neal, *Exceptionalism and the Politics*.

[35] For example, Chomsky, 'International Terrorism'. A more recent development of Chomsky's
thought on the subject appears in Chomsky, *9–11*.

name of freedom, or sanctioned in view of just-war theory. But if it is called terrorism, today, however large or small, whether waged by a hapless suicide bomber in the commercial centre of Stockholm or by a squadron of well-trained paramilitaries in the countryside of Nicaragua, the armed struggle can never be excused. It can only be objected to, and if possible prosecuted.

Sometimes, when social thinkers call attention to a kind of terrorism on all sides of the political divides in the modern world, by governments as well as insurgents, they point to a general condition of terror, taken to be constitutive of modern life.[36] The idea goes back at least as far as Thomas Hobbes: that fear is what makes political society possible. Citizens need to fear authority; they need to be in 'awe' of it, as Hobbes put it, lest authority crumble and the people revert to an anarchist state of nature. Therefore authorities may well wish to foment fear, to seal their authority through the terrorization of a population. Show trials, public executions, military demonstrations, mass arrests, and declared states of emergency, not to mention vigorous everyday police presence on the streets, may all serve to cow a population into obedience.[37] So too may officially aroused paranoia. If the 'common power' can hold a populace 'in awe', as Hobbes puts it, so can fear of an enemy, without or within, imaginary or real.[38] According to Hobbes, the 'reason' why people should be obedient to their sovereign, and their awe of the sovereign will be justified, is their 'protection'; obedience and awe are justified if and only if the sovereign is able to provide security.[39] As history has shown many times since Hobbes's times, one of the best ways for a regime to maintain the support of its subjects is to make them feel that without the regime chaos will ensue. But terrorist organizations have often attempted to prove to a public that nothing but chaos would follow *unless* the regime was changed, or unless the group's specific demands were met. As a general condition, fear is a medium through which regimes and insurgencies attempt to control the will of the majority; fear is an underlying energy of modern political society, and it is over the distribution of this energy that sovereign regimes and terrorists will often struggle.[40]

The origin of the term 'terrorism' seems to underscore this ambiguity, where activities meant to intimidate a population seem to be at once a special case of political violence and a general condition of political life.[41] For the word derives from the French Terror of 1793–4, which according to its primary champion, Maximillien Robespierre, was a campaign undertaken for the sake of 'liberty and equality' and the universal 'destiny of man', but which, according to the philosopher G.W.F.

---

[36] For example, Berleant, 'Art, Terrorism'; Ibrahim, 'Commodifying Terrorism'; Grimshaw, 'Religion, Terror and the End of the Postmodern'. 'This is not a reign of terror', writes Berleant, after describing many of the acts of violence and disinformation today, drawing attention to our general world condition; 'this is an age of terror' (5).

[37] The idea is explored at length in Agamben, *State of Exception* and Braud, *Violences politiques*. A more systematic approach is taken, earlier, in Giddens, *A Contemporary Critique*.

[38] Hobbes, *Leviathan*, 2.17.227.   [39] Hobbes, *Leviathan*, 2.2.272.

[40] For a recent recapitulation of the idea, with a good deal to say about Hobbes and his legacy, see Robin, *Fear*.

[41] For interesting accounts of the genesis of the word 'terrorism' and its development as a philosophy of action, see Redfield, *Rhetoric of Terror* and Verhoeven, *Odd Man Karakozov*.

Hegel, in a shrewd analysis, was waged on behalf of 'subjective freedom' trying to attain to the more objective 'absolute freedom'.[42] Terror seems to arise as a condition of modern society, a violence of, for, and against (potentially) everyone, in the name of humanity.[43] But as Hegel also pointed out, the violence actually showed that the party of universality led by Robespierre was merely a 'faction', 'the *victorious* faction'.[44] Neither the violence nor the freedom and equality on behalf of which it was waged were genuinely universal. Violence in the name of universality was needed precisely because the condition of universality was missing, and factionalist struggle for dominance was at stake.

And so, from its initial use to characterize a brutal government policy to its application to other types of violent behaviour by both governmental and non-governmental agents, the word 'terrorism' undertook its notorious career. The word was often tossed about in the interest of combating phantom enemies, even imaginary worldwide conspiracies: governments against peoples, or associations of insurgents against governments and industries. But it also became the name of a specific form of armed factionalism. Directed mainly against persons and property representing national governments, terrorism in this latter sense was a form of armed struggle intended to undermine political authority and trigger revolution. It was a form of struggle, moreover, to whose terms it behoved a revolutionary to adhere, until such time as the need for the struggle had been overcome. In many minds terrorism had thus become, precisely, an *ism*, with its own forms, agents, methods, and objectives. It would become possible for revolutionaries and insurgents of various stripes willingly to identify themselves as 'terrorists', or even to publish, as the Russian anarchist Gerasim Grigorevich Romanenko would do, a book called *Terrorism and Routine* (1880), embracing terrorist tactics and the terrorist way of life.[45] The self-identification in the late nineteenth century of anarchists, revolutionary socialists, and nationalist separatists as 'terrorists' helped etch in the public mind a characterology of terrorism as well as an ideology, and made it seem (in spite of widespread differences among different individuals and organizations and their aims and methods) as if terrorists and terrorism were the vehicles of kinds of essences, core qualities of personhood and thought, inescapably common to them all. By the late nineteenth century, nefarious yet exciting figures like 'the dynamitard' loomed large in the public imagination in Europe. Nevertheless, there always remained in everyday language the idea that terror could be attributed to other sorts of agents and agencies, who had little in common with anarchist dynamiters. Evil supernatural beings (as in gothic fiction), legendary tyrants like Ivan the Terrible or the fictional aristocrat Ferdinando Falkland in William Godwin's

[42] Maximillien Robespierre, *Report upon the Principles of Political Morality* (1794): <http://www.marxists.org/history/france/revolution/robespierre/1794/political-morality.htm>. Hegel, *Phenomenology*, sections 582–95, pages 356–63; Comay, 'Dead Right: Hegel and the Terror'; Cameron and Goldstein, 'The Ontology of Modern Terrorism'.

[43] Arendt, *Origins of Totalitarianism*, thus developed the idea that 'terror' was the essence of tyranny and totalitarianism, but 'terror' for Arendt was not simply the circulation of fear: it was the elimination of the value of human life, so that everyone had to fear for his or her own survival.

[44] Hegel, *Phenomenology*: section 591, page 360.

[45] See Laqueur, ed., *Voices of Terror*, 83–6.

novel *Caleb Williams* (1794), violent labour movement activists, national separatists, white supremacist organizations, vigilante groups, delusional lone assassins, rogue police squads, crime syndicates, whole governments violently repressing their people—all of them could be said to engage in terrorist activities with no infraction being made against everyday usage. One of the problems was and continues to be the word itself: terrorism, implying terrorization, the dissemination of fear, or somewhat less forcefully, 'intimidation'. For although fear is one of the classic tools of terrorists (and shows up with several different meanings in the abortive United Nations definition), fear is not the only tool, or even the universally essential tool, at terrorists' disposal; and conversely, not all people who use fear as a tool to achieve domination are actually terrorists. Even if fear is a social energy which terrorists and counter-terrorists—not to mention tyrants, hate-groups, and gangsters—commonly try to manipulate, fear is not a *sine qua non* of terrorist violence. (That is why the UN definition vaguely adds 'to compel' as one of the things terrorists may try to do.) The self-appointed terrorists of the nineteenth century claimed to be attempting what was called the 'propaganda of the deed'. They were trying not only to generate anxiety concerning political authority, but more importantly to express and generate support for an idea.

It is against this background of overgeneralizations, accusations, legal confusions, claims to essential identities, and ideologies that political scientists like Walter Laqueur have tried to intervene and bring some clarity. But paradoxically, if Laqueur is correct, one of the ways to bring clarity is to abandon the attempt to try to develop a systematic and comprehensive definition. After all, Laqueur argues, 'people reasonably familiar with the terrorist phenomenon will agree ninety per cent of the time about what terrorism is.... In fact, terrorism is an unmistakable phenomenon.' The signs of terrorism are like the signs of an illness, such as pneumonia, which a professional medical doctor can seldom fail to recognize, even if he or she does not understand all the causes and conditions underlying the signs. (Pneumonia can be either viral or bacterial, yet lead to the same symptoms.) But even Laqueur has to admit that terrorism has at least some minimal characteristics, to be found whenever the phenomenon is recognized for what it is: 'the systematic use of murder, injury, and destruction, or the threat of such acts, aimed at achieving political ends'.[46] And in fact, such a minimalist definition actually conveys a great deal of information.

By *systematic* Laqueur indicates a self-consciously strategic recourse to violence; that is, on the one hand, methodical violence, undertaken instrumentally, and, on the other, objective violence, undertaken for what are taken to be rational ends. And this systematicity is linked, above all, to the coupling of violence with political ends, a coupling which incorporates historical, anthropological, and strategic parameters. For violence is a special form of action, with its own historically determined constraints, and political society is not the only kind of society among the many that have appeared in the course of history. Nor is intervening in political life the only kind of violence possible in the struggle for power. As for tactics, one of

---

[46] Laqueur, *No End to War*. 238.

the things that the coupling of violence and politics implies is that terrorist violence is methodically communicative. Laqueur does not always choose to emphasize this, but the idea is implicit in much of his work and commonplace among many other political scientists. It has even drawn some specialist analyses from the field of communications studies.[47] To say that terrorism is a systematic use of violence to achieve political ends is to say that terrorism is an act of violence whose perpetrators try, deliberately, to enter into public discourse and express something in it. That is how terrorism usually operates, whether its primary effect is intimidation or some other psychological or cognitive condition: it sends a message, by force, or in conjunction with force, to members of one or more publics, to change their minds and compel their behaviour. As political scientist Martha Crenshaw puts it, terrorism is an 'expressive' form of 'aggression'. It speaks to one or more 'audiences', and thus 'targets the few in a way that claims the attention of the many'.[48] Or in Laqueur's own words, 'most' terrorists 'believe in a strategy of provocation', and that is to say much the same thing.[49] To provoke is to incite or arouse, but it is also to summon and invite. The terrorist methodically coerces or destroys, or threatens to do one or the other, and he or she all but inescapably provokes—incites, arouses, summons, and invites—in the process. There is an inescapably communicative dimension to provocation, just as there is an inescapably communicative dimension to any action in the domain of the political. In many cases, perhaps most of them, this communicative dimension is also 'performative' or 'theatrical'. Not only are terrorists acting out the messages they send, they are also acting them out as if on a stage, with one or more audiences in mind. Just by performing—raising their weapons—they are communicating.[50] They are engaging, as we will see, in a form of symbolic exchange, where acting out the violence is already a shift in power relations, already a transformation of the status quo, bringing rewards to some and penalties to others.

But if the minimalist definition implies an understanding of political life in conjunction with communication and violence, it also incorporates negative qualifications. As another political scientist, Bruce Hoffman, puts it, responding to Laqueur, 'If we cannot define terrorism, then we can at least usefully distinguish it from other types of violence and identify the characteristics that make terrorism the distinct phenomenon of political violence that it is.'[51] Some of Laqueur's other statements about the nature of terrorism, as well as Hoffman's, are helpful. In the first place, for a social scientist, as for a historian or a literary critic, the term terrorism is not an accusation. It has no legal standing in academic discourse, and ought not have a polemical standing either. Surely the study of terrorism involves the study of many atrocities, and surely the student of terrorism is not absolved from the responsibility for naming atrocities as such, or of otherwise taking moral or political

---

[47] Matusitz, *Terrorism and Communication*; Tuman, *Communicating Terror*.
[48] Crenshaw, 'Terrorism in Context': 4.   [49] Laqueur, *The New Terrorism*: 37.
[50] An early statement of this idea is Jenkins, *Terrorism: A New Kind of Warfare*. And see Schechner, *Performance Theory*, esp. 194–5. Juergensmeyer, *Terror in the Mind of God*, develops this theme at length. And it is reiterated in Cowen, 'Terrorism as Theater'.
[51] Hoffman, *Inside Terrorism*: 34.

stands with regard to incidents of terrorism organizations that sponsor it. But the term itself, terrorism, for academic and scientific purposes, is neutral. It is descriptive and denotative rather than polemical and connotative.[52] Secondly, the term cannot be used, without causing a good deal of confusion, to describe a general condition. If the term is to be helpful in the identification of individual acts of political violence, or individual organizations and ideologies that give rise to them, it cannot, without obfuscating the issue, be used to identify the nature of political life itself.[53] And thirdly, not all individual, terrible acts committed in the name of political principles and for the sake of political advantage are helpfully designated as terrorism. Some acts of political violence are worse than terrorism; some, neither better nor worse, are simply different kinds of acts of political violence, and warrant different kinds of analysis.

It is easy to see why the Dresden bombing and the Stalinist purges have often been accused of being terrorism and why they might be considered to be far worse, as atrocities, than anything committed by such overtly terrorist organizations as the IRA, the Red Brigade, or Al Qaeda. But one of the reasons why political scientists like Laqueur and Hoffman can recognize terrorism when they see it is that they limit the use of the term to low-intensity conflicts, and usually also to non-state or sub-state agents.[54] Low intensity may of course be in the eyes of the beholder; but for the political scientist the term usually indicates a conflict tangibly and structurally below the level of conventional warfare, where control over territory by two opposed armed groups is contested. Low intensity designates a situation of official peace or the interval of a truce, or a situation of latent rather than overt, or minimal rather than maximal conflict in which express incidents of armed violence are rare. Warfare is warfare: when a war is on, few people in the vicinity of the fighting are unaware that a war is on. Territorial control is at stake.[55] But when an Archduke is assassinated in the city streets, or a bomb is set off in a mosque, few people in the vicinity are unaware that the peace has been violated, and latent conflicts have been, for the moment, made terribly manifest. When terrorism communicates, it disrupts the flow of everyday life; it comes unexpectedly (however much, in retrospect, it ought to have been anticipated); it announces itself as a violation of the peace and expresses a threatening message, demanding some kind of change in a balance of power. As for the raising of the level of conflict *above* that of conventional warfare, that may perhaps be what was undertaken during the Dresden bombing. So might many other episodes of atrocities against civilians in wars both ancient and recent. 'War crimes' is a term commonly used for such atrocities, since they deliberately violate conventions of warfare, including the recognition of the right of civilians to be left in peace. In the early modern period a case in point was

[52] See Crenshaw and Pimlott, *Encyclopedia*: Volume One, Introduction.

[53] This, however, is precisely the tactic adopted by Miller, 'Ordinary Terrorism', where the 'ordinary' is precisely the nation-state in its everyday function as the monopolist, in Weber's terms, of legitimate violence.

[54] Hoffman, 'Current Research'; Laqueur, *The New Terrorism*: 8–10.

[55] A somewhat different analysis of intensity is offered in Tilly, *The Politics of Collective Violence*. For Tilly, given his own method of plotting intensities, the main characteristic of terrorism is asymmetry (233–6).

the Sack of Antwerp in 1576, when the Spanish army, in one of its periodical 'Furies', ran amuck on the streets of the already pacified city, leaving over 7000 people dead.[56] The English poet, George Gascoigne, a horrified eyewitness, compared the spectacle of the dead and dying in the streets of Antwerp to the spectacle of hell in Michelangelo's painting, *The Last Judgement*.[57] Many other cases of early modern excess in war could be cited, along with literary testimonies to it like Shakespeare's Henry V, threatening before the city's gates not to 'leave the half-achieved Harfleur / Till in her ashes she lie buried'.[58] It makes perfect sense, in common language, to talk about the terrorism of armed forces when they exceed the needs of military strategy and commit atrocities against civilians and their property; but that is not a sense of the word 'terrorism' that is useful to the political scientist or historian. One of the most characteristic features of terrorism is its ability to have a tremendous impact under conditions of low intensity. The death of a single person, even the abduction of a person, can seemingly bring a nation to its knees. Terrorism can be attractive to political dissidents precisely because it promises to bring about political change on a large scale at the cost of a small-scale operation. Such of course was the large ambition of John Felton, as he followed the Duke of Buckingham into the latter's residence, and took him unawares.

As for the Great Terror of the Stalinist purges, or for that matter the Holocaust, or the bombing of Hiroshima and Nagasaki, or the devastating reign of the Khmer Rouge in Cambodia (1975–9), or any other horror that could be added to this list, these things are obviously worthy of serious attention, but not as incidents of terrorism. All of them were far worse than terrorism has ever been, in terms both of their death tolls and of the moral challenges they pose—their challenges to the very idea of being human—and they arose out of considerably different circumstances. They belong to another category of violence.

State terrorism is a difficult topic. At a minimum it can be said that states participate in terrorism when they sponsor, assist, or through the deployment of special forces directly undertake acts of violence, in low-intensity conditions, in a foreign country, with the intention of bringing about political change. CIA participation in the undermining of the government of Salvador Allende in Chile through acts of violence, including the assassination of Chilean General René Schneider, is a case in point.[59] Another case in point would be the Libyan government's apparent sponsorship of the downing of Pan Am 103 over Lockerbie, Scotland in 1988.[60] But CIA intervention in Chile was a case where one government engaged in actions against another government, and the downing of the airplane by Libyan agents was probably a case of one government trying to intimidate the people as well as the government of several other nations. When a government turns against

---

[56] Arnade, *Beggars, Iconoclasts*: 244–58; Parker, *The Dutch Revolt*.

[57] Gascoigne, *The Spoyle of Antwerpe*: C1.

[58] Shakespeare, *Henry V*: 3.3.85–6; and see Ruff, *Violence in Early Modern Europe*: 55–7.

[59] See Harmer, *Allende's Chile*; and Shiraz, 'CIA Intervention in Chile'.

[60] There have been a great many published accounts of this affair, some of them contradicting one another. The amateur can only suppose that members of the Libyan government, possibly with Quaddafi's knowledge and support, *probably* sponsored the attack.

its own people, however, when the so-called state terrorism involves domestic violence, and state agents are either ordered or encouraged to harm innocent civilians, it is seldom clear that something on the order of 'terrorism' is involved. Both Laqueur and Hoffman eschew the concept of state terrorism in this sense. And when scholars try to explore the idea of state terrorism, as for example Gus Martin in *Understanding Terrorism*, the result can be unconvincing, for 'state terrorism' usually turns out to be synonymous with violent repression of just about any kind, and even genocide or what some scholars call 'democide' become 'terrorism'.[61] Again, such 'state terrorism', directed by a state against its own people, is often far more objectionable than non-state terrorism. But that does not make 'state terrorism' a particularly helpful locution in such a case. When the totalitarian violence of the Nazi Final Solution or the Khmer Rouge's evacuation of Phnom Penh become taxonomically linked with Stern Gang dynamiters and Palestinian suicide bombers, little light is being shed on either sort of phenomenon.[62]

Nevertheless, it would seem that there have been cases when governments have genuinely engaged in terrorism against their own citizens in the more limited sense. Death squads in El Salvador during the 1980s might be examples, where state-supported agents hunted down the regime's political enemies.[63] The assassinations of prominent opposition leaders in many countries over the past century might be examples too: human rights activist John Paul Oulo in Kenya in 2009, killed in his car by unidentified but no doubt government-supporting assailants in the middle of rush hour traffic;[64] left-wing political leader Manuel Colom Argueta, struck down by an army raid in Guatemala in 1979;[65] the exiled Leon Trotsky, bludgeoned to death by an NKVD agent on the orders of Joseph Stalin, in Mexico, in 1940. Here government agents act extra-judiciously to harm inconvenient citizens and send a message to their supporters. Some killings of this kind have been trumpeted by the government officials responsible for them, as an example to others and an expression of the government's power, so that the message is loud and clear. Most government-sponsored assassinations are kept quiet, never admitted to and never prosecuted; and so the message is subtle. But it would seem in a good many such cases that a form of state terrorism is being practised; that is, terrorist violence undertaken by agents of the government, acting under the orders or with the blessings of government officials.

In the study of the early modern period it is crucial to distinguish between a repressive government harming citizens as a matter of policy and a body of government agents engaging in terrorist violence in special circumstances for the sake of a symbolic political gain. When the Spanish government reconquered a piece of territory in the Low Countries, during what would come to be called the Eighty Years War (1568–1648), the government could take extremely harsh repressive

---

[61] Martin, *Understanding Terrorism*: 110–51. The term, democide, originates with Rudolph Rummel. See especially Rummel, *Death By Government*.

[62] Horgan and Boyle, 'A Case Against' (57), make a similar point.

[63] Americas Watch, *El Salvador's Decade of Terror*.

[64] FIDH, 'Kenya: Assassination': <http://www.fidh.org/en/africa/kenya/Kenya-Assassination-of-Messrs>.

[65] Ball et al., *State Violence in Guatemala*: 21.

measures: executing open adversaries and suspected dissidents and heretics, banning Protestant worship and assembly, plundering wealth, imposing punitive taxes. But such repression was categorically different from the Spanish-sponsored murder of William of Orange, in 1584: an act taking place by an assassin in Delft, behind the lines of a territory and within the limits of a city at peace. That assassination, according to historian Franklin Ford, set in motion a long chain of events, for it declared a kind of open war on monarchs and princes from that day forward, without regard to the rules of combat, and it brought about a long chain of assassinations and attempted assassinations in Europe.[66] But here, therefore, is an important categorical distinction, highly relevant to the study of the period: on the one side, excessive, forceful oppression in an occupied territory; on the other, government-sanctioned violence against specific targets, undertaken in a non-militarized territory where peaceful conditions have prevailed.

There were times when monarchs or other authorities ordered the extra-judicial murder, arrest, or harassment of individuals or groups of individuals who were their legal subjects and not charged with any crimes. Spectacular cases include the assassination of Henry Lorraine the third Duke of Guise, in 1588, by the orders and for that matter in the presence of Henry III, and the assassination of Concino Concini the Marquis d'Ancre in 1613, on the orders of Louis XIII. A more mysterious case probably of the same kind was the murder of Henry Stewart, Lord Darnley, in Scotland in 1570—the husband of Mary Queen of Scots, who probably sanctioned the assassination. Another mysterious case turns up in the conflict between Mary Queen of Scots and Elizabeth I. The latter seems to have ordered the assassination of Mary, only later to retract the order in favour of a judicial execution.[67]

Before the late eighteenth century, again, there was no such word as 'terrorism'. There was no word to describe the incidents, no category of thought, feeling, or observation to which they corresponded. This is, again, the first reason why I call them episodes of 'terrorism before the letter'. But everybody could see that the killings of the Duke of Guise, Concino Concini, and Henry Stewart were illegal; they were extra-judicial; they were crimes committed against individuals who had not been officially charged with any wrongdoing. One could bring a Duke of Guise or a Mary Queen of Scots to trial and execute either if found guilty of a capital offence. But without trial, without so much as a warrant, without any legally valid complaint, one could have a political enemy murdered: one could even, as Henry III would do after Guise's murder, publicly announce, defend, and celebrate the deed. But this was a crime, a 'sur-crime', as it were. And this was a form of what today we call terrorism.

The one political theorist of the early modern period who came close to explaining these crimes or sur-crimes as a special category was a Frenchman, Gabriel Naudé, writing in Rome in the early seventeenth century. He did not focus on all

[66] Ford, *Political Murder*: 160–2. Ford also credits the assassination of the French Admiral Gaspar de Coligny at the beginning of the Saint Bartholomew Massacre in 1572 to have been key in this respect. He could also have mentioned the killing of François Lorraine, the Second Duke of Guise, in 1562.
[67] Fraser, *Mary Queen of Scots*: 657–8.

such crimes, only on those committed by princes and other high-ranking officials. And he called them *coup d'états*—by which he meant not the overthrow of the government but an illegal 'master stroke' of the government, undertaken for the sake of good governance. Violating 'common law', as Naudé puts it, 'without regard to any form or order of justice', these figures attempted to remake government in the image of their own violence and the higher principle it served, the 'public good', or otherwise for 'the safety of the people'.[68] His examples include the assassination of the Duke of Guise in 1588 and the Saint Bartholomew Day Massacre of August 1572.

The point is that though the early moderns had no word for terrorism, they could at least sometimes see, as Naudé did, that violent acts by public officials against their own subjects, undertaken without recourse to the law, but resorted to for the sake of what was called a 'reason of state' or the principle of 'the safety of the people', were justifiable crimes. And it is inevitable that the concept of crime be introduced in this context, just as the concept of justifiability needs to be introduced to it. On the one hand, *crime*: acts of terrorism, or of terrorism before the letter, are inevitably crimes according to pertinent standards of penal justice, of which agents, victims, and observers are well aware. If there is no 'crime' involved in an act of terrorism, then it probably isn't terrorism, but rather some other form of violence. On the other hand, *justifiable*: crimes of terrorism are usually considered by their perpetrators and supporters to be justifiable according to a higher, alternative law. 'Reason of state' or the 'safety of the people' would be among those higher laws. So in the early modern period there would be such laws as the Word of God, or more specifically the right to the freedom of worship, or the right of one religion to eliminate another in the interest of such principles (very popular during the French Wars of Religion) as *un roi, une loi, une foi*: one king, one law, one faith.

Of course, this coupling of criminality and justifiability does not apply only to the terrorism of princes. It also applies to the terrorism of non-state agents, like John Felton. John Felton's supporters—and perhaps Felton himself, given his public statements—seemed to believe that what Felton did was both unambiguously a crime, deserving punishment, and yet unambiguously an expression of a higher law, which made the crime regrettable but necessary and just. And there were many other such cases, some of which played a part in inspiring Felton. In 1589 a young Dominican friar, Jacques Clément, was admitted to a private interview with Henry III, who was stationed at a chateau outside Paris.[69] Clément stabbed the king in the abdomen, and the king died from an infection caused by the wound a few days later. Clément was celebrated by many Catholics as another Ehud, or another Judith, even though Henry III himself was a devout Catholic. Another case: in 1605, a group of Catholic Englishmen led by Robert Catesby conspired to blow up the House of Lords, and kill the king, most of the royal

---

[68] Naudé, *Considérations politiques*. 'Master stroke' is the translation of *coup d'état* given in *Political Consideration upon Refin'd Politicks, and the Master-Strokes of State* (London, 1711), a translation by William King. I will throughout be using the French *coup d'état*, to keep it differentiated from the English 'coup d'etat', which has the modern meaning of a government overthrow.

[69] See Vaissière, *De Quelques assassins*.

family, and perhaps hundreds of other members of the ruling elite. The Gunpowder Plot of course was foiled. But along with the cases of John Felton and Jacques Clément, it provides a picture of criminality coupled, at least in the mind of the perpetrators, with justifiability. Felton, Clément, and the Gunpowder Plotters seemed to have been perfectly aware that what they were doing was against the law. But they also believed that they were justified by a higher form of law. In committing a crime—an offence against the state, as well as against private persons or property within it—they were certain that they were both committing and not committing a crime.

To the minimal definition of terrorism proposed by Laqueur, 'the systematic use of murder, injury, and destruction, or the threat of such acts, aimed at achieving political ends', I am adding another minimal condition: criminality coupled with justifiability. Whether committed by state or non-state agents, terrorism involves the resort to illegal violence and, at the same time, an appeal to a higher justification. It is not certain that all terrorists of all times and places could be characterized in this way. But I am not aware of any exceptions. Of all the many examples of terrorist violence that I have been able to document in the sixteenth and seventeenth centuries, there are no exceptions. It is possible to imagine a killer-for-hire undertaking a political murder for the money and no other reason, or one political rival killing or having killed another rival simply for the sake of getting rid of the rival, or even—this being a common allegation in the early modern period—killers of political figures going about their work simply out of madness or possession by the devil. These would all be cases of political violence without the agent being motivated by a political objective, and there are many examples of them: thugs hired to do the work of political operatives; rivals eliminating the competition; madmen doing the work of political life without understanding that that is what they are doing. But it is hard to imagine someone whom an impartial observer would recognize as a terrorist or a terrorist-sponsoring individual acting without political or politico-religious idealism, and without believing that a standard of justice existed which condoned or even demanded an act of otherwise illegal violence. When an act of violence is recognized to be an act of terrorism, what is recognized is precisely this, that there is, for the perpetrators—if only the perpetrators who hired the thugs or manipulated a madman—a political reason which both motivates and justifies the turn to violence. Criminality and justifiability are linked as concepts through which terrorists and their supporters can proceed to valorize the violence they engage in, or even intend to have violence perpetrated in the first place.

Criminality and justifiability are also, to be sure, concepts through which opponents to terrorism can reject and de-legitimate the violence. That is to say, the detractors of an act of terrorism, using the same concepts, can condemn the violence. They accuse the act of criminality—treason, sedition, riot, abduction, parricide, murder, vandalism, theft—and they allow no qualification or mitigation. They deny the justification. And even more, the detractors can be appalled at the appeal to a justification, revolted by the idea that the perpetrators of a terrorist incident think themselves above the law, acting on behalf of a divine or otherwise transcendent principle. In many cases, the justification of a terrorist incident is considered more heinous than the crime itself. And the response therefore is expressed that there is something inherently wrong with the presumption of the terrorist, the belief system to which the terrorist adheres, or the delusions to which the terrorist has been subject, or even the hypocrisy of resorting to ideological subterfuge, as when a terrorist claims to be acting on behalf of a principle when he is really only saying that as a cover for unprincipled malice. Said Buckingham's biographer, Henry Wooton, about John Felton's motives: 'what may have been the immediate or greatest motive of that felonious conception, is even yet in the clouds'. The appeal to the Remonstrance was the 'fairest cover' for Felton's motives; but 'whatsoever were the true motive,...I think none can determine, but the Prince of Darkness it self'.[70]

That criminality and justifiability are also commonly *contested* in incidents of terrorist violence is not an argument against the idea that the two things go together. On the contrary, the contesting and the linking of criminality and justifiability are both expressions of what Hoffman calls the 'ineluctably political' nature of terrorism. For the political arena is a space of contestation, even if it is also a space where, ideally, contestation is supposed to lead to negotiation, decision, and assent.[71] When terrorists and anti-terrorists disagree with one another, their disagreement is, in the first instance, political. But to Hoffman's idea I would add that this contesting and linking is a sign of the ineluctably *dialectical* nature of terrorist violence. Although some acts of terrorist violence may have what seem to be highly limited objectives—the freeing of political prisoners, the receiving of a ransom, an agreement toward the changing of a national policy—a deeper quarrel is almost always at stake, and usually the deeper quarrel is exactly what the act of violence is intended to address. The quarrel is rendered into violence, or the threat thereof, for either limited or general purposes, yet with a general conflict in mind, which the violence inherently articulates and tries to resolve, irreversibly, in its own behalf. But that is not the end of it, in either case: after the act or the threat, decisions are still to be made, the quarrel is still to be negotiated, and the concepts of criminality and justifiability are still to be contested, dialectically, with words and actions.

Laqueur is right, it appears. Terrorism can never be defined once and for all. Laqueur is right to suggest flexibility, and to stress that even the minimal conditions of terrorist violence can change enormously over time. But then an interesting duality arises. On the one hand, there are minimal characteristics: 'violence', 'politics', 'communication', 'low intensity', 'criminality', and 'justifiability'. On the other, what constitutes any of these characteristics—violence, politics, and so forth—may be subject to great variation. What is 'violent' in 2015—for example, beating a pupil at school for misbehaviour—may not be 'violent' in 1559. What may be 'political' today—for example, the environmental regulation of mining—may not be 'political' or even heard of in an earlier era. And so we face a difficult but useful interpretive problem.

---

[70] Wotton, *A Short View*. 22–4.
[71] On this idea, politics as a space of (peaceful) contestation, the most important texts are probably Arendt, *The Human Condition* and Habermas, *Theory of Communicative Action*. See Chapter 5, section 5.

On the one hand, we may know what we are looking for; but on the other, what we find is sometimes likely to surprise, or to cause us to reassess our notions of violence, politics, and the like. There may be borderline cases, too. In borderline cases, one or more characteristics may be missing, or be modified by other characteristics. For example, when one nation is at war with another nation, but deploys a terrorist tactic—an assassination, say, behind enemy lines, meant to demoralize the opposition—the condition of low intensity is missing in one sense, since a full-on war is being waged, but is present in another sense, since the assassination is carried out *as if* low-intensity conditions prevailed. Or to give another example, when a government or faction tries to intervene in the affairs of another government or faction by sponsoring an *agent provocateur*, like the notorious Yevno Azef (1869–1918) who worked undercover for the imperial Russian government, and actually engineered incidents of terrorist violence that the government blamed on others, the perpetrating organization in effect *simulates* terrorist violence;[72] and still, most observers would be inclined to recognize the violence really to be, in most respects, terroristic, for that is how the violence is supposed to be received by the public. The variety of contexts in which terrorist violence can be undertaken, and the variety of the ways in which what seem to be its basic characteristics can be combined with another, or even simulated, suggests that if terrorism can be recognized alike by most experts in most cases, an indefinite variability nevertheless prevails. From a semantic perspective, the situation may be akin to Wittgenstein's notion of 'family resemblances', where recognizable characteristics are 'overlapping' and 'criss-crossing' rather than intertwined.[73] There is no essence of terrorism, only a range of pertinent resemblances from one phenomenon to another. From a historicist perspective, meanwhile, the situation may be akin to Foucault's concept of an episteme (an idea iterated by Zulaika and Douglass). In given moments of history, politics, violence, and communication, along with low intensity, criminality, and justifiability, may be expressible together—and committable together—by way of an evolving system of 'discourse formation'.[74] The circumstance are right. A political settlement has been institutionalized, which is nonetheless vulnerable to violence. A sphere of communicative action has been developed, in which violence may intervene. Conflicts may rage short of warfare or permanent hostility, and interventions attempting to solve the conflict may take on both a criminality and a justifiability. If Foucault's principles may be correctly applied to the idea of terrorism, terrorism has both a history and a future, and both alike have or will depend upon ever-changing sites of discursive recombination where these characteristics, in one form or another, may appear. What terrorism was, or will be, has depended and will depend on what politics is, what violence is, and so forth, and how these different phenomena can be articulated and acted upon together. What it was, has been, or will be shall always depend upon an unobservable arché-terror which discourse itself has put into place, and whose empirical effects discourse has rendered intelligible.

---

[72] Rubenstein, *Comrade Valentine*. It is such a character that undertakes the bombing of the Greenwich Observatory in Conrad's *Secret Agent*.

[73] Wittgenstein, *Philosophical Investigations*: 27–8.

[74] Foucault, *Archaeology of Knowledge*.

But there is still one more reason why the definition of terrorism is, though serviceable, incomplete. The reason is that terrorism is dialectical. From the scientific point of view, terrorism can be identified from near or far when certain characteristics, or family resemblances of characteristics, are observed. But in the course of the events themselves, as terrorists try to communicate their messages, a chain or a multitude of chains of response are let loose, where the targets and audiences of the violence can comply or resist complying with what the violence is saying, and the message can unwind in many different ways. The combination of criminality and justifiability can be accepted; the opposition defeated. But equally, the combination can be challenged, rejected, refused, or overlooked. Even that which was undertaken as a decisively political act can be responded to as if it wasn't political at all, but merely a criminal misdeed and very likely mad. The terrorists try to make statements; they try to get themselves and their positions *recognized*, brought into the political arena and validated. But equally, their positions can be either *refused recognition* or *misrecognized*. For as soon as they act, the terrorists have entered into a dialectic of recognition.[75] In fact, if the terrorists are not already *in* such a dialectic, in such a struggle for political recognition, the violence they undertake will create one for them. What happens next is history and can progress in any of several ways. The cause can be won. The cause can be lost. Or it can be neither won nor lost, but just be there, a wound in time; and what was taken on one side of a conflict to be an act of 'terrorism', a meaningfully political resort to violence, can be remembered as an outrage of no account. (This is what happened, as will be seen, in the case of the assassination of Henry IV.) In the dialectic for recognition, there are forces that triumph, forces that get repelled and renounced, and forces that do not even register as forces. There are forces so victorious that in retrospect they do not seem like terrorism at all, but rather as outcomes of inevitable historical processes. (Such a reading has often marked responses to the Saint Bartholomew Massacre.) There are forces so successfully repressed that they never even manage to express a grievance, even if traumatic repercussions still seem to be felt for them. (Such seems to have been the case of the Gowrie Conspiracy in Scotland, against James VI in 1600, where the king was nearly killed.) Responding to 9/11, Jacques Derrida called attention to the 'psychic effects' that terrorist incidents are meant to produce. He also called attention to the fact that the effects do not unwind in a simple linear fashion, the terrorist message disseminating its statement once and for all. On the contrary, the effects and messages of terrorism may take, as Derrida put it, 'innumerable detours, an incalculable number of them'.[76] Being as much resisted as received, renounced as commended, terrorist acts—to keep to Derrida's

---

[75] The idea, as I am using it, is adopted from Hegel, *Phenomenology of Spirit*; I am also responding to the reinterpretation of Hegel's position in Kojève, *Introduction to the Reading of Hegel*, its psychologization in Jacques Lacan, especially in *Four Fundamental Concepts*, and to still another reinterpretation, influenced by Kojève, in Francis Fukuyama, *The End of History and the Last Man*. I am, as the reader will see, placing this dialectic in a new context, and certainly removing it from the idea of the 'end of history' which is so important to Kojève and Fukuyama. Rather, in the spirit of Lacan and the later Derrida (especially *Spectres of Marx*), but in the field of the political and historical rather than the psychic or the ethical, I am thinking of this dialectic as open rather than closed.

[76] Derrida, in Borradori, *Philosophy in a Time of Terror*. 107.

metaphor—run into roadblocks, dead ends, faulty passageways, and yet may keep on circulating, this way and that, their messages never quite reaching their destination. And yet the destination of recognition is what was desired at the outset. When terrorism happens, it does so because some sort of determination is sought. Victory is recognition and recognition is determination. But the results are often indeterminate. Maybe they always are. John Felton was a hero to some, a villain to others, and to still others a non-entity. His deed was an act of valour, a scandal, or a mistake. It was soon forgotten. But it was also, in other contexts, when in the 1640s opposition to the powers-that-be became an element of a popular revolution, an event to be remembered.

3. CRITICAL TERRORISM STUDIES

This book is about the representation of terrorism in England, Scotland, France, and a few bordering territories from the mid-1500s to the mid-1600s. It is meant to be a contribution to literary and cultural history, where a variety of texts are read for their textual as well as their supra-textual features: contexts, codes, ideologies. But this book is also meant to be a contribution to 'critical terrorism studies'. There is a journal called *Critical Studies on Terrorism* which has established a set of methodological and theoretical principles as well as a political agenda.[77] There are also books in the field, like one that has already been cited, Zulaika and Douglass's *Terror and Taboo*. The current study is intended to contribute to the field. But it is meant to do so by adding a few things: first of all, an understanding of a specific historical period, early modernity in Britain and France; second, a demonstration of how literary study and especially literary history can enhance the cause of critical terrorism studies; and third, a clarification of some of the terms, methods, and intellectual traditions that may be used for such studies, including those belonging to Kenneth Burke's 'grammar of motives', those belonging to the tradition of close and comparative readings of literary texts, and those belonging to critical theories in the poststructuralist tradition.

The term 'critical terrorism studies' implies that there are forms of terrorism studies which are insufficiently 'critical', or 'self-critical'. Perhaps that is another way of saying that some forms of study are insufficiently dialectical, insufficiently aware of the partisan values, perspectival limitations, or theoretical assumptions that go into making 'terrorism' a field of study, and insufficiently adept at dealing with conflict and contradiction in terrorist and counter-terrorist phenomena. A detractor might quip that all that means is that some terrorism studies, for some scholars, are insufficiently Marxian or poststructuralist, and therefore un-enamoured with dialectical reason.[78] But the larger point seems to be threefold. First, to be critical or self-critical terrorism study needs to be sceptical of the familiar binary

[77] Smyth et al., 'Critical Terrorism Studies'. Also see Jackson et al., *Critical Terrorism Studies*.
[78] See Heath-Kelly, 'Critical Terrorism Studies', on the discipline's specific commitment to 'Critical Theory' and its emancipatory project, stemming from the work of Max Horkheimer. And see Horgan and Boyle, 'A Case Against', for a response against the general case for critical terrorism studies.

oppositions (friends against enemies, and so forth) through which the concept of
terrorism is so often constructed, and the interest of security (preventing terrorism)
gets confused with the interest of understanding (knowing terrorism for what it is).
We have already looked at a major example, where a lack of dialectics, a misunderstanding of how binary oppositions operate to obfuscate as well as clarify; it comes
in the case of Walter Laqueur's metaphor of terrorism as an illness, such that terrorism always becomes that which invades, and apparently invades some version of
'us'. Secondly, such study needs to be aware of the existence of terrorism not just as
a phenomenon but also as a signifier, with an impact that greatly exceeds that of
isolated incidents of violence. As the editors of *Critical Studies on Terrorism* put it,
terrorism 'is a term that generates vast amounts of social and political activity, in-
duces powerful emotions and, through a vast array of social practices, constitutes a
legal and political subject, a cultural taboo, a myth and an object of fear, hatred,
surprise, admiration, "entertainment" and identity'.[79] The study of terrorism in
the field of critical terrorism studies includes the study of the signifier as well as the
phenomenon, and may well concentrate on examining the often troubled relation
between the two. This signifier may develop into what Zulaika and Douglass originally called a 'mythography', a system of 'enabling fictions' that circulates among
terrorists and counter-terrorists alike, among media-makers and media-consumers,
among ideologues, observers, victims, audiences, and perpetrators. When we talk
about terrorism, we talk not only about the thing, but also about what the thing
does to us, and what talking about the thing does to us, and what talking about it
does, has done, or will do to others, as well as, ultimately, what talking about it
does to the nature of the thing itself. The late 'War on Terror' and the American
attack on Iraq are the obvious reference points today, where the idea of terrorism
broke free from its immediate referent and was caused to signify in new ways,
coming to create referents of its own. Saddam Hussein, who had nothing to do
with 9/11, became the terrorist enemy, and 'weapons of mass destruction'—which
Boeing 757s and 767s, in reality, had been made to become—were translated,
phantasmatically, into non-existent arsenals in Iraq. But there have been and will
be other reference points of this kind, other hyper-idealizations of the power of
violent intentions and other hysterias over it. The mythography of terrorism is
dangerous, even if to some people it can also represent hope. But thirdly, the study
of terrorism should therefore be free to draw upon the methods of insights of all
the human sciences, from anthropology to philosophy, not to mention literary
studies, in order to be sufficiently critical about a signifier in the midst of human
culture which both draws upon and intervenes in the committing of violence.

It is no secret that literary artists have played a major role both in constructing
the signifier of terrorism and analysing the phenomenon. The profoundest two
works ever written about terrorism are probably *Demons* by Fyodor Dostoevsky

---

[79] Smyth et al., 'Critical Terrorism Studies': 1. Monographs in the field of critical terrorism studies
that predate the founding of the journal, in the order of their publication, include Zualika, *Basque
Violence*; Simon, *The Terrorist Trap*; Silberstein, *War of Words*; Jackson, *Writing the War on Terrorism*;
Rai, *7/7*; and Muro, *Ethnicity and Violence*. That the writers put 'entertainment' in inverted commas
speaks volumes.

(1872) and *The Secret Agent* (1906) by Joseph Conrad. Another major literary artist, Albert Camus, wrote not only three separate plays on the theme of terrorism (*Caligula* [1938], *Les Justes* [1949], and *Les Posédés* [1959], the latter an adaptation of Dostoevsky's *Demons*), but also an extended meditation on political violence, *L'homme révolté* (1951), where he connected what he called 'metaphysical rebellion' to both terrorist movements and fascism. In the United States, long before 9/11, novelist Don DeLillo was drawing attention to terrorism as a signifier in American life. In *Players* (1977) he imagined a nihilist terrorist conspiracy in downtown Manhattan; in *Libra* (1988) he re-imagined the assassination of John F. Kennedy; in *Mao II* (1991) he dramatized the intersection of fiction-writing and terrorism, and had a character, a novelist, make a famous statement: 'There's a curious knot that binds novelists and terrorists. . . . Years ago I used to think it was possible for a novelist to alter the inner life of the culture. Now bomb-makers and gunmen have taken that territory. They make raids on human consciousness.'[80]

Since 9/11, or even a few years before then, the salience of terrorism as a signifier, or even a spectre of sorts, haunting both elite and popular culture,[81] has brought about a huge growth in critical writing on the subject, focusing on a great many different texts, from popular thrillers to high-minded lyrical poems.[82] Increasingly scholars have found both that the phenomenon of terrorism itself has a writerly dimension, since terrorism involves the communicating of messages, and that the discourse of and about terrorist violence has a long literary history. When it turns out that even so apolitical a writer as Henry James was fascinated (in *The Princess Casamassima* [1886]) with terrorist violence, and that his fascination with it was a fashionable sign of his commitment to realism, we know that we are dealing with something old rather than new, deep rather than shallow, demanding investigation and explanation.[83] As for the early modern period, though no general overview of the role of terrorism in it has yet been attempted, the topic keeps surfacing in pieces: about Milton and Samson, about Ben Jonson and William Shakespeare and the Gunpowder Plot, or about the response of French writers to the Saint Bartholomew Massacre and other incidents.[84]

So far work in literary studies has sat astride rather than contributed directly to critical terrorism studies. The same fate perhaps awaits the current study. But both literature and literary analysis have important insights—not just into ideas or phenomena, but into how terrorism is constructed as a signifier, and how this signifier may be inscribed in symbolic systems, recruited into action, and disseminated

---

[80] DeLillo, *Mao II*: 41.

[81] See Appelbaum, 'Fantasias of Terrorism'; and Jackson, 'The Study of Terrorism'.

[82] The MLA International Bibliography (accessed January 2015) shows 489 peer-reviewed articles on terrorism, for example: over ninety per cent of them were published in 2001 or later. Important monographs on the topic include Melchiori, *Terrorism in the Late Victorian Novel*; Scanlan, *Plotting Terror*; Houen, *Terrorism and Modern Literature*; Gray, *After the Fall*; Versluys, *Out of the Blue*; and Preece, *Baader-Meinhof and the Novel*.

[83] Scanlan, 'Terrorism and the Realistic Novel'; Miller, 'The Inward Revolution'.

[84] Carey, 'A Work in Praise of Terrorism?'; Rudrum, 'Milton Scholarship and the "Agon"'; Gregory, 'The Political Messages'; Mohamed, *Milton and The Post-Secular Present*; Dutton, *Ben Jonson*, '*Volpone*' *and the Gunpowder Plot*; Wilson, *Secret Shakespeare*; Biberman and Lupton, eds., *Shakespeare After 9/11*; Dassonville, ed., *Ronsard et Montaigne*; Vinestock and Foster, eds., *Writers in Conflict*.

through discourse. Imaginative literature adds modifications and complications to the study of terrorism. It qualifies our understanding of the nature of the imagination through which terrorism is identified and the language through which it is represented, highlighting the power of figurative speech, dramatic expectation, narrative point of view, and other dimensions of literary communication: irony, allegory, allusion, and the like, all of which modify the signifier and the signified, and modulate their reception by readers. Imaginative literature complicates our understanding of psychological motivation, the sequencing of actions, the establishing of contexts (historical, geographical, and mental) and the pursuit of ideological, ethical, teleological, and spiritual ends. Zulaika, who began by pointing out the relevance of the anthropological study of terrorists, has recently called upon students of terrorism to think about the model of novelist Truman Capote, in his study of two murderers, *In Cold Blood* (1966). Capote came to understand far more about his criminals—not terrorists, to be sure, but men whose evil was, like many terrorists', at once stark and opaque—than would have been possible without his application of a novelist's sensibility. Among other things, the more Capote came to know his criminals, the more he came to see that a lot of what was in them as human beings was also in himself. Such an insight was ultimately devastating for Capote personally—he was hardly able to write creatively again. But it was astonishingly revelatory of the nature of homicide.[85]

The study of literary *history* has something to add to critical terrorism studies too. Terrorism studies is a profoundly un-historical discipline. The historical understanding of terrorism has been weakly developed and has some gaping holes, including a hole in the place where the period of the current study is located. In a recent 474-page collective effort by terrorism specialists, *The History of Terrorism from Antiquity to Al Qaeda* (2007), there are exactly two paragraphs about the sixteenth century in Europe, and only a few more than that about the seventeenth century—misleadingly devoted to military atrocities committed during the Thirty Years War.[86] A brief search of the journals *Studies in Terrorism and Conflict*, in business since 1977, and *Terrorism and Political Violence*, in business since 1989, show not a single essay concerned even tangentially with the Saint Bartholomew Massacre, the assassinations of Henry III and Henry IV, the Gunpowder Plot, or the assassination of the Duke of Buckingham. The same goes for *Critical Studies on Terrorism*, whose editors endlessly critique the epistemological limitations of other terrorism studies, but whose own anthology, *Critical Terrorism Studies: An Agenda*, refers to no events or texts before the 1960s. (It also fails to refer to a single philosopher of violence, whether an ancient figure like Hobbes or a contemporary like Žižek, and makes no mention of imaginative texts about violence.[87]) The literary

---

[85] Zulaika, *Terrorism*: 37–62. Contrary to Zulaika, there is at least one establishment counter-terrorist specialist who has made a novelist's effort to get inside the mind of a terrorist: Jessica Stern in *Terror in the Name of God*. But one thing Stern did not find in her encounters with real-life terrorists was a reflection of herself.

[86] Chaliand and Blind, *History of Terrorism*: 87–92.

[87] To be fair, most literary and philosophical accounts of terrorism fail to take political science, 'critical' or otherwise, much into account.

history of the present study may thus serve the purpose, even as it focuses on literary production, of reintroducing the history of early modern terrorism in Western Europe to students of terrorism, and showing the relevance of that history for today. As this history of early modern terrorism has to cope not just with events but also with thoughts, as it will engage therefore with such sources and spaces of thought as the Bible, the writings of classical antiquity, the reflections of early modern political philosophers, the polemics of the early modern press, and the powerful dramas of the early modern theatre, this study may make the further contribution of showing how vested Western culture has been in the imaginary of terrorism—how Western culture has been a part of, not apart from, the spread of terrorist violence and its mythographies.

This last point is important. Consider the cases of John Wilkes Booth and Timothy McVeigh. Booth was a Shakespearean actor who had played a major role in *Julius Caesar* along with his two thespian brothers a few months before the evening he shot and killed President Abraham Lincoln, shouting to the crowd in the theatre immediately afterwards a slogan from the legend of Marcus Brutus, which had become the motto of the state of Virginia: '*Sic semper tyrannis*.'[88] Timothy McVeigh, on the day he was caught by the FBI and brought in for questioning with regard to the terrible Oklahoma City bombing (1995), was wearing a tee-shirt with the same slogan emblazoned on it, underneath a stencilled portrait of Abraham Lincoln.[89] The two killers may of course have been deranged, or at least very much deluded in their convictions, and their reading of the legend tells us nothing about the actual killing of Caesar or about Shakespeare's interpretation of it. But it shows that attacks upon the system of government of a Western power can derive their semiotics from Western power and the discourse that has emerged from it and about it.

In fact, they are all but obliged to do so. In the aftermath of 9/11, Derrida, Jean Baudrillard, and Slavoj Žižek all came to the similar conclusion that when such terrorists as the 9/11 hijackers attack a system—The West, America, Global Capitalism—they do so in the language of the system. Derrida thus spoke of terrorism by way of the metaphor of an auto-immune disorder, Baudrillard on the mirrored uses of the simulation by capitalism and its enemies, and Žižek on the controlling fantasy of self-destruction that the 9/11 hijackers replicated.[90] The 9/11 attack was a repetition with a difference, and that was one of the things that was most awful about it.[91] The West had created the technology, the organizations, the semiotics, and the violent fantasies through which its self-purported enemies could terrorize it. If terror is not a general condition of modernity, it is nevertheless situated within the system of modernity. It is in the system materially, as Derrida

[88] Kaufman, *American Brutus*. An irony lies in the fact that the part he played in that performance was Marc Antony.

[89] Michel and Herbeck, *American Terrorist*.

[90] Baudrillard, *Spirit of Terrorism*; Derrida in Borradori, *Philosophy in a Time of Terror*; and Žižek, *Welcome to the Desert of the Real*.

[91] On the aesthetic dimensions of the event, also see Lentricchia and Macauliffe, *Crimes of Art and Terror*.

noted, given for example the fact that Al Qaeda was an offshoot of American efforts to stymie the Soviets in Afghanistan—a case of a defence system striking back against the system it is supposed to defend. And it is in the system semiotically, as all three thinkers noted, given that the language the terrible attacks spoke was perfectly intelligible, and was in fact the West's own language, speaking its own terrible desires. Had the philosophers addressed themselves to Western terrorism against Western targets—for example, the nineteenth-century Irish Fenians against the British government—or Western terrorism against non-Western targets—for example, the murder of Osama Bin-Laden[92]—they would have come to the same conclusion. A language of political violence precedes the committing of political violence, and the language comes from within the depths of the history of civilization.

The literary history of terrorism in early modern Britain and France may at a minimum draw attention to a legacy of an enabling discourse, in Zulaika and Douglass's sense: discourse that puts the signifier of terrorism on a horizon of possibility. Booth and McVeigh drew upon a discourse of tyrannicide with ancient roots that was in fact revived by sixteenth-century humanists before it eventually became part of the American discourse of sovereignty in the eighteenth century. The originators of the 9/11 attacks drew upon fantasies of destruction, again with ancient roots, that were a major theme of tragic theatre and heroic poetry in the sixteenth and seventeenth-century theatre, as writers reflected on the meaning of current events like the Wars of Religion and the Gunpowder Plot. Nothing in the sixteenth century caused terrorism in the nineteenth century or in our own time. But there is a line of descent from the one time to the others. There was a mythography then, there is a mythography now, and the two phenomena are not unrelated.

The boundaries of the mythography of terrorism before the letter in early modern Britain and France, however, as perhaps in any period, are fuzzy rather than distinct. Within the parameters of the mythography lay texts of a great many different genres, written in a great many registers. Some were outright fictions, some were fictional adaptations of true stories, some were accounts or arguments about true events, or about the principles and historical legacies in keeping with which true events were undertaken and became intelligible. Some of these texts only implied a background story, and instead commented on an idea, or celebrated or execrated a fait accompli. Some of the texts were about legends, some of them were about legends that were taken to be true, including stories of biblical lore. Some of them were what the people of the time called 'imitations'; that is, re-writings of revered stories, as Guillaume du Bartas re-wrote the story of Judith and Holofernes (1574–9) with the Wars of Religion in mind, or as Francis Quarles re-wrote the story of Samson (1631) with the Thirty Years War in mind. Some of the texts, like those on the subject of the Duke of Buckingham, were brief poems commemorating the death of a prominent person. Some of them were lengthy heroic poems recapitulating in horror events like the Gunpowder Plot, or, conversely, memoirs of participants in the milieu of the Plot, protesting their innocence, such as the recollections of Father John Gerard and Father Oswald Tesimond.

---

[92] See Chapter 6, section 6.

Some of them were stories set in the deep past, like Shakespeare's *Macbeth* or Jonson's *Catiline*, which were constructed as ways of understanding recent events. Some were allegories, like Spenser's depiction of events in the Low Countries in the Fifth Book of the *Fairie Queene*, where an actual event was twisted into a fantastic fictional event so as to convey another meaning. Some, of course, were outright fictions. Most of the texts of terrorism before the letter can be read as *parables*; that is, as statements both about the real or fictional world they address and as statements about something else entirely. Terrorism was not only a subject of representation, in this period; it was also a pretext for writing about other subjects.

'Mythography' refers at once to a body of historical contents—of common legends, ideas, symbols, current events, and other points of reference—and a system for making statements or constructing narratives and dramas about them. It is as much a system of difference as a system of resemblance. That is, it involves the structure by which *Macbeth* and *Catiline* can not only be assimilated to one another—both of them being energetic responses to political nihilism and its dangers, dramatizing adventures into destructive yet ambitious violence—but also differentiated: the story of a Thane and a monarch as opposed to the story of a Senator, the story of a murder bringing about a tyranny as opposed to a story about murder prevented, and therefore about tyranny prevented. Similarity and difference are both involved: How does an action get made into an object of mimetic attention? How does it get assimilated to other such acts? How does it get differentiated from other such acts?

So a mythography is a system—open rather than closed, responsive as well as productive—through which certain kinds of statements and forms of discourse can be assimilated and yet differentiated from one another, disseminated, and dispersed. And it is, as I have put it, 'enabling'. The discourse of terrorism before the letter is not only a discourse about a kind of combat; it is also a discourse *in combat*, enabling more combat. Real-life stakes are always on the horizon. And a battle is being fought over a dialectic of recognition. What in one text is a heroic effort is in another text diabolical. What in one text is a liberating defeat of tyranny is in another text a seditious blow against law and order. What in one text is a matter of survival, since a nation and its purity of religion are at stake, is in another text a matter of turbulence, undertaken for the sake of turbulence, or on behalf of a family feud. Some texts argue in favour of violence, knowing that the recourse to violence is completely wrong. Others argue in favour of quiescent patience, even in the face of atrocity and an awareness of the moral and existential dangers of timidity. The texts of terrorism before the letter can engage in sophistry, making one thing seem like another, and even war seem like peace, or peace seem like war, or a *coup d'état* seem like a judicial execution. The texts can make death and dying into a spectacle to crow over. Or conversely, they can make death and dying into a drama of suffering that no political action and no arguments will ever justify: real tragedy, as in the plays of Robert Garnier, written in the spirit of the ancient Greek playwrights. The texts can make soldiers of fortune look like representatives of the people of God, in imitation of biblical ancestors, or else like hired thugs, comic figures who were only involved in violence for the money. They can make terrible massacres into premeditated doses of 'physic'; or they can make them into 'unfortunate incidents' for which no redress is possible. It can make the deaths of martyrs into iterations of God's plan for the end of time; and it can make the deaths of innocent people into an outrage that needs to avenged, and that can only lead to more war, and war again until the end of time. These texts not only enter into disputes about the nature of acts, the characters of persons, and the contexts and means of violence, but also the teleology, divine or human, of acts, persons, contexts, and means.

4. THE GRAMMAR OF MOTIVES

There are many ways in which one could assemble the data of terrorism before the letter, create an exposition of the material and provide explanations. The obvious way is to go through the texts one by one, chronologically. But that would not only be tedious; it would also fail to draw the analysis around the main phenomenon in question, not a plethora of texts that in some way address the existence of terrorism before the letter, but a mythography, an evolving system in keeping with which texts about terrorism could be generated and caused to enter into a dialectic of recognition. But how to describe and explain a mythography? There is more than one way of going about it and I have been tempted by other methods than the one I have chosen. If a 'mythography' is in question, for example, a method along the lines of Claude Lévi-Strauss's structural interpretation of myth might be in order.[93] 'Mythemes' might be isolated (for example, 'tyranny'), relations between the mythemes documented, compatibilities, incompatibilities, and variations noted. Processes of mythic invention and reinvention would be highlighted. The method might be old-fashioned, structuralism presumably being dead. But still, one could show, in structuralist fashion, how the discourse of terrorism before the letter functioned as myth (even if it also functioned in other ways), using the tools of mythic analysis. But the analysis would still be missing a crucial element of the discourse of terrorism before the letter, the element of action and, with action, intention.

For terrorism signifies first of all the choice of a tactic.[94] From that choice issues action, or a chain of actions. But what finally, from a structural or presumably mythic point of view, is an action? In the past half century a discipline called the 'philosophy of action' has emerged.[95] The fundamental idea with which the discipline is concerned is that an action is different from a motion. An action is *intentional*; it implies an *agent* and an *objective*: John opens the door. That makes it different from something that happens without the intervention of an intention, an agent, or an objective: a door blows open. There are many theoretical complexities involved in differentiating 'John opens the door' from 'a door blows open'.

---

[93] Lévi-Strauss, 'Structural Study'.
[94] This is the fundamental principle of Crenshaw, 'The Logic of Terrorism'.
[95] A founding text is Donald Davidson, *Essays on Actions*. For a recent overview see O'Connor and Sandis, *A Companion*.

And there are many complexities involved in unpacking the first idea on its own terms, 'John opens the door'. Finding ways to *construct* statements like 'John opens the door' as representations of significant action is one of the prime tasks of the narrative, dramatic, descriptive, or argumentative writer. Finding ways to *interpret* such statements is one of the prime tasks of the reader, the critic, and the historian. Kenneth Burke's theory of a 'grammar of motives' and the 'dramatistic' analysis of texts, though it cannot answer all the questions raised by the philosophy of action, illuminates how statements about action are both constructed and interpreted, as well as how different kinds of statements about action may be related to one another.[96]

The concern in this book is not with statements like 'John opens the door', but with more challenging ones like 'Ravaillac committed parricide', '*sic semper tyrannis*', and 'I told him Yes, in this or what else soever, if he resolved upon it, I would venture my life.' The concern is to parse such longer accounts as the following, taken, like the previous sentence, from Thomas Winter's confession about his involvement in the Gunpowder Plot, upon having been recruited to it by Robert Catesby:

> [Catesby] said that he had bethought him of a way at one instant to deliver us from all our bonds, and without any foreign help to replant again the Catholic religion, and withal told me in a word it was to blow up the Parliament House with gunpowder; for, said he, in that place have they done us all the mischief, and perchance God hath designed that place for their punishment. I wondered at the strangeness of the conceit, and told him that true it was this strake at the root and would breed a confusion fit to beget new alterations, but if it should not take effect (as most of this nature miscarried) the scandal would be so great which the Catholic religion might hereby sustain, as not only our enemies, but our friends also would with good reason condemn us. He told me the nature of the disease required so sharp a remedy, and asked me if I would give my consent.[97]

The critic, reading this statement as a critic, will already be alert to the preponderance of tropes in the characterization of the Plot: 'deliver us from our bonds', 'replant', 'strake at the root', 'God and punishment', 'the disease required so sharp a remedy'. Some of these figures may well be playing the role of mythemes—'delivery and bondage', for example—taken from the language of the Old Testament, and meant to signify a kind of typological condition which warrants a type of violent response. The tropes beg for analysis. And much of what follows will in fact be concerned with analysing the tropes of terrorism before the letter. Especially important, we will see, is synecdoche, where attacks on parts are equated with attacks on a whole, and larger processes and figures related to synecdoche, most notably symbolic exchange and sacrifice. 'Happy is he', writes the Catholic priest Jean Boucher, in praise of regicide, in characteristically synecdoche form,

---

[96] Burke, *Grammar of Motives*: esp. xv–xxiii. Also see Burke, 'Dramatism'; Gusfield, 'The Bridge over Separated Lands'; Jameson, 'The Symbolic Inference'; Signorile, 'Ratios and Causes', and Wess, *Kenneth Burke*: esp. 111–13.

[97] England and Wales, *His Majesties Speach*: Iv.

> who to save Catholic France,
> Overthrows with one blow the whole heretical reign,
> And in breaking its head will break its body.[98]

The trope—killing a part means killing a whole—at once establishes the logic of the action and connects the action to a paradigm of justified murder. If you kill the head, you will kill the body, and thus 'save Catholic France'. The murder of a heretical king will be a form of symbolic exchange, an implicit giving and taking, and, for here is the paradigmatic, quasi-religious warrant for violence, it will also be a kind of sacrifice. Killing the one will at once destroy the many and save the many—salvation being a word commonly used in this period, with deliberate ambiguity, to denote both existential rescue and spiritual liberation—through the death of a sacrificial victim.

So tropes, perhaps even mythemes, are important. Synecdoche, symbolic exchange, and sacrificial murder are concepts that are vital to understanding the internal logic of terrorism before the letter. A related form of symbolic exchange, scapegoating, as in the case of Buckingham, is important too. The concepts help explain how a 'tactic' can not only be strategic in a utilitarianism sense, but in a symbolic sense as well. They help explain the symbolic structure of an action which from the outset is communicative as well as violent, and undertaken not only to end the life of an enemy but also to provide for what the perpetrator takes to be significant social and political change. Symbolic exchange indicates the transaction that comes about when the terms of a tropological relationship are redeemed in an action. Sacrifice, the best known form of symbolic exchange where death or injury are concerned, indicates a traditional form through such a transaction is undertaken, where one thing is given away, 'offered' (and *offer* is etymologically the name both of the act and the victim of a sacrifice, hence the English *offering*), in exchange for something greater than itself.[99]

But first there is the action itself: the murder being imagined, or the kidnapping or sabotaging being planned. First there is the imagined event, in all its complexity. And what Kenneth Burke has shown is that when it comes to action not just one or two but five different 'motives' are inevitably in question, motives to which I have already alluded and which are put together by him as a 'pentad': act, agent, scene, agency, and purpose. Killing a 'head' of state may well amount to killing a 'body' of heretics. But how does the killing come? Who does it? Where does it get done? How does it get done? How in fact does a murder turn out to be a sacrifice, and a crime against the commandments of God and state turn out to be a fulfilment of the commandments of God and state? And why, frankly, must this killing come on? Why does God want men to take divine and human law into their own hands? What purposes does such tearing of the fabric of civil society actually serve? Or conversely, why in any given case does such a killing fail? Or does such an individual measure up to the act he or she would undertake? Or such a time and place prove unpropitious? Or such a killing fail to have the desired effect, or fail to fulfil a legitimate commandment of God or state?

---

[98] Boucher, *Apologie*: n.p.   [99] See Chapter 5 for a more extended discussion.

In any given 'action', according to Burke—'action' again being differentiated from 'motion'—there is always an act or sequence of acts, an agent or a group of agents, a scene or a gathering of scenes, an agency of action or a combination of many agencies, and a final purpose for the sake of which the action is undertaken, or perhaps many purposes. Actions and accounts of actions are constructed out of 'motives', and there are not, in the mix of motives, just one or two but all five, in any given case. Of any action, one may ask the familiar questions of journalism: What? Who? When and where? How? Why? One of Burke's primary concerns, Burke being interested in dialectical materialism, sociology, and psychoanalysis, and being very much opposed to the psychological behaviourism that was a dominant discipline in his day, was to expand the notion of what people do when they act, and how texts go about articulating action. Among the most counter-intuitive of his ideas, but also (as we will see) one of the most productive, concerned the large role that 'scene'—the when and where of an act—played in action. The scene of an act is a 'motive', and so many sociologically minded writers attribute primary causality to social conditions, rather than, say, to agents. The scene is a 'motive', in fact, in its capacity to enable action as a kind of performance, a playing of roles within the context of a time, a place, and purpose. The performative dimension of action is a common concern in Burke, and links his work with performance theory in anthropology as well as in theatre studies. The idea of a 'scene' of action is therefore central to Burke's 'dramatism'. Among another of his important ideas that may seem counter-intuitive concerned the role of 'purpose'. Purposes come in many forms, but Burke's ideas allow us to distinguish between motives ascribed to the agent (psychological instinct, for example) and motives ascribed to the action as a whole, which can include teleological purpose, or the larger purposes of the story that accounts for the action. A death drive can motivate an action, the streets of Paris during a hot month in the summer can motivate an action, and so can an understanding of God's eventual triumph over heresy. Making distinctions of this kind are not unique to the 'dramatistic' method that Burke recommends. In fact, they are commonplace among literary critics and historians. They are the inevitable focal points of humanist inquiry into actions and texts. But Burke challenges us not to be complacent about them, not to worry about what common sense or a currently fashionable model of interpretation may encourage us to think and reduce the motives of an action to one thing or two. Moreover, Burke argues that this is what we must do when we try to account for actions and texts: we must see how the actions and the texts that account for them distribute motivation, not only as specific explanations but as mimetic constructions. And again, we must be clear that this is what we must be doing. Analysing action and accounts of action means examining the distributions of five kinds of motive, from act to agent, from agent to scene, from scene to agency, and from agency to purpose. It also, then, means examining the relations among the motives in any given case, including what Burke calls the 'ratios' between them, as for example the ratio of the agent to the scene: a compulsive thief walking down the street sees a shop whose display window has been broken; a man with murder in his heart sees the king's open carriage coming down the street. Each action is enabled by the coming together of one motive, a nefarious character, in a ratio to another motive, a vulnerable scene, all but inviting its own violation.

The relevance of Burke's dramatism to the critical study of representations of terrorism is this: while providing a framework of analytical clarity, it allows us to expand the notions of motive being brought to bear on the phenomenon. Terrorist actions have acts, agents, scenes, agencies, purposes. They have all five of these things. The differences between different accounts of them are differences not just in temperament or ideology, but also differences in the distributions of motive. Of course, the latter serves the former. Armed with an ideology or a temperament, perhaps armed as well with a gut reaction to an event, or to certain personal or public fidelities, opportunities and ambitions, the writer, writing, distributes motives, and puts them in relation to one another. But such choices of motivations may also help determine ideology. Each serves the other. In either case, the system for distributing these motives, as a question of both similarities and differences, of continuities and dispersions, and thus of generating enabling fictions, is the mythography of terrorism before the letter.

There is nothing reductive about the dramatistic analysis of mythography in this sense; nor is there any straightforward methodology in it. Mythography is expansive, and dramatism can be as nuanced as the critic can make it. But mythography is also fuzzy, and dramatism does not come with a sure-fire methodological apparatus. Looking at terrorism before the letter from the point of view of its mythography will mean rethinking not only the texts involved but also the terms being used to describe them and the procedures through which texts and terms are analysed. It will involve critical intuition aimed in the direction not only of interpretation but also of answering basic theoretical questions. In the context of terrorism before the letter, the true story of Jacques Clément assassinating Henry III, or the legendary story of Samson bringing down a temple or theatre, what, after all, is an act? What is a person? What is a scene? What is an agency? What is a purpose? All kinds of questions may be raised when an anonymous John opens a door. But when an identifiable individual apparently takes it upon himself or herself to change the course of history through a single signal act of violence, when the event occurs or is aborted, when the aftermath comes and history is changed but seldom, finally, in the way the individual intended, when writers come to report the story in a way that explains, justifies, condemns, or exploits the purposes of the individual for ends that are the writers' own—what then is an act, a person, a scene, an agency, or a purpose? The prospect of acts like these prompted Renaissance poets to rethink their assumptions about human behaviour, and can challenge us to do the same.

5. THE WAY FORWARD

Terrorism is a concept that can lead to a lot of confusion. For terrorism is at once a highly specific recourse to violence and a phenomenon that appears to look very different from one context to another, and often *is* different. In addition, terrorism is a term that summons confusion, since it is applied to so many things and since it has taken on a number of connotative as well as denotative applications. I have tried to clarify the matter by insisting that the word 'terrorism' in not an accusation, but a specification, whose value lies in its utility to the analyst analysing it. I have also tried to clarify it by saying that terrorism always involves politics, violence, communication, criminality, and justifiability, but that each of these terms is subject to considerable historical and geographical variation, as well as contestation. To understand this variability it helps to think of Wittgenstein's theory of 'family resemblances' and Foucault's theory of 'discursive formations'. In many different contexts, politics, violence, communication, criminality, and justifiability *can* come together in an incident of terror, and *can* be written about in advance or in reaction to an incident, *given* a range of material variables, a family of recognizable concepts, and a formation of discourse that provides for their convergence with intelligibility and functionality.

The historical range of actions and texts which involve the phenomenon has often been misunderstood. Terrorism studies is not for the most part a historical discipline, and the glance into history by people interested in terrorism, especially terrorism before 1789, has been tentative. I am trying to correct for that. And I am trying to establish a role that literary history can play in the general study of terrorism and particularly in what is now called 'critical terrorism studies'.

A non-reductive methodology is needed for the study of terrorism before the letter, although the final justification for the method for it must come from the results it yields, and not in preliminary conjectures. If terrorism can be seen to have played a long role in the *longue durée* of Western European history, and if it can also be seen then to have become part of the political and imaginative language of Western Europe, then a method equal to the language is needed. A method is needed that cuts through the ideological disputes and generic differences between texts and is able to highlight common structures of formation, differentiation, and diffusion. A method is needed too that asks basic questions about its subject matter, down to the level of its fundamental grammar and semantics. Burke's dramatism is such a method, though in practice it is less a 'method' than a 'heuristic', a way of making distinctions, discovering fields of inquiry, and raising questions about fundamental terms and principles. Again, the proof is in the pudding. The value of this non-reductive and somewhat improvisational method, applied to a phenomenon which itself has fuzzy borders, can be proven only in the results, and in the usefulness of the method in coming to them.

In any case, what was enabled by the discourse of terrorism before the letter in the sixteenth and seventeenth centuries was both action and response, both tactic and text. A good way to think about this discourse is to focus on its participation in a dialectic of recognition. In a general sense, what the terrorists and writers are trying to establish is an answer to a riddle of history. *What shall we be conscious of in the realm of the political?* So far as consciousness is considered in a Hegelian sense, as a process of intelligence that is both subjective and objective (and hence both mental and material), this is the question that the texts (as well as the terrorists) of 'terrorism before the letter' can be seen to be struggling to answer.[100] The

---

[100] Neither Foucault nor Wittgenstein, two other thinkers from whom I am adopting my ideas, would have condoned my appeal to Hegelian consciousness. In this respect I have to confess to devising a rather hybrid model of understanding to think about terrorism before the letter. But I believe it works, and the proof will come in the results.

observation of one of Don DeLillo's fictional characters, expressing himself in a quasi-Hegelian frame, is worth keeping in mind. Terrorists 'make raids on human consciousness'. They do so in modern times and they did so in early modern times too. But writers writing about terrorism attempted to make raids as well. They attempted to raid a zone of political consciousness and communication, a public sphere where decisions needed to be made about how society should be organized, who should rule, how they should rule, how national and other civic boundaries should be drawn, how wealth should be distributed, and what religion should be practised. The dialectic of recognition is a dialectic where positions and position-takers have to make themselves seen, acknowledged, valorized, accepted—or else comes either failure or more dialectics, and probably more violence.

Let me be clear about my own position. I loathe violence, but I know that in some cases violence has proven to be necessary to protect a people or bring about beneficial social change, major and minor. Justice cannot always wait and the coming of modernity often demands revolution. I condemn terrorism, and I believe that history shows that terrorism is not only in itself usually morally wrong but also counter-productive.[101] I go along with the Russian Bolsheviks about this. Writing in 1911, Leon Trotsky insisted that the Russian Communists renounce all terrorist action. For the 'confusion' caused by terrorist violence can only be 'short-lived'. Soon afterwards, 'the smoke from the explosion clears away, the panic disappears, the successor of the murdered minister makes his appearance, life again settles into the old rut, the wheel of capitalist exploitation turns as before; only police repression grows more savage and brazen. And as a result, in place of the kindled hopes and artificially aroused excitement come disillusion and apathy.'[102] In brief, whether or not terrorism is always morally wrong, terrorism is almost always strategically weak, since it provokes reaction by its powerful adversaries, sympathy for its victims, and disappointment for its supporters. But sometimes terrorism has had an impact on history of a very different kind. Sometimes it works, at least in concert with other efforts at social change. Many successful nationalist movements of liberation—America's in the eighteenth century, Ireland's and Algeria's in the twentieth—were unthinkable without at least some recourse to terrorist violence. Sometimes, not quite working, terrorism nevertheless has made so deep an impression on 'human consciousness' that it has brought about uncanny effects. The Saint Bartholomew Massacre, a main subject of this study, did not put an end to the Wars of Religion or eradicate Protestant militancy, but it landed a serious blow to the cause of Protestantism in France, putting an end to its growth as a popular religion and rousing a large number of Protestants to emigrate. Sometimes terrorism has worked, as it were, ironically. Trotsky wrote about disillusionments of terrorism not knowing that in a few years one such terrorist adventure, by Serbian nationalists assassinating an Archduke, would launch Europe into the most destructive and pointless war it had ever fought up until then—and inadvertently bring about the conditions that would make for a successful

---

[101] On the question of morality, see Nathanson, *Terrorism and the Ethics of War*.
[102] Leon Trotsky, *Terrorism*: <http://www.marxists.de/theory/whatis/terror2.htm>.

communist revolution in Russia. That is what Derrida indeed would call a 'detour'. To understand history is among other things to understand the role that violence and ideas about it have played in it, and will continue to do so, even when the violence has unanticipated effects and ideas about it, right, wrong, and in between, circulate about it indefinitely.[103]

Understanding terrorist violence and the languages attached to it means understanding a pair of mysteries, a mystery of a faith and a mystery of hysteria: faith in the power of violence, such faith in it that multitudes are drawn to resort to it, even in the face of the many prohibitions against it, the many failures of violence to accomplish its goals, and the evidence of its horror; such hysteria as causes multitudes to overreact to it, whether for or against, and not to see what is frequently their own complicity in it. I am by no means original in this. The pairing of faith and hysteria on the subject of political violence is the main theme of many versions of the story of the assassination of Julius Caesar, including Grévin's and Shakespeare's. This pairing is even evident, and sometimes shown to be problematic, in the doggerel written on the occasion of Buckingham's murder. Says another poem:

> ... then Felton, did the land
> Receive a speedie cure by this just hand:
> Thou stabb'st our desolation with a stroke,
> And in one blow didst free us from the yoke
> Of foreign bondage, that to buy our peace
> Unconduit'st all thy blood, and did'st not cease
> 'Till thou had'st wrought thy unexampled deed
> Of our redemption, and had'st made him bleed
> That gras'd the lives and fortunes of us all,
> Which thou hast timely rescued by his fall.[104]

How can anyone believe that 'desolation' can be removed with the stroke of a dagger, or that scapegoating a prominent victim could lead to a nation's freedom, peace, and redemption? Only faith and hysteria, modes of accepting a myth, in advance or in reaction to an act of violence, can lead to the adoption of such a delusion.

The appeals of faith and hysteria, in cases like the legendary murder of Caesar, or the present-day murder of Buckingham, have nevertheless been widespread, and frequently followed. In texts, they may not only be sometimes exposed as hollow errors, but also celebrated as emotions of hope, or as subjects of the dramatic or the historic sublime. Faith can be sublime. Hysteria can be sublime. Identification with either a hero or a victim can be awe-inspiring. There is no question that faith in the power of violence and hysteria in reaction to it have been driving forces behind many events—and it is perhaps the case that sometimes the faith and the hysteria have been rightly placed, even if one can sense that beneath the historical triumph of violence is often an unmanageable irrationality.

---

[103] The point is elegantly argued in the Introduction to Edwards et al., *Age of Atrocity*.
[104] *Poems and Songs*: 69.

I am repulsed by all these tales of violence. Yet I am fascinated by them too. I get excited by them, even when I don't agree with the reason why the author wants to excite me. There is something inside me which is terroristic, impatient, angry, subversive, and aching to destroy. There is something in me which finds gratification in these texts. There is an idea in my head that sometimes, to bring about human emancipation, we need a symbolically potent act of violence, a blow against injustice that will take care of the problem, undoing it once and for all. But if I have a terrorist inside me, yearning for creative destruction, I also have a victim there, who suffers continuously, in sympathy with other victims, and which always says to the impulse toward violence: 'Thou shalt not.' The victim sits side-by-side with my conscious moral sense, which tells me that violence is always wrong, even when it is necessary.

Joseba Zulaika is therefore right as well. We need to work like novelists, and find the sources of violence and responses to it not only outside of us but also those that are within us. We need to study the consciousness of aggression and vulnerability that is constitutive of us as humans. Yet we also need to work like other kinds of students of life. To get at this faith in violence, or conversely to get at the hysteria that can arise about it, to understand these things from the inside, we need not only to surrender to the myths that enable them, and acknowledge the terrorists and victims within us, but also to decompose the myths, break them down into their elements, query them, dissolve them into the truths, the half-truths, the misunderstandings, and the lies that ultimately form them.

1

Terrorism Before the Letter

1. THE STORIES

Among the oldest of the stories that early modern Europe inherited about terrorism before the letter, and one of the simplest—we have already seen it alluded
to in the case of John Felton—was an anecdote from the third chapter of Judges.
The people of Israel, Scripture says, 'having done evil in the eyes of God', were
conquered and ruled by Eglon the king of Moab for eighteen years. But then the
people of Israel 'cried to the LORD' and 'the LORD raised up for them a deliverer,
Ehud . . . a left-handed man'. Ehud was given the job of delivering tribute to Eglon,
who was by now the well-established peacetime ruler of the Jewish territory. So
Ehud 'made for himself a sword with two edges, a cubit in length; and he girded it
on his right thigh under his clothes'. After delivering the tribute to Eglon, he turned
to him privately and said, 'I have a secret message for you, O king.' The king sent his
attendants away, 'And Ehud came to him, as he was sitting alone in his cool roof
chamber. And Ehud said, "I have a message from God for you."' Eglon rose from
his seat. 'Ehud reached with his left hand, took the sword from his right thigh, and
thrust it into his belly.' The king immediately died.[1]

'I have a message from God for you.' Perhaps there is comic irony in Ehud's language, since after all a sword thrust is not a 'message' in any common sense.[2] The
humour is emphasized by English translators of the Bible, including both the Authorized King James Version and the New Revised Standard Edition translators.
The Vulgate, the standard Latin translation, uses the term 'verbum': the word for a
'spoken word'. 'Verbum Dei habeo ad te', the Latinized Ehud says. The early modern
French bibles do the same thing. 'J'ai une parole de Dieu pour toi', the French
Ehud commonly says: a parole, a spoken word. The idea seems a bit attenuated in
the Latin and French versions. But in any case, the violence, ironically or not, is a

---

[1] Judges: 3:14–30. In *New Revised Standard Version*. All quotations from the Bible will be from this
text. The story of Ehud and its political morality have been the subject of some controversy among
modern biblical scholars. See Niditch, *War in the Hebrew Bible*; Tollington, 'Ethics of Warfare';
Chisholm, 'Ehud: Assessing an Assassin'; and Christianson, 'A Fistful Of Shekels'. For a more general
background on how the Ehud story works as a text and a historical document see Halpern, *First Historians*. A recent study of the influence of the Ehud story in early modern England concentrates on the
revolutionary period: Holstun, *Ehud's Dagger*. The story of Ehud and all the rest of the Judges was
given an elaborate, chapter-by-chapter analysis by the puritan minister Richard Rogers in 1615: *A
Commentary upon the Whole Booke of Judges*. (On Ehud, see 164–88.) Rogers's treatment of the Samson
story will be discussed in Chapter 6, section 5.
[2] See Handy, 'Uneasy Laughter'.

'message' or a 'word'. It communicates meaning. And the perpetrator is a messenger
of that meaning, the bearer of a word that comes from a higher source, and speaks
to a wider audience.

The meaning, however, is not self-sufficient. For the violence has implications
and consequences. It is important in this story that Eglon was 'a very fat man',
and that when the sword entered his belly, 'the hilt also went in after the blade, and the
fat closed over the blade, for [Ehud] did not draw the sword out of his belly; and
the dirt came out'. This is brutal violence; the Bible insists on it, dwelling on the
impact of the blow. It is grotesque violence, too, beginning with the monstrosity
of Eglon's body and the filth it expels.[3] The Bible implies that the brutality of the
blow and the grotesqueness of the victim are also part of the message. But crucially
important as well is the fact that the violence would have political consequences.
Ehud leaves the king dead in the royal chamber and escapes, unsuspected of anything. The king's servants wait outside for a while, thinking that the king (the narrative still in the mode of the grotesque) was 'only relieving himself in the closet of
the cool chamber'. Finally, when Eglon after a long while 'still did not open the
doors of the roof chamber, they took the key and opened them; and there lay their
lord dead on the floor'. Meanwhile, Ehud summoned his countrymen and said to
them, 'Follow after me; for the LORD has given your enemies the Moabites into
your hand.' In the absence of the leadership of Eglon they went out against the
Moabites and slaughtered a good 10,000 of them, all 'strong, able-bodied men';
'not a man escaped'. Israel triumphed and ended up ruling the region in peace for
the next eighty years.

So, Ehud delivered a message. The message was from God. The recipient was
first of all Eglon. The effect was first of all Eglon's disgusting death. Later on, the
effect was insurrection, leading to a change of government, Israeli hegemony, and
a long stretch of peace. Eglon was not the only one ultimately to get the message:
the whole of both Moab and Israel was eventually informed. And so this crime
against a sovereign, perpetrated in a time of peace, and motivated by neither personal ambition nor a personal grudge, only rather by the political aspiration of a
people whose hope was warranted by the will of God, took its place in the long
history of the Jewish nation, and in a Holy Scripture every word of which was in
principle both exemplary and true. A representative of the people, called upon by
God, with a single blow not only killed a man, but sent a message with the power
of changing of power.

Nor, again, was this the only such story in the annals of the sixteenth and seventeenth centuries. Just as popular was the story of Judith, the legendary widow of
the fictional Judean town of Bethulia. Having enticed the Assyrian general Holofernes with wine and a promise of sex, Judith killed the man in his sleep, cutting
off his head with his own sword. Holofernes had himself once 'spread terror among
the Israelites', the Deuterocanonical Book of Judith says; but now the terror was
reversed: when the leaders of the Assyrian army found out about what Judith had

---

[3] And so has the violence been traditionally interpreted. But see Stone, 'Eglon's Belly', which argues
for a less grotesque but no less brutal act of violence.

done, 'they tore their tunics and were greatly dismayed'; when the rest of the men found out 'they were amazed at what had happened' and 'overcome with fear and trembling' (Jud 14:19–15:2). The Assyrian army fled in panic, the Israelites pursued them, and soon, after a general slaughter, Israel was free again and prosperous. Judith herself was honoured, even 'famous' for the rest of her long and happy life (Jud 16:23). Once again, a single blow against a sovereign (though Holofernes's sovereignty is never actually recognized by the Judeans, his being a sovereignty-to-come, as the Judeans prepared to surrender) sent a message to friends and foes alike, a message with the power of changing power.[4]

As for classical history, there was always at hand, among many other political murders and treasons, the assassination of Julius Caesar by Marcus Brutus, a descendant of the founder of the Roman Republic, along with Cassius and a few other conspirators, when they ganged up on the dictator in the halls of the Senate and brought to realization a prophecy made to Caesar about the Ides of March. The conspiracy ended disastrously; in Shakespeare's words, it 'let slip the dogs of war'.[5] But for many literate people of the sixteenth and seventeenth centuries Brutus was a hero, and it was not the disaster that followed but the expression of intention, courage, and the spirit of political self-determination that mattered.[6] After taking it upon himself to murder his cousin, the Duke of Florence Alessandro de' Medici, in 1536, Lorenzino de' Medici wrote from the safety of exile an *Apologia* in which he compared himself specifically to Marcus Brutus. He acted, he said, for the good of his country and for no other reason, killing a tyrant and an oppressor.[7] Several prominent republican-minded painters—among them Andrea Mantegna, Sandro Botticelli, and Vincenzo Catena—had already taken Judith as a subject, depicting her as a hero of chastity, valour, and political independence. A statue by Donatello of Judith beheading Holofernes had been placed in one of the city's main public squares.[8] Now, at about the same time as Lorenzino murdered Alessandro, no less a figure than Michelangelo Buonarroti would sculpt his own version of the bust of a heroic Brutus.[9] (Michelangelo would also paint his own version of the story of Judith on the ceiling of the Sistine Chapel.) A century later, when the English playwright James Shirley would dramatize the assassination of Alessandro on stage, he would have the dying man cry out at his assassin, though not without irony, 'Thus Caesar fell by Brutus'.[10]

Both the Bible and classical history are full of tales of political violence, of course. The story of Ehud is contained in the same book of the Old Testament that

[4] For extended discussion of the Judith text and its place in the Bible, see Appelbaum, 'Judith Dines Alone'; Moore, *Judith: A New Translation*; and Otzen, *Tobit and Judith*.

[5] Shakespeare, *Julius Caesar*, 3.1.276, in Greenblatt, *Norton Shakespeare* (all citations from Shakespeare will be from this edition).

[6] On the pros and cons of Brutus's behaviour from a Shakespearean perspective, see Miola, '*Julius Caesar* and the Tyrannicide Debate'.

[7] Medici, *Apology*: 3–18. For the Italian and further background see Medici, 'Apologia'. And see Baker, 'Writing the Wrongs of the Past'.

[8] Crum, 'Severing the Neck'; McHam, 'Donatello's Bronze'.

[9] Gordon, 'Gianotti, Michelangelo, and the Cult of Brutus'. Also see Hampton, *Writing from History*: 1–3.

[10] Shirley, *The Traitor*: 5.3.67. And see Chapter 3, section 4 of this volume.

includes the story of the woman, Jael, who assassinated the Canaanite general Sisera (Judges 4–5), and the story of Samson (Judges 13–16), and the episode where he brings down a temple and kills 3,000 people.[11] Meanwhile, from the same body of sources as the story of Caesar and Brutus came other stories of symbolically significant political violence: for example, the legend of Darius III, the Persian leader killed by his subordinates Bessus and Nabarzanes, in the age of Alexander the Great; the legend of Catiline and the failed Second Conspiracy, immortalized by Sallust and Cicero; the legend of Pompey, assassinated on the orders of Ptolemy, upon his arrival on the shores of Egypt; the legend of Cinna (Gnaeus Cornelius Cinna Magnus), who conspired against the life of Augustus, but was detected beforehand, apprehended, and pardoned.

The Bible and classical antiquity both provided a legendary backdrop of violence where something like terrorism before the letter was involved. In most, the few or the one were targeted to claim the attention of many. Killing Eglon, Holofernes, and Caesar appalled their supporters and rallied their opponents, leading to insurrection in the first case, a military rout in the second, and, in the third, a civil war, although a peaceful restoration of the Republic was originally intended. But there were variations. In the story of Jael, killing one man, Sisera, was a matter of finishing a job that had already been accomplished by killing all the rest of Sisera's army. In the stories of Samson and Catiline, one population was targeted to claim the attention of another population. Samson wins a signal battle of resistance, a massacre, culminating in the terrible hope working its way throughout the Book of Judges, that the Hebrew God, acting through one human agent, might overturn a multitudinous oppressor completely. Catiline plans, but fails, to overturn the Roman government by targeted assassinations, arson, sabotage, and rumour. In the stories of the murders of Darius and Pompey there is yet another variation, the targeting of the one to claim the attention of another one, though the 'one' in this case has the power of a great many: Darius being murdered to make an impression on Alexander; Pompey being murdered to make an impression on Caesar. And then there is the participation, in the giving and receiving of violent messages, of divinity. In the biblical stories, there is always the presence of God, standing by as both initiator and observer, having agents act on behalf of both His people and His Self. In the classical stories, for want of monotheism, this sort of super-audience for the violence is missing; but at least in some versions, an element of the divine nevertheless enters into the picture, as perpetrators approximate themselves to sacrificers, propitiating the Roman gods, and doing the Roman people a holy service.

Most of these stories highlighted the heroism of the individual, armed with little more than his or her own courage and wits; and they showed how violence could have an impact well beyond the tactical removal of an inconvenient person. The violence of figures like Ehud terrified and expostulated. It provoked people into

[11] See Niditch, *War in the Hebrew Bible*: 111–17; Tollington, 'The Ethics of Warfare'; Jantzen, *Violence to Eternity*: 13–148. For a counter-intuitive but fascinating feminist reading see Bal, *Death and Dissymmetry*.

action. And it did these things precisely with a view to political concepts of collective identity, equity, and freedom—'ancient liberty' in most cases, in keeping with an ancient covenant: not a new and revolutionary freedom, but liberty all the same.

The stories were complicated, fashioned with cunning symbolic particulars, from Ehud's left-handedness and Judith's femininity to Brutus's descent from Lucius Junius Brutus; or from Elgon's disgusting obesity and Holofernes's lecherous drunkenness to Caesar's falling sickness. So of course were many of the other legends—Samson's hair, Catiline's crimes, as they were said to be, 'against nature'. They were complex elaborations of basic structures of conflict. History came qualified with complexity and particularity, and if it provided any lessons for later times it could only do so after specific choices of interpretation were made. Even the selection of a certain story over others as model of understanding or of action was an act of interpretation. One could choose to celebrate the grandeur of Brutus, but one could also choose to celebrate the resourcefulness of his rival Antony or, better still, the dignity of his other rival Caesar Augustus.[12] The story of Brutus could be a model for republican virtue in the face of a would-be tyrant, as it was in sixteenth-century Florence, but it could also be a model of treachery in the face of a benign and necessary ruler, as it would be, for example, in Georges de Scudéry's stage play, *La mort de César* (1636).[13] The story of Ehud could be a model for people in France who wanted to celebrate what had been accomplished by a man they took to be their own Ehud, Jacques Clément, the killer of Henry III. But Clément's detractors took pleasure in showing how he was no Ehud at all, but rather a deluded fool, duped by his Machiavellian masters, the Catholic Leaguers. 'First of all', writes a detractor, denying the analogy between Clément and Ehud, 'Ehud was called upon by God to do what he did', while Clément most definitely was not. Secondly, 'Eglon was not the king of Israel, and Ehud was not his legitimate subject.'[14] (That last assessment, by the way, is probably incorrect.)

As for the person of Samson, whom Ehud seems to prefigure, feelings about him were often negative or at least ambivalent. Some seventeenth-century writers began to explore his potency as a figure of devotional militancy, culminating in the protagonist of Milton's *Samson Agonistes* (1671, and therefore outside the chronological limits of this study).[15] But most references to Samson, especially in the sixteenth century, dwelled on his seduction by Delilah. Though he was potentially a superhero among terrorists, writers in Britain and France, along with painters from Italy and the Low Countries, were more likely to portray him in a cautionary manner as an example of the dangers of effeminate distraction. Samson was at once a case of absolute political violence and of political violence *manqué*, as if what mattered was not so much his ultimate success but rather his temporary failure. Samson was someone who had literally slept with the enemy and who sometimes

[12] See Shapiro, *Political Communication*: 95–8 and 128–30.
[13] See Dutertre, *Scudéry*: 275–9.
[14] *Advertissement sur deux discours imprimez*: 22.
[15] Gregory, 'The Political Messages', notes that Milton deliberately paired Samson with Ehud in his *First Defense*.

seemed to be a threat even to his own people. According to Boccaccio, who placed Samson among the 'princes' whose 'fall' required documentation, the moral to the Samson 'tragedy' was that, in John Lydgate's translation, the good prince should 'your counsel well to keep', even if your own personal Delilah should 'complain, cry and weep!'[16] Yet this same figure could 'rouse' himself, as Milton would put it in *Areopagitica* (1644), identifying Samson with the English people as a whole. In two surviving statues made in Florence, a bronze model by Michelangelo (1528) and a marble-work by Giambologna (1562), Samson is a Herculean warrior rising above his enemies, waging his famous jawbone in a fierce struggle. In these cases, as in Milton, Samson seems to be a figure of republican virtue struggling against enemies who would try to pull him down to their own level, even as his own effort must be to attack his enemy and literally beat it down.[17] Then, in the seventeenth century, a few retellings of the Samson story appear before Milton and the English Revolution where Samson seems to stand for a principle of religious as well as political resistance, such that, as one author would put it, God gives 'His promise in the death of Samson, / As by a metaphor'.[18]

There were many kinds of stories of political violence in the example of antiquity, including acts of violence against rival officials and civilians which were atrocities but not quite terrorist incidents.[19] They involved warfare or other forms of high-intensity conflict, or they lacked an overtly communicative or dialectical dimension. But they nevertheless could become a part of early modern discourse when real incidents of terrorism were being responded to or imagined. In the early books of the Bible, as the people of Israel settle into the Promised Land, the Lord often commands His people to annihilate the enemy, to put a 'ban' (*hērem*) on them, including women, children, livestock, and property.[20] (The ban effectively prevented post-battle assimilation of gentiles and gentile goods into Israeli society.) The legacy of the first mass violence against Egyptians and Canaanites continues into the era of Judges and Kings, though the register of the violence becomes more nuanced when Jewish society becomes more technologically advanced and elaborately organized. In 1 Samuel 15 Saul is rejected by Samuel as king of Israel because he did not obey God's command 'to utterly destroy the sinners Amalekites, and fight against them until they be consumed' (1 Samuel 15:3). He had spared the Amalekite king and much of the nation's cattle. Trying to make up for Saul's negligence, Samuel calls for the Amalekite king and singlehandedly hacks him 'in pieces' (1 Samuel 15:33).

---

[16] Lydgate, *Fall of Princes*, Part One: 183–4.
[17] Milton, *Areopagitica*: 34. See Hill, *Milton*: 428–48. Hill cites a number of writers who, like Milton, identified Samson with the English people and their cause against episcopacy and royalism; but none of them before 1642. *A Remonstrance Against Presbytery*, by Sir Thomas Aston (1641), actually thinks of the Samson story as a cautionary tale against the destruction by people, the mob, afflicted with blindness of the 'pillars of our state', which Aston takes to be the 'freedom' guaranteed by 'our ancient laws' (Hill, 430). In other words, for Aston Samson is a bad thing, and so are revolutionaries who would emulate him.
[18] Wunstius, *Simson*: 5: 53–4. And see Chapter 6, section 4 of this volume.
[19] See Jantzen, *Foundations of Violence*, for a mythographic overview.
[20] Collins, 'The Zeal of Phinehas'; Niditch, *War in the Hebrew Bible*: 28–77.

The story of David and Goliath—extremely popular among Renaissance artists, and another analogical source for the story of Judith—combines motifs familiar from the Ehud story with the story of pitched battle. Again, it is not quite terrorism: David and Goliath meet man-to-man, on an open battlefield. The high intensity of the conflict is qualified, however, by the imbalance of the fighters and their means of fighting, which is reversed by the imbalance of the consequences. 'This very day the Lord will deliver you into my hand', David tells Goliath,

> and I will strike you down and cut off your head; and I will give the dead bodies of the Philistine army this very day to the birds of the air and to the wild animals of the earth, so that all the earth may know that there is a God in Israel, and that all this assembly may know that the Lord does not save by sword and spear; for the battle is the Lord's and he will give you into our hand. (1 Samuel 17:46–7).

As in Judith, the sight of their beheaded military leader causes the Philistine troops to flee in panic.

In Psalms, David gives thanks to God for his military achievements:

> I pursued my enemies and overtook them;
> and did not turn back until they were consumed.
> I struck them down, so that they were not able to rise;
> they fell under my feet.
> For you girded me with strength for the battle;
> you made my assailants sink under me.
> You made my enemies turn their backs to me,
> and those who hated me I destroyed.
> They cried for help, but there was no one to save them;
> they cried to the Lord, but he did not answer them.
> I beat them fine, like dust before the wind;
> I cast them out like the mire of the streets (Psalms 18: 37–42).

But individual political murder—assassination—had its place too. In King David's dying words, he commands his son Solomon to murder Joab, a former commander in the Israeli army and a relative by marriage, because of earlier offences and because of his opposition to some of David's policies. 'Act therefore according to your wisdom', says David, 'but do not let his grey head go down to Sheol in peace' (1 Kings 2:5–6).

These are but a few examples, from Judges, Kings, Samuel, and Psalms. There are many others, all the way through the books of the prophets and the Apocrypha. From the story of Exodus forward, the Hebrew people were a political or 'ethno-nationalist' people, an 'Israel'; their religious violence was also a political violence and it was often ruthless.[21] In consequence, when religious rivalries heated up during the Reformation, and when those rivalries began to have political and economic consequences, the example of the Old Testament could both foment and structure violence, not to mention justify it: typologically, metaphorically, allegorically, and analogically. In later books of the Bible, written about either a diaspora

---

[21] Hassner and Aran, 'Religion and Violence'.

or imperial rule over Jewish people in Judaea, for example Esther and the Books of the Maccabees, violence could both avenge and liberate. In Esther, when a genocidal plot against the Jews in Persia is discovered, the king not only takes action against the plotters but allows the Jews to arm and organize themselves and take revenge against any of their foes. Slaughter follows. In 1 Maccabee, when a large Syrian army comes to punish the Jews for rebellion, Judas Maccabeus inspires his small band of guerrilla warriors by telling them, 'It is easy for many to be hemmed in by few, for in the sight of Heaven there is no difference between saving by many or by few. It is not on the size of the army that victory in battle depends, but strength comes from Heaven.... We fight for our lives and our laws. He himself will crush them before us.' After the Jews win the battle and rout the army, 'Judas and his brothers began to be feared, and terror fell on the Gentiles all around them' (1 Maccabees 3.18–25).

Meanwhile, in the secular history of the ancient world being so avidly studied by French, English, and Scottish humanists of the period, political violence is the dominant theme: empires fought for, won, and lost, or conversely, independence fought for, won, and lost. If the story of Caesar's assassination loomed large in the early modern imagination, so did the story of Caesar's conquests, and the wisdom with which Caesar governed the Empire he had enlarged. Both Henry IV and James VI and I identified with Caesar, and were pleased to find poets comparing them to the Roman dictator. In *Basilikon Doron* James VI and I recommended Caesar's *Commentaries* as perfect reading. 'I have ever been of that opinion', he wrote, 'that of all the Ethnic Emperors, or great Captains that ever were, he hath farthest excelled, both in his practise, and in his precepts in martial affairs.'[22] Henry IV commissioned a volume by Antoine Bandole, *Parallèles de César et d'Henri IV*, that appeared first in 1599 and then in an expanded version in 1609. An anonymous *Devise du grand Henry IV où il est comparé à César* was published in Utrecht in 1598. The *Pax Romana* was much admired, as was, in France, the Carolingian peace of the early Middle Ages; and humanist thought was increasingly pacifistic, following the lead of Erasmus, and even of King James.[23] But few educated people were under the illusion that peace was not the offspring of warfare, conquest, and suppression, or that both ancient and modern history had not been a story of battles, wars, and territorial sovereignties won and lost. Again, although peace might be the desideratum, armed conflict was the legacy, and the language of armed conflict, empire, and resistance was the language of historical and political consciousness.

Early Christianity seems to have signalled a great change from the militarism of traditional, nationalist Judaism to the cosmopolitan pacifism of Jesus and his followers, but there are undercurrents of violence throughout the New Testament, including the displacement of violence onto an apocalyptic future.[24] Early

---

[22] James VI and I, *Basilikon Doron*. Quoted in Kewes, 'Julius Caesar': 160. Kewes develops an important discussion of the figure of Caesar in Renaissance England.

[23] See Appelbaum, 'War and Peace'.

[24] Jantzen, *Violence to Eternity*; 149–88; Krueger, 'Christianity and Violence'; Steffen, 'Religion and Violence in Christian Traditions'.

Christianity, following a tradition biblically established in the Book of Daniel, added the stories of martyrdom, violence against believers because they bore witness to the faith, so that sufferance of violence by, as it were, militant innocents, resisting secular authority, became a large part of the historical imagination. History since Christ was the history of violence suffered—an idea that would come to be important not only for the cult of saints fostered by the Catholic Church, but also for the history of early Protestantism, which produced popular books of martyrs in French, English, and German, and continued to promote myths of martyrdom well into the seventeenth century.[25]

After Christianity became the religion of the Roman Empire, and then of what remained after the Empire's collapse, Saint Augustine firmly reconciled proactive political violence with religion by way of just war theory.[26] Augustine was a realist; he knew that Christianity would not survive if Christians always turned the other cheek. But Augustine mainly believed in (just) war as an active, even punitive force in the world: 'It is beneficial that the good should extend their dominion far and wide, and that their reign should endure, with the worship of the true God, by genuine sacrifices and upright lives.'[27] In *The City of God* Augustine both separates and correlates human and divine history, so that the break from the war-making of Jews to the peace-making of Jesus also marks a continuity in the violent history of the City of Man, on its way, on behalf of Christians, to assimilating to a City of God. The meaning of warfare has changed for Augustine, but not its importance in the ongoing affairs of men. As for individual acts of political violence, however, there Augustine draws a line: Christians, for Augustine, can justifiably turn to violent measures only when they act on the orders of legitimate state authority.[28] Similar scruples would be reiterated by Protestant monarchomachs in the sixteenth century, who believed that tyrants might be deposed, but only on the authority of 'public' persons officially responsible for the general welfare.

The Middle Ages brought with it, along with feudalism and refinements of Augustine's position and a number of crusades, a new code of violence, chivalry, and a great many stories to accommodate it. But though there would be periodic 'revivals' of chivalry in the sixteenth and seventeenth centuries, and periods when chivalric rituals and poetic conventions became fashionable, chivalric codes seem at the most to have an indirect, residual effect on the later period.[29] I refer to the aestheticization and courtly regulation of violence that we associate with chivalry as well as the cult of manly prowess and honour for its own sake that we also, rightly, associate with it.[30] Chivalric romances continued to circulate—it is said that Henry IV of France's favourite book was *Amadis of Gaul*[31]—but contemporary political and religious conflict seldom fit a model to which chivalric convention

---

[25] Boyarin, *Dying for God*; Castelli, *Martyrdom and Memory*; Knott, *Discourses of Martyrdom*; Lestringant, *Lumière des martyrs*; Monta, *Martyrdom and Literature*.
[26] Langan, 'The Elements of St. Augustine's'.
[27] Augustine, *City of God*, 138.
[28] Augustine, *Reply to Faustus*: Chapter 22. Mattox, *Saint Augustine*: 56–9. Lee, 'Selective Memory'.
[29] Ferguson, *The Chivalric Tradition*; Saul, *For Honour and Fame*.
[30] Kaeper, *Chivalry and Violence*.   [31] Babelon, *Henri IV*: 113–14.

could apply. Only a severely modified, even deconstructed medievalism could make texts like *Gerusalemme liberata* and *The Fairie Queene* succeed as narratives.[32] Meanwhile, new breeds of stories about political violence were circulating in print. One of them, which the French dubbed *histoires tragiques*, began appearing in 1559, with the first volume of Pierre Boaistuau's translation of six tales by the Italian writer Matteo Bandello, and went on with considerable success into the seventeenth century.[33] Another, already mentioned, based on a genre going back to Boccaccio, were tales of the falls of princes, sometimes called 'tragedies'. The most significant compilation in the period under study was the English *Mirror for Magistrates*, which went into fourteen editions between 1559 and 1620.[34] Few of either the *histoires tragiques* or tragedies of princes feature episodes of what might be called terrorist violence. But some do. Boaistuau's adaptation of Bandello's story of Mahomet and Irene (1559), for instance, which would also appear, in English, in William Painter's *Palace of Pleasure* (1566), as well as in a lost play by George Peele (1594?), is an unusually clear demonstration of how violence can be used as a political message, and will be discussed at length in Chapter 5. And there are other stories which run toward terrorism—perhaps most famously, for students of English literature, Bandello's story of the Duchess of Malfi. But the main point is that the writers and readers in the late sixteenth and early seventeenth centuries, in Britain and France alike, become enthusiastic over relatively new forms of secular, predominantly realistic storytelling, featuring politically and socially prominent individuals and their brushes with violence, either as victims or perpetrators. These stories do not just recount violence; they structure it, 'emplot' it, mythically and ideologically.[35] (The same can also be said of the new national historical chronicles appearing in the press, like Holinshed's *Chronicles* [1577; 1587].) And whether or not the violence they dealt with was directly political, they disseminated ways of thinking about violence which put it in the context of the nation-state, the established legal system, and a personal morality with both a spiritual and a legalistic dimension. It might have taken Shakespeare to make the murder of Richard II into a gruesome and pitiful outrage. But in the rudimentary *prosopopeia* in the *Mirror for Magistrates* (the *prosopopeia* itself becoming a useful genre for ruminating on violent political death[36]), we already hear a dead Richard II, speaking from beyond the grave, claim the following:

> For when king Henry knew that for my cause
> His lords in mask would kill him if they might,
> To dash all doubts, he took no farther pause
> But sent sir Pierce of Exton a traitorous knight
> To Pomfret Castle, with other armed light,

---

[32] Bolzoni, 'An Epic Poem of Peace'; Lewis, *Allegory of Love*: c. 6.

[33] See Carr, *Pierre Boaistuau's Histoires*; Biet, Introduction, *Théâtre de la cruauté*.

[34] See Winston, '*A Mirror for Magistrates*'. For an overview of the *histoires tragiques* taken together with the falls of princes and tragedy on the stage, see Tibor and Németh, 'Les histoires tragiques'.

[35] The idea of 'emplotment' is explored in Ricoeur, *Time and Narrative*, and White, *The Content of the Form*.

[36] See Chapter 3.

Who causeless killed me there against all laws.
Thus lawless life, to lawless death [it] draws.[37]

This is, in Richard's mouth, an expression of the logic of the *coup d'état* before the letter, as well as a *cri de coeur*. A law was broken and a lawless man was killed, for the good of the ruler of the state, sadly so but and in some way rightly so as well. Richard's death is both tragic and sovereign, a violation of right and a cautionary example.

If there were old sorts of stories which could be used to model political violence undertaken by individuals, guerrilla fighters, and armies, to justify assaults against non-combatants and even genocide, to build or challenge empires, and to combine secular and religious objectives in battle, there were also new sorts of stories underscoring the nature of the *tragique*. The appearance of the prose stories coincided with the invention of vernacular tragedy for the stage, where many different kinds of violence, including terrorism, committed by or against members of the elite, could become both sovereign and melancholy. (What is in question, the *tragique*, is similar to what Walter Benjamin said about the German *Trauerspiel*, the grief drama, where history is the usual subject, and where tyranny and martyrdom, cruelty and suffering, are frequently conflated.[38]) From the divine heroism of Ehud to the providential martyrdom of saints and the lawless pathos of Richard II, the period thus had a wide range of mythic models to draw upon as it tried to come to terms with the idea of terrorist violence.

2. HISTORY AND ITS TEXTS

It was during an expression of a chivalric revival that a key event in the history of political violence took place: the death of Henry II of France, during a joust, by an accidental thrust through the eye. The joust took place to celebrate a pair of dynastic marriages (between Henry's sister and the King of Spain, and Henry's daughter and the Duke of Savoy) as well as, more generally, the signing of the Treaty of Cateau-Cambrésis, which had stipulated the marriages.[39] With Henry II's death, the French crown would pass to his fifteen-year-old son Francis II, the latter soon to die and pass the crown to his nine-year-old brother Charles IX. The young and weak kings brought instability to the crown at a moment when strength was needed, for religious controversy was heating up and taking on political and economic dimensions. Already in various parts of France Protestants and Catholics were involved in skirmishes against one another. The 'rites of violence', as Natalie Zemon Davis called them, and which Denis Crouzet went on to document at length, had begun.[40] In 1557, a man named Caboche, a cleric with a grudge over the prosecution of his Protestant brothers for heresy, approached the king with a weapon in his hand, reportedly crying out, 'King, I have been sent by God to kill

---

[37] *The Mirror for Magistrates*: 117–18.   [38] Benjamin, *The Origin*: esp. 73–4.
[39] Haan, *Une paix pour l'éternité*.
[40] Davis, 'The Rites of Violence'; Crouzet, *Guerriers de dieu*.

you.'[41] So authority was being challenged by religious conflict even before Henry II succumbed to an accident, and the central government after his death required a strength of resolve that young, regent-supervised princes could not provide. But in the larger scheme of things, taking England and Scotland into account as well as France, and looking forward from 1559 to the middle of the seventeenth century, it was not just instability that was introduced by Henry's death and concurrent developments, but also, as it were, a stable condition of instability—a condition through which conflicts could arise, resolutions could be sought and power could be at once expressed and contended which itself had certain long-lasting features.

Internationally, the Treaty outlined the boundaries of major territories in Western Europe—including Spain, Italy, France, and England—that by and large survived until 1648 and the Treaty of Westphalia. Some hoped that the Treaty would stabilize the religious situation in Europe too, in favour of Catholicism. But it wasn't to be. And if the outward territorial limits of the chief states of Western Europe held firm, internecine conflict, often supported from without by rival foreign powers, was rampant.

Four-and-a-half months before the Treaty of Cateau-Cambrésis was signed—this being one of the reasons Henry II was keen to have the treaty formulated and passed—Elizabeth I succeeded to the throne of England, and England was officially reconverted to Protestantism. In May 1559, not long after the Treaty was signed, Scottish Protestants led a rebellion against Mary of Guise, the Queen Regent of Scotland and what was called the Auld Alliance with France; eventually the rebels would go so far as to occupy Edinburgh and sign a treaty with England. After Mary of Guise died, under the strain of war, in June 1560, French and English troops alike left Scotland, and by August Scotland had declared its independence both from France and Rome, and had set up its own constitutionally validated church. In December of 1560, Mary of Guise's daughter, Mary Stuart, who had been married to Francis II, suddenly found herself a motherless widow, and, in spite of the Scottish Reformation and its parliamentary disposition, began making plans to return to Scotland to take up duties as its queen.

England, Scotland, France, the three nations tied together by old dynastic affiliations and rivalries, and now three corners of a political contest where religion too was a major point of dispute, yet where all three countries also had something to fear from the outside powers of Spain, the Holy Roman Empire, and the Papacy, and so often formed alliances—those are the nations with which this book is predominantly concerned. The three nations shared a great deal even as they varied in size and technological and administrative development, and even as they alternated between being allies and rivals. Their fates were politically intertwined from the outset, and in more ways than one. Mary of Guise and her daughter Mary Stuart were respectively the sister and niece of François the second Duke of Guise and his brother the Cardinal of Lorraine, who up until the death of Francis II

---

[41] Carroll, *Martyrs and Murderers*: 92. Clouas, *Henri II*: 559–60.

controlled the regency of France.[42] Events in Scotland had a major impact on the political fortunes of the Guise, which meant it had a disproportionate impact on the political makeup of the larger country across the sea. The violence of the Scottish Reformation in 1559 even helped trigger the violence to come in France. Historian Stuart Carroll claims that 'the first shots in France's civil war were fired in Scotland. The overthrow of the Guise regime there in 1559 inspired their French co-religionists with similar patriotic ideals to resist the "foreign" tyranny at home and call the Guise clan to account at the hitherto moribund Estates-General.'[43] Meanwhile English foreign policy was primarily directed toward balancing hostility and alliance toward its Scottish neighbour on the one front and France (along with Burgundy) on the other.[44] That had been its priority since the late fifteenth century, and now with the rise of Protestantism in Scotland, France, and the old Burgundian territories, England had become party to a dangerous new sort of international movement of which it was itself, unwillingly, a leader.

In the Chronology, attached to this chapter as its Appendix, I list major events and terrorist incidents in England, Scotland, and France from 1559 to 1642, along with major texts about terrorist violence. I do not claim that the list is exhaustive. The focus is on major incidents in the sense of incidents which had national repercussions, and were spoken and written about often. There were many minor incidents, of course, especially in France. For example, Le Roy Ladurie tells the story of an 'uprising' in Romans, in 1579–80—a revolt of the peasantry and urban labourers against the large landowners, powerful burghers, and government officials of the area, which anticipated the series of Croquant revolts that would begin to come a couple of decades later. It was an overdetermined event, as Le Roy Ladurie tells it, related to the Wars of Religion but not exactly of them, responding predominantly to economic inequities; it ended, for the rebels, in disaster. But on the way to the uprising, there were incidents in 1578 like 'the burning of the noble landlord of Dorbain's castle, followed by his murder'.[45] This was very much an incident meant to send a political message to the local and national governments, as well as to avenge deeds committed by Dorbain. It would probably be accurate, and helpful, to call it an incident of terrorism before the letter. It would probably be accurate as well to place the incident in the context of a dialectic of recognition, where the rebels were trying to make themselves and their cause of equality of taxation observed, valorized, and accepted as policy. But the only two extant records of the incident (according to Le Roy Ladurie) are obscure, one submitted in a letter to the Queen Mother, Catherine de Medici, which she may never have read, the other recorded in a private journal. The incident shows that people did not have to operate on a national stage to engage in terrorist violence, that there was more than one public sphere in which rebels could try violently to intervene, and that behind the more sensational events, like the assassination of a king, there was a more

---

[42] See Carroll, *Martyrs and Murderers*, for an excellent account of the role the Guises played in these struggles.

[43] Carroll, 'The Rights of Violence': 156–7.

[44] Doran, *Elizabeth I*.   [45] Le Roy Ladurie, *Carnival in Romans*: 132.

general culture of dissent, protest, and violence, not to mention, as the rebels of Romans would find out to their loss, a culture of violent suppression.

Nevertheless, the focus of this study is on the incidents that were well known to the public, having a national impact, becoming either *causes célèbres* or scandals. There are plenty of events as it stands in the Chronology: at least twenty-seven, up to 1628, depending on how one counts the Saint Bartholomew Massacre (for there were many copycat massacres that have been identified by the one name). As for texts, there are over seventy (again, depending on how one counts multiple editions and adaptations), ranging from a number of dramas about Julius Caesar and his assassination, including Shakespeare's, to polemics over the Saint Bartholomew Massacre and narratives of the Gunpowder Plot. In the bibliography at the back of this book approximately 200 additional works about terrorism before the letter are listed, some only a few pages long, some of them voluminous histories of the time whose authors find themselves continuously challenged to make sense of religious ferment and political violence. 'Harangues', 'deplorations', 'arraignments', 'detections', 'admirations', 'thanksgivings', and 'execrations', along with 'true and exact reports' and 'last wills and testaments', flow from the press in both Britain and France in reaction to terrorist violence; this study will try to do justice to as many as possible.

The French Wars of Religion broke out in 1562, triggered by the Massacre at Vassy, and would go on until 1598, a few years after Henry IV had converted to Catholicism. In between the great military campaigns of the Wars, in times of peace, however uneasy, or behind the lines of combat, terrorist incidents could take place, like the assassination of François Lorraine the Second Duke of Guise in 1563, or most prominently, on what was supposed to be the occasion of the peaceful unification of the realm, in Paris in August 1572, sealed by the marriage of a Catholic Valois princess and a Protestant Bourbon prince, the Saint Bartholomew affair.[46] What massacres were and why it is useful to categorize them as incidents of terrorism before the letter will be discussed in subsequent chapters. But in a word, these massacres were mass murders, undertaken in asymmetrical conditions of conflict, with the aim of making bloody statements about religious toleration and thereby of altering a balance of power. They largely succeeded. But just as shocking to France, and just as much a spur to literary production, would be the murders of the second and third Dukes of Guise and of the successive Kings Henry III and Henry IV. When Henry the third Duke of Guise was assassinated in 1588, Pierre Matthieu, a member of the Guise faction, promptly composed a *Guisiade* that went through three editions, a tragedy where the duke is slain just off-stage by a gang of conspirators, and then lamented by a Chorus. The play (falsely) reports that Henry himself was among the murderers, and has him cry out at the end: 'We are two no longer; now I am the King!'[47] When Henry IV the King of France was assassinated by the fanatic François Ravaillac in 1610, Claude Billard, courtier

---

[46] The irony of the Massacre in this respect was noted by contemporaries. See, for example, *Relation du massacre*: 88–9. A recent study of it in just this light is Crouzet, *La Nuit de la Saint-Barthélemy*.

[47] Matthieu, *Guisiade*, trans. Hillman, Act 5 Argument: 264.

and poet, immediately set about writing a *Mort d'Henry le Grand*, which similarly dramatized a great man's death. The play was possibly performed within months of the assassination at court, and if it was not performed, it certainly circulated in manuscript there. The mourning widow, the Queen Marie de Medici, may well have watched herself on stage mourning the death of her husband. The former mignon of Henry III, now one of the great governors of France, the Duke d'Epernon, may well have watched himself reporting how he had been in the carriage with the king, how the knife had gone into the king's chest, how the blood had spilled out.[48]

A final sensational assassination in France takes place in 1616, the murder of Concino Concini the Marquis d'Ancre in 1616. Then the chronicle of terrorist violence, though not literary output concerned with the subject, goes quiet. Louis XIII and his chief councillors, Charles de Luyne and Cardinal Richelieu, certainly faced a good deal of opposition, even armed opposition, from within the nation as well as from without. But neither the crown, the councillors, nor their opponents resorted to terrorist violence to resolve their differences. When the Wars of Religion were renewed in the 1620s, they were fought in pitched battles where control over territory and sovereignty was at stake. That includes the devastating siege of La Rochelle and adjacent territories (1627–8), which led to the all-but-total surrender of the Guyenne Huguenots to the crown (who were nevertheless granted freedom of worship in return for military surrender) and, among other things, the humiliation of an English army and hence the assassination of Buckingham. Soon after came what was probably the most notorious attempt at a *coup* in the period, aimed against the ministry of Richelieu, which came to be called the Day of the Dupes (1630). But the *coup* itself, a failure in any case, was bloodless. Follow-ups to the attempt to wrest power away from the Cardinal and exert authority over the king were undertaken in the form of armed battles fought for control over territory. When a leader of the insurrection, the Duke de Montmorency, was captured, after a military siege, he was formally arraigned and executed publicly as a traitor. Many were unhappy to see a famous duke put to death; but they were not scandalized by it. The execution was legal.[49]

Why there were no more major incidents of terrorism for a long while in France is a matter of speculation. Perhaps the notoriety of earlier incidents, and their failure to deliver what the perpetrators were seeking, warded people off. It cannot be said that there was less political violence in France after 1616, not with the tax revolts in the countryside, adventures like Montmorency's campaign against Richelieu, and the central government's preoccupation with wars of territorial sovereignty, both on the home front against Huguenots and on the foreign front against Spain and even sometimes its putative ally England. But in national affairs, the terrorist option is not known to have been chosen in the 1620s and '30s.

[48] Billard, *Mort d'Henry IV*; Biet, Notice, *Tragédie sur la mort*, in Biet, *Théatre*: 938–50; Lancaster, *Claude Billard*; Zamparelli, *Theater of Claude Billard*; Zonza, 'Tragédie à sujet actuel'.
[49] Erlanger, *Richelieu*: 2.313–25; Kamil, *Fortress of the Soul*; Moote, *Louis XIII*: 199–219.

The major episodes of terrorist violence in Scotland and England similarly came early, with the exception of the assassination of the Duke of Buckingham in 1628. After Buckingham's death, the story went around that Buckingham had refused to protect himself by wearing a shirt of mail under his clothes, even though he knew that he was unpopular and he had already received a death threat. 'A shirt of mail', he is reported to have said, 'would be a silly defence against any popular fury. As for a single man's assault, I take myself to be in no danger. There are no Roman spirits left.'[50] Buckingham may have been right, in part. For Buckingham was no Caesar, and it would appear that Felton did not sacrifice him in the spirit of the senatorial Brutus. (None of the extant poems commending Felton compare him to Marcus Brutus.) But certainly in the 1630s no one prominent came forward to show himself a Roman.

In any case, earlier in the period, when terrorist plots were thick on the ground, members of the royal family were the prime targets. In Scotland, the status of Mary Stuart and her son James were the main points of contention; the struggle being waged not only over whether either figure was to survive or die but also over which faction had control over the meaning of their reigns for religious practice and secular governance. In England, Elizabeth was a target of several assassination attempts, and it was only two years into his reign as King of England that James was the central target for the conspiracy of mass murder known as either the Gunpowder Plot or the Powder Treason. After the Plot, there was a good deal of uneasiness in England, and rumours circulated about other plots in the making. But no other nationally prominent episode of terrorist violence would take place besides the murder of Buckingham.

During the earlier years of uneasiness over the successions in Scotland and England and over relations, possibly dynastic, with France, writers expressed their engagement with the problem of sovereignty, power, violence, and religion in a great many ways. The Old Testament, ancient Rome, Carolingian France, and pre-Tudor Britain all provided considerable fodder for writers in circumstances of state censorship where it was difficult publicly to discuss politics directly. So too did the affairs of contemporary France.[51] Huguenot writing, including monarchomach texts, circulated widely, either in translation or in the original Latin or French; and, in general, literature from France, including works by Ronsard, Montaigne, Garnier, and Du Bartas—all of whom responded to the political violence in France—was taken very seriously. Episodes like the Saint Bartholomew Massacre and the murders of Henry IV and Concino Concini were widely reported, and even often found representation on the stage. Christopher Marlowe's *The Massacre at Paris* is the prime case in point, along with the several plays about French politics written by George Chapman, including *The Revenge of Bussy d'Ambois*, which includes a fictionalized account of the murder of the third Duke of Guise at Blois. But there were others. Among the many lost plays of the English Renaissance are *The Civil Wars in France, Parts 1, 2 and 3*, by Thomas Dekker and Michael Drayton, and the

---

[50] Gardiner, *History*, vol. 6: 348.   [51] Coldiron, 'French Presences'.

anonymous *Marquis d'Ancre*.[52] Meanwhile many stage plays that have survived, though they do not deal directly with current events in France, clearly take them as a subtext. An example, listed in the Chronology, is Thomas Lodge's, *The Wounds of Civil War* (1587), which includes a modern French assassin killing for hire among the politically contending Romans of the first century BCE. Another may well be Shakespeare's *Love's Labour's Lost* (1595?), which takes place at a fictionalized court of Henry of Navarre, and seems to refer to the death of Henry III.[53] Henry of Navarre (later Henry IV) was a popular subject in English writing. A search of the Early English Books Online (EEBO) database shows over fifty texts published before 1611 concerning the career of Henry IV of France, and over fifteen published over the next two years concerning his murder.

There would seem to be an easy distinction to make between writings about affairs in one's home country and writing about affairs abroad, just as there would seem to be an easy distinction between writing about the affairs of the past and affairs of the present. On inspection, however, the distinctions do not hold except on the most literal of levels. Affairs in France, Scotland, and England were intertwined in ways that the academic habit of dividing the study of history into the study of different nationalities often conceals. The same is true of literature. If a work of poetry, like (say) Du Bartas's *La Judit*, gets translated both in Scotland and England, and circulated in both countries with the blessings of one of Du Bartas's greatest admirers, the king, are *The Historie of Judith* or *Bethulians Rescue* still entirely 'French'? Are the poems still mainly a parable about wars of religion over 'there'? The binary oppositions of the here and the there, the now and the then, though required as distinct categories on the level of literal understanding, are constantly being deconstructed in the allegorical work performed by literary texts, so that what matters there and then also matters in the here and now in all kinds of ways. It is true that there was a lot more traffic going in the direction from France to Britain than the other way.[54] This was the case both in the sense of literary influence and in the sense of interest in current events. But that does not lessen the significance of the traffic; it only qualifies it. The British Isles were unavoidably peripheral in the sixteenth and seventeenth centuries, even if being peripheral could sometimes prove to be an advantage, or lend itself to that false assumption of centrality known as insularity.

By far the most culturally important act of terrorism for the English and Scottish culture, in any case—an event that doesn't seem to have much interested the French[55]—was home grown, the Gunpowder Plot. The Plot gave life to the nation's first secular holiday, though dedicated to a godly 'thanksgiving', which came with its own secular rituals of scapegoating, public bonfires, and festivity; it inspired dozens of memorial texts in print, including many narrative retellings of the plot and castigations of papacy, the Whore of Babylon, in general; it inspired stage plays

---

[52] *Lost Plays Database*: <http://www.lostplays.org/index.php/Main_Page> (24 December 2013).
[53] Wilson, 'Worthies Away'.
[54] Lee, *The French Renaissance in England*; Salmon, *The French Religious Wars*.
[55] I have found only two texts from 1605–6 published in France that directly report on the Plot, one apparently a translation of The King's Book.

like *Macbeth*, *Volpone*, *Catiline*, and, indeed, Thomas Dekker's *Whore of Babylon*; and it became the occasion of an untold number of homilies, delivered in parish churches and many times issued in print.[56] It brought about a kind of hysterical paradigm of Protestant-Catholic relations in Britain, which would continue to be influential during the English Revolution and the Restoration, where Catholic perfidy was now and forever to be met with a self-congratulatory Protestantism.[57] A text with the following long title was reprinted thirteen times between 1606 and 1640: *Prayers and thankesgiving to be used by all the Kings Maiesties loving subiects for the happy deliverance of His Maiestie, the Queene, Prince and states of the Parliament, from the most traiterous and bloodie intended massacre by gunpowder the 5 of November 1605/set forth by authoritie.* Catholicism survived in England, and some members of the nobility continued to practise it openly, including Charles I's devoted wife Henrietta Maria; but Catholicism was also widely resented as a source of danger to the commonwealth and a form of arrogantly sectarian apostasy. Perhaps not surprisingly, the Plot was frequently coupled in people's minds with the Saint Bartholomew Massacre in France. Such a massacre as actually occurred in Paris or as might have occurred in London, the idea went, was an expression of the fundamental impulse of Catholics in Britain and abroad. The scandal of the Plot may have discouraged other English Catholics from thinking about armed resistance anymore; the success of anti-Plot propaganda encouraged Protestant triumphalism, as well as anti-Catholic hysteria, and would eventually play a role in the outbreak of the Civil Wars in England, even though Catholicism had little to do with the controversy between Parliament and the crown.[58]

In the Chronology I have included several narratives of the Gunpowder Plot written in verse, including John Milton's early effort *In quintum novembris* (1626) and Phineas Fletcher's dual-language (Latin-English) *Locustae and The Locusts, or The Apollonyists* (1627) as well as several prose accounts, including memoirs by two of the priests involved, John Gerard and Oswald Tesimond. That the Plot continued to attract literary output into the 1620s says something about the cultural work the story of the Plot was made to perform. The story had taken on a life of its own, and it had become useful in ways that could never have been anticipated. Milton and Fletcher may have been responding to the Plot not only to commemorate a national moment of grace, but also to spur on a continued engagement against the Spanish in the context of the Thirty Years War. As Milton's poem argues that there is no denying the providential destiny of the British or English people, so Fletcher's poem argues that there is no trusting the Catholic enemy, and no business to be done with them. They have to be destroyed.

In the 1630s, in France and Britain alike, a handful of interesting texts on the subject of terrorist violence appear, but in a context where terrorist violence is not

---

[56] Appelbaum, 'Milton, the Gunpowder Plot'; Appelbaum, 'Shakespeare and Terrorism'; Appelbaum, 'The Gunpowder Plot'; Cressy, *Bonfire and Bells*; Hardin, 'The Early Poetry'; Dutton, *Ben Jonson*; Nowak, 'Propaganda and the Pulpit'.

[57] Marotti, *Religious Ideology*; Tutino, *Law and Conscience*.

[58] Hurstfield, 'A Retrospect' and Okines, 'Why Was There So Little' provide sometimes contrasting, sometimes complementary views of the political impact of the Plot.

a major issue in current real-life affairs. These include several retellings of the death of Julius Caesar and its consequences, Thomas May's *Continuation of the Subject of Lucan's Historicall Poem till the Death of Julius Caesar* (1630), and Georges de Scudéry's *La mort de César* (1636). May had also written a Latin tragedy, now lost, about Julius Caesar at about this time. By now in any case the literature of terrorism before the letter has become self-reflexive: authors are commenting not only on ancient sources with an eye toward a contemporary context but also on the local literature of the recent past. By the 1630s, in other words, if not sooner, the mythography of terrorism before the letter had developed to the point of autonomy. It was becoming self-referential. If in the early 1500s writers drew upon ancient stories, by the 1630s writers could draw both upon the ancients and their own immediate predecessors. There were bodies of national literature which dealt with the idea of terrorist violence, even if the idea remained unnamed, and all the different threads of thought and action, of political conflict and structures of feeling, remained unidentified. It was possible for authors to write about terrorism as a familiar if nameless topic, and to do so possibly with an eye toward current events, even in a period when terrorist violence was not a threat to domestic peace.

In the late 1630s, a period of personal (that is, non-parliamentarian) government in England and of continued centralization of authority in France, war comes again. France throws itself into the Thirty Years War in Germany and a Franco-Spanish War beginning in 1635. England retreats from involvement in Germany, but in 1638 the first skirmishes of what historians would call the Wars of the Three Kingdoms break out, with the Scots and then the Irish rebelling against the English, and the English invading both countries.[59] Soon enough would follow the Civil Wars in England and the Fronde rebellions in France. These developments can be seen to be expressions of conflicts going back to the sixteenth century which on other occasions inspired terrorist incidents; they are part of what historians have called a 'General Crisis' of the seventeenth century, which had been stoked by a number of individual crises in the sixteenth century. But at the point of the break-out of these newer armed struggles, this study must come to an end. It must end, on the one hand, when the literature of terrorism before the letter has become an autonomous field of myth, and, on the other, when new sets of conditions for political struggle and political discourse come to dominate the scene.

To explain why the period after 1642, if not sooner, needs to be excluded from this study would require a separate study. But here are a few historical landmarks: in France, the death of Richelieu in 1642, followed a few months later, in 1643, by the death of Louis XIII; in France again, the rise to power of Cardinal Mazarin as the chief minister of the regency of Louis XIV, the beginnings, as mentioned, of the Fronde, and the beginnings too of a new sort of discourse, the *Mazarinade*, mocking the minister and undermining conventional political authority;[60] in the British Isles, after horrible episodes of violence in Scotland and Ireland, a Revolution

---

[59] Woolrych, *Britain in Revolution*: 89–233. On Ireland, see the essays collected in Edwards et al., *Age of Atrocity*.

[60] See Ranum, *The Fronde*.

in England; with the Revolution the expiration of the censorship of the press, the closing of the theatres, an explosion of political pamphlet literature, and the development of a whole new class of political philosophy, created by people like Hobbes, Milton, Harrington, and, collectively, the Levellers, all arguing on behalf of constitutional government and a strong central state, whether authoritarian or democratic.[61] At first, a good deal of the language of terrorism before the letter would serve. Pierre Corneille would present his *Cinna* (1642) as a kind of coda to years of personal violence being undertaken as political violence. *Cinna* is a post-Julius Caesar story, and a renunciation of the kinds of conflicts that were built into both the real story of Julius Caesar and all the incidents and anxieties that made the story so popular in the sixteenth and early seventeenth centuries. In Britain, as stories about atrocities in Ireland were spread abroad, failures in Scotland reported, and new forms of unrest began to be felt in towns like London, models of political reaction based on the experience of terrorism before the letter would sometimes serve. In 1642, in response to news about a conflict conventionally known as the Irish Rebellion, an official document would appear in London called *An act of state, made by the Lords justices and councell of Ireland, for the observation of the three and twentieth day of October yeerly, to be a day of thanks-giving, for the discovery and prevention of the horrible conspiracy and plot of the papists, to massacre all the protestants in that Kingdom.* The document is only five pages long and it is a poor reflection of the many raids, skirmishes, and incursions that took place at the time, as many Irish lordships rose up against the English plantation and sometimes against one another, or then again as English military units attempted to quell rebellion and expand English hegemony.[62] But it is noteworthy that the document repeats language that was common from reports about the Saint Bartholomew Massacre and the Powder Treason. In other words, if the Irish were rebelling against English rule, the official account (and many to follow) transformed the idea of an uprising for the sake of national liberation into the idea of a nefarious massacre of the godly, as understood from the legacy of terrorism before the letter.

Circumstances would change, however. The suggestion is not that there was no more discourse about terrorism after 1642. Quite the contrary. Because it had taken on a life of its own, it became useful in new kinds of ways. But circumstances had changed, and fresh analysis, outside the scope of this book, would be required to do justice to them. It was one thing, in 1590, to represent the Saint Bartholomew Massacre on stage as at least in part a call for militancy against papacy. It was another, in 1642, to represent it in pamphlet literature, at a time of public demonstrations on the streets of London in favour of overthrowing the English episcopacy and supporting the Parliament against the king.

The period from 1559 to 1642 is more or less the subject of this book, then, with a focus on the triangular relations between England, Scotland, and France: a period with at least twenty-seven major incidents of terrorist violence, the last one

---

[61] Of the many accounts of this turn of events, I hope I will not be faulted if I cite my own book, *Literature and Utopian Politics in Seventeenth-Century England* along with Smith, *Literature and Revolution.*

[62] See Edwards et al., *Age of Atrocity.*

coming in 1628. There were also major wars going on in this period, taking place apart from but with respect to the England-Scotland-France triangle of relations: the Eighty Years War in the Netherlands (1568–1648), in which both the French and the British were often involved; the Wars of Religion themselves, first from 1563 to 1598, and then again in the 1620s; the Thirty Years War in Germany (1618–48); the Franco-Spanish War (1635–59). Society on the level of everyday life as well as warfare was much more violent than it is today, even if this was also a major period for what Norbert Elias called 'the civilising process'. The timocratic-warrior ethics of medieval life was being laid aside in favour of civility and central-ized authority. The modern notion of 'crime', where wrongdoing was to be punished by the state rather than the family or friends of its victims, was coming to dominate the regulation of social life.[63] There was a 'judicial revolution' during this period. Law enforcement was codified, wrongdoing was criminalized and thus subjected pre-eminently to state authority, and the application of sovereignty was more and more equalized throughout the territorial limits of the nation.[64] In pol-itics, nevertheless, conflicts were again and again being decided by recourse to violent measures, large and small, for reasons both personal and public. The con-trol of wealth was always an underlying issue, again for reasons both personal and public. Thus the 'General Crisis'. The crisis came to a head in the middle seven-teenth century, and even exploded into a worldwide crisis at that time, where not only the Wars of the Three Kingdoms would break out but even similar wars in Spanish America and China, not to mention Poland, Germany, and Italy. This crisis stemmed in the first place from the break from feudalism and the rise of the modern nation-state. It stemmed in the second place from problems in stabilizing political and economic conditions in the new nation-state, and especially from difficulties the new states faced in financing themselves, and the new classes of pro-fessional and landowning men contended over financial matters of their own. It stemmed too, in Europe, from religious ferment, and from the internationalization of trade, both of which complicated loyalties.[65] New forms of power legitimation were required, demanded, and then thwarted, again and again: and so crises emerged, leading up to the big crisis.

Unfortunately, the idea—or rather the metaphor—of a crisis can only go so far as a key to explanation. For it assumes conditions of normality out of which the abnormal conditions of a crisis emerge—as if history were ever somehow 'normal'. The idea of a general crisis, however apt in certain circumstances, should not cause us to see the period coming before simply pathologically, as if the story of the

[63] Briggs, *Crime and Punishment in England*; Brown, *Bloodfeud in Scotland*; Carroll, *Blood and Vio-lence*; Elias, *The Civilising Process*; Gaskill, *Crime and Mentalities in Early Modern England*; Muchem-bled, *A History of Violence*; Ruff, *Violence in Early Modern Europe*; Sharpe, *Crime in Early Modern England*; Spierenburg, *A History of Murder*; Spierenburg, *The Spectacle of Suffering*.

[64] Lenman and Parker, 'The State, the Community and the Criminal Law'; Ruff, *Violence in Early Modern Europe*: esp. 73–116. Ruff succinctly defines the judicial revolution as 'the progressive exten-sion of state criminal law to supplant infra-judicial means of conflict resolution' (73).

[65] Parker, 'Crisis and Catastrophe'; Parker, ed., *Europe in Crisis*; Raab, *The Struggle for Stability*; Salmon, *Society in Crisis*; Stone, *Crisis of the Aristocracy*. For recent re-evaluations of the crisis thesis see Dewald, 'Crisis, Chronology'; and De Vries, 'The Economic Crisis'.

sixteenth and seventeenth centuries was the story of an illness which kept on getting worse and worse until a decisive crisis came on. I am not opposed on principle
to examining historical events in terms of what came after them. Nor am I opposed
on principle to the idea of crises. As will be seen in what follows, there were many
incidents in the sixteenth and seventeenth centuries that the people involved
considered to be crises of one kind or another. It was in order to resolve crises—
especially what I will call 'crises of meaning'—that many terrorist plots were
hatched. These ideas need to be treated seriously. So too does the general instability
in Scotland and France (and by implication in England) that came with the death
of Henry II.

But the idea of a 'General Crisis' is in the end more vaguely descriptive than
precisely explanatory. And to get at the period in question and its terrorism before
the letter, additional modes of explanation are called for. These include historical
dialectics, as in the dialectic of recognition I have referred to, as well as a 'grammar
of motives'.

3. POLITICAL THOUGHT AND THE
POLITICAL IMAGINATION

The period from 1559 to 1642 is important in the history of political thought,
even if the achievements may pale in comparison with political writings of the later
seventeenth century. Among the highlights were Jean Bodin, *Six livres de la répub-
lique* (1576), written on behalf of absolutism and the indivisibility of state sovereignty; Justus Lipsius, *Politicorum sive Civilis Doctrinae Libri Sex* (1589), translated
into French as *Les Six livres des politiques* (1590) and into English as *Sixe Bookes of
Politickes or Civil Doctrine* (1594), a conservative tract concerned with law and
order and 'prudence' under a prince, governing a sovereign state; Giovanni Botero,
Della ragion di Stato (1589), translated into French as *Raison et gouvernement d'estat
en diz livres* (1599), similar to Lipsius's work but more rationalized in its appreciation of the uniqueness of the state as an institution; and two works by James VI
and I, the already mentioned *Basilikon Doron* and *The True Law of Free Monarchy*
(both 1599), which argue for benign absolutism, given the 'freedom' of both the
state and its sovereign. These works all participate in the formation of the modern
doctrine of sovereignty and central authority, and still within the time period in
question is an early work by Thomas Hobbes, *Elements of Law* (1640), where
Hobbes begins his systematization of the principles of sovereignty which would
find its mature expression in *Leviathan* (1653).[66]

All of these works point toward the slow but sure creation of the modern nation-
state, and the dominance of its 'sovereignty' over more and more realms of social
life, along with the codification of crime and law enforcement and the rise of a

---

[66] For a classic summary of political theory in the period see Skinner, *Foundations*. Also see Burgess, *British Political Thought*; Keohane, *Philosophy and the State in France*; Salmon, *French Religious
Wars*; Tuck, *Philosophy and Government*; Waszink, Introduction; Marin, 'Pour une théorie baroque'.

'public sphere'. Well before the development of the coffee house public sphere of which Jürgen Habermas wrote, there was already developing, in France and Britain alike, a kind of 'public-ness' of governance, a sphere of communicative action where political questions were being decided by public and conciliar opinion as well as by the force of 'representation'.[67]

Conversely, and still more germane to the question of terrorism, are works in the area of resistance theory and monarchomachy: Étienne de La Boétie's *Discours sur la servitude volontaire* (written in 1552–3, and published in 1576); François Hotman's *Franco-Gallia* (1573), establishing the constitutional basis of church and state in the French territories; Théodore de Bèze's *De jure magistratuum* (1574), a monarchomach text; and especially (because of their stridency) George Buchanan's *De jure regni apud scotos* (1579), and the anonymous *Vindiciae contra tyrannos* (1579).[68] As the civil authority of the state became more and more central to the political imagination, and 'reasons of state' acquired moral authority, so too, under the pressures of the Wars of Religion and similar conflicts, did the idea of the right—a legitimate, codified right—to resist tyrannical civil authority. There was a Spanish, Jesuitical version of resistance theory too, as evidenced in the widely cited *De rege et regis institutione* by Juan de Mariana (1598). All of these works reflect on how to respond to tyranny—tyranny being understood to be either the condition of coming into power through illegitimate means or else the exercise of power for illegitimate ends. Illegitimate ends ranged from corrupt self-enrichment to religious persecution or the imposition of heresy.[69] The idea of 'tyrannicide' is never far from the agenda of these writers, although few go so far as to advocate violence directly, and with the exception of *Vindiciae* and to a smaller extent *De jure regni apud scotos* none have recourse to violent language; that is, language meant to do damage in its own right or to stir the reader into violent action. Resistance theory is rational political theory, and it hesitates to dwell on the violence at the root of its own reasonableness—the 'law of conquest' as James VI and I and many others put it, which originally established most early modern states. Nor does it ever do more than hint at the modern idea of revolution—the creation of an entirely new political order out of the destruction of the old. That would not appear in European discourse until the late 1640s and 1650s, and even then only tentatively. Although there are structural continuities between the political violence of the pre-modern and the modern periods, going back to the peasant wars of the fourteenth century,[70] revolution in the modern sense was not yet reckoned with or articulated, and the word 'revolution' in our modern sense—the fundamental and irreversible transformation of the conditions of political or economic society—was not yet in use.[71]

---

[67] Habermas, *Structural Transformation*; Lake and Pincus, 'Rethinking the Public Sphere'. And see Chapter 5, section 5.

[68] See Giesey 'The Monarchomach Triumvirs'.

[69] For a summary of European beliefs and important writings on the subject of tyrannicide, see Mousnier, *Assassination of Henry IV*: 86–105. On tyranny in general see Bushnell, *Tragedies of Tyrants*.

[70] Zagorin, *Rebel and Rulers*; Bourgeon, *L'assassinat de Coligny*; Bercé, *Revolt and Revolution*.

[71] Williams, *Keywords*: 270–4; Appelbaum, *Literature and Utopian Politics*: 155–6 and *passim*.

Ancient liberty, as already mentioned, was the great appeal.[72] One might resist on certain occasions; but what one resisted was a corruption of a previous condition, and even then one had to be cautious; violence was not to be entered into lightly; usually it shouldn't be entered into at all, especially not by 'private persons'.[73] It did not really have the power to recreate, to express new meanings, to found a new political condition. At best it could only restore, and so, theoretically, it was not usually to be recommended.

Farthest along in taking violence seriously, that is in thinking about violence as a productive force in the remaking of a constitutional state, is a work already alluded to, Naudé's *Considérations sur les coups d'états*. Printed in an edition of twelve, in Rome, far from the France that was Naudé's main concern, the *Considérations* openly congratulated all those sovereign rulers who had recourse to the exceptional violence of the *coup d'état*. His main examples include the Saint Bartholomew Massacre (allegedly ordered by Charles IX), the assassination of Henry Lorraine Duke of Guise (ordered by Henry III), and the assassination of the Marquis d'Ancre (ordered by Louis XIII). Not all of the masterstrokes he discussed were so sensational, or even terroristic. When covert means were available, Naudé thought them preferable. And among the masterstrokes were expressive acts that were not in themselves violent. On several occasions Naudé approvingly mentions the lies and myths that rulers have propounded to legitimate their rule in the eyes of the people; for example, that the rulers were demigods, born of heavenly parents. In a Machiavellian vein, he praises deception, whether religious or secular, as an original tool of the well-governed state. But a good part of the text is devoted to exceptional violence that re-founded the legitimacy of sovereignty by sending a message to the public as well as by actually harming one or more victims: the *coup d'état*, properly so-called.

Here is the one direct statement of the idea of communicative, law-giving violence—and it comes not in the discourse of resistance to tyranny, but in the discourse of resistance to sedition, in the name of the reason of state. And still, the argument hesitates, ultimately adopting a defensive rather than offensive posture, and failing to embrace its Machiavellian perception that violence could govern by terrorizing the subjects of the kingdom. Instead, the argument ends up thinking of violence as being merely instrumental, in conditions of states of emergency. These 'masterstrokes' of political violence, Naudé insists, must be 'defensive rather than offensive'; they must 'conserve rather than aggrandise, and protect against deceptions, villainies, and dangerous conspiracies or surprise attacks rather than commit them'. The higher law to which they adhere, as we have seen before, is that 'the supreme law is the safety of the people'.[74] Yet still, they are only a means to an end. And the end Naudé imagines is not of a regeneration or expansion of the public good, but only its repair or rectification. In other words, the 'supreme law' is already and ever in effect. He wants dangerous people removed from the state before

---

[72] Pocock, *Ancient Constitution*; Zagorin, *Rebels and Rulers*: 2.167. Also see Bercé, *Revolt and Revolution*: 4–33.

[73] The point is underscored in Davis, 'Rites of Violence': 65.

[74] Naudé, *Considérations*: 107–8.

they can accomplish the harm they are inclined to inflict; he wants them either surgically extracted or else medicinally purged, so that the state can get back to being what it already was, which is to say, lawfully secure. That is why, when considering the success of the *coups d'état* of the past, Naudé repeatedly asks whether they succeeded in completely eliminating the danger against which they were undertaken. And that is why, according to Naudé, the Saint Bartholomew Massacre, which he applauds rather than condemns, was not entirely successful. It did not entirely rid the king, Charles IX, of 'the Admiral and his accomplices'; it did not kill *all* of the Huguenot leaders. Do not start something you cannot finish, says Naudé. And Charles never really finished what he had set out to do, since some Huguenot leaders escaped the Paris riots, and the follow-through in the provinces was incomplete. It would have been necessary instead 'to imitate expert surgeons, who, while the vein is open, extract the blood to the point of making the patient faint, in order to cleanse the blood of all its ill humours'.[75]

Elimination—we have seen the idea trumpeted in Old Testament appeals to 'the ban', as well as in David's admonition to his son Solomon about a political rival. We have also begun to see it in terms of sacrifice and symbolic exchange. 'Let us be sacrificers, not butchers', as Shakespeare's Brutus puts it, in a trope that would be repeated often, and which will be analysed at length in what follows.[76] Here, in Naudé's *Considérations*, elimination is in a different guise: elimination of an enemy or obstacle as a form of purging, phlebotomy. But why does purging work, and how does it do so, apart from stopping one or more individuals from being, possibly doing something detrimental within the system that harbours them, and communicating the law of right that justifies it? The metaphor of a medical purge was not uncommon when theorists thought about the efficacy of political violence; so was the metaphor, encountered in the verse by Boucher, of decapitation. 'The nature of the disease required so sharp a remedy', we have heard Robert Catesby say about his apparent plan both to bleed the nation and decapitate it with gunpowder.[77] If an ill body politic could be purged of bad blood or ill humours, or be subject to the removal of its own vicious head of state, the body could be cured. But how can it be assumed that when a seditious person is killed, the sedition dies along with him, or that when a tyrant is killed a tyranny is killed as well—or even that without a 'head' of state a body politic would prosper? The theorists of the day could not answer such questions (no more than could some of the terrorists themselves). In fact, they had trouble even to ask them. The metaphors depended on notions of original conditions, of ancient liberty or some other pre-existing conditions of peace and health, to which elimination was supposed to cause the state to return. The metaphorically based concepts didn't account, and probably couldn't account, for the changes that violence inevitably brings about. They were weak on the idea of how violence was coupled with communication. Nor did they take into account the possible attractions of violence for its own sake: elimination for the

---

[75] Naudé, *Considérations*: 121. It should be noted that Naudé is not saying he would have approved of the slaying of all heretics, only the political and military leaders among them, the *huguenots de guerre*.

[76] Shakespeare, *Julius Caesar*: 2.1.166.　　　[77] See Chapter 1, section 4.

sake of elimination, a kind of message-sending violence where violence was both the vehicle and the tenor of the message.

'I would there were more Romes than one to ruin', says Catiline in Ben Jonson's play by that name. 'More Romes?' replies his interlocutor, parodying famous words by Alexander the Great. 'More worlds!'[78] Such words are meant to expose the hollowness of the Catiline conspiracy, and such similar plots as, perhaps, the Powder Treason, to which the play seems to allude.[79] But in exposing the conspiracy's hollowness, Jonson also evokes an idea that had parallels in a number of imaginative responses to terrorism: another idea without a name at the time, what today we call nihilism. Well before the word nihilism was coined and the concept became an object of intellectual attention ('nihilism', according to the *OED*, is roughly the same age as 'terrorism', and similarly comes into English from the French, in response to events connected with the French Revolution)—well before the word for it was coined, there is Jonson in *Catiline* satirically exposing the idea, and even putting it into a set of contexts which he expects his audience to understand: the Roman Republic, the writings of Sallust and Cicero, the Gunpowder Plot, contemporary controversies over Roman and contemporary history, the conventions of Jacobean theatre.[80] Jonson was neither unique nor original in highlighting this impulse toward destruction for the sake of destruction. The same idea appears in works as diverse as a tract about iconoclastic violence in France in the 1560s,[81] and a play about Samson, published in France in the 1620s. 'I want', says the title character of *Samson le fort*, 'to totally undo [desfaire] the Philistines / By fire, by blood, by homicidal weaponry, / And make their wheat-bearing fields and their vines to burn.'[82] In England, meanwhile, in a poem, another 'prosopopeia' written about participants in the Gunpowder Plot with whom Jonson may have been personally familiar, the ghost of one of the conspirators, Thomas Percy, is made to speak: 'I never did regard Religion', he says.

> A brain I had conceiting cruel plots,
> And what did I respect Religion,
> Since nothing fell into my luckless lots
> But what might work a general Confusion,
>   What was devised, but Country's monarchy
>   Even in one day to make an Anarchy.

And as the ghost goes on to put it: 'All my desire was bloody massacre'.[83]

This is a long way from 'I have a message from God for you.' But it is an outpost of the same territory. And if it is not visible in the constructive political theory of the day, but only in historical and creative literature, that is only more evidence as

[78] Jonson, *Catiline*: 3.595.
[79] Luna, *Jonson's Romish Plot*; Worden, 'Politics in Catiline'; Lemon, *Treason by Words*: 139–55.
[80] Boehrer, 'Jonson's *Catiline*'.
[81] *Remonstrances sur la diversité des poëtes* (1563), quoted in Christin, *Révolution*: 65.
[82] Ville-Toustain, *Samson le fort*: 10. See Chapter 6, section 3.
[83] Hawes, *Prosopopoeia*: B4.

to why looking at theoretical writing and at the concepts they express, or even, in the Pocock-Skinner tradition, looking at as 'ideas in context' are not enough if one wants to understand the phenomenon of terrorism before the letter. To examine how political violence really worked, or might have worked, one does better to turn to the historians, polemicists, and creative writers of the period. Or else, one does better to submit even theoretical writings, like the *Considérations*, to the kind of analysis to which one would submit histories, polemics, and creative writings, and examine their many dramatistic motives. An idea like elimination in any of the many forms it takes—purging, surgery, decapitation, sacrifice, removal of an obstacle, martyrization, the 'ban', or else plain murder, butchery, massacre—has to be seen not only as an idea but as an action: something with a who, what, where and when, how, and why: and something that however uncannily and dialectically, with its pentad of motives, communicates something demanding recognition.

Moreover, the violence has to be seen as an action *represented*, and therefore as an action mimetically *in use*. It is easy, when examining a phenomenon like terrorism before the letter, to make the mistake of thinking that one is examining something that happened, in and of itself. Certainly one has to think about what happened in and of itself outside the world of the text; the texts themselves demand it. And one is not wrong to try to speculate about what really happened in any given case—what really happened when Catiline raised a conspiracy, or when Robert Catesby broached the idea of the Gunpowder Plot—or to try to separate fact from fiction, evidence-backed assertions from fanciful misrepresentations, serious analysis from unscrupulous polemics, and so forth. But the subject of this study is terrorism *as represented*, terrorism as an element in a discourse, terrorism as an idea, theme, emotion, or psychological characterization which is being articulated for purposes that belong to the discourse. Those purposes can be quite complex. They can involve a brushing against something like destruction for the sake of destruction only to discredit it, or perhaps instead to offer a logical explanation of evil, or urge a frisson of recognition among the ambitious, or a summoning of an angry sublime. The discourse of terrorism before the letter places phenomena like nihilism in the contexts of acts, agents, scenes, agencies, and purposes. For terrorism is not only represented in the mythography: it is also used. It gets used as writers place themselves somewhere within the dialectic of recognition that their response to terror places them in. It gets used as writers, at the same time, indulge in literary play, and construct parables out of stories featuring terror. Like the parable in general discussed in Franz Kafka's story, 'Of Parables', a literary account of terrorism before the letter may at any time communicate two different and incompatible meanings: one that is a meaning for life, for conduct and moral decision; another that is a meaning for literary speculation, the parable as a parable, the puzzle as a puzzle.

People complain, says a narrator, about parables. 'All these parables', told by the wise men of the age, 'really set out to say merely that the incomprehensible is incomprehensible, and we know that already.' Daily life is a struggle, and the parables of the wise are of no use to it. And yet daily life is the 'only life we have'. The story continues:

> Concerning this a man once said: Why such reluctance? If you only followed the parables you yourselves would become parables and with that be rid of all your daily cares.
>
> Another said: I bet that is also a parable.
>
> The first said: You have won.
>
> The second said: But unfortunately only in parable.
>
> The first said: No, in reality: in parable you have lost.[84]

The literature of terrorism before the letter is a literature *in combat*, I have said, a literature struggling over the parameters, structures, and contents of political consciousness. But it speaks in a combat zone where there is a meeting between real-life issues and the parables that can be constructed about it. That Julius Caesar was assassinated we can all agree. But was he sacrificed, executed, butchered, slaughtered, eliminated, apotheosized, or forever defamed? Was his death an expression of virtue, of malice, of error, of historical necessity? Was it an unfortunate incident leading the way to the golden age of the Roman Empire, or a fatal crime that brought about a chain reaction of other fatal crimes? We still talk about Julius Caesar. But is that because the past weighs upon us, because we have transcended the past, because the past remains as a model for the present, or because what we really want to say about the present is unsayable? Or is it because, regardless of what might be taken as a practical application to the present, what really counts is the language itself, the impulses and imaginaries it articulates, the fears and hopes it sublimates, the assertion of incomprehensibility at which it ultimately throws up its hands, the tale of Julius Caesar being a sublime yet desperate sign for the incomprehensible?

How terrorism before the letter gets used by letters, and why it gets used the way it does, through what processes of articulation, and what contexts of the imagination, of ideological contestation and literary play, in reality and parable alike, is the subject of the next five chapters.

APPENDIX. A CHRONOLOGY OF MAJOR EVENTS AND LITERARY WORKS

Death of Mary of England, accession of Elizabeth I (1558: official coronation in 1559)

Death of Henry II of France, accession of Francis II (1559)

Heresy trial and execution in Paris of Parliamentary Councillor Anne du Bourg, assassination of Prosecutor Antoine Minard (1559)

> Boaistuau and Belleforest, *Histoires Tragiques* (Volume 1, including story of Mahomet) (1559)

---

[84] Kafka, 'Of Parables'.

Amboise Conspiracy (1560)

> Jacques Grévin, *César* (1559–61?)

Death of Francis II of France, accession of Charles IX (1560)

Outbreaks of iconoclastic (Protestant) and anti-heresy (Catholic) violence throughout France (1560–2)

> Jacques de La Taille, *Daire* (1561)

Mary Stuart takes up residence in Scotland as 'Queen of Scots' (1561)

Massacre at Vassy (1562)

Outbreak of the first War of Religion (1562)

> Pierre de Ronsard, *Discours sur les misères de ce temps* (1562–7)
> Thomas Norton and Thomas Sackville, *Gorboduc* (1562)

Assassination of François Second Duke of Guise by Jean de Poltrot (1563)

Assassination of David Riccio in Scotland (1566)

Assassination of Henry Stewart, Lord Darnley in Scotland (1567)

> Robert Garnier, *Porcie* (1568)

Assassination of James Stewart, Earl of Moray, in Scotland (1570)

The Ridolfi Plot against Elizabeth (1571)

> George Buchanan, *Ane Detectioun of the duinges of Marie Quene of Scottes* (1571)

Saint Bartholomew Massacres (1572)

> *Cantique general des catholiques sur la mort de Gaspard de Coligny* (1572)
> François Belleforest, *Cinquieme Livre des Histories Tragiques*, including *Amleth* (1572)
> François Hotman, *De Furoribus Gallicas* [translated in England as *A true and plaine report of the furious outrages of Fraunce*] (1573)
> Nicolas Barnaud, *Le Reveille-matin des Français* (1573)
> Camille Capilupi, *Le Strategeme, ou la ruse de Charles IX, Roy de France, contre les Huguenots rebelles à Dieu et à luy* (1573)
> Garnier, *Cornélie* (1574)
> Guillaume Du Bartas, *La Judit* (1574; revised 1579)

Death of Charles IX, accession of Henry III (1574)

> François de Chantelouve, *La Tragedie du feu Gaspar de Coligny* (1575)
> Simon Goulart, *Mémoires de l'Estat de France, sous Charles neufiesme*, Second edition (1578–9)
> George Buchanan, *De jure regni apud scotos* (1579)

LIVERPOOL JOHN MOORES UNIVERSITY
LEARNING SERVICES

George Buchanan, *Rerum Scoticarum Historia* (1579)
Pompee. Tragedie nouvelle (1579)
Vindiciae contra tyrannos (1579)
Le tocsain contre les massacreurs et auteurs des confusions en France (1579)
Guillaume Du Bartas, *La Judit*, expanded second edition (1579)
Amboise, Adrien d', *Holoferne. Tragedie sacrée extraite de l'histoire de Judith* (1580)

Attempted assassination of William of Orange (1582)

Ruthven Raid, kidnapping of James VI of Scotland (1582)

Assassination of William of Orange (1584)

Thomas Hudson, trans., *Historie of Judith* (1584)

Execution of William Parry for plotting to assassinate Elizabeth I (1585)

Babington Plot against Elizabeth I (1586)

Execution of Mary Queen of Scots (1587)

Thomas Lodge, *The Wounds of Civil War* (1587?)

Assassination of Henry Third Duke of Guise at Blois (1588)

Assassination of Henry III by Jacques Clément (1589)

Pierre Mathieu, *La Guisiade* (1589)
Charles Pinselet, *Le Martyre de frere Jacques Clement* (1589)
Jean Boucher, *Vie et faits notables de Henry de Valois* (1589)
Anne Dowriche, *The French Historie* (1589)
Simon Belyard, *Le Guysien* (1592)

Assassination Plot by Pierre Barrière against Henry IV (1593)

Assassination of President Brisson in Paris by Leaguers (1593)

Christopher Marlowe, *The Massacre at Paris* (1590–3)

Execution of Rodrigo Lopez for plotting to assassinate Elizabeth (1594)

Thomas Kyd, *Pompey the Great His Cornelia's Tragedie*[Translation of Garnier's *Cornélie*] (1595)

Execution of William Parry for plotting against Elizabeth (1595)

Attempted assassination of Henry IV by Jean Chastel (1595)

Gabrielle De Coignard, *Imitation de la victoire de Judith* (1595)
Discours sur la mort de Monsieur le Président Brisson. Ensemble les arrests donnez à l'encontre des assassinateurs (1595)

Jean Boucher, *Apologie pour Jehan Chastel* (1595)

Heyn, Pieter *Le Miroir des vefves: Tragedie sacrée d'Holofernes et Judith* ([1580] 1596)

Jean Crespin and Simon Goulart, *Histoire des martyrs persecutez et mis à mort pour la verité de l'Evangile* [Augmented Edition] (1597)

William Shakespeare *Julius Caesar* (1599)

The Gowrie Conspiracy (1600)

The Earle of Gowries Conspiracy Against the Kings Majestie of Scotland (1600)

Jacques de Fonteny, *Cleophon* (1600)

Antoine de Bandole, *Les Paralleles de César et Henry IIII* (1600)

William Alexander, *Darius* (1603)

George Chapman, *Caesar and Pompey* (1604; pub. 1631)

The Bye Plot (1604)

The Gunpowder Plot (1605)

The King's Book [i.e. *His Majesties Speach*] (1605)

Herring, Francis, *Pietas Pontificia* (1606)

William Shakespeare, *Macbeth* (1606)

La Liberté vangée, ou César Poignardé (1606) [85]

Edward Hawes, *Trayterous Percies & Catesbys Prosopoeia* (1606)

Thomas Middleton, *The Revenger's Tragedy* (1607)

William Alexander, *Monarchike Tragedies, Second Edition* [incl. *Darius* and *Julius Caesar*] (1607)

Thomas Dekker, *The Whore of Babylon* (1607)

John Gerard, *Narrative of the Gunpowder Plot* (1607?)

Oswald Tesimond, *The Gunpowder Plot* (1607?)

Richard Jean Nérée, *Le Triomphe de la ligue, tragoedie nouvelle* (1607)

Tragedie of Caesar and Pompey or Caesars reuenge (1607)

Francis Herring, *Popish Piety* (1610)

Assassination of Henry IV by Ravaillac (1610)

George Chapman, *The Revenge of Bussy d'Ambois* (1611)

Ben Jonson, *Catiline* (1611)

---

[85] An anonymous reprinting of Grévin's *César*, with some changes.

Claude Billard, *La Mort de Henry le Grand* (1611)

Georges Du Peyrat, *Recueil de diverses poésies sur le trepas de Henry le Grand* (1611)

Pierre Matthieu, *The Heroyk Life and Deplorable Death of the Most Christian King Henry the Fourth*, trans. E. Grimeston (London, 1612) (French edition, *Histoire de la mort déplorable du Roi Henri le Grand* also 1612)

Richard Rogers, *Commentary on the Whole Book of Judges* (1615)

Thomas Campion, *De Puluerea Coniuratione* [On the Gunpowder Plot] (1615?)

Assassination of Concini, Marquis d'Ancre (1616)

Théodore Agrippa d'Aubigné, *Les Tragiques* (1616)

Francis Herring and John Vicars, *Mischeefes Mystery* (1617)

Pierre Matthieu, *La conjuration de Conchine* (1618)

Ville-Toustain, *Tragédie nouvelle de Samson le fort* (1620)

George Hakewill, *A Comparison Betweene the Dayes of Purim and that of the Powder Treason* (1625)

Conspiration des dames: a plot against Richelieu (1626)

John Milton, *In quintum novembris* (1626)

Phineas Fletcher, *Locustae* and *The Locusts, or The Apollonyists* (1627)

Assassination of the Duke of Buckingham (1628)

Thomas May, *A Continuation of the Subject of Lucan's Historicall Poem till the Death of Julius Caesar* (1630)

James Shirley, *The Traitor* (1631–5)

Francis Quarles, *The History of Samson* (1631)

Georges de Scudéry, *La mort de César* (1636)

Guérin de Bouscal, Guyon, *La mort de Brute et de Porcie* (1637)

Charles Chaulmer, *La mort de Pompee* (1638)

Gabriel Naudé, *Considérations sur les coups d'états* (1639)

Pierre Corneille, *Cinna* (1640–2)

Henry Wotton, *Short View of the Life and Death of George Villiers, Duke of Buckingham* (1642)

2

Act

1. KILLING NOE MURDER

The act itself was always decisive. Even in cases where a plot has failed to come off, the act that might have been was the *sine qua non*. In many accounts of the Gunpowder Plot, a prime example, indignant authors took pains to make their readers recoil at the horrendousness of what might have happened. King James was among them. In his speech to Parliament a few days after the discovery of the Plot, the king dwelled on it. There are three 'forms...by which mankind may be put to death', he said. The first was by men, the second by animals, and the third 'by insensible and inanimate things: and amongst them all, the most cruel are the two elements of Water and Fire; and of those two the Fire most raging and merciless'. The king was appealing to the pathos of the act. But he was also appealing to its moral character, viewed from the point of view of the victim, with an eye toward the culpability of the perpetrators. Attacked by an animal or another human being, a man may resist and play a role in his own fate. He may well escape, due to his own efforts. Moreover, in the case of being attacked by another man, 'Who knoweth what pity God may stir up in the hearts of the actors at the very instant?'[1] It is better to be confronted man-to-man at a moment of assault or even animal-to-man than to be submerged underwater or trapped in a burning building, not only because drowning or being burnt alive is especially painful or frightful, or because one is more likely to escape the clutches of an animal or a man, but also because morality and mercy may be at hand. Even animals have sometimes shown themselves to be capable of pity, James asserts. But the elements are only cruel, knowing neither pity nor mercy, and fire is the cruellest. All the more reason to be outraged by the Gunpowder Plot, then: 'What can I speak of it, I know not. Nay, what can I not speak of it? And therefore I must say with the Poet, *vox faucibus haeret* [my voice sticks in my throat].'[2] That the act that might have been, the raging fire, was so horrendous as to be 'unspeakable' would become another commonplace of the discourse of the Gunpowder Plot.[3] 'I sing Impiety beyond a name', wrote the poet Richard Crashaw some years later. 'Who styles it any thing,

---

[1] *His Majesties Speach*: B3.   [2] *His Majesties Speach*: B2.
[3] Herman, 'A Deed without a Name'.

knows not the same.'[4] But notice that James *also* says that the Plot was so horrendous as to demand *a lot* of words: 'what can I *not* speak of it?'

Notice, too, that even when James focuses on the act in and of itself, he brings in the rest of the pentad of motives. He has to specify *agents* (the actors and the victims) and the *agency* (fire from an explosion). He has already called attention to the *scene*—the House of Lords, where he was now speaking, and where the act was supposed to have taken place—and he is inquiring, now, as to what *purpose* the Plot was supposed to have served, and also therefore what measures the government ought to take in the future. The act, the agents, the scene, the agency, and the purpose: they are all there, implied in the king's every word. They are present, moreover, not only in what the king is talking about, 'a roaring, nay a thundering sin of fire and brimstone, from the which God hath most miraculously delivered us all', but also in what the king *himself* is *doing*.[5] The king (*agent*) is delivering a speech (*act*), on a special occasion in Parliament (*scene*), with the willing attention of a sympathetic audience with the powers of a court of law (*agency*), in order to make sense of the Plot and direct the minds and hearts of the public in the direction he wants to direct them (*purpose*). On the one hand, there is a pentad of motives regarding what the author has *represented*, a version of the story of the Gunpowder Plot. On the other hand, there is a pentad of motives regarding the *representation*, the action of articulation and communication.

It is not hard to make distinctions among the motives, and to separate an act from an agent, a scene, an agency, or a purpose, but it is hard to talk about any one element of motivation without talking about the others. For all of them require one another: there is no purpose without an agent, no agency without a scene, no act without an agent, an agency, a scene, and a purpose. But in this matter of the act, in situations of terrorism before the letter, the essence of the act has a powerful role to play that is all its own.

The French refer to the *passage à l'acte*, the decisive moment when agent, scene, agency, and purpose all switch, together, into assault against a target.[6] The act is a passage, especially, given the causes and consequences, the terrorist act. It goes. It transforms. If successful, the terrorist act may make the living into the dead, and yet also turn a silence into something spoken, and create out of a common citizen— the one doing the killing—a valorous hero or a traitorous villain. In Aristotelian terms, the central terrorist act functions as a *peripeteia*, a turning point. But as the act is something accomplished by an agent, the act is also a passage of the agent and by the agent: a passage of the agent *into* action, the French say, and thus into the role of a *provocateur*.

[4] Crashaw, 'On ye Gunpowder-Treason', in *Steps to the Temple*: 350.
[5] *His Majesties Speach*: B2.
[6] Pierre Henri Castel, 'Passage à l'acte': <http://pierrehenri.castel.free.fr/Articles/Passageacte.htm>. The term has frequently been absorbed into the discourse of French psychoanalysis, but Lacan distinguished between *passage à l'acte*, which involved conscious intentionality, and the English term, 'acting-out', which involved the unconscious. Castel himself distinguishes between the *passage* as a 'brutal exit from a scene' and the 'acting-out' which leaves the scene in place, and is meant to do so. A young woman in despair, hurling herself off a bridge, has made a *passage à l'acte*. Freud's Dora, neurotically coughing whenever sex is mentioned, is acting out.

Early modern writers were commonly fascinated by the *passage*. They could ignore or de-emphasize it, if they wished. They could even, as will be seen, opt for a contrary model of terrorist action where the model of the heroic/villainous *passage* was eschewed for the model of the '*accident misérable*', an 'unfortunate incident', an event without a premeditated cause. Then, even in the case of horrific massacres, violence would be, if not excusable, at least incompletely culpable. The act would have arrived without anyone precisely willing it to come. Especially if viewed from the side of apologists, much that would otherwise seem an outrage could thus find a kind of excuse by being framed not as a bold *passage à l'acte* but as an unfortunate incident whose causes were remote rather than direct, ambiguous rather than clear, many-sided rather than one-sided, a fault of the victims as well as the perpetrators.

Nevertheless, terrorist action would usually seem to involve something direct, clear, and one-sided: a remarkable audacity, at once moral, psychological, and historical; a 'thundering sin'; or else a masterstroke of national deliverance, like the 'one blow' we heard about in the case of John Felton, which was said to 'free us from the yoke'. The singularity of the event fascinated, amazed, appalled, or maybe even inspired and stimulated admiration. 'What can I speak of it, I know not. Nay, what can I not speak of it?' Whether right or wrong, it would seem to involve what was at once a magnificent nullification and a horrible assertion. When one considered how, with a single blow, a concord was made into discord, a certainty was rendered uncertain, life was turned into death, and, perhaps most curiously, an individual at rest was made into a hero or a villain, one thought about the power of action in and of itself.

But the *passage* was not self-sufficient. For the writer responding to the idea or the memory of a terrorist event, there was not only the *passage* to take into account, but also the result of the *passage:* direct and indirect consequences; open and covert efforts to control, resist or nullify the consequences; the roads and detours of the meaning of the act as it effects worked their way through society; the acts of mourning, punishment, and revenge that the act might lead to, where once again the meaning of the act would be rehearsed, renounced, ritualized, transvalued, exorcised, or vindicated. From an attack on the body of a victim or a body politic might well come an attack on the body of a scapegoat, as from an assault on the dignity of the state might well come an affirmation of its power. Or conversely, from an attack on an oppressor might well come a carnival of sacrificial glee. The message of terrorist violence was ambiguous from the start, and it had to be disambiguated. And so a writer would have to take not only the message of the violence into consideration, but also the byways of its interpretation and clarification. Moreover, if a writer really was to take the event into account, there was the origin of the act and its messages to consider; for acts do not come from nowhere; they have causes and erupt out of a sequence of other acts. The decisive *passage* was always really an attempt to resolve a conflict—a struggle over meaning as well as over power—that may well have originated in another decisive *passage*. At the origin of the terrorist assault there was almost always a crisis, which the assault was meant to resolve, although resolution seldom came, or at least seldom came in the way the terrorists anticipated.

2. THE HEROIC EFFORT

It could be momentous, the *passage à l'acte*, especially in the most famous cases of terrorist violence. The time has waited, the time has come, the moment is here, the moment is now, and the times will never be the same.

'Brutus show yourself', says Brutus to himself in front of his fellow conspirators in Jacques Grévin's *César* (1559–61):

> Consecrate today your life to the long reach of memory…
> Do it today, Brutus, do it, do it, that Caesar die
> So that forever you are remembered
> As the enemy of the cruel tyrant.

Brutus's comrade Cassius joins in the conversation, and Cassius is even more fervid:

> I feel my heart [he says], my blood, my spirits, my courage
> Burst and boil and burn and bound up
> All conspiring to one end, emboldening me
> To spill Caesar's blood, and with the greatest audacity –
> Upright, hands ready – to confront him, face to face.
> Armed with such a will I want, I want to plunge
> My dagger in his breast, and clutch it there
> Until he dies, so that I may say that I
> With one blow have killed both Caesar and the Empire.[7]

The repetitions (along with the mixed metaphors) are all in the original French: do it, do it, do it: I want, I want [*fais, fais, fais; je veux, je veux*]. And they indicate not just emotion, but a sense of how the act at hand is going to interrupt the flow of time.

Shakespeare's assassins express similar ideas. Here is Shakespeare's Brutus, in *Julius Caesar* (1599) at the same moment, deliberating about what he is about to do to the title character:

> Between the acting of a dreadful thing
> And the first motion, all the interim is
> Like a phantasma, or a hideous dream.

The act is momentous, and as it is violent and murderous too, it is dreadful. It is hard to think past the idea to the thing itself. But Brutus has already made his resolution, or at least he wants to think he has made his resolution:

> 'Speak, strike, redress!' [He is reading an anonymous missive.] Am I entreated
> To speak and strike? O Rome, I make thee promise:
> If the redress will follow, thou receivest
> Thy full petition at the hand of Brutus![8]

---

[7] Grévin, *César*. 381–3; 430–8. And see Pineaux, 'César dans la tragédie'.
[8] Shakespeare, *Julius Caesar*. 2.1.63–65; 2.1.55–58. I discuss the critical context in 'Shakespeare and Terrorism'. Among the most pertinent, recent analyses for understanding the function of the

In *Macbeth* (1606), before killing Duncan, his king, Macbeth goes through much the same process, though with more dread than ever troubled Brutus, and also more hope, imagining that the fatal moment might annihilate all the moments to come and slip the present into an eternal future:

> If it were done when 'tis done, then 'twere well
> It were done quickly...

Two things happen at once. The momentousness of the event fills the man with a longing for impetuosity, mixed with moral reservation. But at the same time, this very mixture of longing, resolution, and hesitation gives birth to a vision of the transcendence of time altogether: 'the be-all and the end-all' he will allude to in a moment would allow him to 'jump the life to come'.[9] It is an expression of Macbeth's *failure* to be another Brutus, even as he prepares to commit what he knows will be an 'assassination', that when he finally resolves himself to act it will be because his wife has come up with a plan for effective dissimulation. Macbeth will not take responsibility for what he does. He will not play the terrorist, actually—a point that I think Shakespeare is eager for us to see, if only by way of the contrast between Macbeth and Brutus in similar crises.[10]

The lead-up to the *passage* is in most cases indicative of the moral and social character of the violent blow. There is seldom any doubt in the minds of the perpetrators, in narratives and dramatizations of this type, that recourse to violence is immoral and illegal. The question is whether the violence will also serve a higher moral purpose and express a higher law. Virtually every telling of the story of Cassius and Brutus has them worrying about this, and the worrying itself indicates the character of what they are doing. It reflects well on the perpetrators if they show themselves to have scruples, to be capable of doubting themselves and fearing for their own courage, if not also for their lives. When the agents of terror do not worry enough, when they show themselves to be altogether certain about what they are doing, about how and why and what the results will be, they come off as fanatics, overcome by their own ambition, pride, and obstinacy or even by what was commonly referred to as 'frenzy', a kind of madness—in the language of early modern humoral psychology, a kind of overheating of the blood. This is what we find in later, unsympathetic accounts of Cassius and Brutus, as in George de Scudéry's *Mort de César* (1636) and Guérin de Bouscal's *Mort de Brute et de Porcie* (1637)—both written very much in the spirit of political absolutism, with a view toward the reign of Louis XIII and his minister Cardinal Richelieu. The plays show

decisive act in *Julius Caesar* are Hadfield, *Shakespeare and Republicanism*: 160–81; Nutall, *Shakespeare the Thinker*: 171–93; Wilson, "A Bleeding Head Where They Begun'"; Gil, 'Bare Life'; Wills, *Rome and Rhetoric*; and Lucking, 'Brutus's Reasons'.

[9] Shakespeare, *Macbeth*: 1.7.1–7. On *Macbeth* and political action see Norbrook, '*Macbeth* and the Politics'; Sinfield, *Faultlines*, 95–108; Coddon, 'Unreal Mockery'; and Wilson, 'Blood Will Have Blood'.

[10] That Macbeth is not a terrorist in any meaningful way, although he imitates some of the patterns of terrorist behaviour, does not detract, however, from the idea that the play *Macbeth* is nevertheless a *response* to terrorism, and in particular to the Gunpowder Plot. On that score see Holderness and Loughrey, 'Shakespeare and Terror', and Appelbaum, 'Shakespeare and Terrorism'.

the rebellious spirits of the murderers of Julius Caesar to have been, in short, too hot.[11] But traces of this immoral (or amoral) frenzy are perhaps even to be found in the more positively depicted conspirators of Grévin, Shakespeare, and the Scots poet Sir William Alexander Stirling, publishing a closet drama, *The Tragedie of Julius Caesar*, in 1607.[12] That is why Grévin's Cassius is ready to 'burst and boil and burn' and that is one of the reasons why Shakespeare's Cassius is looking for a 'show of fire' in Brutus, and Stirling's Cassius urges his co-conspirators that they must act 'whilst of our band the fury flames most hot'. Passing *into* this act means passing, heatedly, into what is at once a violation and a transcendence. The great heroes of terror, such as Shakespeare's and Grévin's Brutus, are aware that they may be violating something in themselves when they pass into action—the very love they bear for Caesar, for example—and so they will need an excess of resolve and passion and maybe even heat to spur themselves into action.

So far as the *passage à l'acte* is understood to involve a transformation of the condition of the state, into it must come a power of momentous impact and transcendence: this *one* blow must have multiple effects. It must not only violate moral and legal codes, it must also surpass and replace them. 'That I may say that I / With one blow have killed both Caesar and the Empire', as we have seen Grévin's Cassius put it. But how can any one act have such a power? If the act is *heroic*, whether for good or evil, heroism itself is at stake. Heroism itself is *on trial*, and heroism has to be *proved*. Hence, in the first place, the act can never be banal; it has to challenge the moral integrity of the agent as well as the norms and laws of the state. Hence, in the second place, it has to be undertaken in a spirit of sublimation. A pathway of action has to be found through which 'killing [is] noe murder', as a radical of the English Revolution would later put it, trying to arouse support for the assassination of Oliver Cromwell: or through which, to give other kinds of examples, kidnapping is not kidnapping, but rather rescue (as in the case of the Amboise Conspiracy of 1560), massacre isn't massacre but rather an extirpation of heresy (as in Catholic accounts of the Saint Bartholomew Massacre of 1572), and the destruction of property isn't destruction but rather a twilight of the idols (as in the case of Huguenot iconoclasm of the 1550s and '60s).[13] There may seem to be sophistry involved in what the terrorists tell themselves and others sometimes; but there is also sincere belief, beginning with a belief in the power of violence to change the terms through which moral and legal judgements can be made.

The metaphor of the sacrifice is therefore constantly summoned in heroic accounts of terrorism before the letter. 'Go to the Senate and wait for the arrival of the victim', says Brutus to the other conspirators in Scudéry's version of the drama. 'My hand wants to conduct the victim to the altar, / And give the mortal blow to save you all.'[14] 'Let us be sacrificers, but not butchers', says Shakespeare's Brutus.

---

[11] See Dutertre, *Scudéry*: 61–86 and 256–85.

[12] For a general overview, including important information about Alexander, see Kewes, 'Julius Caesar in Jacobean England'.

[13] Allen, *Killing Noe Murder*. And see Holstun, *Ehud's Dagger*: 305–66.

[14] Scudéry, *Mort de Cesar*: 3.2.682–3.

'Let's carve him as a dish fit for the gods.'[15] In both Scudéry and Shakespeare the actual killing is nothing like the spectacle of a victim at an altar, or the carving of a sacrificial lamb; it is rather messy and brutal. The playwrights intentionally ironize the moment, highlighting the contrast between expectations and results. But it is in the direction of a sacrificial moment—a good and true one, or a counterfeit sacrifice, as the case may be—that dramatizations of this type try to portray the *passage*. In the pathway of the act will already come a kind of transcendence, since the killing will be a ritual observance rather than a slaughter, a 'carving' at the table of an altar rather than a butchery in the stalls. And once accomplished the ritual observance will overcome any scruples that might have been made against it in advance. On the one hand, the heroes of terrorism before the letter have to show themselves to be psychologically heroic, to have mastered something in themselves, and faced down their own scruples and fears. On the other hand, they also have to undertake the act of violence in a spirit of transcendence, which usually means a sort of ritual transformation. They have to believe in what they are doing, and believe that what they are doing will overcome the objections that might be made against it.

Another paradigmatic case of the *passage* is therefore the story of Judith, the subject of a great many discussions in the period, and four full-length works published in French, as well as two separate English translations of the first of them, Du Bartas's *La Judit*.[16] Unlike the Roman story, the Judith story involves an unambiguously successful sacrificial murder. No messy brutality comes with the blow that severs Holofernes's head from his body. (In two famous paintings of the sacrificial moment, however, by Michelangelo Caravaggio and Artemesia Gentilleschi, both in the Uffizi, Judith kills Holofernes as if slaughtering a calf: blood flows and Judith seems a bit squeamish, but the job is done.) Certainly, however, the Judith story involves heroism, and hence a heroic test, where the heroine has to master something in herself, and also undertake the act of violence in a spirit of ritual purity.

'Now is the time', says the Judith of Guillaume Du Bartas's *Judit*, in a northern English translation, as the heroine contemplates killing Holofernes in his bed:

> go to it,
> And save thy people: Nay, I will not do it.
> I will, I will not. Go, fear not again.

This psychomachy at the verge of a critical act reflects not only on the danger Judith is exposing herself to but also the moral enormity of her situation. She is about to murder someone; only her certainty that she is pursuing a higher, divine aim can move her forward. She reasons with herself and finally comes to a decision. 'Nor is it profane, but holier it shall stand / When holy folk are helped by my

[15] Shakespeare, *Julius Caesar*. 2.1.166–72.
[16] See Appelbaum, 'Judith Dines Alone', for further background on the text in the Bible as well as the text by Du Bartas. The most important secondary material includes Lépront et al., *Judith et Holopherne*; the essays collected in Vander Kam, ed., *No One Spoke Ill of Her*; Otzen, *Tobit and Judith*; Poirier, *Judith: echos d'un mythe*; Sproxton, 'Peut-on définir'.

hand.' The end will not only justify the means, it will sanctify them. And she will not therefore be guilty of a crime. 'All murder is not for murder always taken.' The examples of Ehud and Jael inspire her. Slaying a tyrant is not mere 'homicide'. As for the danger she runs, unlike Macbeth, who needs to know that he can cover up the murder of Macduff before he sets himself to it, Judith is sure that no extra preventive measure is required. 'God brought me here; God will deliver me.'[17]

So Judith is resolved, *sainctement resolue*, as the original French puts it. It is true that Judith has resorted to guile, a common feature of terrorist aggression. Guile and fraud are characteristic of the terrorist act for early modern writers just to the extent that terrorist violence is neither open combat nor symmetrical. Judith's trickery is classic. She has beguiled her man with female charms and a promise of sexual favours. Her aggressive femininity, which seduces in order to kill, is a mark of the imbalance between herself and her foe.[18] Waged by the weak against the strong and the righteous against the wicked, terrorism may well depend on agents who are prototypically 'feminine'—forced into a condition of weakness, passivity, and dependency, though also capable of constancy and passion. But Du Bartas's Judith (like the Judith in other versions[19]) has no scruples about using her feminine wiles in this way; it is part of her artillery of virtue. And so she is resolved, she thinks. Yet when she comes near the bed where Holofernes has passed out, drunk, she debates with herself once again: 'Alas my heart is weak for such a deed.' She prays for strength. She gets it. She takes up the sword, Holofernes's sword, 'which oft had bathed the world in human blood'. She loses her resolve. 'Fear wrest the sword from her; and down she fell.' One last prayer turns the trick. 'O God (quoth she) now by thy mighty force / Restore my strength.' And then:

> This said, with pale annoy,
> She rudely rose, and stroke this sleeping *Roy*
> so fell, that from his shoulder flew his poule [head]
> and from his body fled his Ethnic [pagan] soul
> hie way to hell.[20]

It is a clean executioner's stroke that Judith delivers. Just one blow does the job—even though the Bible specifies that two blows and a bit of slicing was required. Just one blow: and that's the end of it.

Or is it? The myth says that a single heroic act can deliver a nation. Du Bartas's alteration of the biblical story serves to emphasize the idea, but even Gabrielle de Coignard's later *Imitation de la victoire de Judith* (1595), another heroic poem, where the two blows are restored ('Ayant frapper deux fois le tyran elle tue'), the

---

[17] Du Bartas, *Historie of Judith*, trans. Hudson: Gv2.
[18] The theme is developed at length in Stocker, *Judith, Sexual Warrior*.
[19] In *Le Miroir des vefves: Tragedie sacrée d'Holofernes et Judith* (1596) Protestant author Pieter Heyns has Judith deliberate at length over the right to commit tyrannicide in Act 3 scene 2. She considers not only the ends of the action but also the means, including deceit. But the ends justify the means, she decides, and so this Judith too resolves herself to act. Praising Judith's accomplishment when she makes it back to Bethulia, one character cries out, 'O bonne deception! O tromperie salutaire! Et louable abus!' (5.4).
[20] Du Bartas, *Historie of Judith*, trans. Hudson: 92.

logic is pretty much the same.[21] Out of a single act against a single victim comes the transformation of a whole community, or even of two whole communities, the home society's and the enemy's. The elimination of the *one* doubly transforms the *many*. But how is that possible? 'Our great god of all', says Du Bartas's Judith, to the townspeople of Bethulia, while bearing the head of Holofernes, 'hath broke this night the whole Assyrian power'.[22] (This line is a close translation of the Bible.) Or as Judith puts it to the Jewish people in the version of the story by Adrien d'Amboise, a Protestant drama for the stage (1580):

> I bring with me liberty and life,
> The unique peace of my dear country:
> I leave behind me fear and terror,
> Fright and despair, death and horror.[23]

The Assyrian military, when it finds the decapitated body, is horrified, intimidated, and demoralized. The people of Bethulia are by contrast encouraged, emboldened, rallied into battle. The murder has been received as a double-edged sacrifice, deadly to the whole Assyrian cause and life-restoring to Israel. 'Woe woe to us', says the second in command among the Assyrians, in Du Bartas's version, upon discovering Holofernes's corpse, 'a slave ... / In slaying Holofernes hath slain us all'.[24]

Let me summarize here. In these heroic efforts there is not only a dramatic intensity, but also a moral, social, and historical shift. The agent passes into aggressive action, even though the agent has legitimate moral scruples against doing so, not to mention doubts and fears. The heroism of the effort signifies some of the act's moral value, although that morality can come in an ambivalent form, as in some of the representations of Brutus. But also at stake is a transformation, magic-like, where the sacrifice of the one may well have a great bearing on the many, or even on more than one social group, as when Judith's killing of Holofernes both terrorizes the Assyrians and rouses the Judeans. This heroic effort, dramatized through a *passage à l'acte*, is paradigmatic: it is one of the chief models through which terrorism before the letter is undertaken.

But there are qualifications to consider. For there are cases, as in James's account of the Gunpowder Plot, where we are required to see the event from the point of view not of the triumphant perpetrators of violence but of the real or intended victims. Not heroes committing heroic acts, but some other kind of agents and acts are required—diabolical characters, committing diabolical acts, in imitation of heroism perhaps, but not pulling it off in reverse. Moreover, there are cases, again as in James's account of the Plot, where the act is a kind of blank. It hasn't occurred, and yet its effect is tremendous. It exists as the idea of an event, but not as an event itself. To tell such a story is both to recreate the diabolical act as an intention and to narrate its failure—a common enough formulation in thrillers in the twentieth and twenty-first centuries, where super-agents or super-heroes thwart the disastrous

---

[21] Coignard, *Oeuvres Chrétiennes*: 445, line 1336.
[22] Du Bartas, *Historie of Judith*, trans. Hudson: 92.
[23] Amboise, *Holofernes*: 5.1315–19.
[24] Du Bartas, *Historie of Judith*, trans. Hudson, *Judit*: 95.

LIVERPOOL JOHN MOORES UNIVERSITY
LEARNING SERVICES

plans of super-terrorists in climaxes of destruction averted, but rather rare in the early modern period, except in the case of Gunpowder Plot-inspired stories. After all, it is the event that marks rupture and transformation. It is the event that forms the primary object of hope and fear. But there is at least one major alternative in the grammar of terrorism before the letter, which could be used to mitigate the problem of personal responsibility, and even to reduce the moral impact of the violence: the act as an 'unfortunate incident'.

3. *ACCIDENTS MISÉRABLES*

This is the case when a decisively violent action expresses not a heroic or would-be heroic decision but rather fortuitousness. This event lacking heroic effort is the *res per accidens*, expressing a violence that up to then was latent rather than manifest.

Consider the shooting of Admiral de Coligny in the lead-up to the Saint Bartholomew Massacre. And consider, as a starting point, the version of the shooting rendered in Christopher Marlowe's *The Massacre at Paris*, published in 1595, itself based on prominent Huguenot accounts.[25] The Saint Bartholomew Massacre will be examined frequently in this study, with respect to both French and English accounts, and to pro-Protestant, pro-Catholic, and non-partisan ones. The event was complex. For 'Saint Bartholomew' refers to five different knots of events:

1. The failed assassination attempt against Admiral Gaspard de Coligny, by gunshot, on 22 August, following the wedding of the Protestant Henry of Navarre and the Catholic Marguerite de Valois.

2. The storming of Coligny's residence, and the murder of Coligny and many of his supporters, high-ranking Huguenots, and soldiers, in the early hours of 24 August.

3. The pursuit of *huguenots de guerre*, led by Guise and other royal officials in the next few days and nights following the murder of Coligny.

4. The outbreak of mass violence against civilians, over the course of the next five days, taking the life of 2–5,000 individuals, including women and children, accompanied by looting, torture, and sexual assault.

5. The outbreak of copycat massacres in the Provinces, though against the command of royal decree, with widespread death and destruction in Toulouse, Bordeaux, Lyon, Bourges, Rouen, Orléans, Meaux, Angers, La Charité, Saumur, Gaillac, and Troyes.

Any account of the Massacre would seem to require a difficult disentangling, distinguishing sovereign violence from popular violence, and between politic-

---

[25] The text we have is obviously corrupt and abbreviated, and the language is tepid, but it probably gives a good indication of the kind of drama Marlowe actually wrote. On the play's relation to history see Briggs, 'Marlowe's *Massacre at Paris*'.

ally tactical violence, rioting, and looting, and genuine terror from other forms of havoc. It is and always has been a controversial subject. But let us look then at how Christopher Marlowe shows the initiating event, the injuring of Coligny.

The Queen of Navarre has suddenly died; characters in the play—the Prince of Condé and the young Henry of Navarre, along with the Admiral, gathering near the Louvre—are convinced that she has been poisoned. (Whether she was actually poisoned was a matter of some controversy in real life.) The Admiral speaks:

ADMIRAL.   Come, my lords, let us bear her body hence,
              And see it honoured with just solemnity.
As they are going, the SOLDIER dischargeth his musket at the LORD ADMIRAL.
CONDÉ.   What, are you hurt, my Lord High Admiral?
ADMIRAL.   Ay, my good lord, shot through the arm.
NAVARRE.   We are betrayed! Come, my lords, and let us go tell the king of this.[26]

Notice the anonymity of the soldier, the lack of any dramatic preparation for the incident, the very blandness of it all. It just—happens. Though a legend, based on the testimony of supposed witnesses, soon spread about who the assassin was, a certain gentleman from Normandy named Maurevert or Morevel, the man was never taken, his motives were guessed at but never determined, and the story of how he came to the chamber, from whose window he fired the shot (or shots), how he resolved himself to act out a personal revenge, or follow orders from higher ups (it was assumed that he had once been associated with the Guises), how he had told himself 'do it do it do it', or whatever he said to himself—almost no one ever even tried to recount it.[27] Why that is so is worth returning to. By itself this act, precipitating the Saint Bartholomew Massacre, 'brought down the king and the kingdom from the great felicity it up to then had enjoyed', according to one contemporary.[28] But as no one ever came forward to take responsibility for it, and no one was ever caught, so no one was ever able to explain it. Unless another identifying cause for the gunman's behaviour could be brought forward—the identity of someone who had hired or commanded him to shoot the Admiral (one of the Guises, say, or the King of Spain) and with the identity of this 'someone' a political cause, either national or international, in the name of which the Admiral was shot—this most momentous of incidents in French political history would have to go down as a stray occurrence, with no essential meaning. Even Marlowe would allow the incident of the shooting of Coligny a character of this kind. If the murder of Julius Caesar is almost always heroic, the attempted murder of Coligny is usually unheroic, even timid. It does not come to pass according to the heroic pattern.

---

[26] Marlowe, *Massacre*: 3.1–6.
[27] Crouzet, in *La Nuit de Saint-Barthélemy*, 462–8, has asserted that Charles de Louviers, sieur de Maurevert, publicly known as the assassin of one of Coligny's lieutenants a few years earlier, was certainly the shooter of 1572; but the evidence Crouzet musters is still mainly circumstantial.
[28] Burin, *Response à une epistre*: 16.

There were ways of characterizing acts like the shooting of Coligny as good or bad regardless of how they were accomplished. Marlowe, following his sources, knows that the shooting was bad, and insinuates that it was part of a vast Catholic conspiracy against the Protestant cause. The king himself was reportedly upset. 'What, always some new trouble!', he is supposed to have said. 'Will I never have any peace and quiet?'[29] So the act could be morally assessed, for or against, irrespective of how the act was dramatically framed. In retrospect, many ultra-Catholics showed themselves to have been gladdened at the first shooting of the Admiral, above all because it led to what they took to be the morally correct killing of the Admiral a few days later. But the pattern through which the event was unwound, and the protagonists were shown, or not shown, to have arrived at a *passage à l'acte*, had a significance of its own.

It could even have a significance for those who wrote in support of the attempted assassination. For it could be said that the shooting of the Admiral was important precisely because it was timid and unsuccessful. It could be argued that the shooting was supposed to fail.[30] The anonymous shooting of the Admiral was supposed to rouse passions among the Catholics and the Huguenots and precipitate an armed conflict. It was an *acte provocateur*, the mysteries of which were to further suspicions of each side against the other. One could go even further and argue the shooting was an example of the workings of chance in outbreaks of political violence, where chance intersects with moral purposes.

Such an argument is implied in the very strange but competent anti-Protestant play published in 1575 (it is not known if it was ever performed on stage) called *La tragédie du feu Gaspar de Coligny*, by François de Chantelouve. A mischievous Jupiter, father of the gods, upset at the violent ambitions of the Protestant leader Gaspar de Coligny, tells his son Mercury to orchestrate a failed assassination attempt:

> I do not wish that [Coligny] should die,
> But be convinced that he may try
> Henceforth to kill the King his lord,
> For that blow will excuse afford...[31]

That is, if someone tries to assassinate Coligny, Coligny will use the attempt against him as an excuse to plan a reprisal, and conspire against the life of the king. And then the king, should he find out about the conspiracy in advance—and no doubt he will find out, since he has spies everywhere—will be moved from his admirable, temperamentally peaceable disposition to take pre-emptive action against Coligny and the Huguenots. Jupiter wants to incite the Huguenots to plot to kill the king, and thereby incite the king to kill the Huguenots.

---

[29] Garrisson, *1572*: 78.

[30] That is how Denis Crouzet, in *Guerriers de Dieu* (2: 29), imagines the Coligny assassination attempt: 'Le coup tiré par Maurevaut, avait-il vraiment but de tuer l'Amiral, ne devait-il pas seulement le blesser?'

[31] Chantelouve, *Tragedy*, trans. Hillman: 3.1.681–4. Hillman's introduction provides valuable commentary.

So from a divine point of view the event was no accident; it was a perfectly well-thought-through gambit, engaged through the instrument of an *agent provocateur*. Yet from an earthly point of view an accident was exactly what it was. A disposition and readiness to act, the Huguenots against the king, the king against the Huguenots, was kindled to combustion by a misfired weapon, shot by an unknown assailant. The Chorus that narrates the shooting and its consequences, defending the justice of the king's behaviour—the king was justified in what he did, according to the Chorus, even if he was not temperamentally disposed toward violence and needed a little accident to shake him up—in ordering a massacre a few days later. If Coligny gets what is coming to him, it is nevertheless chance or fate and not an evil disposition or murderousness on the part of those who gave it to him:

> All things are mutable
> In a world of rise and fall;
> Only inconstancy
> Constant in this world can be.[32]

This appeal to chance and inconstancy, a commonplace of Renaissance thought that would be codified as a principle of political philosophy and neo-stoicism by Justus Lipsius and Pierre de Charron, expresses not just a rhetorical figure but also a world view. Human affairs are fragile and uncertain; the wheel of fortune turns and it is only the constancy of one's own soul that one can rely on. But the appeal to chance—in the middle of a story about the slaughter of what would amount to thousands, apparently at the order of the nation's king—also expresses an excuse, based on a refusal to recognize human responsibility for human crime. Accidents will happen. Or to put it another way, humans have to do what they have to do because the universe is inhuman, and it forces awful decisions upon humans, including the decision to order a pre-emptive massacre of one's likely enemies.

The same kind of appeal would be made in the case of the first great religious massacre of the post-Cateau-Cambrésis era, the Massacre at Vassy.[33] François Lorraine, the second Duke of Guise, the leader of this 'massacre'—though he himself would never use that portentous word—was asked to explain what happened before a council of nobles. In his speech before the council, reprinted in a pamphlet soon afterwards, Guise made a concession: 'Il est vrai', he said, 'que c'est un accident misérable.' We might wish to translate 'accident' as 'incident': 'it is true that it is [was] an unfortunate incident'. But *accident* here carries the sense not only of 'incident' but also, as the French dictionaries put it, an *évènement imprévu*—an event unforeseen, unexpected. And what Guise really wants to emphasize is that the incident wasn't planned; there was no conscious intention on his part, or on the part of his soldiers, to break up a Protestant service and injure a number of worshippers. He and his men were simply coming through town, as it was their right to do, when they were harassed by the Protestants, who, interrupting their own service, threw rocks upon them from the roof of the barn they were using as

---

[32] Chantelouve, *Tragedy*: 3.2.769–73.
[33] For a recent account of the event, see Carroll, *Martyrs and Murderers*: 1–20.

a church. Then gunfire was shot (by whom no one knows) and his own men took steps to protect themselves. Things eventually got out of hand, and as many as one hundred people (all of them Protestants) were killed or injured. If anything was to blame for this *accident misérable*, Guise said, it was the laxity of the Calvinist ministers, 'who preach nothing but an unlimited liberty of sedition'.[34]

There is a blame game going on here, as elsewhere in the discourse of terrorism before the letter. The blame game is a product of polemics, where accusations fly back and forth for the sake of scoring points. But it is also something more: the blame game *channels* the meaning of the violence for the sake of arriving at a defensible ideological position. The blame game is an expression of a response to terrorism's demands for recognition, where either acceptance, refusal, or the incomprehension of misrecognition is required. One way or the other, this violence, in its meaning, would have to be exploited. But it is first of all to be noted that while the Duke of Guise blamed stray characters among the Protestant worshippers for starting the violence, and blamed Protestant preaching for indirectly encouraging it, he was above all stressing, by calling the incident an unfortunate accident, that the massacre hadn't been *planned*. And hence, as we see from the point of view of the analysis of action, there was no *resolve* to take into account, no moral dilemma to negotiate, and no hesitation.

Spontaneity could nevertheless be motivated, as Guise himself understood; unpremeditated violence could erupt in the instant of a Machiavellian *occasione*, when long-entertained objectives found a sudden opportunity for fulfilment. Surely Guise saw the rock-throwing of Protestant worshippers, aimed at his soldiers, as something at once unpremeditated and motivated. The Protestant worshippers found a chance, fortuitously, to grasp the occasion and express themselves, given what their ministers had been preaching to them: they threw rocks. And Guise may have understood the reaction of his men in the same light too: given a long-smouldering conflict between the forces of law and order and the forces of Protestant 'sedition', once the Protestants began throwing rocks the forces of law and order had a chance to express themselves, and resist the challenge to authority.

Back in the realm of legend and fictional embellishment, in a structurally similar situation we find the *Amleth* of Belleforest (1572), the title character translated into a 'Hamblet' or 'Hamlet' by an anonymous Englishman in 1608 (he uses both spellings), whose version I will be quoting from. *Amleth*, a prose fiction, is very much the key source to Shakespeare's *Hamlet* (or of the ur-Hamlet Shakespeare may have imitated), but it is also very different.[35] Fashioned out of medieval material (Saxo Grammaticus's *Gesta Danorum*) but rewritten for a French readership caught in the religious troubles of the 1570s, *Amleth* is an overtly political work, speaking on behalf of principles of native, collective, and traditional sovereignty. Belleforest's Amleth has been cheated of his right of succession not only by a murderous uncle, but by a whole ruling class (likened perhaps to power-grabbing Huguenot nobles) which has openly acknowledged that a murder has taken place and condoned it, allying themselves with the uncle. Amleth's revenge thus takes on an

[34] *Discours au vray et en abbregé*: 116.   [35] See Stabler, 'Melancholy, Ambition'.

overtly public character in Belleforest's story. And part of the revenge, unlike anything contemplated in *Hamlet*, is mass murder. Like the Massacre at Vassy, and like some accounts of the Saint Bartholomew Massacre, although this time written from the Catholic side, there is an element of the accidental, the unforeseen in the murder of Amleth's victims.[36]

The massacre comes when, at the climax of the main story, Amleth the hero spontaneously decides with one blow to slaughter the nobility of Denmark. Upon his return from England, according to Belleforest's elaboration of the old story, Amleth gave a banquet at the royal palace to celebrate his return.

> At the banquet the hero gave the noblemen such store of liquor, that all of them being full laden with wine and gorged with meat, were constrained to lay themselves down in the same place where they had supped, so much their senses were dulled, and overcome with the fire of over-great drinking... which when Hamlet [sic] perceiving, and finding so good opportunity to effect his purpose and be revenged of his enemies, and by the means to abandon the actions, gestures, and apparel of a mad man, occasion so fitly finding his turn, as it were effecting itself, failed not to take hold thereof...

Amleth observed the 'drunken bodies filled with wine, lying like hogs upon the ground', sleeping and puking, and so he

> made the hangings about the hall to fall down and cover them all over; which he nailed to the ground... and presently he set fire in the four corners of the hall, in such sort, that all that were as then therein not one escaped away, but were forced to purge their sins by fire, and dry up the great abundance of liquor by them received into their bodies, all of them dying in the inevitable and merciless flames of the hot and burning fire...

The slaying of the uncle, in open but unequal combat, follows immediately after. Amleth has been motivated for years, feigning madness, waiting for the right opportunity. And it all results not from a resolution taken, but from the mere fact of 'finding so good opportunity... occasion so fitly finding his turn'.[37]

Belleforest's Amleth is not simply exacting a private revenge, as I have said. In Belleforest's hands Amleth's revenge, extending to both a massacre and an execution, is thoroughly political, a public act meant to rearrange power relations in Denmark. It is also thoroughly horrible, an act of sacrificial terror. In fact, the Danish public, when they wake up to the disaster, are by and large appalled. But Amleth delivers what Belleforest calls a 'harangue' to re-orient their affections. Let no right-thinking man 'be moved', Amleth asserts,

> nor think it strange to behold the confused, hideous, and fearful spectacle of this present calamity: if there be any man that affecteth fidelity... let him not be ashamed beholding this massacre, much less offended to see so fearful a ruin both of men and

---

[36] The element of chance survives in *Hamlet* as Hamlet's turn toward the 'Providence in the fall of a sparrow', the idea that he should just 'let be', and the apparently fortuitous circumstances under which he dies.

[37] Belleforest, *Hystorie of Hamblet*: 109. The translation is commendably accurate, but it shows some awareness of Shakespeare's version of the story. A modern edition of the French original is included in Biet, *Théâtre de la cruauté*.

of the bravest house in all this country: for the hand that hath done this justice could not effect it by any other means.

An interesting locution: 'justice' could not be effected 'by any other means': a common pretence for terrorism before the letter. As we saw in the case of Robert Catesby's call to blow up the House of Lords, the commonplace that desperate diseases call for desperate remedies is frequently repeated.[38] Necessity in this case is a pretext for the legality of transgressive violence, as in Naudé's notion of the *coup d'état*. As for Fengon, the dead uncle,

> I pray you remember this body is not the body of a king, but of an execrable tyrant, and a parricide most detestable. Oh Danes! the spectacle was much more hideous when Horvendile your king [Amleth's father] was murdered by his brother.

It turns out that Amleth has accomplished nothing less than the restoration of ancient liberty. The corrupt uncle was 'a tyrant and murderer of his brother: one that hath perverted all right, abolished the ancient laws of our fathers, contaminated the memories of our ancestors…'. To complete the occasion of his harangue, Amleth ceremoniously leaves the dead body to the Danish public for ritual desecration.

> I have left Fengon whole, that you might punish his dead carcass…to accomplish the full punishment and vengeance due unto him, and so satisfy your choler upon the bones of him that filled his greedy hands and coffers with your riches, and shed the blood of your brethren and friends. Be joyful then (my good friends); make ready the pyre for this usurping king: burn his abominable body, boil his lascivious members, and cast the ashes of him that hath been hurtful to all the world into the air…Let not a trace of a parricide be seen, nor your country defiled with the presence of the least member of this tyrant without pity, that your neighbours may not smell the contagion, nor our land the polluted infection of a body condemned for his wickedness…[39]

4. AGAINST COMMON SENSE: THE MESSAGE AND ITS DISAMBIGUATION

Amleth's is a case of mixed motivation with regard to the act. On the one hand, the act exemplifies heroic effort. On the other hand, it comes about fortuitously. As in the case of Guise's account of the Massacre at Vassy, the account of Amleth's violence shows a situation for which the usual metaphor (I have already found myself forced to use it more than once, and Belleforest of course makes it literal) is

---

[38] It of course makes an appearance in Shakespeare's *Hamlet*, 4.3.8–11, though in the mouth of Claudius: 'Diseases desperate grown / By desperate appliance are relieved / Or not all.' Shakespeare's Hamlet is *not* a terrorist, and for interesting, well-known reasons, including the fact that the murder of his father was private and secret and no one colluded in it: only Belleforest's Amleth rises to the dignity of a terrorist.

[39] Belleforest, *Hamblet*: 113–14. The speech is adapted from a similar speech in Belleforest's source, Saxo Grammaticus's *Historiae Danicae*, but Belleforest has modernized its political context, emphasizing the notions of 'tyranny' and 'massacre'. Belleforest is also responsible for the significant detail that the murder of Amleth's father was public, and that the nobles of Denmark were complicit with the murder.

'combustion': a conflict is ready to ignite, once the conflicting parties come into contact with one another in a hot and dry enough situation. But as in other cases, Amleth's behaviour is decisive. It announces a passage into a new condition for both Amleth and the society over which he is meant to preside. That Amleth's story, written by the fervently royalist anti-Huguenot Belleforest, may also encode another excuse for such massacres as the Saint Bartholomew affair is a stunning and troubling sidelight.[40] But a correlative of the Belleforest's siding with massacre on behalf of legitimate sovereignty is that the massacre is shown to be at once necessary and unplanned, and to that extent both just and unintentional.

Common sense, in response to such acts of terrorist violence, has few tools for understanding situations of this kind, or really for any of the major acts of violence that have been highlighted so far. The Gunpowder Plotters against the King and the House of Lords; Brutus and his fellow conspirators against Julius Caesar; Judith against Holofernes; an anonymous assassin against Coligny; a squadron (in phase two of the massacre) against Coligny and his protectors; a regiment of armed soldiers against unarmed worshippers at a church in Vassy; the Prince of Denmark against a gathering of nobles: these would seem to be characteristic *fights*, rivals against rivals, with the outcomes of either failure or victory. But there is much more to these incidents, obviously, for their effects are so great. And why? Common sense (and I use the term descriptively, not pejoratively) can appeal to the status of the antagonists: as high-ranking officials or low-ranking attackers, as rogue military troops or innocent non-combatants. It may also appeal to the asymmetries and the illegalities of the attacks. These conditions in themselves tell us that there is something exceptional about the incidents. Common sense may even appeal to the fact that there are political purposes involved in the violence, strategic and ideological. But there is a power in these fights that is still unaccounted for. They cause a transition of circumstances that well exceeds those of the immediate participants. In keeping with the status of the antagonists, the asymmetries and illegalities of their conflicts, and the political purposes of the perpetrators, but also in keeping with other factors as yet unaccounted for, these acts of violence are forcefully symbolic. In fact, they are so forcefully symbolic that they constitute history-transforming events even when they fail to occur, or when, having occurred, their perpetrators can claim that they were merely *accidents misérables*.

That a psychology of fear is incorporated in the events goes without saying. Life and death, freedom and bondage, security and danger are all at stake. But a psychology of hope is incorporated in them as well—a hope that may be difficult for victims to fathom, but that is central to the very possibility of the *passage á l'acte*. Fear, yes, but fear because of a hope: that is one of the real conundrums. One party can be afraid because another party is hopeful. And vice versa. More generally, then, as I have been arguing from the outset, what is at stake in major terrorist incidents is meaning: the syntax and semantics of an uncanny political action, delivering the message of terrorist violence. It is to this message, its initiation, its

---

[40] See Belleforest's own direct contribution to the pamphlet controversies of the day, *Advertissement sur les rébellions*.

unveiling, its communication and progress, the struggle for recognition that is undertaken on its behalf, and the resistance that might be waged against it that all texts concerned with terrorism before the letter must address themselves, whatever their political and social orientation, and whatever their generic approach.

One of the chief signs of the symbolic power of the act in itself, but also a chief qualification of that power, is the fact that the act, even as a message-delivering blow, is never isolated. It comes from somewhere, as I have said. It has its origins. And it goes somewhere. In fact, in case after case, the discourse shows the message of the violence to be at once complete and open-ended. On the one hand, the act must be self-substantiating; it must in itself have the power of disrupting the historical situation and changing the power relations of the moment. It is an act of transcendent justice and it must be *complete*. On the other hand, the act is never really complete. Much remains, in the aftermath of the blow, to be said, heard, and interpreted by the people who have survived it. After the destructive disruption, there must come a clarification of the meaning of the destruction and appeal to the consent of the public—or else there must come a resistance to that meaning, a challenge to its integrity and logic.

The case of *Amleth* is characteristic. First Amleth kills the nobility of Denmark and his uncle. He brings about his revenge. There was no other way. And he stands before the people of Denmark putatively as their champion and leader, having eliminated tyranny. But what he has brought about is also a 'confused, hideous, and fearful spectacle', a 'calamity'. It was a massacre, after all. So secondly, Amleth has to explain what has happened. He has to assure the public that he has accomplished 'justice'. And in a gesture characteristic of the discourse and practice of early modern terror, he has to call upon the public to finish the job of making the calamity into an act of justice, asking it to signal its assent and finish the act by mutilating a corpse. Leaving aside the nobles, who have been burnt to ashes already, 'I have left Fengon whole, that you might punish his dead carcass'.

To this process of clarifying and ratifying the meaning of an act of terrorist violence, gruesome though it may be, I give the neutral name 'disambiguation'. The act, in all its horror and hope, has to be unwound, explained, justified, and ratified if it is to succeed, or otherwise, if it is to be resisted, disparaged, vilified, and rejected. The meaning of the act has to be rendered unambiguous. The most prominent example of this in the literature is the case of the murder of Julius Caesar. 'Liberty! Freedom! Tyranny is dead!' the conspirator Cinna cries out immediately after the death of Caesar in Shakespeare's play. 'Run hence, proclaim, cry it about the streets.' He is followed by Cassius saying much the same thing, and then Brutus, elaborating:

> Stoop, Romans, stoop,
> And let us bathe our hands in Caesar's blood
> Up to the elbows, and besmear our swords:
> Then walk we forth, even to the market-place,
> And, waving our red weapons o'er our heads,
> Let's all cry 'Peace, freedom and liberty!'[41]

---

[41] Shakespeare, *Julius Caesar*. 3.1.77–8; 3.1.107–11.

It is not enough just to kill or sacrifice Caesar. One also has to let people know what the killing means, and require their consent. Recognize the act, in other words, the conspirators are crying in the streets. Recognize the act in its violence and what the violence *means*. Caesar is dead. And by all means, acknowledge and consent to *this meaning*: peace, freedom, and liberty. Brutus and Cassius in Grévin's *César* make similar pronouncements. 'Breathe easy, O Roman liberty' says Brutus, in *César*. 'Citizens, see here this bloody dagger, / This dagger, citizens, can boast / Of having done its duty.'[42]

The problem, of course, is that the public can fail to recognize what the terrorist is saying, or refuse to do so. Though Amleth succeeds, Brutus and his fellow conspirators fail. 'What enchants you thus', Brutus says to the public, the Chorus of William Alexander, Earl of Stirling's *Julius Caesar*,

> that ye abstain
> That which ye should have taken to receive?
> Where be those inundations of delight
> That should burst out through thoughts overflow'd with joy,
> Whilst emulous virtue may your minds incite
> That which we conquer'd have, at least t'enjoy?[43]

The failure of the Roman conspirators was legend, and all kinds of explanations were offered for it, including the idea that the Roman people were unworthy of the message of liberty. The status of the corpse of Caesar provided interesting explanations too. If the body of Fengon remains to be desecrated by the people, with the desecration serving to complete the process of disambiguation, Caesar, it is often implied, instead of being a 'dish fit for the gods', ends up desecrated in the act of murder. Caesar's bloody wounds are 'poor poor dumb mouths' according to Shakespeare's Antony, deriding the dignity of the assassination. The wounds 'ope their ruby lips' to beg, dumbly, for Antony to speak for them and cry 'Havoc!'[44] What becomes disambiguated is the message not of liberty but of treachery, not of a divine sacrifice for the good of Roman republicans but a bloody sacrilege against the interests and the sensibility of the people. The message may have been ambiguous at first, but in the end its meaning for the majority was clear, and the meaning was treachery and an imperative of vengeance. And so the people cry out: 'Revenge! About! Seek! Burn! Fire! Kill! Slay! / Let not a traitor live.'[45]

The story of disambiguation can unfold in any number of ways. In lost causes, told from the point of view of those who have lost, the message of terror can come out in the martyrdom of the would-be heroes, which is what happens in Shakespeare's *Julius Caesar*. Or the message can come in the guilt of the would-be heroes, which is what shows up in Garnier's reflection on the assassination of Caesar, *Porcie*. 'Nous tuâmes César pour n'avoir point des Rois', complains the title character of Garnier's *Porcie*, 'Mais au meurtre de lui nous en avons fait trois.' We killed Caesar in order to be rid of kings, but in murdering him we have created three

---

[42] Grévin, *César*. 5.1.1031–8. [43] Stirling, *Caesar*. Bb3–Bb3v.
[44] Shakespeare, *Julius Caesar*. 3.2.216;3.1.262–76.
[45] Shakespeare, *Julius Caesar*. 3.2.195–6.

(that is, the triumvirate of Antony, Octavius, and Lepidus). The message, in the end, is that the conspirators were wrong, and should have let things alone. A tragic error has been committed.

The disambiguation can also come, as in accounts of the Amboise Conspiracy of 1560, in a combination of the martyrdom of the would-be heroes with the guilt of the would-be victims. That was an episode where a large band of Protestant soldiers gathered to storm the palace at Amboise, kill the king's guards, abduct the king, and thus free the king from the regency of the Guises. According to pro-Protestant literature, which called the Conspiracy a 'tumult', the aim was to let the French people communicate their will directly to the king, having freed the king to act in their interests. They were betrayed by a spy, however, and caught by the royal, Guisard army before even getting close to the fortress they were planning to invade. They were rounded up by the dozens and summarily executed in public, in the middle of Amboise, and their corpses were publicly abused. But according to a pro-Protestant reporter, the conspirators had by the very fact of their death become martyrs. 'Having prayed to God in a loud voice and called upon Him to judge their cause, they died with such constancy that even their enemies were compelled to weep.' Meanwhile, the table turns on the would-be victims. The highly respected Lord Chancellor, François Olivier, who had served in that capacity under both Francis I and Henry II, falls ill, and the message of protest, suffocated in the slaughter of the Huguenot soldiers, gets expressed all the same:

> Something happened that many thought to have been sent by God to warn the Guises not to continue with their cruelty, to wit a grievous malady which suddenly seized Chancellor Olivier, as a punishment for his disloyalty. For knowing that the cause of the prisoners was just, and being Chief Justice, Olivier nevertheless let himself be ruled by the appetite and ambition of the Guises. Now, being suddenly stung with remorse, he fell sick with extreme melancholy, so that he sighed without cease, miserably muttering against God and troubling his own person in a strange and frightening manner. In this torment he was visited by the Cardinal of Lorraine [one of the Guise brothers]. Olivier could not see him, but he sensed his presence and cried out these words: 'Ha! Cardinal, you have caused all of us to be damned!'[46]

Olivier would die soon after. And so the message, originally intended for delivery by way of violence against the Guises and the royal palace, is ultimately delivered by way of remorse at retaliation against the conspirators. The heroes of the Huguenot cause (Huguenot being a term originally of derision, and first applied to French Protestants at this time) have been made into martyrs. And the defenders of the Guisard faction have reiterated the message the Huguenots wanted to send by falling ill and damning themselves.

In more straightforward cases, where the act has been successful, the blow delivered and a cause of justice triumphant, one success is followed by another success, all the way to the desecration of the corpse of the chief victims. In Du Bartas's version, the story of Judith ends not only with a routing of the Assyrian army, but with a carnival of retribution, first performed against the head of Holofernes,

---

[46] *Histoire de tumulte*: 29.

affixed to Bethulia's rampart, and then against the headless corpse, found in the Assyrian camp among the other Assyrian corpses. At the rampart,

> There, fathers came, and sons, and wives and maids,
> who erst had lost amongst the Heathen blades,
> There sons, their parents, mates, and lovers dear,
> with heavy harts and furious raging cheer,
> They pilled and pared his beard of paled hew,
> Spit in his face and out his tongue they drew,
> which used to speak of God great blasphemies,
> And with their fingers poached out his eyes,
> The rife remembrance of so late an ill,
> Made vulgar folk such vengeance to fulfil.[47]

Then, after the head is torn apart, what Du Bartas, in the original French, calls the *sot populace* descend upon the headless corpse in the Assyrian camp, and cut it into pieces, as if preparing to make a cannibal-feast of it.

The completion of terrorist violence through the desecration of the corpse in this case is mythic, legendary. It articulates a paradigm. Yet it is important to note that such an attack on the corpse does not take place in the Bible. In Scripture, what happens to Holofernes's headless body is left unsaid. The people celebrate their victory over the Assyrians by plundering the enemy camp, and then holding a festival in Jerusalem. So Du Bartas makes a significant departure from the original text in this regard. He has the people of Bethulia do to Holofernes, the evil general-oppressor, what Belleforest has the people of Denmark do to Fengon, the evil uncle-king. Though there are sources for stories of this kind of behaviour both in the Bible and the legends of Greco-Roman antiquity, it would seem that this focus on the body of the enemy was an especially acute preoccupation in early modernity. Denis Crouzet documents a great many cases of the desecration of corpses following religious violence, at the horror of which the essayist Montaigne recoiled in his famous piece, 'Of Cruelty', and some of which are graphically documented (from a Catholic point of view) by the *Théâtre des cruautés* by Richard Verstegan.[48] The great religious massacres of the period featured any number of instances where it was important not just to kill an enemy, but to insult his or her body and ultimately to be rid of it, to tear it up, burn it up, or flood it away downriver. A Christian burial was no apt conclusion to the killing of a heretic, who didn't deserve one, and whose moral pollution was also corporeal. The desecration of the corpse, so important to the legends retold by Belleforest and Du Bartas, seems to have been a key element of the religious violence of the period, and imported into the legends. But there was also a judicial precedent. For particularly heinous crimes had long since been the occasion for particularly gruesome punishments, both during execution itself and in the aftermath, when something had to

[47] *La Judit*, 6.215–24. Hudson, *Historie of Judith*, sig. GvR3.
[48] Crouzet, *Guerriers de Dieu*.

be done with the criminal's tortured, mutilated body.[49] Most famously, a desecration of the corpse was practised upon convicted traitors. The opening of Foucault's *Discipline and Punish* features a late example of the drawing and quartering of a still-living regicide, in the mid-eighteenth century. Had Foucault wandered into earlier centuries he would have found even more gruesome examples, where the people directly participated in the punishment. They do not just watch the spectacle. When the moment comes, they take hold of the criminal's body and punish it anew. One such episode of popular violence, the punishment of the regicide François Ravaillac, will be scrutinized in the next chapter. It is an example of how the mythography of terrorism tried to extract meaning not just out of the event but also out of the *person* of the terrorist. But the point to be made here, in the context of the act of terrorism and the sequence of actions that follow from it, is that such desecrations as feature in the stories of Belleforest and Du Bartas seem to respond to both of the impulses just mentioned, the religious and the judicial. The obscenity of desecration may purify the social body while also reasserting the body politic's principles of sovereignty and justice.

Such seems to have been the motives of Belleforest and Du Bartas in following up successful terrorist violence with desecration. With the humiliation and dispersion of the corpse comes the final disambiguation. There is no question anymore as to what the terrorist attack may have meant. An oppressor has been destroyed, and with him the oppression. Such an answer would seem to have come in the case of the desecration of the corpse of Gaspard de Coligny, after he was a second time attacked during the Saint Bartholomew Massacre. Coligny was killed, defenestrated, and beheaded, with a number of reports going so far as to say that the head of Coligny was not only paraded around the streets of Paris, but delivered to the Pope in Rome, and received with thanks.

Such an answer too seems to have come in the case of the Concino Concini affair of 1616.[50] About this affair accounts in favour of the assassination—and all published accounts in French were in favour of it—were agreed; the ascendance of the foreigner Concini, a Florentine, to a position of great power under the regent Queen, Marie de' Medici, Louis XIII being yet an adolescent, was an insult to the integrity of the kingdom. It was an insult all the more threatening in that the Queen and the Marquis were favourably disposed toward France's traditional enemy, Spain. 'The king seeing himself enslaved, in the middle of his own state, and fearing that such violent designs would go all the way to the taking of his life...', one document puts it, leading up to an obvious conclusion—the sentence hardly needs to be completed. The king will have needed to take action. The king will have needed to resolve himself to give the order for a *coup d'état*. 'My lord', the young Louis XIII is told by one of his closest advisers, angling for the murder of Concini, 'you will always be badly followed as long as you don't make yourself the leader'.[51]

[49] Silverman, *Tortured Subjects*; Spierenburg, *The Spectacle of Suffering*. Vestegan, *Le théâtre des cruautés*. Montaigne, *Essays*, in *Complete Works*, Book 2, Essay 11.
[50] For background see Boucher, *Concino-Concini*; and Delamare, *Concino Concini*.
[51] Marillac, *Relation de ce qui s'est passé*: 451.

When the time came for the blow, the decision having been taken, the order given, and the moment ripe to surprise the victim, Vitry and his men found Concini with his men heading toward the royal palace, about to cross the Pont du Louvre. Pierre Matthieu, whom we have already encountered, an author of many plays and polemics dealing with the political violence, and at the moment working as an official historian for the crown, put it this way:

> Vitry confronted Concini at the foot of the bridge, and putting his hand on Concini's shoulder told him he had orders to arrest him and take him prisoner. 'Me?' said the marquis. He made a gesture to take up his sword along with several of his men. But at that instant, the Sieur of Vitry, whose sword was sheathed, and whose pistol was in its holster, said 'Kill-Kill': at which words Concini received three pistol shots in the stomach from the Sieur of Hallier and the Sieur of Persan. Concini did not fall, but other shots followed and felled him, and suddenly those who had put their hands to their swords to defend the marquis, seeing that what had happened had been ordered by the King, asked pardon, and the others withdrew.

'Kill-kill': those words, *Tuë-tuë*, ring through the narratives of terror during the French troubles, and here they are again, spoken on the orders of the king, though in a situation where disproportion reigns, the king thinking himself otherwise defenceless against Concini, and Concini himself shown to be defenceless on the streets of Paris, even when accompanied by a group of defenders.

What follows is predictable: 'The corpse was left stretched out on the Pont du Louvre, and a little later thrown in a little nook where waste was swept. Many came there to see it, with an infinity of oaths, reproaches, and mockeries.' In fact, according to Matthieu, a festival followed. The body was said to be such a pollution that no disposal of it, whether by water, earth, or fire, was good enough for it. It was taken to the Louvre and then 'torn into a thousand pieces' and dragged through the streets. Nor was the murder and desecration without effect. Matthieu is not being ironic, or not only ironic, when he explains what happened next. 'This death changed everything; war was changed into peace, rain into bright skies, hail and thunder into fine weather; the mute spoke and those who spoke went mute.' And more: the assassination had the effect of making the king into a real king: 'He who had been regarded as a mere child was now recognized for his wisdom and his great and magnanimous courage, for being the true son of Henry the Great.' By this one act, in fact, the king is said to have restored to the people their 'liberty'. It seemed as if with the death of this one victim came 'the death of an infinite number of enemies'.[52]

Note the sequence here. An act is undertaken to shift the balance of power in France. The act is undertaken in public, but as a surprise. A variation on the usual conditions of asymmetry are acted out: the attackers with guns, the victim and his retinue with swords. After a moment of confusion, survivors who could have reacted belligerently are said to 'see[…] that what had happened had been ordered by the King'. The *legitimacy* of what might have been construed as a cruel and

---

[52] Matthieu, *Conjuration de Conchine*: 266–82.

illegal ambush has somehow been *communicated* to the survivors. The message is unambiguous, and so men of arms ask for pardon and withdraw. Then a ritual of desecration is undertaken, performed not by the few but by the many, in celebration of the fact that eliminating the *one* has *liberated* the *many*. And as the ritual disambiguation comes to a climax, a magnificent change is thought to have come over the nation, and the death of the one even seems to have meant the death of *many other* enemies. France has been transformed, and so has much of the rest of Europe. End of message.

5. ORIGINS

An account of origins nevertheless remains to be fleshed out. And origins there were, for early moderns were trained to think that actions had origins as well as consequences, that nothing came from nothing. If a party of Huguenots conspired to kidnap the king and eliminate his protectors, if a party of Catholics conspired to blow up Parliament, if a king found reason to order the murder of one of his councillors, there had to be a reason for it which could be located in the sequence of acts leading up to the decision and the eventual *passage à l'acte*.

But what was it? Each case was different, of course, but more often than not, when writers reflected on the event, the terrorist incident originated in a crisis. This would not always be the sort of crisis contemporary historians might appeal to—for example, a failure in governance, the weakness of a regency, the unpopularity of a new monarch, or an onerous new tax policy. Sometimes the origins were held to be supernatural, and the crisis cosmic. In Milton's account of the Gunpowder Plot, therefore, the story begins with the irritation of the devil at the success of the English people in preserving the true religion. In Garnier's tragedies, *Porcie* and *Cornélie*, which reflect on the murders of Caesar and Pompey, the story begins, Seneca-like, with the vexation of a Fury, who wants it made clear that the Roman Empire will not last forever, and deserves punishment for a variety of offences. These beginnings are allegorical, of course. Whether they are ever supposed to be understood on a literal level too is unclear. But they signal that for writers like Milton and Garnier, to understand an evil course of events is to understand how evil gets into the world, and how then perhaps some kind of supernatural force in the universe prompts people into committing evil deeds.

Texts arguing on behalf of terrorist violence, or ambiguously with regard to it, cannot so easily summon the supernatural to get the action going, for a heroic impulse is required, not a temptation. God intervenes easily enough in the biblical story of Ehud: 'When the Israelites cried out to the Lord, the Lord raised up for them a deliverer, Ehud son of Gera, the Benjaminite, a left-handed man.'[53] But in most stories, even if the hero may assume that God is on his or her side, the urge to action comes from the hero. 'Listen to me', says Judith to the leaders of Bethulia, in the biblical version of the story. 'I am about to do something that will go down

---

[53] Judges 3.15.

through all generations of our descendants. Stand at the town gate tonight so that I may go out with my maid; and within the days after which you have promised to surrender the town to our enemies, the Lord will deliver Israel by my hand.'[54] God, or the gods, may be behind any action whatsoever, of course, to the pre-modern mind; and God is certainly assumed to be behind the actions of all Christian heroes. But the heroic action not only requires a heroic *passage à l'acte*. It also requires an action of commitment, prior to the event. 'I told him Yes', we have heard Thomas Winter claiming to have said to the ringleader Robert Catesby; 'in this or what else soever, if he resolved upon it, I would venture my life'.[55] One can waver after committing oneself to a cause or a plot, of course; but such a wavering would be a significant element of the sequence contingent upon this first binding of the hero to a cause. This is a primary act of faith.

And still, there comes something beforehand: a state of emergency. Again and again, stories of terrorism before the letter either narrate or refer back to a state of emergency. This emergency should not be subsumed under the idea of the 'state of exception' that has become so much a part of modern political thought, under the influence of Carl Schmitt and Giorgio Agamben.[56] The two phenomena are related. And when a state official calls for a *coup d'état*, in the early modern period, he may well be expressing, in part, the logic of Schmitt and Agamben's 'state of exception', where sovereignty gets defined by its ability to violate the laws of sovereignty. But in the world of terrorist violence one does not need to be sovereign to declare to one's own satisfaction that a state of emergency exists, and that one has a sovereign right to respond to it. All that one needs is the perception that a crisis is at hand, and that it is imperative to do something about it.

This crisis is what comes at the origin of the action of terrorism before the letter. It can be narrated and explained, reflected upon at length, or only implied. It can be attributed to both natural and supernatural causes. It can be debunked by a sceptical discourse or satirical allegory. What looked like a crisis was only a blip in the normal course of events, or it was a crisis only to those who were evilly disposed toward the well-being of the society. Milton's Satan believes there is a crisis, although the existence of Satan, 'the cruel tyrant' as Milton calls him, is itself a condition of crisis. And when Satan recruits the Pope to initiate the Gunpowder Plot, he plants in the Pope's mind the idea of an utter emergency. 'Are you asleep, my son?', he says to the Pope as in a dream. The Pope is neglectful then, the devil says, and in great danger: 'If you choose to drowse on your soft bed, and if you refuse to shatter the waxing strength of the enemy, then will that enemy fill the Tyrrhenian Sea with his soldiery, and plant his gleaming standards on the Aventine hill. He will break the relics of your fathers, and burn them with fire. He will tread with unholy feet upon your sacred neck, yours whose shoes kings once rejoiced to kiss!'[57]

Disposed as many of us are, using common sense, to think that what matters in struggles of this type are conflicts of interest matched with conflicts of opinion, we

---

[54] Judith 8.33–34.   [55] *His Majesties Speach*: Iv.
[56] Schmitt, *Concept of the Political*; Agamben, *State of Exception*.
[57] Milton, *In quintum novembris*: 92–112.

may find it difficult to understand the spirit of Milton's language here. Surely this is madness. Surely it is absurd for Milton to think that the Pope was in any way involved in the Plot, or that the Pope was so afraid for the survival of his religion (his main enemy being little England) that he would instigate so underhanded and desperate a conspiracy as the Gunpowder Plot. And surely, conversely, if Milton was nevertheless right and the Pope was involved, then the Pope himself, or any-body who thought like him, was mad. Nor were early moderns themselves incap-able of thinking that fanatics on either side of a conflict were suffering from the delusions of the insane. But at the origin of a terrorist plot in the sixteenth and seventeenth centuries, this is what we find: the story of what at least one interested party imagines to be a desperate emergency. And the emergency has two parts: on the one hand, an order of symbolic meaning is under threat, a culture, a religion, or a sovereignty being challenged by the claims of an alternate order of symbolic meaning; on the other hand, survival itself is under threat. The challenge of one order against another is at once symbolic and existential. Such a crisis is what would-be terrorists perceive: something has happened to cause a rupture in condi-tions of the symbolic and existential order. In agreement with this account would be all the heroes so far alluded to, all the good terrorists, as it were: Brutus, Judith, Amleth, the Amboise conspirators, the killers of Concino Concini. For that matter, all the villains, the bad terrorists alluded to so far, would seem to be in agreement too: the Gunpowder Plotters, the would-be assassin of Gaspard de Coligny, the soldiers at Vassy. 'Good' or 'bad' is of course a judgement call, which the writers make as they tell their stories, and a figure who is good in one story, Brutus for example, may be bad in another. But either way, when an episode of terrorism comes, it has its origins in the perception of a state of emergency. Brutus sees an emergency in the Republic, Judith sees an emergency in Judaea, Amleth sees an emergency in Denmark, Jupiter sees an emergency in Paris, the Gunpowder Plot-ters see an emergency in England: in each case the emergency is different, devel-oping out of unique circumstances, and finding unique means of resolution; but in each case the emergency has this same general character. A system of meaning is under threat, and at the same time a system of life, and lots of real lives, are under threat as well.

The relation between the symbolic and the existential in these cases provides another challenge to common sense. But it is important. Would-be terrorists, finding themselves confronted with a choice of committing themselves to a cause, and later confronted with the choice of committing themselves to a signal act of violence, respond to what they take to be a general state of political emergency, where both an order of meaning and the survival of a community are at stake. Whatever might be the fate of the individual, who may or may not 'venture' his or her life for the cause, the fate of the community and at the same time the fate of the order of meaning that sustains it are under threat, opposed by an inimical pol-itical power. Even if a cultural or religious rivalry is at the root of the problem, or if cultural or religious integrity seems to be what is especially in danger, the crisis comes on a political level, and it is at the political level that crisis will have to be resolved. For it is precisely at the political level that orders of meaning and orders of survival are combined. As the Judith of Adrien d'Amboise puts it, as she prays for strength, 'Holoferne mort Béthulie vivra / Et le Tyran vivant le Cité périra.' 'If Holofernes dies, Bethulia will live: And if the tyrant lives, the city will perish.'[58] The city, the *polis*, is at stake; a 'tyrant' is what endangers it; and only one or the other may survive.

The identity of a community's symbolic life with its existential survival is a problem that even early modern fanatics perceive and have difficulty solving sometimes. Why would France die if France was no longer Catholic? Why would Denmark die if it were 'corrupted' by the presence of a parricide? The identity of meaning and life is not a problem in the stories of the Book of Judges, where the existential survival of Israel is always the theme, and always bound up with whether the state remains faithful to the Lord; but in later books in the Bible, as in later history and literature, the two ideas may sit uneasily together. Perhaps France does not have to be Catholic to survive, only majority Catholic. Perhaps Denmark could survive a corrupt regime and recover later. Moreover, it was a commonplace that sometimes communities are plagued by God as a form of chastisement. A threat to the practice of religion on the part of persecuting an enemy, or a threat to a nation on the part of a tyrant, may be a divine ordeal, meant to test the stamina of the faithful. Patience is required; and if patience is what comes, the people most likely will survive. But still, when a plan to resort to terrorist violence arises, agents are there who entertain few doubts about the urgency of the danger they face, or the need to use violence to defend against it. Missing from all early modern accounts of the assassination of Caesar that I am aware of is the idea that, in view of Caesar's regal popularity, the republican-minded senators ought to improve their republicanism, and reach out to the people. Missing from all accounts of the Judith story is approval of the idea that the Bethulians might solve their crisis by patient negotiation. According to the logic of terrorism before the letter, a life or death situation is at hand, and a yes or no is required. The whole first half of the Book of Judith can be read as a delineation of events where symbolic threats are transposed into existential threats, and vice versa, until the coming of the great crisis where the people of Bethulia are alone, surrounded, dying of thirst, and tempted to drink and eat unholy things. Apologies for the Amboise Conspiracy and the assassination of Concino Concini read much the same way. It is not only the case that something needs to be said in the public sphere, or said for that matter with violence. It is that violence is thought to be capable of both eliminating an existential-symbolic threat and overcoming the discourse that enables it.

Milton dramatizes this urgency of terrorists in the course of ridiculing them. But his ridicule is doubly ironic, for he has the Pope panic over an actual expression of commonly known Protestant intentions toward Catholicism: they 'will smash your ancient relics and burn them on the pyre, and trample your holy neck beneath his profane feet'. This was what the French, English, and Scottish iconoclasts of the sixteenth century endeavoured to accomplish; and it was what the English and Scottish iconoclasts of the seventeenth century would endeavour to

---

[58] Amboise, *Holoferne*: 1260–1.

accomplish again. The rhetoric is of a piece with the official English rhetoric about the Gunpowder Plot, and the scapegoating ceremonies that by now were a habit of English life, and it was of a piece too with the ambitions of radical Protestantism, to the cause of which Milton was not yet but would soon be sympathetic.[59]

But Milton then adds an important qualification. 'Do not attack [King James and the English people] with war and open conflict', Satan advises the Pope; 'that would be fruitless labour; rather make skilful use of fraud'. In the beginning of the story of a terrorist plot there comes not only the perception of a crisis demanding resolution, but also the perception of an asymmetry of means, and the choice therefore of strategy that is not only unlawful but also underhanded. Everything that follows, whether the perpetrators can resolve themselves sufficiently, whether in fact the plot is really a 'plot' or rather an *accident misérable*, a dagger to the abdomen of a foreign tyrant, or a massacre of an attack by firearms against unarmed citizens, whether the act in any case succeeds or fails, whether the message of the violence is recognized or spoiled, assented to or rejected, is consequent upon this dual perception: something is fundamentally wrong, but the only way to rectify it is to do something else that is fundamentally wrong.

And so there is the origin. In the mythic world of terrorism before the letter, questions of survival get conflated with questions of value and meaning. And so solutions to problems of survival, value, and meaning are on the road toward coming with a conflation of life-threatening violence, a transvaluation of value and a message of life-enhancing terror. 'Liberty! Freedom! Tyranny is dead!' Of course, out of that origin, much else can be made, much else can happen, and the roadway of terrorism may be blocked in any number of ways. Neither the act of terrorist violence nor the success of the terrorist message is ever inevitable. But that is why successful parties to terrorism may go to such lengths to disambiguate and ratify the act. That is why the act itself is such a challenging *passage*. And that is why, at the origin of the action, the writer may go to such lengths to testify to the necessity of its being undertaken, or otherwise prove that the violence was from the beginning a tragic or ridiculous mistake.

The terrorist action, as early moderns and their ancient predecessors represent it, is a sequence of acts. A life-threatening, culture-threatening disruption is observed to have taken place. And then, either one or more persons commit themselves to doing something about it or else one or more persons find themselves thrust into having to commit themselves. Now the observation of a threat and the commitment to action can be right or wrong, reasonable or insane. But a pattern is being followed. The moment of the act comes, rightly or wrongly. With the act it is believed that a major transformation has taken place. But then comes a final struggle either to ratify the act or resist it, to express its meaning throughout the public sphere and have it recognized, or else to contradict, defer, or belittle its meaning, and have the public reject it. Again and again this pattern is expressed, though with an indefinite number of variations. And this is the mythography of terrorism before the letter, on the level of the act; a mythography that permeated French,

---

[59] On Milton's changing sympathies, see Campbell and Corns, *John Milton*.

English, and Scottish literature from 1559 to 1642, and that all too often was enacted in real life as well, as political and religious conflicts irrupted into terror.

That is why the *passage à l'acte* is often so dramatically powerful. That is why the crucial moment will so often come in a prayer. 'Give me strength this day, O Lord God of Israel!', Judith cries out as she raises the sword (Jud 13.7). That is why, in the absence of a God to pray to, Roman characters have to resolve themselves by stoical self-examination. And it is why, conversely, a writer reflecting on an event may take pains to minimize the drama, to displace the action into an accident. So much is riding on this event. In question is not just the completion of a deadly mission, with all the risks it entails, but the meaning of the mission too. The event has to signify and signify fully, even if afterwards much work will inevitably remain to be done, and even if from the arrival of the moment itself the significance is subject to doubt, resistance, and indifference.

To consume a government by fire—was that an act of justice, or an act of horror? In retrospect it may seem that King James was certainly right, that the 9/11 of early modern England would have been a catastrophe beyond imagination. 'This offense', the jurist Edmund Coke would go on to say at the trial of the surviving conspirators, 'is such, that no man can express it, no example pattern it, no measure contain it.'[60] The whole scale of the conspiracy was wrong. But that is because Coke (and we along with him) look at what might have been from the side of the intended victims. We are happy to extract, as the meaning of the event, along with Coke, that it was monstrous, cruel, and wrongheaded—even that it was motivated by superstition or else by a misunderstanding of religious doctrine. We are happy to *resist* the meaning of the intended violence. But from the opposite point of view, if the Plot had succeeded, who knows what the climate of discourse would have been in the end? Who knows how its message would have been disambiguated?

---

[60] *A True and Perfect Relation*: D3V2.

3

Agents

1. OF CHARACTER

Consider Milton's Satan one more time. 'I have wandered the whole world', he says, flying over Albion, 'and here I have found the only cause for tears: these are the only people to rebel against me, scorn my rule, these alone have power greater than my arts. Yet if my efforts have any effect, not long shall they continue unpunished.'[1] A crisis, a decision, an expectation; a scene (Albion the strong), an agency (terror), and a purpose (punishment, vindication, self-assertion) are all contemplated here: and here is Satan himself doing the contemplating. He begins with a certain aim in life and finds himself in the middle of a customary mission, and he comes to us with an identity: the 'proud tyrant', the narrator calls him, and if we are not sure at first why he is a 'tyrant' we certainly know that he is proud and evil and a trouble-maker who bears all good people ill will.

This chapter is about agents, the ones who act and the ones who suffer, the ones who help and the ones who hinder, the ones who look on and celebrate an act of terrorist violence and the ones who behold and find themselves crippled with grief. This chapter also examines the meanings that are introduced into the discourse of terrorism before the letter by having agents recognized as characters of one sort or another. If Guy Fawkes is a deluded fool, then the Gunpowder Plot may have the added meaning of foolishness; but if it is Satan who is behind the whole operation, considerably more meaning is added to it. The victory of the discovery of the Plot is not only victory over misguided soldiers; it is also a victory over evil itself.

At a minimal level, agents are what A. J. Greimas called 'actants', grammatical subjects from whom, to whom, and through whom the structure of narrated action is realized; or what Tzvetan Todorov called *hommes-récits*.[2] Even actants or *hommes-récits* have meaning in themselves, in most forms of narratology, however: the actant role of the hero, the helper, the opponent, and so forth. Satan of course comes ready-made as an opponent. But the meaning depends on the narrative context, and can be either minimal or maximal. In the act of opening a door or even flying through the air, the actant may function as the barest of subjects: not yet even a hero or an opponent, the actant is simply the subject of an action, the change from one state of affairs to another, a going from here to there, or from stasis to activity. But in the act of being outraged at the sight of a prospering

---

[1] Milton, *In quintum novembris*: 40–5.
[2] Todorov, *Poétique de la prose*: 33–46; Greimas, 'Actants'.

Protestant country, swearing to commit oneself to a cause of vengeance, and being so supernaturally endowed as to put the Plot into motion, with the help of the Pope, the actant is a bare subject no more. Common sense tells us that such an actant was never just a bare subject. Even when a subject merely opens a door it may be assumed that the subject has inclinations and intentions to be reckoned with, and possibly a great many of them. And Satan is already known to us; he comes with a reputation. But it is up to the narrative or drama, or the implied story behind an argument, to show how a subject could arise who is capable of acting human-like, whether in opening a door or in expressing outrage, and whose doing so has a meaning for both the subject and us. It is up to the narrative to demonstrate not only what the subject did, but who the subject is, and what the relation between doing and being might be. Milton can be congratulated for having produced an adequate Satan, a figure more than equal to the task of setting the Gunpowder Plot in motion and, later on in Milton's career, in the context of *Paradise Lost*, becoming a grand enough figure to have produced even evil itself in the context of the human world.[3] And yet sometimes narratives fail to satisfy our common-sense demands, or deliberately refuse to do so.

Not too long ago it was popular among social scientists to speculate on the psychology of the terrorist. A good deal continues to be written on the subject, but careful writers no longer speculate about a general psychology of terrorism. For there are too many different kinds of terrorists, it is clear by now, for any one psychological model to fit a plurality of cases, and evidence of any special terrorist pathology or personality profile is thin even in individual cases.[4] There may be problems with the application of psychological thought to terrorism of any kind. One influential school of thought advises that terrorists should be understood as rational actors only. 'For the only real difference between terrorism and conventional military action is one of strategy.'[5] And again, many apparently reasonable and well-adjusted people have committed themselves to terrorist causes. But such a position proceeds from too neat a divide between rational and irrational, or healthy and deranged people, or for that matter between any analysis of strategic behaviour and any analysis of psychological behaviour—as if 'psychology' only applied to the people suffering from derangement or committed to delusional behaviour. Such a position can be faulted for taking too narrow a view of the psychological. It can be faulted as well for taking too narrow a view of the community of agents involved in incidents of violence. For terrorists do not operate in the theatre of terror alone. Their victims, their audiences, their supporters, and their detractors operate there as well. Satan, the Pope, Judith, not to mention real-life terrorists like Robert Catesby and François Ravaillac, are impossible to understand either as actants or as psychological beings without reference to the circumstances under which they have taken action, including the circumstances, in short, of other people.[6]

[3] Appelbaum, 'Milton, the Gunpowder Plot'.
[4] Hogan, 'The Search for the Terrorist Personality'.
[5] Ruby, 'Are Terrorists Mentally Deranged': 15. And see Kruglanski and Fishman, 'The Psychology of Terrorism'.
[6] This is a central argument in Crenshaw, 'Relating Terrorism'.

There is no tyrant-slayer without a tyrant, or a people imagined to suffer from the tyrant's oppression; and no mass murderer without a mass of innocent people who may be thought by terrorist logic to be complicit with an onerous regime, or worthy of being killed because of the symbolic value of doing so. Nor of course are the characteristics which may be attributed to actants only 'psychological'. They are social, anthropological, and historical too.

The general question is this: what does a *discourse* of terrorist violence require the reader to know or feel about the agents and victims and other concerned parties to the act of violence? Since the subject here is mainly the discourse as a literary phenomenon, the general question leads to the specific question of what literatures of various kinds, at various times and places, can accomplish with what in literary terms is usually called 'character'. But since the subject here is also discourse and literature as historical phenomena, it can also be asked how the literature of terrorism before the letter addressed the historical issue of character itself. On the one hand, the idea of character, along with the tools for representing and examining character, has a history. On the other hand, the idea of terrorist violence raises questions about character that are all its own, and so too then does the history of terrorist violence and its representation.

Raymond Williams might have included 'character' among his 'keywords'.[7] The idea of character evolves over time like the ideas indicated by other keywords, and in fact it is precisely in the sixteenth and seventeenth century that character acquires its most common modern meanings. In the Middle Ages, according to the *OED*, at least as early as 1315 a 'character' was 'a distinctive mark impressed, engraved, or otherwise formed; a brand, stamp'. Eventually, the character of an individual was the individual's distinctive mark—often a quality like irascibility or generosity, or a social status, like the chivalric dignity of Chaucer's Knight.[8] Only in 1647 is there clear evidence of character coming to mean 'the sum of the moral and mental qualities which distinguish an individual or race, viewed as a homogenous whole'.[9] Most extended treatments of the concept of character in narrative, unfortunately, neglect this or any other history of the idea and use of character, and are synchronic rather than diachronic in their approach to the subject.[10] Beginning with a canonical body of literary representations of character, they deduce from that canon a structure—sometimes syntactical, sometimes semantic—of *hommes-récits*. But for the age of Calvinism and cases of conscience, of *histoires tragiques*, Garnier, Montaigne, Marlowe, Jonson, Shakespeare, and Corneille, character must be seen as a phenomenon undergoing change, emerging toward new horizons of representation and understanding. Distinctive marks are becoming homogenous wholes; persons are coming to have personalities.

[7] Williams, *Keywords*.
[8] Fowler, *Literary Character*, discusses such figures as 'social persons'.
[9] The idea is probably already implied in Aristotle's *Poetics*.
[10] I include among such works the following, listed in order of the date of appearance: Docherty, *Reading (Absent) Character*; Phelan, *Reading People*; States, *Hamlet and the Concept*; Lynch, *The Economy of Character*; Woloch, *The One vs. The Many*; Vermeule, *Why Do We Care*. Somewhat different in approach is Hamon, *Personnel*.

One way of explaining this, following a humanist tradition that goes back to Henry James and E. M. Forster, is to say that writers are becoming more and more equipped to present characters who are unique rather than common, round rather than flat, vividly individual rather than stereotypical, emotionally and cognitively complex rather than one dimensional, evidently aware of themselves as conscious agents, motivated by multiple factors and impulses rather than single factors and impulses, subject to change over long stretches of time rather than limited to a single quality of existence over time, consistent in their actions or else, as Aristotle originally put it, 'consistently inconsistent', and, often most important, capable of nevertheless demonstrating steadfastness in the face of challenges to their integrity or survival.[11] The homogenous whole of the character is the unity fashioned out of these complications. The 'personality'—another word just coming into use in the modern sense in the seventeenth century—is the word that would eventually be used to describe this quality of the complex whole.

Another way of explaining this emergence of character and personality, however, in the spirit of the structuralists who helped raise the question, is to refer to what Roland Barthes called 'the ideology of the person'.[12] Putting aside the question of what people actually are outside of discourses about them, Barthes proposes that certain discourses about persons (his example being the realist novel) create illusions about persons which are nevertheless taken to be necessary and true. For Barthes the main one is the illusion of the person itself. The person is both the unity of what can be observed about the individual—the individual's traits, experiences, histories—and something left over, a 'precious remainder', an 'inductor of truth'. One of the things Barthes is talking about is the impression fictional texts may give that the person is independent of the things that are said and shown about him or her. Hamlet is in some sense, in our experience, independent of the words and deeds evident in *Hamlet*, just as, or almost just as, since he is historical as well as fictional, Julius Caesar is independent of anything that happens on a stage play called *Caesar*.[13] What is *not* said or shown about Hamlet or Caesar may even become an important part of our experience of him.[14] But another thing Barthes is talking about, more important here, is the idea that texts participate in the practice of fabricating the idea of the person, the person as a social construct the value of which is a part of the ideology of the social.

Barthes is especially interested in the idea that character is put forward as a kind of 'truth' or as a 'seme' that indicates truth. Apart from plot, theme, and other elements of dramas and narratives, there is a truth within or through the person,

[11] Aristotle, *Poetics*: XV.   [12] Barthes, *S/Z*: 191.
[13] Explaining the difference, from a semiotic point of view, between a fictional character and a historical character placed in a narrative or drama is a tricky business. But see Gallagher, 'What Would Napoleon Do?'
[14] Greenblatt, *Will in the World*: 303–25, argues that the power of the unseen in the establishment of character is a Shakespearean discovery. However, in *Meditations on a Hobby Horse* (9–11) E. H. Gombrich already argued that Renaissance realism began with the notion that artists did not need to paint the whole of a person because persons existed independently of what was actually shown about them.

that 'precious remainder'. In pre-modern literature, if this is not a 'personality', perhaps it is something that could be called the soul, or that which, according to Hamlet, one may have 'within which passes show'.[15] And if it is a quality that is often apparent among fictional characters, so it may be a quality observed or constructed in historical and contemporary figures. Brutus is a character, in this sense. The Duchess of Malfi, withstanding torture, is a character in this sense. And so too, as creatures of discourse, are the real-life terrorists Jacques Clément and François Ravaillac.

The stories of terrorism before the letter put considerable pressure on their main characters. They require them to face up to sizeable moral obstacles, to encounter transgression, danger, and horror. They challenge them to try to change the course of history, or otherwise resist historical pressure. And they put them in communities of agents who are similarly challenged. Moreover, they confront their characters with the problem of responsibility. In Paul Ricoeur's philosophy of narrative, a character's identity is tied to the condition of owning or 'authoring' his or her actions.[16] To author an action is to be responsible for it: yes I did it, and yes I intended it, or else, I intended something else but, I admit, this is what resulted. But just such ownership or authorship is frequently put into question by narratives of terrorism before the letter. That is, the narratives ask whether the perpetrators of crimes are really the perpetrators of crimes, or really responsible for their actions. Or else, they ask about the complicity of victims, or the complicity of perpetrators with other persons and social forces. In addition, in the distribution of the action among various actants, the stories manipulate point of view, sympathy, and identification. To whom do the stories of terrorist violence really belong? In the construction and distribution of character, writers may well wrest control of a story from one set of persons to another, and thereby from one set of interests and ideologies to another. And there may arise the question of truth itself; that is, the question not only of who the agents in stories of terrorism really are, but what their being who they really are tells us about the meaning of violence. If one kind of story can insist that the basic truth of an episode of violence lies in what really happened, another can insist the truth lies in who the people doing or suffering the violence really were, and how the doing and suffering affected them. For Barthes that is what happens when there is a 'surplus of meaning' in the character, when the character means more than the story that is told about him or her.

What follows, then, is a discussion of four related topics: the fundamental actantial roles at the core of the story or drama of a terrorist incident, that is of its 'agon'; the distribution of characters in the unfolding of a story or drama; the individualization of character, which may work for or against the apparent ideology behind an agon; and finally the surplus meaning of character, the meaning that cannot be confined to the story, or the meaning that is demanded of a story but not supplied because it is over-supplied, about which I will use the character of the assassin François Ravaillac as an example. In the agon a basic set of actantial

---

[15] See Maus, *Inwardness and Theatre.*   [16] Paul Ricoeur, 'Narrative Identity'.

relations are established at the core story of terrorist violence. In the distribution of characters a whole society of individuals may be arranged around the core story, and the story itself re-focalized, in a sense re-signified through character. In the individualization of character the story may come to acquire a psychological and moral bearing which outweighs many other considerations, including the purposes behind terrorist action and the representation of it. And as for surplus meaning, here we will see, in the case of Ravaillac, a demand made on character which character cannot satisfy, that character be a reliable and absolute 'inductor of truth'.

2. THE AGON

At the heart of the story, so far as the arrangement of character is concerned, are two adversaries or groups of adversaries, who have been placed in opposition to one another. A political conflict is involved which may require a recourse to violence. This political conflict has a generalized aspect, since it is about ideas and social groups as well as individuals, and since its resolution has to be public and communicative. But the political conflict has a personal aspect as well. It is lived, enacted, and struggled through by agents, who find themselves in adversarial relationships. The agents are competing for political hegemony and the competition between them is the agon of terrorism before the letter. Of course this agon can be viewed from many angles, explained in keeping with a great many causes, and resolved in a great many different ways, in keeping with a great many conscious and unconscious purposes. But from the point of view of the concept of the agent, in the first place, a competition between adversaries is at stake. In addition, this competition almost always comes with the same basic actantial structure. In the discourse of terrorism before the letter, the core struggle is almost always acted out between either of two sets of adversaries: either a tyrant and a tyrant-slayer, or else a martyr and a traitor. There can be plural adversaries—tyrants and slayers, martyrs and traitors. There can be helpers, people who assist the tyrants, and so forth; and there can be hinderers, people who get in their way, as well as observers, people who see and comment on the action. There can be shifts in roles, as when a tyrant-slayer goes down in his efforts and ends up a martyr, or as when a drama shifts its point of view, and someone who seems like a tyrant-slayer turns out to be nothing of the kind. And there can be dual roles: the tyrant who is also a traitor, the tyrant-slayer who is knowingly on the path to becoming a martyr, given that he is undertaking a suicide mission. But at the core of any conflict of terrorist before there would always seem to be an agon including either of the two sets of adversaries.

Whether the prime contenders are tyrants or martyrs, or tyrant-slayers or traitors, depends on the writer's attitude toward the struggle. In the Judith stories, Holofernes is unquestionably a tyrant, Judith a tyrant-slayer. In published stories about the murder of Henry IV, the king is unquestionably a martyr—dying because he was good rather than bad, a witness to virtue rather than an exemplar of vice—and Ravaillac his killer is unquestionably a traitor. But there are cases that can go either way, like the Caesar-Brutus story, or the contemporary cases of the slaying of the second Duke of Guise in 1563, the third Duke of Guise in 1588, or Henry III in 1589. There were writers for whom these latter figures were tyrants and deserved to die, and writers for whom they were martyrs, who shouldn't have been killed but, having been killed, bore witness to a higher cause. Also, there are variations when not a great leader is the target but some other sort of adversary—a mob, a retinue, symbolic objects. When the Massacre at Vassy flared up, those who decried it tried very hard to make the Duke of Guise and his soldiers not only into very bad people, but into traitors—one of the key Huguenot arguments at the time being that Vassy was a royal protectorate and not a part of the Guise's private domain, the Duchy of Lorraine. Those bad, intolerant people, subverting the laws of the monarch (which guaranteed freedom of worship) were traitors to the nation, and their victims, surely, were martyrs to the state. When iconoclastic violence flared up in such a way to take on the characteristics of terrorist violence, inanimate objects could take on the actantial role of tyrants, and their attackers as tyrant-slayers. For the idol has a power over the idolaters, which the iconoclast needs to crush. Even a place, a building, as in the case of the Gunpowder Plot, where the terrorists had multiple targets and objectives, could symbolically embody a tyranny, and thus become a target in the agon initiated by an ambitious tyrant-slayer. Had the House of Lords actually been blown up, like other scenes of disaster—Ground Zero comes inevitably to mind—it may well have been credited with the actantial character of a victim; the building might have been memorialized in some way, so that the site of the disaster would have been caused to bear witness to what it had suffered, as if the building were a person.

The tyrant and the tyrant-slayer, the martyr and the traitor: these actantial roles at the core of terrorism before the letter are already ideologically meaningful. No agent performing any of the roles is simply a bare subject. The agent belongs to a world where tyranny, resistance, martyrdom, and treachery are key principles of social and political understanding, and the corresponding actantial roles establish inevitable relations of power, conflict, value, personhood, and agency. It is key that the roles are both complementary and asymmetrical. A non-complementary agon, say a tyrant against a traitor, would not be impossible; but it would be hard for such an agon to express any political value apart from a bare struggle for domination, and it would be hard therefore for it to count as terrorism. A different kind of response would be required from a struggle between a tyrant and a traitor. A symmetrical agon would be possible too: a tyrant against a tyrant, a traitor against a traitor. But again, it would be hard for such a contest to express any political value apart from the bare struggle for power. A different kind of response would be required. Terrorism, in the sixteenth and seventeenth centuries, begins with this double condition for the agency of the actor: in the first place, a complementary agon, in the second place an asymmetrical one: tyrant against tyrant-slayer, or traitor against martyr.

It is with this agon that the message of terrorism begins, not in the sense that with the existence of these actants an episode and its meanings literally *start*, but in the sense that this agon, requiring opponents of a certain kind, is structurally *required*, and the story of terrorism cannot go on without it. When the agon comes, the message of terrorism already contains this meaning, that either a tyrant and a tyrant-slayer or a martyr and a traitor have come into violent contact. Terrorist violence is not unique in encompassing actantial roles of this kind; all sorts of violence may be defined by the degrees of complementarity and symmetry between their participants.[17] But terrorist violence during the sixteenth and seventeenth centuries is perhaps unique in encompassing precisely these particular roles most of the time, and using the expression of these roles to construct political messages. Consider some of the prime examples: Judith and Holofernes, Brutus and Caesar, Amleth and the nobles of Denmark, the Gunpowder Plotters and the king and his House of Lords. The psychologies or character profiles of these agents and victims may be quite different from case to case, but their actantial roles are structurally the same. And it is first of all the delegation of these actantial roles, where Holofernes is structurally the tyrant and Judith is structurally the tyrant-slayer, or where Gunpowder Plotters were structurally traitors and King James along with the House of Lords is structurally a potential martyr, that the meaning of the terrorist incident is communicated. In fact, when polemics fly over real-life incidents of terror, they fly first of all over the delegation of actantial roles. Which is which? Who is the tyrant, who the traitor? In controversial cases, as in the killing of Henry III in 1589, the issue was precisely over the nature of the participants. Of course, what Jacques Clément did, stealing upon the king, abusing the latter's good nature, and killing him with a blow to the abdomen, was illegal, immoral, and, so far as its detractors were concerned, 'parricide' and 'treason'.[18] But if Henry III was a tyrant, and Clément a tyrant-slayer, the case was altered. Then, as Jean Boucher put it, what Clément did was 'praiseworthy, as against a public enemy, who had been condemned by the courts, and towards whom all obligations of respect and duty had been lifted'.[19]

Showing the participants to be one thing or another and establishing the actantial relations among them comprises a big part of the work of the text of terrorism before the letter. An especially important way of doing this was through exemplarity, a common feature of early modern thought.[20] I have already noted the case of John Felton in this regard. One (anonymous) poet puts the following words in Felton's mouth:

> I know what Phineas did; and Heber's wife,
> And Ehud, Israel's judge, with Eglon's life:
> And I did hear, and see, and know, too well,
> What evil was done our English Israel:
> And I had warrant seal'd, and sent from heaven,
> My work to do: and so the blow is given.[21]

---

[17] See Collins, *Violence: A Micro-sociological Theory.*
[18] See for example *L'assassinat et parricide commis*, in Goulart, *Memoires de la Ligue*: 3.587–90; and Serres, *A General Inventorie*: 736.
[19] Boucher, *Apologie pour Jehan Chastel*: 17.
[20] Hampton, *Writing from History.*   [21] *Poems and Songs*: 73.

The poet is not only justifying Felton here; the poet is also characterizing him. Felton is similar to Phineas, Jael (Heber's wife), and Ehud; he is both choosing and being chosen to act as they did, under analogous circumstances.

But even the legendary figures could be modelled on earlier figures. In most versions of his story, including Plutarch's (though not Suetonius's), it is important that Marcus Brutus is descended from Lucius Junius Brutus, that supporters of action against Caesar would exhort him to imitate his ancestor and be a 'true' Brutus, and that the action as a whole could be thought of as repetition of the event that founded the Roman Republic. Ehud, for his part, is the second in a series of twelve 'judges', characterized as 'deliverers' of Israel after Israel would 'do evil in the eyes of the LORD', and God would hand them over to domination by a rival people. The judges do not imitate or invoke one another, but they reiterate a pattern. Many of them come from an obscure or deprived background. They are marked out by idiosyncrasies: Ehud being left-handed; Deborah a woman, assigned to lead a patriarchal society; Jepthah the disinherited son of a prostitute; Samson a Nazirite, born to a barren couple, pledged to long hair and the avoidance of alcohol in a land where wine was the common beverage. The battles of deliverance are frequently asymmetrical, the numbers uneven. The godliness of the event is signalled by the asymmetries of the killings.

So Brutus, Ehud, and other legendary terrorists were *already* formulated through exemplarity. Their identities were matched with the identities of others, who played analogous roles in the history of their nations. And then, in the sixteenth and seventeenth centuries, both fictional and real-life terrorists could be matched to exemplary figures of history, as also could their victims. Sixty-five years before John Felton's moment of fame, in 1563, a minor nobleman and soldier, Jean de Poltrot de Méré, assassinated François de Lorraine, the second Duke of Guise, the man who had been involved in the Massacre of Vassy, and who was now chief general of the royal army.[22] Poltrot underwent a similar fate of having a number of anonymous poems circulated in his praise, even while being sentenced to death for treason. 'As David slew the giant Philistine', says one,

> As Judith beheaded Holophernes
> So Méré you bravely killed this mutineer
> Who had done such wrong to the children of God.[23]

Another establishes a parallel with Brutus:

> If for having put a tyrant to death
> Brutus acquired such great renown,
> Méré you deserve even more strongly
> That your glory should always be known,
> For you owe nothing to that valiant Roman
> In the counsel and constancy you assert.[24]

---

[22] For background see Ruble, *L'assassinat de François*; and Vaissière, *De Quelques assassins*.
[23] *Poésies protestantes*: 23.　　[24] *Poésies protestantes*: 24.

The shooting and killing (from behind and in the dark of night) of the second Duke of Guise in February 1563 was a far more consequential event than the assassination of Buckingham.[25] It so shocked the French nation that even while Poltrot was executed as a traitor, the regent Catherine de Medici hastened to arrange a truce and issue the Edict of Amboise, which granted limited rights of assembly and worship to the Huguenots and called a halt to military engagement between Huguenots and the crown. Under interrogation, Poltrot himself claimed that his aim in killing Guise was to bring the nation together and put an end to the armed conflict between Protestants and Catholics. But public opinion was 'radicalized' in response to the assassination.[26] Even as it brought peace, the assassination stoked hostilities and hardened ideological differences. Protestants and Catholics became more suspicious of each other's intentions—as well the latter at least might, given the evidence of the Protestant poetry about Poltrot. Meanwhile, members of the Guise family, refusing to acknowledge the political message Poltrot claimed to have sent, got it into their heads that Gaspard de Coligny was responsible. Coligny was away in Normandy at the time—he was not part of the fighting in Orléans—and he openly denied the charge.[27] But the killing of the second Duke of Guise thus had the unintentional effect of igniting a feud between the Guise family and Coligny's clan. That feud played a role in the assassination of Coligny nine years later, as the Saint Bartholomew Massacre got underway, and it may have played a role in the failed attempt against the life of Coligny that helped trigger the Massacre.

If Poltrot, however, was another David or Judith, he was guiltless. In fact he was a hero, acting on behalf of a persecuted religious minority. And if Poltrot was another Brutus, again he was a guiltless hero. There was an essential difference between the two kinds of heroes, all the same. Although both the Jewish figures and the Roman one committed acts of political violence, the political principle on behalf of which the former fought was predominantly religious, and the latter predominantly secular. So the poets were saying something significant in their choice of exemplars. They were even anticipating differences between monarchomach theories, which would sometimes emphasize the primacy of religion over politics, and other times stress the secular values of sovereignty, security, and justice. The anonymously authored *Vindiciae contra tyrannos* would argue that a people do not owe allegiance to a ruler who prevents them from obeying the law of God; George Buchanan's *De jure regni apud scotos* would argue that magistrates have the right to depose a ruler, violently if necessary, who has violated the national constitution, religion having little to do with it.

Characterization, even on so slender a ground as drawing a parallel between one person and another, may thus have important ideological consequences, implying arguments on behalf of a political theory. It has norm-establishing consequences as

[25] Carroll, *Martyrs and Murderers*: 289–97. Also see Ruble, *L'assassinat*; Sutherland, 'The Assassination'; and Vaissière, *De Quelques assassins*.

[26] Wilkinson, 'Homicides Royaux'.

[27] Coligny, *Response à l'interrogatoire*. The 'response' was soon translated into English and published in London.

well. In the first place, it classifies not only the author of a violent act, but also its victim. Moreover, it can make a hero *representative* of a people. A good terrorist never acts on his or her own behalf. The good terrorist acts on behalf of the people to whose community he or she belongs. As we saw in the previous chapter, part of the story of the terrorist incident involves an 'action of commitment'. But in every case examined so far, the good terrorist is not only someone who decides, selflessly, to save a community, but also someone who already belongs to that community and wishes to represent it. The good terrorist may be exceptional in some way— left-handed, female, or the like—but he or she can never be an outsider.

Exemplarity, however, was not the only way the agent in an agon could be iden- tified and characterized. Simple accusations, with perhaps some evidence, could work. Said another poem about Poltrot and Guise, the latter, 'the butcher of Vassy', had been a danger to the state. He had been a

> proud tyrant who held in thrall
> The young king, his mother, and all the blood of France,
> That devilish tyrant who with his mischief makers
> Filled all of France with orphans,
> Supposing by that means to build a ladder
> For climbing above the king, whom he held under his wing.[28]

'Pride' was a weighty accusation in cases like this, along with tyrant-hood. In the case of Guise, along with his pride came stories of atrocities: as a military com- mander (although working on behalf of the Crown) he had made a lot of people into orphans; as a regent of France, when the young Francis II was still alive, he had shown his colours during the Tumult of Amboise. As a proud tyrant, more- over, Guise had been ambitious. This was a charge that would also be levelled against Gaspard de Coligny, David Riccio, Henry the third Duke of Guise, Con- cino Concini the Marquis d'Ancre, and George Villiers the Duke of Buckingham. As tyrants of ambition they were not actual monarchs; but they aspired to dom- inate a monarch, or even to replace one. Sometimes claims of proud ambition could be levelled even against sovereigns in power, like Henry IV (or, as we have seen, Milton's Satan). It was intrinsic to the nature of these persons that they would stop at nothing to further themselves, which was one of the main reasons they needed to be eliminated.

To do justice to the tyrannical impulses of such figures, writers sometimes amp- lified their failings, or discovered new kinds of vices to accuse them of. The trad- ition of the tyrannical character went back to Plato.[29] The tyrant was not only a person who had usurped the power he held and ruled his people corruptly; he was also himself inherently corrupt, and unable even to rule himself. The most no- torious of such out-of-control tyrants, in polemical literature discussing real-life figures, was Henry III. Henry's main crime of character was subtlety and a measure of tolerance for Protestantism; but the polemical literature, especially after he

---

[28] *Poésies protestantes*: 4; 20.
[29] Bushnell, *Tragedies of Tyrants*. And see Mousnier, *The Assassination of Henry IV.*

ordered the assassination of Henry the Duke of Guise in 1588, was violently abusive. Never calling him by his true title, but rather by his family name, Henri de Valois, the literature made Henry into a murderer, an atheist, an abuser of his people, a sexual pervert (sodomy was the main charge), and even a witch.[30] Along with that egregious character came a programme. According to polemicist Charles de Pinselet, 'All the actions and gestures of Henry de Valois were directed toward no other end but to ruin the Apostolic and Roman Catholic Christian Church.' The monarch wanted to 'condemn good faithful Christians ..., advance atheism and heresy as much as he could, and, not being content with bitter tyranny, ... despoil Catholics by an infinitude of taxes'. This came in a book significantly entitled *The Martyrdom of Brother Jacques Clément*.[31] Having first fulfilled the role of a tyrant-slayer, the good and courageous Clément was killed on the spot by Henry's guards, and so in his actantial role he shifted from being a killer to a martyr.

But traitors too could be subjected to creative characterization in this manner, as for that matter could tyrant-slayers and martyrs. In addition to or in place of appeals to historical exemplarity, writers could establish actantial roles by assigning conventional ideas such as tyranny and martyrdom to their characters, by delineating novel characteristics that complemented conventional ones (Henry's sexual perversion, for example), and by describing personal histories and ambitions that also complemented stereotypes.

In many stories, the uniqueness of an agent needed to be stressed. Such was the case especially with real-life, horrifyingly bad terrorists, for whom new types of characterization sometimes needed to be supplied. What conventional ideas could be associated with such people as the Gunpowder Plotters, attempting what all observers acknowledged to be an unprecedented strategy of mass murder and insurrection? Even some victims of terrorism could cry out, as it were, for a high level of individualization. Transcending familiar notions of good or evil, or even of personality, some agents were not only assigned fulsome qualities of habit, disposition, and ambition, but were even caused to be the vehicles through which new types of character could be delineated.

At the core of nearly every story of terrorism before the letter, however, there was, again, an agon between a tyrant and a tyrant-slayer, or between a traitor and a martyr. Or to be more precise, there was almost always at least one of these two different types of contest, with one or more individuals playing either one or the other actantial role. The names of different exemplary figures from the history of political violence were in the first place code words for these roles.

And the general significance of the centrality of these actantial roles was this: it established a major part of the mythic magic of terrorist violence. Again and again,

---

[30] Most of the extant polemical literature on the subject of Henry and Clément is collected in L'Estoile, *Les Belles figures et drolleries de la Ligue*. Some of the most telling of the polemics are listed in the bibliography of primary sources included at the end of this study. A whole play was devoted to the polemics as well, Pierre Matthieu's *La Guisade*, which went through three editions in 1588–9. On the historical situation see Le Roux, *Un régicide au nom de Dieu*; and Polachek, 'Le Mécénat meurtrier'. On the general atmosphere of polemics see Racaut, *Hatred in Print*.

[31] Pinselet, *Le Martyre de frere Jacques Clement*.

when the actantial roles were ideologically well defined, as in all of the examples given so far in this chapter, violence was taken to have an extraordinary power. The person of the chief victim of violence came to be identified with the principle he was held to stand for and even with the power of the principle's enforcement. Killing a tyrant meant (or was supposed to mean) killing both the man and the tyranny he represented. The two were held to go together, the person and the principle, the will of the person and the principle in force, since power itself in these cases was understood, as if magically, to be at once systemic and personal. The obverse of the idea of 'the king's two bodies' was a part of this, what can be called 'the tyrant's two bodies'.[32] Thus we hear a triumphant Amleth make the following announcement to the people of Denmark: 'I have washed the spots that defiled the reputation of the queen', he says, 'overthrowing both the tyrant and the tyranny.'[33] Similar sentiments were echoed in different versions of the stories of Judith, Brutus, and Samson—not to mention those who celebrated the heroic accomplishments of such real-life killers as Jean de Poltrot, Jacques Clément, and John Felton. It was by no means a unanimous idea among early moderns that tyranny was personal rather than systemic. In *Discours sur la servitude volontaire*, La Boétie argues that tyranny operates by collusion; the whole of a society cooperates in the propagation of oppression, and the whole of society is to blame when a tyrant reigns.[34] (There is never a suggestion in La Boétie's book, therefore, that the problem of tyranny can be solved by murdering the tyrant.) Many history books and moral tracts similarly warned that it was not the character of an individual leader that was decisive so much as the character of the people over whom the leader presided. But when homicide was considered as a solution to the problem of tyranny, the assumption was that tyranny is personal and individual as well as corporate, and that attacks against the person amount to attacks against the corporate power. If, in the case of the king's two bodies, when one body dies (the mortal part) the other body still lives, in the case of the tyrant's two bodies, when the mortal tyrant dies the body of tyranny dies as well.

3. DISTRIBUTION

There is little question, then, that the competition between two reciprocal antagonists was usually at the core of the characterological life of terrorism before the letter. But there had to be other sorts of characters in any account of a terrorist incident. Tyrants have associates, aides, and friends as well as people over whom they exercise oppression; tyrant-slayers too are part of a group of differently placed types of individuals. If violence operates by sending a message, there must be agents who are able to receive the message and act or suffer in response to it: interested observers, casual bystanders, collateral victims. Moreover, even if an agon is at the core of the story, the agon and its agents need not be the main focus of the

---

[32] Kantorowicz, *The King's Two Bodies*.   [33] *Historie of Hamblet*: 116.
[34] La Boétie, *The Politics of Obedience*: esp. 48–50.

discourse about it. In the Book of Judith, the contest between the Assyrians and the Jews is intricately balanced, even at the moment of recognition: first the Jews see what Judith has done, then the Assyrians see what she has done; first the Jews rally at the site of Holophernes's head, and prepare for battle; then, in their own camp the next morning, the Assyrians are 'overcome with fear and trembling', and on their own initiative flee the scene even before the Jewish soldiers arrive (Jud 14–15). But though the core story remains the same as in the Bible, there is no such focal balance in Pieter Heyns's *Le Miroir des vefves: Tragedie sacrée d'Holofernes et Judith*, which shifts the attention of the reader or playgoer to interested observers of the action.

The play itself was written to be performed by schoolgirls at Heyns's college for girls, in Antwerp, where a perfectly modern Parisian French was the medium of instruction. *The Mirror for Widows* was performed in 1582 and published in 1596, along with several other schoolgirl plays by Heyns. There are no male parts but one, Achior, the Assyrian official who goes over to the Jewish side and converts (a part that was probably played by Heyns). There is no violence enacted on stage. Instead, the characters, most of them allegorical figures and some of them real women involved in the action, talk about the assassination, about what led up to it and how and why, and what its implications are for the lives of women, and especially for widows, for whom Judith serves as a paragon. Among the characters are History, Docility, Worldly Widow, Curiosity, Rumour (*Fama*) who has the most lines, Judith, Judith's servant Abra, and an interesting character Heyns invents, Holofernes's Mistress (*Pallaca Holoferni*). Without substantially changing the story, Heyns re-focalizes it. In this story about the killing of a tyrant, the tyrant is never seen. Or rather, the tyrant is never seen except in retrospect through the eyes of women who have been affected by him, including a woman who is jealous of the attention he is paying to Judith.

The neo-classical conventions of French theatre lent themselves to dramas where the core action was re-focalized through characters whose main role was to respond emotionally and intellectually. If epic accounts like Du Bartas's *Judit* place the hero and the victim at the centre of attention, dramatic accounts could well put bystanders or members of the public there. The story of terrorism before the letter might then concentrate on the effect of the violence rather than its perpetration, and it might ask the reader or playgoer to think about terrorism as something whose messages have to be processed, whether we like it or not. A Chorus could be brought into a drama, and play the role of a public responding to the behaviour of the greats, or of an apparently impartial commenter on the action. Messengers may report an action, and with their message serve not only as reporters but as interpreters of the action, and as initial registrars of affective response.

In French drama female characters were frequently key. It was one of the innovations of Muret's Latin *Julius Caesar* (1550) and Grévin's *César*, which was based on Muret's work, to make Calpurnia a central figure. Caesar's wife and her premonitions of disaster were already a part of legend, and discussed by both Plutarch and Suetonius. But in Muret Calpurnia dominates a scene; in Grévin she dominates two scenes. (She is present in Shakespeare's play too, of course, but she does not dominate any scene.) While Caesar and Brutus contest over the meaning of leadership, sovereignty, tradition, loyalty, and freedom, Calpurnia worries about whether her husband and bedfellow will survive another day, given her dreams and other presentiments. While the partisans of Antony and Brutus face off to deter- mine the fate of the Republic, Calpurnia gets the news of the death of her husband and reacts.

> O strange event! O cruel day!
> O dream, no longer a dream, but now a truth
> Too truthfully given! That my Caesar is dead
> By the sword of Brutus! O miserable fate!
> Is that how heaven puts our fortunes in the balance?
> Is that how one good deed is rewarded by another?[35]

Scenes like this de-centre the political battle which otherwise seems waged at the heart of the drama. The political battle requires the violence to fall out either on the side of the sur-crime of national deliverance or the heinous crime of parricide and treason. But the character of a collateral victim responding to the violence introduces a third point of view, where even higher values may be at stake. It sug- gests to the audience that the real meaning of terrorism lies in the suffering and puzzlement it causes for those who have survived it.

In his two great plays about assassination and civil war in Rome, *Porcie* and *Cornélie*, Robert Garnier makes widows the focus, and there is no ambiguity as to why he does so.[36] (A third play on the theme of civil war in Rome would be *Marc Antoine*, where the focal character is Cleopatra; but in that play assassination and terror are not at issue.) Porcie and Cornélie are secondary victims of political vio- lence; they are survivors, and it is to the plight of such victims that Garnier wants to direct attention. What both women have to face is the meaning of the disasters that have befallen them and their society. For Porcie, this is the failure of the assas- sination of Caesar to have the effect intended, thus the coming of civil war and ultimately the death of her husband and the cause he stood for. Porcie's complaint is not only about personal loss and disappointment; it is also about what the dis- aster she faces says about the order of the universe and the meaning of life. She does not quite die on stage, but she passionately summons her death. Her body being found by her Nurse, Porcie's death is then lamented by a Chorus of Young Women along with the Nurse: 'Brutus has died twice!' And the Nurse passionately resolves to kill herself as well.

The title character of *Cornélie* has to deal not with one but three dead beloveds: her first husband Publius Crassus, her second husband Pompey, and finally her father Scipio. Like Porcie, Cornélie confronts not just personal loss but a public crisis, and she imagines her own fate to be tied to the fate of the Republic. The loss of Pompey is especially painful. Crassus died in battle, Scipio died by his own hand (rather than allowing himself to be captured by Caesar's forces), but Pompey—to whose identity she was most strongly attached—died at the hands of assassins, and

---

[35] Grévin, *César.* 917–22.   [36] See Jondorf, *Robert Garnier* and Lebègue, *Les Guerres civiles.*

she was there to see it. The means of his death was a kind of insult she has to live down.

> But he is dead, (O heavens), not dead in fight,
> With pike in hand upon a fort besieged,
> Defending of a breach; but basely slain,
> Slain traitorously, without assault in war.[37]

The story was told by both Plutarch and Lucan. Having lost the Battle of Pharsalia against Caesar, Pompey wandered through the eastern Mediterranean looking for a place where he could re-establish himself and his fortune, and perhaps even re-collect his troops. Eventually he was invited to visit Egypt. But the reigning monarch Ptolemy, deliberating with his aides about what to do about Pompey, came to the conclusion that the Roman general would be too dangerous to have around. He might well tyrannize over the Egyptians, or else cause his rival Caesar to re-invade Egypt and play havoc there. The best thing to do would be to kill Pompey and offer him as a token of fidelity to Caesar. (A similar logic obtains in the story of the killing of the Persian king Darius, as represented in both French and English literature: Darius is offered as a token to Alexander.[38]) So Pompey sails to Alexandria, his wife Cornélie and other close associates with him. Pompey's ship anchors close off the coast, and Pompey embarks on a boat and lands. He is greeted ceremoniously, and then fatally attacked by three of Ptolemy's men armed with daggers. 'I saw him, I was there', says Cornélie, 'and in mine arms / He almost felt the poniard when he fell.'[39]

It makes a great difference to Cornélie that Pompey died 'traitorously'. In early modern France, as in early modern Rome, the means of one's death express a value on the scale of an honour code. To be killed by a social equal is far more honourable than to be killed by underlings, who ought to revere their superiors. (One of the assassins was a Roman soldier who had served under Pompey, and all Egyptians possibly still owed him deference.) To be killed under unequal conditions is dishonourable: another French word for being killed under such conditions, as will be seen in the next chapter, is *massacre*, and the massacre fouls the honour both of the perpetrator and the victim. It also makes a great difference, of course, that Pompey died in front of Cornélie's eyes. It almost goes without saying: to see a loved one murdered before one's eyes is horrifying. But in Cornélie's case, as in Porcie's, the personal loss comes wrapped in the indignity of being a victim to terrorism, a terrorism whose message one must fervidly reject.

> O barbarous, inhuman, hateful traitors [proclaims Cornélie]
> This your disloyal dealing hath defamed
> Your King and his inhospitable seat
> Of the extremest and most odious crime
> That 'gainst the heavens might be imagined.

[37] Garnier, *Cornelia*, trans. Kyd: 2.178–81.
[38] Jacques de La Taille, *Daire* (1561) and William Alexander, *Darius* (1603). Both plays are similar in emphasis, exposing the perfidy of the men who killed the Persian leader.
[39] Garnier, *Cornelia*, trans. Kyd: 2.184–5.

> For ye have basely broke the Law of Arms,
> And outraged over an afflicted soul;
> Murdered a man that did submit himself,
> And injured him that ever used you kindly.[40]

Here is the obverse of the story of Judith, where a violation of the laws of hospitality comes to express not a form of necessary guile in which 'killing is not for murder always taken', but rather an outrage, concentrated into an 'extremest and most odious crime'. Among Cornélie's other quandaries is the fact that she has no means to redress the crime. Another is that it is impossible for her to assent to what the murder was supposed to signal: the utter triumph of Caesar and therefore the utter defeat of the Republic.

As the play continues, Caesar attempts to show himself magnanimous, and Cassius and Brutus begin to think about assassinating Caesar. As a comment on the contemporary Wars of Religion, *Cornélie* is clearly meant to delineate, by way of parallels with ancient Roman stories, a breakdown in traditional codes of conduct, in peace as in war. The play was written in 1574, and so the author, a member of the Pleiades group and a friend to *politique* councillors Michel de l'Hôpital and Guy Du Faur Pibrac, had already lived through the assassinations of the second Duke of Guise and the Admiral of France, Gaspard de Coligny, as well as the execution of the Prince of Condé in the course of the Battle of Jarnac, not to mention a number of mass murders.[41] But Garnier does not only illustrate and comment on the breakdown of order. He places the experience of the breakdown, concentrated into the outrage of Pompey's assassination, into the person of someone who is a victim, a survivor, and a witness.

In Garnier's work the episode of violence puts its survivors to a test that they believe to be unfairly directed against them. Within the character of the survivor, while the survivor not only thinks and feels but also struggles for a reason to live or die and the resolution to follow the dictates of reason, the final meaning of the terrorist incident comes. What matters from this characterological perspective is not whether the perpetrators of violence were right or wrong, or whether the cause on behalf of which the violence was undertaken is to be accepted or rejected, but whether the victimized survivor can adequately respond to the moral shock of the disaster that has befallen him or her.

One of the reasons Garnier liked to focus on female characters, as he did in all his tragedies, is that unlike male characters, the women do not have the opportunity to respond to disaster by revenge. Like his fellow *politiques*, Garnier wanted to see the cycle of violence of his own time come to an end, and wanted to argue that respect for law, authority, kinship, and the common bonds of humanity was required to end it. But the tragic power of the plays of Garnier comes not from pacifism; it comes from his perception of the powerlessness of pacifism in the face of unrelenting aggression. Garnier has been called 'the first real tragedian' because

[40] Garnier, *Cornelia*, trans. Kyd: 3.3.32–40.
[41] See *Declaration, et Protestation du Tres-illustre Prince*. And for more on Condé, see Chapter 4, section 3.

he begins with the premise that 'life is unjust'.[42] But to that must be added that 'life is unjust' in Garnier's frame of mind precisely when the means to redressing injustice are either unavailable or unacceptable. To the avenger, the injustice of life is never complete and definitive; it can always be rectified through violence.[43] In Greek tragedies like Euripides's *Hecuba* and *Medea*, which Garnier probably knew first hand, even women are given the option of redressing a grievance through murder. But vengeance is not an option in Garnier's plays, and the choice of female protagonists all but guarantees it. To someone committed to non-vengeance and hence to peace, injustice may well prevail. Placing the focus on women, Garnier creates characters on whom pacifism has been imposed. Placing the focus on survivors of political violence—mainly terrorist violence in *Porcie* and *Cornélie*, open war in the others—Garnier constructs a drama of the traumatized, where the action of the play is devoted to the internal agon of the survivor, as she struggles to decide how or even whether to live.

When polemicists argue over the meaning of a violent incident, one of the key points of dispute is what to think about survivors, or how to be one. And apart from polemics, in other dramas and stories besides Garnier's, where tragedy is near, the subject positions of survivors must too be arranged, and lines of empathy, identification, indifference, or contempt established. When Shakespeare puts the Roman crowd into the drama of *Julius Caesar*, he is creating a collective character which is challenged to survive an outrage and decide how to live in the aftermath. A similar problem is encountered in George Chapman's *The Revenge of Bussy d'Ambois* (1611–13), where the main character Clermont d'Ambois, seeing his patron the Duke of Guise assassinated, resolves to kill himself.[44]

4. THE INDIVIDUAL: AGAINST IDEOLOGY

Most of the characters discussed so far express, in their persons, an ideology. They may or may not express the words of their ideologies; they may or may not make arguments about them. But their actantial roles, which are already ideologically coded, correspond to the other traits that go into making their persons 'homogenous wholes'.

But there are times when the individualization of the character—the homogenous whole he or she is identified with—works at cross purposes. Characters are constructed with a view toward modifying or even undermining the political messages they are sending or receiving as actants. Hypocrites are cases in point, people who do one thing and believe another. A simple example is the title character of Shirley's *The Traitor* (1631–5). Based, as we have seen, on the life of Lorenzino de Medici, and the assassination of his cousin the duke, the play turns Lorenzino into a dissimulator. Says a collaborator, after he and Lorenzino have killed the Duke of Florence, 'You told a tale once of a commonwealth / And liberty.' 'It was to gain a

---

[42] Turzio, Introduction to Garnier, *Porcie*.   [43] See Kerrigan, *Revenge Tragedy*.
[44] See Chapter 6, section 2.

faction of discontented persons', Lorenzino replies, 'a fine trick to make a buzz of reformation.'[45] A mere Machiavel in Shirley's retelling of the story, the 'traitor' Lorenzo says one thing and means another; political idealism is exposed as an excuse for usurpation. And so many characters in stories and polemics of terrorism before the letter show themselves to be simple hypocrites, who take advantage of the political ideals of others to further their own ambition.

But under the pressure of terrorist incidents, many characters show themselves to be hypocrites of a new kind, a new depth, either comic or tragic. And sometimes the personality of an agent can modify or undermine ideology on the strength of personality itself. Character in itself, of the perpetrator or the victim of violence, becomes a key focus of the writer; it becomes more interesting than much of the story, and modifies what might otherwise be the ideological clarity of the agon behind it.

A case of newly tragic hypocrisy appears in Chantelouve's *Tragédie du feu Gaspar de Coligny*. This is a play, it will be recalled, that turns the murder of Coligny, and by implication the whole of the Saint Bartholomew Massacre, into a good thing, warranted by the law of self-defence. Another tyrant of ambition, as Chantelouve depicts him, Coligny is also a demonic atheist. When the play opens, Coligny is alone, a Doctor Faustus *avant la lettre*, invoking a range of dark supernatural powers, almost incoherently, and not without an element of the ridiculous:

> O Death, O Rage, O Fire, O Pluto, O Furies!
> Come, cover me with your bitter furores,
> O Satan! O Calvin! Open to me the gates of Hell…

Considering his lust for power, Coligny chooses the dark powers over God, 'who frightens children and women', and finally decides to renounce 'all religion', even the religion of de Bèze.

> I ask myself to overturn the faith
> Of both Pope and Calvin, and fleeing all Law,
> Which would restrain me under its empire,
> I alone will be exempt from Law: I want to be King.[46]

Charging a religious militant, as Coligny surely was, with hypocrisy and atheism was a common rhetorical ploy. The aim was defensive. If a dissident could claim that he was suffering religious persecution, then his motives were based on what he took to be faith, and his dissent could be understood as an honest rebuke to the powers harassing him. Of course, such a dissident could be stigmatized as a heretic—but the charge of heresy against fellow subjects, over a decade since the French Troubles began, seems to have lost some of its force. The sincerity of the antagonist might be based on a falsehood, a heretical idea, but still, it was sincere. So it might be more powerful rhetorically to charge the antagonist with only pretending to be religious for the sake of pursuing an irreligious ambition.

---

[45] Shirley, *The Traitor*: Act 5: sig.Kr2.   [46] Chantelouve, *Tragédie*: 4–5.

As an apologist for the murder of Coligny like Chantelouve could make Coligny into a tyrant of ambition who needed to be stopped at all costs, so, we have seen, could apologists for other murders, even the assassination of King Henry III. But in the case of Chantelouve's play, Coligny is not only accused of ambition, irreligion, and the like. As a dramatist Chantelouve has tried to get to the inside of the mind and will of Coligny. He has tried to make his hypocrisy, atheism, and will-to-power into a form of personhood. And this personhood is supposed to act as a refutation of ideology: there is no ideology where the champion of Protestantism lives, only a will-to-power which cynically exploits ideology. There is nothing terrible about killing such a person as Coligny; there is not even anything political about it anymore. But there is something terrible about looking into the soul of such a person: we get a glimpse of the awful abyss over which human nature is capable of teetering. We stare down, vertiginously, at the depths to which such a figure may descend.

We get a similar picture in a play critical of the character of Henry the third Duke of Guise, *Le Triomphe de la ligue*, by Richard Néré. 'I feel a thousand executioners in my conscience', says the duke. 'And what I imagine in my troubled heart / Is nothing but iron, fire and blood, nothing but hideous massacres.'[47] This was a play published in 1607. Like Chantelouve's tragedy, the play apologizes for a murder, this time the murder of Guise on the orders of Henry III. Guise, in the play, is another dark soul who uses religion as a cover for his ambition. He acquires another dimension of character for us when we see him not only aspiring to power but being afraid for himself and his 'troubled heart' as a result. Guise has presentiments. He dreams that he is going to be torn apart by lions. The dream predicts, he fears, his 'final torment', by which he means both the manner by which his death is to come and his damnation to hell for being a man of blood. Not just ambitious and violent but Faustian in his bargaining with the forces of death, Néré's version of Guise sees his own impossibility as a human being. He shall have to be killed.

And this, again, is about a *victim* of terrorism, a man who is shown to have deserved to meet a terrorist death. But about perpetrators of terrorism similar kinds of individualization could be expressed. A comic case comes in Thomas Lodge's *The Wounds of Civil War* (1586), a play about the conflict between Marius and Sulla in republican Rome, a generation before the advent of Pompey and Caesar. Incongruously, as was mentioned earlier, the task of murdering a captured Marius is assigned to a half-French, half-English-speaking Frenchman named Pedro, who refuses to commit the murder until he is paid ('de fault avoir argent, me no point de argent, no point kill Marius') and then finds himself unable to carry out the assassination anyway. He is too much in awe of legitimate authority.[48]

A more troubling case comes in a fictionalized portrayal of the real-life assassin William Parry, in Thomas Dekker's *The Whore of Babylon* (1607). 'How are my spirits / Hauled, tortured, and grown wild!', he says,

[47] Neré, *Triomphe de la ligue*: 102.
[48] Lodge, *Wounds of Civil War*, Act 3. For the politics of the play, see Hadfield, 'Thomas Lodge and Elizabethan Republicanism'.

> On leaves eternal
> Vows have I writ so deep, so bound them up,
> So texted them in characters capital
> I cannot raise them but I blot my name
> Out of the book of sense.

When arrested after a failed attempt on Elizabeth's life, Parry (called 'Paridel') tells his captors, "Tis welcome; a black life ends in black fame.'[49] As Pedro is a ridiculous man recruited to achieve the political goals of people whom he cannot understand, Parry is an anxious desperado, recruited by Jesuits to 'relieve' the English people of religious tyranny. Parry understands all too well what he is doing, and for that reason, in the end, he cannot do it.[50] When he comes face to face with Elizabeth, and readies to strike her, he sees his own 'tortured', criminal desperation.

Early modern playwrights, in France and England alike, often aspired not only to produce sharply drawn characters, but also to produce what in Barthes's terms would be called a 'surplus' of character. If the meaning of terrorist conspiracy, in a play like *The Whore of Babylon*—a play, by the way, that discusses plots against Elizabeth, but that is probably thinking about the Gunpowder Plot—begins with crisis, it may come to an end with a revelation of character. Jesuits and other Catholic officials may nefariously plot against the life of a beloved queen, for the sake of promoting their whorish religion, but it is within the personality of a man like Parry that the key to the evil is to be found.

In the hands of the writers who have come to be the most admired of the period, the humanity of the characters could all but overwhelm the politics of a story. I think of this above all with respect to Shakespeare, but perhaps the most significant humanization of the political in the context of terrorism before the letter comes in Corneille's *Cinna*. The chief antagonists of the play, Cinna and Augustus, are so humanized that the very terms of tyranny, treachery, resistance, freedom, and authority on behalf of or against which each can claim to be acting are rendered nugatory. The two main characters seem to fit the usual actantial roles, at first: either a tyrant and a tyrant-slayer, or a traitor and a martyr. Cinna has launched a conspiracy against Augustus, in the name of ancient liberty; Augustus has committed enough crimes against his own people, in his struggle to ascend to power, to apparently warrant the name of a tyrant. But the conspiracy never comes off. Instead, Augustus both confounds the conspiracy and pardons everyone involved, turning his enemies into allies, and launching the golden age of Augustan rule—in the words of a recent critic, bringing about a 'converted world, where war has turned into peace, violence into sweetness, and hate into harmony'.[51]

Back in 1922, Gustave L. van Roosbroeck already identified the two current events that were probably on Corneille's mind when he wrote *Cinna*.[52] Most obvious was a tax revolt in Corneille's home town of Rouen, which broke out in 1639

---

[49] Dekker, *The Whore of Babylon*: 5.2. 125–80. And see Krantz, 'Thomas Dekker's Political Commentary'.

[50] In real life, too, Parry was a hard man to fathom. See Parry, *A True and Plaine Declaration*.

[51] Landry, '*Cinna* ou le paradoxe': 452.   [52] Roosbroeck, 'Corneille's *Cinna*'.

and was suppressed by the central government in 1640, just as *Cinna* was first being performed on stage. More parallel to the events of *Cinna* was an incident of 1626, called *La conspiration des dames*, where a group of disaffected nobles plotted to assassinate Cardinal Richelieu and transform the crown's policy for succession. In both cases, sedition threatened the authority of the central government, though only the latter can be categorized as a terrorist plot; and in both cases, the sedition having been suppressed, Richelieu showed clemency to the offenders. Corneille himself claimed to have been inspired by the tale told of Cinna in an essay by Seneca, 'Of Clemency', and retold by Montaigne in his essay, Book I Chapter 23, 'Various Outcomes of the Same Counsel' (an essay that also deals with the assassination of François Lorraine the second Duke of Guise). In *Cinna* Corneille has made the story of Augustus's clemency into an allegory in praise of his patron, Richelieu. But he has also come to express a kind of post-ideological account of political ideology.

Corneille does not eschew political language, but he has created a world where character precedes the political, and outweighs it as a motivation. Characters act the way they do—including conspiring to assassinate the new emperor—out of mixtures of self-interest and idealism, passion and reason, a rage for personal vengeance mixed with a desire for universal justice. They even act out of a recognition of the power of exemplarity. Cinna is a descendant of Pompey, and he wants to prove himself worthy of his ancestor, not to mention the high-born woman he wants to marry. The political action is supposed to be undertaken by way of the pure logic of political action. Everybody seems to be aware of that. Rhetoric goes back and forth about tyranny and treason and the conspirators plan to carry out the murder in the spirit of a sacrifice. But the characters cannot sort out the political from the entanglements of their desires. Rivalry for the logic of the main female character along with countervailing bonds of loyalty, lineage, and brotherly affection undermine the conspiracy. Cinna is made to look a hypocrite—not only in the eyes of others, but more importantly in his own. And when Augustus has the chance to follow-up the bungling of the conspiracy with the usual logic of political retribution—the show trial and execution of traitors—instead he forecloses the process and proposes a transcendence of the political conflict. Instead of punishing the conspirators, he will elevate them. Instead of begrudging their intentions, he will forgive. 'Let the conspirators come to know Augustus / Has learned everything, and wishes everything to forget.'[53]

In transcending a political conflict and the language behind it, Augustus of course remakes the politics of his state, and brings to it a new political language. *Cinna* is not an apolitical play, and it feeds into the development of absolutist ideology in France. But *Cinna* remakes politics by means that rely upon what appear to be non-political elements: personalities, whose needs and dreams outweigh the ends of political action. Clemency and absolutism together allow personalities to thrive as personalities, at peace with one another. When Augustus tells his would-be assailants that he is ready to forgive and forget and even to bestow wealth

---

[53] Corneille, *Cinna*: 5.3.1778–80.

and privilege on them, he also argues that there is no alternative. My argument here is that there is no alternative because Corneille has constructed a new kind of character for political drama, a character whose significance as a person transcends his or her significance as an actant, or for that matter his or her significance as a political animal.[54]

Whether this is a remarkable insight into how politics works, and why absolutism could seem like a reasonable solution to French intellectuals in the seventeenth century, is a question that may be left to others to answer. But it seems to correlate with the thought of Corneille's contemporary, Thomas Hobbes. I say this in view of the humanist and liberal impulses of Hobbes's thought, as well as the mechanistic and repressive impulses.[55] Human nature is capacious, in the thought of both Corneille and Hobbes. Hence comes the capacious characterization of Corneille, and Hobbes's famous admiration of William Davenant's *Gondibert*.[56] But in that capaciousness also comes a kind of natural warfare of person against person and even of individuals against themselves. Hence a benign absolutism comes as a solution to conflict, a power that is exercised in the recognition that people cannot govern themselves, but must be placed in 'awe' of sovereign power.

5. RAVAILLAC THE SCAPEGOAT

The idea of character was especially tested, deliberated, and struggled over in the real-life case of François Ravaillac, the assassin of Henry IV, in whose defence no one ever came forward. In Ravaillac's case there seemed to exist that 'precious remainder', that thing left over, that illusion of a hidden and inaccessible interiority, which was definitive of who he was and therefore of what he did. It was not the interiority of a great man, or even an intelligent man, but it was an interiority which was at once demanded and denied. Ravaillac was a terrorist whose political purposes could only be divined by way of his hidden psychological purposes; he was a man whose historical truth was his personality—his terrorist personality— but whose truth was therefore ineffable, and never to be grasped. The triumph of character in the case of a play like *Cinna* may well represent a triumph of humanism over ideology. But in the real-life case of Ravaillac the triumph of character signified the failure of humanism and ideology alike, for the character of Ravaillac could never satisfy the demands that onlookers placed upon it.

François Ravaillac of Angoulême (1578–1610) set upon Henry while the king and a couple of aides were in a carriage on a narrow street in Paris, making their way toward the offices of the Arsenal, a garrison on the banks of the Seine (now the site of a public library, where much research for this volume was undertaken). The carriage coming to a stop in a seventeenth-century traffic jam, the end of the street being blocked by merchants' carts, Ravaillac rushed up to the carriage and

---

[54] A similar observation about character in Corneille, though with respect to *Oedipe*, is made by Jacques Rancière in *The Future of the Image*: 116.
[55] See Appelbaum, 'Flowing or Pumping?'   [56] Hobbes, 'The Answer'.

stabbed Henry twice in the chest, the second time severing his aorta (or his cava vena, according to some reports) and all but immediately killing him. When Ravaillac was apprehended a moment later, one of Henry's aides, the Duke of Epernon, wisely cautioned Ravaillac's captors not to kill him. Instead, Ravaillac was brought into custody, interrogated over several days, and brought to trial. Ravaillac confessed to his interrogators, openly and articulately, obstinately sticking to the same story. And most of the details of what he told his interrogators were easy to confirm.

Ravaillac acted out of religious conviction, and he apparently acted alone. He had heard sermons saying that Henry IV was still a heretic and a tyrant, notwithstanding Henry's conversion to Catholicism and his pacification of the realm, and he had heard it said that tyrannicide was legal and heroic. He had determined that Henry IV was not doing enough, at the very least, to stamp out heresy, and had heard rumours that Henry was going to wage war against Catholics, perhaps even against the Pope—rumours that were to some degree true, since Henry was getting ready for a campaign against a Habsburg principality at the time (the visit to the Arsenal being preparatory to that campaign). He had heard rumours too that the Huguenots, whom Henry was not doing enough to suppress, were planning a Christmas Day Massacre, on the scale of the Saint Bartholomew Massacre and in retaliation for it. A poor man and a loner, but not uneducated, having worked as a legal representative and a schoolteacher in his native Angoulême, he had made several visits to Paris on business, with another intention in mind as well: to speak to the king, to try to get the king to change his mind about tolerating the Huguenots, and, if unsuccessful, to kill him. He had planned once, he said, to meet the king to tell him that he suffered from a temptation to commit regicide. And in fact, the urge to commit regicide had come to him often, sometimes in visions.

Ravaillac, however, was straightforward and nonplussed during his interrogations. He was perfectly capable of seeing the criminality of what he had done, and to admit to it, and even to recognize that what he thought he was doing at the behest of God may well have been a temptation of the devil. Sometimes in his examination and trial he seemed confused. His interrogators were able to point out contradictions in some of his ideas, and Ravaillac was not always able to get around them. But usually Ravaillac was self-assured, knowing that he had done what he had to do; he never broke down under pressure, or for that matter, until the day of his execution, under torture.

The most interesting part of Ravaillac's story may be the reaction he evoked in his interrogators and observers. 'I can get nothing out of him', his first examiner complained on the day of the murder, coming back to the royal palace to report to the queen's council. That's because, said Jacques Nompar de Caumont de la Force, as reported in his memoirs, 'you don't know how to handle people like that. Let's go back, I know how to make him talk.' The memoirs go on, in the third person:

> They returned then with permission from the leaders of the Council to examine this parricide, who had been put in the hands of the archers of the Royal Guard, and brought to the *hôtel de Retz*, in order to discover who the culprits were.... On arrival the Sieur de la Force said to the prisoner: 'Wretch, you thought you had succeeded in

killing the king, but he is not dead.' 'Yes he is,' Ravaillac said; 'he is, and if he wasn't, I would kill him again.'[57]

And so on, even as torture was applied to him. It was difficult to accept that Ravaillac had acted alone, although Ravaillac insisted on it again and again. It was even more difficult to confront the face of the crime and see nothing in it but the face of a crime.

Ravaillac's interrogators, like other members of the audience of what Ravaillac had done, were looking for a kind of depth, a wellspring of tactical, psychological, and ideological causation. And they could not find one. The tactics, the psychology, and the ideology were shallow. Even Ravaillac's madness, such as it was, was unsatisfactory. For Ravaillac was placidly intrepid. He did not seem to be hiding anything and he did not seem to *have* anything to hide. He was aware of what he did and why he did it and he was by-and-large unrepentant. He seemed more absurd than deranged, more fixated on a difficult-to-account-for objective than wild, delusional, or ferocious. If he admitted that he had visions sometimes, which encouraged him in his mission, visions alone were not out-of-the-ordinary; for Counter-Reformation Catholicism promoted mystical experience. The main problem—and in this Ravaillac can be compared to any of a number of apprehended terrorists of modern history— was that Ravaillac's personality, faulty though it may have been, did not fit the requirements of the guilt that needed to be associated with him. It was not equal to the anger and the indignation that his interrogators and the public experienced and wanted to vent against him. Beneath his exterior of bland, foolish obstinacy there was no dark and terrible conspiracy to confess, no authors behind the author; and there was no terrible, evil *character* either.

The problem appears most vividly in a pair of literary responses to Henry IV's assassination, both of which have already been mentioned, and both of which, in the face of this stubbornly unsuitable face, worked to supplement what was known about Ravaillac with more characterization. The first is Claude Billard's stage play, *Mort d' Henry le Grand.* Henry le Grand is commemorated in it as a Mars and a Hercules, a son of Jupiter. As for Ravaillac, a 'parricide, a traitor, a renegade', there is not much to say at the level of propositions. Billard finds it necessary to bring in Satan to explain and dramatize the crime. Like similar figures in Gunpowder Plot narratives, Billard's Satan is motivated by jealousy. Satan once thought that he was going to triumph over the people of France, he asserts in an opening soliloquy, and never more than during the Wars of Religion, when all of France was delivered to 'rage, pillage, and inhumanity'. But then Henry IV came on the scene, this 'vanquishing monarch', acting less with the help of others than with the strength of his own 'heart and mind' and an 'angel of God, who made him invincible'. Satan's hopes were utterly disappointed when Henry abjured his Protestantism and became a Catholic. So the jealous Satan wants revenge.

Ravaillac is Satan's instrument, chosen because Satan wants to land a sudden blow by the unsuspected hand of an unknown 'rogue, a renegade' before Henry's

---

[57] *Procès de Ravaillac.* In *Archives Curieuses*, 1ere 15:113–41. For a similar account, see L'Estoile, *Journal du règne de Heni IV*: 3.98–101.

guardian angel has a chance to prevent it. And when we finally meet Ravaillac, we encounter a man possessed:

> Demons, rages, furies, terrible Acherontides
> Who guide, who push, who press, homicidally,
> My parricidal hands, who give me courage,
> But who force me to confront that conqueror...
> Why do your brilliant flames, your bloody vipers,
> Every night, at all hours, hiss into my two eyes,
> Transporting my senses, putting me in a fury,
> Throwing me beyond myself, bringing down the horror
> That this barbarous blow, this wicked enterprise
> Gives birth in me...?[58]

Like other treacherous assassins in the dramatic literature, this Ravaillac is not incapable of seeing that what he is doing might be wrong, or anticipating the consequences of what he is doing. But he cannot help himself:

> I have to be the murderer of a king
> Who has never done me wrong: cruel, abominable,
> Abortion of Satan, I am so miserable,
> Damned like Judas, wanting to assassinate
> The mild and kindly king, who once pardoned
> Me of a misdeed, giving me grace,
> Me, deserving death, and not clemency,
> Me, deserving torture, shackles and chains...

When the moment comes, Ravaillac goes through his own drama of hesitation and resolution. Though the moment resembles dramatizations of the stories of Brutus and Judith, even to delineating a struggle between hesitation and resolution, it is unique, I think, in Renaissance drama, so far as it shows the psychomachy of a real and recent assassin.[59]

> There he is in his coach. O God! My hand trembles:
> That's trouble; do I dare confront him?
> His footmen will come and push me off.
> But forget their repulses, like a wild animal
> I will go massacre him: if my blade reaches him,
> It's done, it has to be, I am no longer myself,
> The blow comes from the demon who has taken me to himself.

Meanwhile Satan watches over him. 'Go ahead,' Satan says,

---

[58] *Mort d'Henry*: 37.
[59] Comparison can be made with Jacques de Fonteny's *Cleophon* (1600), which depicts the assassination of Henry III. There the assassin is made into the dupe of nobles who want to wrest power away from Henry mainly out of love for power. And the assassin is completely impassive as he ponders what he is about to do, speaking to his facilitators:

> I put myself in peril, but of my will;
> If the execution answers to my desire
> Be assured that the king will soon lose his life,
> Nothing will stop me. Adieu... (4.1.1007–10)

no one will see anything, you will be invisible,
Me, I will guide your hand and make you capable of anything…
What! You're trembling, you coward; but don't be afraid
Of their strength and number: it's me, it's my fury
That animates you, driving you forward and inflaming you with horror.[60]

This effective if melodramatic rendering of the assassination very carefully exonerates Ravaillac of any motive but possession by the devil. The devil has his reasons, which include Henry's religion; but it is not religious fanaticism that the devil either appeals to or takes advantage of, and Ravaillac says and thinks nothing about it. Ravaillac acts out of an impulse to kill a king that he himself cannot explain, except to recognize that the impulse is irresistible and comes from the devil.

So there is Billard's *Mort*, which deserves to be more widely known. In demonizing the impulses behind Ravaillac's act, and in making Ravaillac into a madman, the play defuses some of the political implications of the assassination. If the devil did it, if a madman did it, then there could not have been a cabal behind him, or even a human agitator or two, and so there could be no one else to recriminate or pursue, whether native Catholic extremists or foreign agents. The court for which Billard wrote the drama had an interest in de-politicizing the murder in just this way. Henry's widow Marie de' Medici would pursue a more pro-Spanish and pro-papal foreign policy than Henry had; in fact the immediate rise in power of the next great victim of assassination, Concino Concini, would be an expression of this turn in court politics toward Italy and Spain. Billard would be performing a service to Marie de' Medici by making the non-political motives of Ravaillac intelligible, precisely for being non-political.

But Billard is also reaching toward a new understanding of characterological motivation, and in at least two respects. In the first place, by means of the soliloquy he constructs a theatrically dialogical character; that is, a character who is in dialogue (literally, but also figuratively) with himself and his audience. Billard has Ravaillac in effect *confess* to the audience, as he had never done during interrogation. He has Ravaillac in effect *recognize* the authority of the audience members and the society they represent, even as he also *exhibits* his defiance of that authority in front of them and *declares* at once his guilt and his weakness, his inability to prevent himself from doing evil. In the second place, though Billard shifts attention away from immediate political issues, he also shifts attention toward the metaphysics of the agent and patient of terror. Nothing is said in the play about Henry tolerating both Protestantism and Catholicism and bringing both Protestants and Catholics into his government, or about how Catholics in France or abroad might resent this. But much is made of the fact that Henry was both a consummate warrior and a man of peace, who militarily pacified France. Ravaillac's evil, spurred by the devil, is the evil of war-making itself, war-making as a principle of the human condition, competing against the principle of peace. The character of Ravaillac, performed by an actor on a stage, is a demonstration of the truth of this principle—the truth that shows this principle to be both dangerous and contemptible.

[60] *Mort d'Henry*: 37; 39.

The second work to discuss is Matthieu's *Mort déplorable*, which was translated within a year of its French publication as *The Heroyk Life and Deplorable Death of the Most Christian King Henry the Fourth* (a very good translation, from which I have been and will continue to be quoting). When Matthieu takes up his pen to write about how the unthinkable actually happened, he borrows (as we have seen) the conceit developed in Bandole's *Parallèles*, which had been reissued with additions in 1609, and makes the last day of Henry's life very much like the last day of Caesar's, complete with presages, premonitions, and warnings, where Henry's wife the queen plays the role of Caesar's Calpurnia, and others, observing things like natural disasters and odd conjunctions of planets, play the role of seers.

Matthieu retreats from the conceit, however, at the crucial point. For like Billard, he will not allow that Henry's murder was political. For Matthieu, Ravaillac's evil begins and ends in Ravaillac. That is what must be emphasized. In Ravaillac's character is the sum total of what Ravaillac represents. So unlike what the parallel between Henry and Caesar might suggest, the assassination of Henry did not express a conflict of political principles. Even the idea of diabolical possession, which Matthieu appeals to from time to time, is ultimately unhelpful. For Ravaillac does not represent a case, as far as Matthieu is concerned, of metaphysical rebellion. He only represents the case of himself.

To get something *out* of this character, to get a rationale for what Ravaillac had accomplished out of Ravaillac himself, is hardly possible. Matthieu can condemn and belittle the man; he can diagnose him; but he cannot wrest from the figure he recreates an answer to the questions that most trouble him. Why, really, did you, Ravaillac, *do* that? Why, really, did *you* do that? And why *that*? How can someone like you have upended our national community? Matthieu will paint a vivid picture of Ravaillac from the point of view of someone who is repelled by him, but to round out the picture he will have to put the character of Ravaillac to the test of the story of his public torture and execution, and even then he will worry that he has come up short.

Here is how Matthieu introduces Ravaillac, while bringing in some essential facts about him, such as his once having attempted to join the monastic order of the Feuillants:

> The force of man was weak and fearful to attempt on the person of this Prince [Henry IV]: Hell spewed forth the author from her bottomless pit. This wretch had led a bad life, and among those who knew him was accounted a cast-away and a desperate fellow. He had a long time followed a suit in law about a succession, and having lost it, misery enforced his father and mother to beg, necessary poverty made his resolution voluntary: He threw himself into the monastery of the Feuillants, and was thrown out again by reason of the weakness of his brain. Those who lodged him told me since that he was wholly subverted, and that the word Huguenot would turn his folly into madness. His mind was still amazed, wavering and superstitious, susceptible of all impressions, and ever resenting the depravation of his humours. He that walketh mad a mile never cometh home wise. The more his folly was apparent the more he thought it was hidden, and the duller he was the more he presumed of wisdom, and not accounting himself to be sick, he did not care for health …[61]

[61] Matthieu, *Heroyck Life*: 105–6.

Ravaillac is almost indistinguishable from any of a number of other traitors contemned in European literature at the time, with the exception of his 'superstition' and what we would now call his fanaticism. This is not the superstition of an individual simply in error, as Voltaire in the next century might put it; nor is it the fanaticism of someone overly dedicated to an abstract cause.[62] It is a superstition coupled to 'folly', a folly coupled to 'madness', and a fanaticism that has no intellectual content apart from hatred.

Matthieu himself had been present at some of the interrogations. He walked away from the questioning with the impression that Ravaillac was mad and possessed, and there was nothing to be done about him. 'I then perceived that melancholy had troubled his spirits with her fumes, had made him capable of diabolical suggestions and impressions, that torture would sooner make trial of his obstinacy, than enforce his conscience.' Matthieu seems to believe that Ravaillac was telling the truth, that he had acted alone. Like Billard, and for similar reasons, Matthieu does not want to go hunting for conspiracies to which Ravaillac may have been recruited. Nor does he want to entertain the kinds of suggestions that openly circulated about that earlier regicide, Jacques Clément, namely that the fanatic had been encouraged by people in the Church to kill the king. Ravaillac had claimed to find support for regicide in sermons he had heard, and people had to wonder what had been said to him in confession when, as he attested, he mentioned his urges to kill the king to his confessors. But Matthieu ignores the idea that anyone in the Church was involved, even indirectly or mistakenly. After all, Henry had converted to Catholicism; he had allowed Catholicism to flourish. And when Ravaillac had tried to join a religious order, when he had tried to follow in the footsteps of the controversial Jacques Clément, he had been rejected.

So there it was. Or was it? Matthieu claims that he was opposed to torturing Ravaillac. Nothing would come of it. It would 'sooner make trial of his obstinacy, than enforce his conscience'. That torture would 'enforce conscience' was an assumption of French jurisprudence; confessions made under torture were more rather than less dependable than confessions rendered voluntarily.[63] They had the advantage of touching the 'conscience', which meant not only getting a sincere and repentant admission of guilt, and an open avowal of any extenuating circumstances involved in the crime, such as the involvement of collaborators, if any there were; but also getting, in exchange for punishment, an expiation. French justice seemed to want of its criminals not only the painful experience of judgement, the writing of the Law on the body of the guilty, but also a return of the criminal to the fold of God. It wanted the satisfaction of public rage; the criminal had to suffer. But it also wanted a reassertion of divine goodness; the criminal had to be redeemed, or else, which was worse but always an option, insensibly hurled into hell.

---

[62] See Voltaire, 'Fanaticisme', in *Dictionnaire Philosophique*: <http://fr.wikisource.org/wiki/Page:Voltaire_-_%C5%92uvres_compl%C3%A8tes_Garnier_tome19.djvu/83>. And for general discussion, Toscano, *The Fanatic*: 105–11.

[63] Silverman, *Tortured Subjects*.

Matthieu is not the only eyewitness account of the execution of Ravaillac. There are several others, and they do not all agree on important details.[64] Above all, they do not all agree on what his execution meant. For some, it seems that Ravaillac actually repented in the end; for others, Ravaillac seemed unable to repent, and the forced repentance Ravaillac expressed in public was insincere or incomplete. Matthieu alone is ambiguous on this point; but his ambiguity is tactical. It is an ambiguity which communicates the idea that *our desire* in our interaction with the character Ravaillac is unequal to *Ravaillac's desire*. Ours is in fact much greater, deeper. We *crave* something out of conspirators and traitors, even if they conspire in a cabal of one, but what we crave may be more than they can give us. King James once referred, as we have seen, to the 'mystery of iniquity'.[65] Matthieu also appeals to such a mystery, to the opacity of evil, even as he also shows how unsatisfactory being left with that mystery can be.

Ravaillac did not, on Matthieu's account, only receive the usual punishment of a homicidal traitor, the public humiliation of being dragged through the streets, the forced *amendes honorables* in front of church doors and on the scaffold, the torturing with pincers and burning lead and oil and flames, the mutilation of the genitals, the drawing and quartering; he received all this in the course of a punishment that would be meted out against a crime committed in broad daylight and thoroughly investigated that was still a mystery. Here is the final decree against the murderer, as summarized by Matthieu:

> [The court] condemned him to make an honourable amends before the great gate of the Cathedral Church of Paris, naked in his shirt, holding a burning torch in his hand of two pound weight, and to declare, that wickedly and treacherously he did kill the King with two stabs of a knife in the body: from thence being brought to the Greve,[66] upon a Scaffold, his paps, brawns of his arms, and calves of his legs, to be torn with burning Pincers, his right-hand holding in it the knife wherewith he committed the murder to be burnt off with fire of brimstone, and on the places where he shall be torn with pincers, molten lead to be cast, scalding oil, burning pitch and rosin, wax and brimstone melted together. That done, his body to be drawn and dismembered with four horse, his members and body consumed with fire, and scattered in the wind, his goods confiscate, the house where he was borne to be razed down to the ground, his father and mother to be banished forth of the realm of France, and his other kinfolks enforced to change their names.

Part of the intention was simply a confirmation of the criminal's guilt, in the criminal's own words. Part of the intention was to make the condemned suffer as long as possible, experience pain and humiliation for as long as possible. Part of the intention—and we have seen this before, as in the case of Fengon's body at the hands of Amleth and the people of Denmark—was annihilation, the annihilation in this case not only of the body but of the name and even, paradoxically, the living

---

[64] These include *Supplice, mort, et fin; Discours veritable sur la mort de François Ravaillat*; L'Estoile, *Journal du règne d' Henri IV*: 3.103–7; De Thou, *Abrégé de l'Histoire*: 10.274–7.

[65] *His Majesties Speach*, B1v.

[66] Place de Grève, the public square used for major executions, now the plaza in front of the Hôtel de Ville.

memory. Matthieu himself notes that in the spirit of the decree, in the course of his long narrative he has never once used the convicted man's proper name.

But something still more was wanted, the light of some additional truth. For that additional truth tortures were applied:

> Before the prisoner was brought to the Greve, they gave him the buskins, which drew from his mouth the former words, but far greater cries then the first torture. It appeared by him, that although he had the charm of silence, so much boasted of by sorcerers, yet he had none against pain. At the first wedging he cried out, O my God take pity on my soul, and forgive me this offence, but not if I have concealed aught. The second wedging ended the torment…

Next the condemned, still conscious, was brought to a church, forced to confess again and beg forgiveness, the *amendes honorables*, and brought to reiterate one more time that what he did he did alone. 'The Doctors could get no more of him.'[67] Some kind of progress was made, in Matthieu's eyes, as Ravaillac was paraded before another church; Ravaillac was confirming in public, by himself, and in a sufficiently penitent voice, though under pressure, what judicial procedure had already determined. But the final truth was still missing:

> He made an honourable amends before Our Ladies Church, falling prostrate on the earth, he kissed the end of the Torch, and seemed to have his heart broken in pieces with repentance. In prison he had uttered diverse blasphemous speeches, against the piety, justice, mercy, and other good intents of the king. The queen commanded Testu, knight of the watch, to look to him that he did not so in the streets; but already, before he came forth of the Conciergerie, he had testified an extreme grief, for having held so bad and impious opinions of this great king. Being pressed with remorse of his own conscience, he did detest his crime, for when [the priest] Doctor Filsac would have given him absolution, and willed him to lift up his eyes to heaven, he answered, I will not do so, for I am unworthy to look thereon, and he was contented that this absolution should be converted to his eternal damnation, if he had concealed aught of the truth.

The crowd, as he was brought to the square, was nevertheless remorseless against him, taunting him while he stood on the scaffold, and taking pleasure in the pain exacted from him:

> When [the executioners] had pinched him with the pincers he cast forth grievous cries: Then they poured molten lead, scalding oil, burning pitch, wax, and brimstone on those places burnt by the pincers. This pain was the most sensible and piercing of all his punishment, and he showed it by the lifting up of his whole body, the beating of his legs, the panting of his flesh. All this was not sufficient to move the people to pity; when all was done, they wished it might begin again.

The process continued, and again the executioners tried to extract a new confession out of him, a naming of names, or an explaining of motives, and again the crowd was remorseless, now trying to get in on the act of punishing him:

[67] L'Estoile's account confirms these details, but L'Estoile's imagination is focused on the matter of whether Ravaillac had any accomplices.

If in this torment they used any pause, it was to give the hangman time to breathe and to the prisoner to feel himself to die, to the divines to exhort him to tell the truth. He said that he knew none other than what he had so often before uttered, and that he should be very foolish, perceiving his body in that lamentable case to abandon his soul to a worse. The horses began to draw, but not fast enough to the people's minds, whereupon divers to help them began to pluck the ropes. Finally, with the help of the crowd, the execution was just about done: and then it was taken altogether out of the executioner's hands. The executioner perceiving that all his members were broken and crushed in pieces, that the horses were tired, and that he was in the agony of death, would have cut him in four quarters, but at the first stroke, the impatient people snatched him forth of his hands, the lackeys gave him a hundred blows with swords, every one gat a piece, and dragged it through the City.[68]

What we see here is something that will again remind us of the famous opening scene of Foucault's *Discipline and Punish*, which recounts the execution of the third most famous regicide in French history, the failed assassin Robert-François Damiens. But there is something in this scene that is missing from Foucault's account. In this case at least, *pace* Foucault, power, the sovereign power of the monarch and the state, did not simply inscribe itself on the body of the condemned. Power also tried to extract something from it, even to extract something from it that wasn't there. Not a surplus but a deficit was at stake in cases like this: a deficit in the meaning of that thing we call character. Nor was the power in question merely the might of the state and the sovereign. The power was also something else, something that admiring historians call the popular will, or plebeian carnival, and that less admiring historians ascribe to upwells of ritual violence. We will shortly begin to look more closely at this crowd, at the scenes of violence to which it is drawn or from which it is repelled, and at the purposes of power and resistance and order and disorder toward which terrorism summons it. But for now, from the point of view of the crowd, we are looking at the agent of a treason. Whatever motives and impulses Ravaillac acted upon, he in the first place acted. The discourse surrounding him could not disguise that fact. From a position of passivity and exclusion—a 'cast-away, a desperate fellow'—he rose to be a fallen angel of history. And that was perhaps the worst indignity of his crime. By what right can anyone take such a responsibility upon himself?

No doubt Matthieu allows himself to get carried away as he describes the rage of the crowd at the spectacle of the condemned. But if Matthieu gets carried away, it is for a reason. He was hired by Henry early in his reign, both in spite of Matthieu's connections with the Guises and the Catholic League and because of it, to be an official court historian and spokesman. He was one of Henry's first official ideologues. So this document, *Histoire de la mort déplorable de Henry IV*, was a kind of closing of accounts, though Matthieu continued to be employed by the court and wrote this work partly for its benefit. With this closing of accounts Matthieu tried to dramatize a merging of a popular will with the will of the sovereign: even, on the occasion of assassination, the snatching of the public will out of the hands of the sovereign and into the hands of the people, in honour of the dead king, and on behalf of both the sovereign and themselves.

[68] Matthieu, *Heroyck Life*: 179–83.

We must take Matthieu's account with a grain of salt, as the extreme reactions of the crowd it relates are not entirely confirmed by other versions of the affair. At a minimum the document shows us how the assassination was meant to be appropriated by the official discourse of the realm; it was taken up and processed for the sake of constructing a myth of Henry the Great that matched the will of the people with the will of the state.[69] Nor was the myth without foundation. No doubt the majority of the people of France were unhappy about the assassination, and no doubt the event focused national attention on the importance of king, country, law, and order. The establishment was the victor in the wake of Ravaillac's anti-establishment gesture. This is a common effect of terrorist violence, as has already been observed; its message is mauled in the reception of it, and it comes to signify just the opposite of what it intended. An act intended to disrupt the public order succeeds in causing a disruption, but ends up reinforcing the solidarity of the populace with the powers that be. But as for the character of the terrorist, Matthieu had to admit to a fact that makes him uncomfortable.

The people gathered in the Place de Grève coming to take part in the act of punishing the condemned regicide, the hangman found himself left with nothing to finish the punishment on. He was supposed to set the quartered body of the condemned man aflame, and scatter his ashes to the wind. But there was nothing left of Ravaillac but his shirt. Meanwhile, the hacked-up body parts were paraded through the streets. 'The people dragged these wretched relics up and down the City, in the same manner as the Maenads did tear the body of Orpheus', wrote Matthieu. The festival of scapegoating proceeded apace, much like the festival Matthieu would later dramatize concerning the case of Concino Concini:

> At the last, [Ravaillac's body] being divided almost in as many pieces as there be streets in Paris, divers fires were made in sundry places, and chiefly there where the King was slain: The Swiss [guards] burnt one piece of it before the Louvre. Little children were seen in the streets to carry straw and wood to the fire. There were some who having drawn certain pieces of that body up and down the City, gathered them together on the Greve, and by burning them, made an end of the execution.

Next, however, comes Matthieu's unpleasant admission:

> It seemed that this so just and exemplary punishment would in some sort have comforted the public grief; but the satisfaction was not equal to the offence, nor the comfort to the sorrow. The wounds of hearts were opened again when men remembered that the causes of [the king's] death were wrapped up in impenetrable darkness, and when many cried out, That this murderer at his death had retained some after-thought.[70]

Just as the murder of Henry IV tried and failed to kill a principle of kingship along with the person of the king, so the carnival of the public execution apparently failed to kill the principle of treason along with the traitor. Darkness remained. Some after-thought remained. And after the after-thought, though the traitor was dead, the treason remained. It was as if treason, like a king, was a phenomenon with two bodies, and only the mortal body of it could be destroyed.

[69] See Chapter 6, section 2.   [70] Matthieu, *Heroyck Life*: 184–5.

4

Scene

1. SAINT MÉDARD

'The scene contains the act' is what, according to Kenneth Burke, we normally think when we consider the relation or 'ratio' between the act and the scene.[1] The 'scene' in this sense is like a stage setting, and in fact the word 'scene' comes from the Greek *skene*, meaning tent, booth, and eventually stage. The scene is a container of actions; it is a situation from which, through which, and especially within which a sequence of events may occur.

But what are we to think, then, of the following, a journalistic (yet obviously biased) account of an episode of iconoclastic violence, in Paris, in 1561?

> On the day of Saint John, two days after Christmas, this great flood of debauchery [i.e. Parisian Huguenots] went to hear a preaching at the Place of the Patriarch, and because it was a feast day the Catholics sounded Vespers, after the sermon, in their church, Saint Médard, where the people had assembled as usual. The Huguenots took offense at the sound of the bells, and alleged that they had been rung in order to interfere with the word of the Lord. And without other provocation they ran to sack that poor church, which was not yet finished, breaking down all the doors, entering with swords in their grips, pistols in their hands, striking without scruple and committing outrages against the poor naked people, thinking of nothing but making war.

Not merely iconoclasts, the Huguenots went on to beat some of the church officials, and injure some of the parishioners, killing a priest. But the greatest outrage, as the writer represents it, was reserved for the building itself.

> They dashed the holy sacrament into pieces and threw it on the ground, destroying it. They did not leave a single image alone, striking against its head, as if against a live and sensible saint. They smashed most of the windows, broke many of the altars, stole ornaments, chalices, relics, and generally anything they could get their hands on. Gabaston, a knight of the Guard, entered the church on horse, coming up to the main altar and cried out in the corrupted tongue of Gascony: *Sack everything, sack everything.*[2]

It could reasonably be asked whether this incident really involved a case of terrorism before the letter. The writer of this account wants his readers to think of the event as a kind of military adventure, a sacking and pillaging of an enemy compound. But there were other points of view. In the period from 1560 to 1562, following upon the accidental death of Henry II and leading up to the outbreak of

---

[1] Burke, *Grammar of Motives*: 3.   [2] Sainctes, *Discours sur le saccagement*: 372.

war between Catholics and Protestants in France, dozens of episodes of internecine violence erupted throughout the kingdom. Most characteristically, Catholics attacked Protestants while they were worshipping, and Protestants attacked the icons of Catholic churches when few people or none were present.[3] But there were also cases of Catholics attacking Protestant property, and of Protestants setting upon Catholic worshippers. Here, at Saint Médard, the violence is characterized as a war against a citadel, with the 'sacking' of the citadel-like church being the main aim of the attackers, but an assault on 'poor naked [unarmed] people' is shown to be part of the process as well. In fact, one of the Catholic clergymen was killed, and many other Catholic worshippers were wounded. But when confronted with the facts of the case, the officials of the city and the kingdom used terms like 'blasphemy', 'sacrilege', 'sedition', and 'mutiny'.[4] As blasphemy the incident was an assault against the Church; as sedition it was a crime against the state. However, a Protestant writer was able to express an opposite point of view, according to which the 'mutiny, tumult, and sedition', as he called it, was started by the Catholic clergymen inside the church.[5] The bells of the church—just across from the home where the Protestants assembled—were rung as a deliberate provocation, an act of acoustic violence against the Protestant worshippers, and when some Protestants went to the church to ask the Catholics to desist, the Catholics responded with physical violence, taking a Protestant prisoner, shutting themselves inside the church, and sounding a 'tocsin'— an alarm bell—to the city, to call in the town militia and stir up more violence. According to the Protestant author, the interior of the church was vandalized by the Catholics themselves, who took apart the stones and images of the church to use as weapons to hurl at Protestant intruders. And in any case, whatever damage the Protestant intruders may have done to property or life and limb, on their account they were acting in self-defence.

If any of this violence can be said to amount to terrorism before the letter, it is because, for all the personal animosity expressed in the attacks and counter-attacks, the struggle was waged over competing systems of meaning, and each side was trying to send a message to the other about freedom of worship.[6] But consider again, then, the nature of the scene of the tumult. Certainly it comprises a situation out of which the incident arose, but if it also 'contains' the action, it can only do so in a special sense. For in this case the scene out of which the violence arose was also an object against which the violence was waged. And even more to the point: it was only *because* the scene could be an object of violence that the event took place at all. The personal violence of a lone assassin, like Ravaillac, can be seen in a symbolic or legal sense to have violated the scene of the streets of Paris when he assaulted the royal carriage, for he breached the peace. The riot of Saint Médard goes even further, and reveals a deeper involvement in the situational context. The

---

[3] This is the recurrent analysis in Crouzet, *Guerriers de Dieu*. On iconoclasm see *Guerriers de Dieu*: 1.395–620. Also see Christin, *Une révolution symbolique*.

[4] *Discours et procédures faites.*

[5] *Histoire véritable de la mutinerie, tumulte et sedition faites par les Pretres Saint Medard contres les Fideles.*

[6] See Diefendorf, *Beneath the Cross*: 49–62, esp. 61–2.

symbolic violation was also a real violation, against the very *scene* of the city of Paris; it was precisely because the scene was vulnerable as an object of suffering as well as a site of action that the violence was possible in the first place.

Following Natalie Zemon Davis, one might call what happened at Saint Médard a 'rite of violence'.[7] One side or the other in this dispute took the law into its own hands, performing justice in imitation of authority. But one of the limitations of the notion of a 'rite of violence', as opposed to the notion of an incident of 'terrorism before the letter', is that the concept of a 'rite' implies a kind of containment, at once spatial and temporal. Rites, according to the *OED*, are 'prescribed'; they are determined beforehand; they are enactments of a ceremonial moment whose coming and going amounts to an 'observance' of a previously encoded sequence and space. Without doubting that such 'rites' even to the point of violence will have occurred in early modern Europe, and that the riot of Saint Médard may even have been one of them, I have to add a pair of qualifications here. This riot approaches the conditions of terrorist violence. It does so because the fight is about sending political as well as religious messages. Moreover, the violence rises to this level precisely so far as it violates the conditions of a 'rite'. This violence is not a self-contained observance or exaction of ritual justice: it is an assault against structures of containment, against the very scene in which and through which it is supposed to assert its message.

There is the matter of form and matter to attend to. If we think of the violence as having been provoked by the sounding of the church bells, though an element of the scene is vital to the action, the cause is nevertheless 'proximate', to use the Aristotelian term. One event triggered another. And behind the provocation were one or more agents. A person rang the bell, perhaps on the orders of another person. But when the scene is a motive of the action, it is not because the scene acts as if it were a person. The scene is rather a spatiotemporal configuration of formal, material, and final causes. No bell ringing without the bell: that is the *matter* in this instance. And no bell ringing either without the existence of a church, and even a Church: that is a dimension of the *form* of action in this case. The scene is a 'motive' of the action because church bells were available for the ringing; because in the Latin Quarter of Paris traditional Catholics and new-fangled Protestants co-existed and worshipped side by side; and finally because Paris was a city of Catholic churches and seminaries, a city where Catholicism was in the business of *expressing* itself—with bells, among other devices, and at Vespers, among other formal occasions. And Catholicism in Paris was supposed to have a future.

One of the reasons it may seem odd to think of the riot at Saint Médard as an incident of terrorism is precisely because it was a riot. There do not seem to have been any agents premeditating the violence. There does not seem to have been a drama of resolution. Nor would it seem that there was any effort undertaken to disambiguate the violence, except so far as writers later went to the effort of writing polemical tracts about it, and the government took legal measures against the culprits involved, determining who was really guilty in this dispute and who

---

[7] Davis, 'The Rites of Violence'.

innocent. But for all we know there were certain agents who premeditated the violence and who undertook their own dramas of resolution. And perhaps the polemics (along with court documents) relating to the incident are precisely the kinds of disambiguations that the incident required. As it stands, it is hard to say what really happened that day, except that at the end of it, a priest was dead and several others wounded, the interior of a church was damaged, and thirty-one people were arrested—all of the detainees, however, being Catholics. Eventually the Catholic prisoners were released and two officers of the guard, including Gabaston, the one who is said to have cried out, *Sack everything*, were arrested, tried, and executed. If the riot was triggered by a dispute over apparently mischievous, politically provocative noise, it was modified by royal guardsmen, who seem to have held Catholics responsible for the uproar, or else who found themselves on the side of Protestants in the midst of a 'sedition'; and then it was finished by the decrees of the royal court and the efforts of the royal executioner.

One way or the other, though, it appears that thinking about this rite of violence as also a kind of anti-rite, where a structure of containment both motivates the violence and gets victimized by it, is a useful way of thinking about how the violence *signified* in this instance, how it meant what it meant not only as an act or as an expression of character but also as a disturbance of a *scene*.

2. THINKING ABOUT THE SCENE

Thinking about the scene means setting aside other priorities with respect to motivation, like the act and the agent, and thinking about the priority of circumstance. Time as well as space is involved in this. With respect to any given act of terrorist violence, we may ask how the space and time of the violence was organized, with what kinds of materials, structures, or laws, on what sort of occasion, with a view toward what future horizon. Even more to the point, with respect to any *representation* of terrorist violence, we can ask about the significance and motivational power the author attributes to the scene. To the extent that scenic motivation dominates a story, the story itself may approach the condition of a sociological, social historical, or even eschatological analysis. What happens when the violence happens is a function of the proximate, material, formal, and final causes that are, in sum, *in place at the time*.

Scenic motivation can be found in all sorts of accounts of terrorism before the letter, even in ones where the act or the agent seems to predominate. In the middle of *La Judit*, following Scripture Du Bartas introduces the character of Achior, who explains to Holofernes the long history and territorial investments of the Jews, implying that under certain conditions, to try to conquer them would be futile. Achior not only places one story, Holofernes's attempt to reconquer Israel, in the context of another story, the history of Israel; he also places the first story in the situation of a scene which will determine its outcome, and provide its underlying motive.

Just because the greatest political conflicts of the day were also conflicts of competing religious systems, each with its own mandate, scenic motivation played a recurrent role in terrorism before the letter, full of implications not only for how acts were accomplished and how persons came to accomplish them, but also for how individual acts of violence came to have significance and speak in a public sphere. Scenes in the period imply teleologies, which means that scenic violence might take on the quality of a final cause, and signify the advent of a historical destiny. The pattern of violence in Judges, noted in the previous chapter, where everything seems to depend upon the hero, is also a pattern of territorial skirmishes, coming to an end with the massacre at the conclusion of Samson's story. 'Do you not know that the Philistines are rulers over us?' says a crowd of Judeans to Samson, after he has attacked and killed a number of them. 'What then have you done to us?'[8] To *us*: we inhabit a territory, in other words, over which the Philistines are sovereign and in which we are subject. So when you hurt them, you hurt us. Territoriality and sovereignty are combined in a scene in which the majority of Judeans feel trapped, but against which only Samson rebels.

I am going to discuss Samson later, however, in Chapter 6, on 'Purpose', where the latter seems actually to be the most important issue. Here I want to focus on incidents where it seems that the question of scenic violence is the most important. As I have indicated, all stories of terrorism before the letter (and indeed all stories) can be analysed in view of the scenic motivation. But stories about scenic violence per se—violence of the scene and against the scene—are the special interest of this chapter, for it is with regard to them that the analysis of scenic motivation awards the highest payoff. The stories come in many forms. Riots or 'tumults' and 'seditions', the preferred words in the 1560s in France, are the subjects of some of them. They are often polemical in nature. In fact the words 'tumult' and 'sedition' are a function of polemics, since they denote an unjustified disruption of the peace. But there were also stories about greater threats, when what might have been a tumult turned or threatened to turn into an especially destructive episode of violence. War or civil war were among those threats, of course. But a new kind of threat was on the horizon: what would eventually be called the 'massacre'.

As a historian who does not believe that one cannot have terrorism before the word terrorism was invented, I do not believe that one cannot have massacres before the word massacre was invented. But the origination of the word, in French and English at about this time, indicates a new sensitivity, responding to what was in fact a new upsurge in internecine violence. What was frequently associated with the *massacre*—not always, but frequently—was a sensitivity to what was scenic or anti-scenic about it. The *massacre* was an outrage that approached the condition not only of an act of what we now call terrorism but also what we now call atrocity, and one of the reasons for that was that the violence was felt to be anti-scenic; it violated the proprieties of time and space, the material, formal, and teleological structures of civil life. The massacre not only involved the killing of innocents, and often in a great number; it was also an outrage against the possibility of society.

In what follows I will explain the idea of the *massacre* at length, and I will go on to discuss several texts that try to come to terms with it: first, a work that predates

[8] Judges 15.11.

the use of the word 'massacre' in English, *Gorboduc*; second, a pair of similar works from several decades later, written by English Jesuit priests, who try to come to terms with the Gunpowder Plot, in some respects apologizing for it; and third, a series of texts that deal with the Saint Bartholomew Massacre, culminating in d'Aubigné's *Les Tragiques*. Some of the worst violence and some of the most troubling thoughts about violence occurring in the period under study are in question here. Always human lives are at stake, and there is much suffering. But just as bad, it would seem, is the damage this violence seems to wreak against civil society. The world of the massacre is a world attacking itself.

3. THE 'MASSACRE'

Sometimes the word 'massacre' was used in the sixteenth and seventeenth centuries as the word 'terrorism' is commonly used today. Very bad violence, very unfair violence, ideologically motivated yet perverted violence against innocents—a 'massacre' could mean this just as an act of 'terrorism' could be thought to mean this today, and it could mean it in French and English alike, the word having come to English by way of the French no later than 1572. But the etymology and eventual use of the word tell an even more interesting story.[9]

The word comes from an old French word *macecre* or *macecle* with roots in Arabic indicating two things: on the one hand a butcher's shop or slaughterhouse; on the other, in a more recent application, the decapitated head of a deer, removed at the end of a hunt, when the deer is first cut open and the dogs are fed the viscera, the 'quarry'. The slaughterhouse, or else the offering of the decapitated and eviscerated deer: that was the *massacre*. Then, at about the same time as the beginning of the Wars of Religion, the word became applied—if not for the first time, at least for the first time as a common word—to the killing of humans. According to the *Dictionnaire historique de la langue française*, by around 1560 the word could mean 'to kill by striking with fury; to bludgeon'. Then by no later than 1564 it had taken on the additional meaning 'to kill defenceless victims'. I find the term used a year earlier, that is in 1563, to describe the riot at Vassy. But the two meanings, one indicating fury, the other indicating the defencelessness of victims, often went hand in hand. The first printed work in French using the word *massacre* in its title that I have been able to document appears in 1569, and it refers to the killing of the Prince of Condé in the aftermath of the defeat of the Protestant army he led at Jarnac; the title calls this the *inhumain et cruel massacre commis en la personne de feu Monseigneur le Prince de Condé*. (The document itself repeats this accusation, also

[9] My analysis of the etymology of 'massacre' is mainly in agreement with that in David El Kenz's in 'Le massacre, objet de l'histoire'. But it differs in some points. El Kenz has not taken evidence from the *OED* into account or all the literary evidence I cite above. Further background on the emergence of the idea of the massacre, though with an eye toward visual art, is found in Jacobus, 'Motherhood and Massacre'. Many of the paintings known in English or French as 'The Massacre of the Innocents / La massacre des innocents' do not use the word 'massacre' in their original language titles, but equivalents of 'murder' or 'slaughter', for example the Italian *strage*.

calling the massacre 'barbarous', in violation of the 'law of arms'. Condé was reportedly denied ransom or deference and shot in the back.) The next titles all refer to the Saint Bartholomew affair of 1572, where it seems that a third meaning is added, where a 'massacre' is also a 'massive' sort of killing, *en masse*, as it is said in French. The first works in English to use 'massacre' in their title refer to the Saint Bartholomew affair, and perhaps communicate the triple meaning. But not all uses of the term combine all three meanings. Traces of the earlier double meaning, fury plus a defenceless victim, without the indication of something 'massive' about the number killed, occur both in Shakespeare, in the 1590s, and in an English-language publication of 1606, where a 'massacre' is said to have killed a single victim.[10] Meanwhile, the one event in France that attracted the most titles using the word massacre was the murder of the Duke of Guise at the Chateau of Blois, at the hands of Henry III and his henchman, followed by the execution of his brother, the Cardinal of Lorraine; for example *Dialogue sur les nouvelles de la mort de monsieur de Guyse, et de son frère Cardinal, massacrez à Blois* (1589). Guise, as we have seen, was killed in the king's antechamber, which he had been invited to visit, by a large group of royal guardsmen, with multiple stab wounds, and much of the nation was outraged. In 1588 there appeared Matthieu's *La Guisade*. The play was meant to contribute to the anti-royalist propaganda of the time. In it, the king, claims a messenger, watched the duke die with a 'regarde execrable, / D'un oeil demy ouvert ce massacre effroyable' (a deplorable look, with a half-open eye on that frightening massacre).[11]

A massacre was a murder or mass murder that outraged sensibilities. The fury of the act, the unfairness of the act, and the amplitude of the act were all beginning to elicit the word 'massacre', as well as qualifiers like 'inhuman' and 'cruel'. A massacre was an unfair and unlawful killing. It was a disproportionate killing, the armed against the unarmed, the strong against the weak, the aware against the unaware. But it was above all a killing which wounded the scene of human life. I do not wish to overstress the significance of the use of the word in itself. Sometimes, faced with the enormity of a massacre, where not just innocent people but a whole scene of life was subject to annihilation, writers stretched for other words, or argued that the enormity was unspeakable, beyond language. We have already seen James VI and I allude to the idea, seconded by jurist Edward Coke and the poet Richard Crashaw.[12] But the Gunpowder Plot and Saint Bartholomew affair were often mentioned in the same breath and the word 'massacre' could be used confidently to characterize the Plot too. We have also noted the case of Edward Hawes's, *Prosopopeia*, where 'all' of a conspirator's 'thoughts' are said to have been 'bloody massacre'. That a new word, 'massacre', came into being in such contexts indicates, along with the new idea of an infraction without a name, that at least some people were sensitive to the notion that a new kind of terrible violence was

---

[10] Shakespeare, *Richard III*: 4.3.2; *Horrible Murther*.   [11] Matthieu, *La Guisade*: 4.2.

[12] Coke, Speech, in *A True and Perfect Relation*, D3v2; also see Nicholls, *Investigating Gunpowder Plot*; Fraser, *The Gunpowder Plot*: 230–73; Nowak, 'Propaganda and the Pulpit'; Herman, 'A Deed without a Name'; Crashaw, 'On ye Gunpowder-Treason', in *Steps to the Temple*: 350.

being committed, or that some people were experiencing a new way of being morally affronted. The offence seems to have had an unspoken subtext, that a 'massacre' or crimes associated with it were offences against the scene of political and
civil society. It was bad enough to kill one or more people ferociously or cruelly, or
to kill many defenceless people; but in doing so to attack the very basis of civil society, apparently to send a message of doom to civil society, was a new enormity of
which Europeans were now aware. Along with massacre came what many saw as
chaos or confusion.

4. *GORBODUC*

Nationalist feeling was sometimes connected with this new awareness. Civil society, as I have called it, was also, in many instances, national society, and vulnerability to something like a massacre could mean that the nation-state could be at
risk. The danger was perceived early in our period, even before the word 'massacre'
had become a part of the political vocabulary. I have mentioned before *The Mirror
for Magistrates* together with the vogue for *histoires tragiques*, all collections for
stories where the weaknesses of rulers and the instability of states are explored. The
play *Gorboduc* can be added to the list, except that *Gorboduc* goes even further than
most of the other stories about the fall of princes. Just as the troubles in France
were beginning, and as Elizabeth was still consolidating her reign, what has often
been called the first English tragedy was performed, and this *Tragedie of Gorboduc*
actually concludes not only with the fall of a prince but the fall of a whole royal
family, the collapse of the kingdom, and a chaos of mass self-destruction. It imagines a massacre where a whole nation turns against itself, in a massive scene of
rape, pillage, parricide, and even infanticide. Written by Thomas Norton and
Thomas Sackville, *Gorboduc* was acted in 1561–2, first at the Inns of Court and
then at Whitehall, in front of an audience that included the queen. It was published in quarto in 1565. It is supposed to be a cautionary tale about the dangers
of 'division'. In 1590 it was reprinted along with an excerpt from John Lydgate's
The Serpent of Division, a prose narrative originally produced in 1432 about the
civil wars in Rome at the time of Julius Caesar, ending with Caesar's assassination.
But *Gorboduc* was not only about 'division', in the manner of later plays like
1 Henry IV, *Julius Caesar*, and *King Lear*; it was also an unsubtle plea for Elizabeth
to marry a fellow English person, namely Robert Dudley, who sponsored the play.
The idea was in the air that the queen should marry a foreign prince, even though
Dudley was available and a favourite of the queen. So the play argues against both
division and foreign alliances which could lead to division. But in doing so, it also
presents something remarkable. Like two contemporary plays in France, Grévin's
César and La Taille's *Daire*, it imagines the state as a spatiotemporal system subject
to tragic collapse, a scenic system where conspiracy can arise and political leaders
can kill one another, and undermine the system itself. But even more, unlike the
two French plays, *Gorboduc* imagines a massacre. It is a doubly cautionary tale

where it is shown that if its warnings aren't heeded, if division and foreign alliance are allowed to arise, there lies on the horizon a kind of massacre to come.

The violence is atrocious. A brother kills a brother. The mother kills the surviving brother, accusing him at once of being both a tyrant and a traitor. The people rise and slay both the mother and her husband, the queen and king. The people are 'contemning quite both Law and loyal heart', one courtier says, and another adds that the people still 'threaten' surviving relatives, to 'uproot the race' of the late queen and king.[13] After still more popular violence, another courtier predicts that the nation in time will finally collapse catastrophically, in a general massacre:

> And thus a thousand mischiefs shall unfold
> And far and near spread thee, O Britain Land;
> All right and law shall cease, and he that had
> Nothing today, tomorrow shall enjoy
> Great heaps of good, and he that flow'd in wealth
> Lo, he shall be reft of life and all,
> And happiest he that then possesseth least.
> The wives shall suffer rape, the maids deflowered
> And children fatherless shall weep and wail:
> With fire and sword thy Native folk shall perish.
> One kinsman shall bereave another life,
> The father shall unwitting slay the son,
> The son shall slay the sire and know it not:
> Women and maids the cruel soldier's sword
> Shall pierce to death, and silly children lo
> That playing in the streets and fields are found
> By violent hand shall close their latter day.[14]

As an argument about division and alliance *Gorboduc* will seem to the modern reader far-fetched. But it was taken seriously in its own day, and was evidently intended to participate in conversations not only about succession and alliance but also about the political constitution of England in general and the balances required among different sectors of government.[15] And the vision of a massacre to come coincides with an innovative idea: that what matters in a state is what matters in a nation, defined as a territorial legacy: 'O Britain Land', the character here puts it; 'the common Mother of us all', another puts it in the same scene, 'Our Native Land, our Country that contains / Our wives, children, kindred, ourselves and all'.[16] On the one hand, the scene—the territorial nation—is promoted as a principle of action; on the other, the scene therefore becomes vulnerable to self-destruction, a massacre in the complete sense of the word. Whether *Gorboduc* touched upon a real danger to the state, or whether it rather enlarged the threat to the point of paranoia, it made a statement about the vulnerability of the state

---

[13] Norton and Sackville, *Gorboduc*: 5.1.6–12.
[14] Norton and Sackville, *Gorboduc*: 5.2.365–80.
[15] Pincombe, 'Robert Dudley'; Winston, 'Expanding the Political'.
[16] *Gorboduc*: 5.2.98–100. And see Vanhoutte, 'Community, Authority'.

to forces from within, so powerful that they could end up crushing the state itself and all its people.

5. THE STATE OF THE GUNPOWDER PLOT

The Gunpowder Plot was a massacre avoided. It attracted all sorts of discourses, as already noted. But discourses emphasizing a scenic element were common. After all, the Plot was directed against a scene, the House of Lords, and that House and the people in it represented the nation. Moreover, the discovery of the Plot aroused patriotic feeling, pride in the territorial heritage and destiny of the state. We have already seen how that affected the young John Milton, and a similar response is evident in a narrative of the Plot by Phineas Fletcher in 1627, *Locustae and The Locusts, or The Apollonyists*—a work in two versions, one Latin and one English. For both writers, the Plot was an attack on the territorial and providential integrity of the nation. Thinking about the Plot thus meant thinking about the national framework it was trying to destroy, the scene of sovereign English life. For Fletcher, that meant thinking especially about the Jesuit mission to England, which Fletcher imagined as a kind of foreign invasion that had the effect of poisoning the minds of all too many subjects of the kingdom, eating at the state from within.

But even the Jesuits who were really involved in the affair could be inclined toward a scenic understanding of the event. Certainly that is the case with two similar works that circulated only in manuscript in the early modern period: the first later published as *The Condition of Catholics under James I: Father Gerard's Narrative of the Gunpowder Plot* (1871); the second an unfinished work translated from Italian and published as *The Gunpowder Plot: The Narrative of Oswald Tesimond alias Greenway* (1973). Both texts were accounts by English Jesuit priests who had been intimate with the Gunpowder Plotters and had escaped England shortly after the Plot's discovery. Writing from the safety of the Continent, Gerard and Tesimond tried to give honest accounts of the incident to the curious. They were also, however, concerned to exonerate themselves and the Jesuit mission of any responsibility for the Plot. And in the face of both the scandal raised by the Plot and an apparent defeat of the Catholic cause in England, signalled by among other things the execution of their leader, Father Henry Garnet, they tried to construct consolatory versions of the events. As narrators, apologists, and comfort-givers, they thus often focused on the circumstantial and eschatological dimensions of the event: conditions that made the Plot possible and plausible even if it was also evil. By that means they rendered the failure of the Plot as a cause for hope.

An excellent recent account of the Jesuit mission in England up to the time of the Powder Treason, with glances toward Gerard and Tesimond, appears in Alice Hogge's *God's Secret Agents* (2005). As the title of the book indicates, however, Hogge's account has the air of a thriller. The Jesuit mission to England was in fact a kind of adventure; and it is not unreasonable to think of the story of the Jesuits, and of the Gunpowder Plot that undid them, as a tale of 'heroic adventures made up of flight, pursuit, capture, and escape', as the *Oxford Dictionary of Literary Terms* defines the genre of the thriller.[17] But though such a kind of rendering of events has great appeal to twenty-first-century writers and readers, and was not unknown in the pre-modern era, at least so far as the Gunpowder Plot was concerned it was not of much appeal. The only early modern literary account that took pains to narrate the intrigue of the Gunpowder Plot, where schemes were laid, conspirators recruited, and plans were put secretly into action one by one, is Thomas Campion's Latin poem, *De Puluerea Coniuratione* (1615?). For most writers, including Milton and Fletcher, the intrigue was not important. And as for the two Jesuit writers who in fact lived lives of flight, pursuit, capture, and escape, what was important about the story of the Plot had little to do with suspense, even the suspense of their own confrontations with danger. What was important was the context, the destiny of the Catholic Church. Although they accounted for what happened with narrative clarity, their main concern was to explain what happened in view of its circumstances, past, present, and future.

It was thus not inappropriate for its modern editor to title John Gerard's memoir *The Condition of Catholics under James I.* The word Gerard uses repeatedly is 'state', or 'state of affairs', as in the heading of the first chapter of the book: 'The State of Persecuted Catholics at the Queen's Death and The King's Entry, with Their Hopes of Relaxation by Him, Whereof They Failed'.[18] A state of affairs had arisen over the years, from the beginning of Elizabeth's reign, which had made life nearly insufferable for most Catholics. Gerard catalogues Catholic grievances, and takes pains to show how the situation kept getting worse and was apt to worsen further. Prohibitions and inhibitions, a legacy of persecutions, penalties, imprisonments, and executions, and a trend where repressive forces were growing in influence all came to impose a kind of 'desolation' on Catholics in England. 'Every prudent man will easily conceive', Gerard concludes,

> what was like to be the sense and feeling of all Catholics in this so great increase of their long-endured afflictions, in this utter despair of any help from His Majesty (in whose promised clemency all their hopes were placed), and in a certain expectation of other most cruel and newly-invented laws to be further imposed upon them at the next Parliament as against traitors not worthy to live in a commonwealth....In what other state could they be but a general and most afflicting desolation.[19]

The only relief from oppression and affliction comes toward the end of Gerard's account, where he describes the execution of Father Garnet, a martyrdom in Gerard's eyes.

> This holy seed of Father Garnett's slaughtered body falling upon the earth did bring forth great fruit. His mortified and divided parts did quicken and unite the minds of many that were before distracted with fears and uncertain reports, and his innocent blood did water the field of Christ in this country, and brought forth a plentiful harvest.[20]

[17] <http://www.oxfordreference.com> [18] Gerard, *The Condition*: 17.
[19] Gerard, *The Condition*: 49. [20] Gerard, *The Condition*: 299.

In fact, Gerard has little evidence to offer that Garnet's death was a genuine martyrdom and inspired an upsurge in Catholic feeling.[21] His tone is bitter rather than hopeful. The condition of Catholics in England at the time of his writing is actually worse because of the discovery of the Plot, he has to admit; and so he concludes his account with a chapter devoted to 'A Catalogue of Laws Made against Catholics'. In the midst of it all there was that decision a few years earlier, made by a handful of men who were unable to 'endure' oppression:

> being resolved never to yield or forsake their faith, they had not patience and longanimity (sic) to expect the Providence of God.... They would not endure to see their brethren so trodden upon by every Puritan, so made a prey to every needy follower of the Court or servant to a Councillor, so presented and pursued by every churchwarden and minister, so hauled to every session when the Justices list to meet, so wronged on every side by the process of excommunication or outlawry, and forced to seek for their own by law, and then also to be denied law, because they were Papists; finally both themselves and all others to be denounced traitors, and designed to the slaughter. These things they would not endure now to begin afresh after so long endurance, and therefore began amongst themselves to consult what remedy they might apply to all these evils (and few greater than these by the daily destruction of innumerable souls, as they alleged at their death) ...[22]

Gerard is not quite excusing the conspirators. He is not denying them moral agency and hence culpability. But he places that agency in a ratio with circumstance where the latter exceeds the former. It almost seems as if the conspirators' greatest fault was impatience, because apart from impatience and their choice of 'unfit means', they are following the logic of the moment. They have come to the situation of a crisis at once symbolic and existential. A 'daily destruction of souls' is going on, and their own destruction could be next.

Oswald Tesimond's book follows a similar pattern. According to Frances Edwards, its editor and translator, Tesimond and Gerard both worked from a Latin manuscript written by another hand, adding their personal perspectives to the original.[23] In any case, Tesimond's account likewise begins with an assessment of the condition of Catholics in England up to 1605, and comes to summary statements like, 'From what has been said, it will be clear at this point to everyone that the Catholics in England arrived at the nadir of their miseries. There was no more hope for them.'[24] For Tesimond English Catholics were undergoing a 'persecution'. 'Indeed', he says at one point, 'it seems to me that the persecution now going on in England is a good deal harsher than that of the primitive church or succeeding ages.'[25] But Tesimond is clearer about the difference between the majority of Catholics and the few men who conspired to blow up the House of Lords, and he is also clearer about the enormity of what the latter were up to. The majority 'encouraged one another to expect relief from Divine Providence alone as they waited on God with true patience and fortitude, and painfully made their way

---

[21] But see Rogers, 'An English Tailor', recounting the myth surrounding Garnet's 'martyrdom'.
[22] Gerard, *The Condition*: 50–1.   [23] Tesimond, *The Gunpowder Plot*: 9–11.
[24] Tesimond, *The Gunpowder Plot*: 52.   [25] Tesimond, *The Gunpowder Plot*: 37.

through hard times. They urged and exhorted one another so that by good example and decency they would find a way of softening the hardness in the hearts of their enemies.' The 'few', however, had 'kindled within them a just desire, as it seemed to them, of retribution. They burned to liberate themselves and their friends from this cruel servitude and oppression.' Obviously, Tesimond is appealing to characterological as well as to scenic motivation. The majority of persons were patient and brave. The few were too hot: they 'burned'. But still, a kind of scenic logic seems to determine what happened next. 'But at last they found a remedy for these evils which was no less lacking in pity and humanity than the very authors of such evil. Led by anger and desperation, they decided to open a way to new and better hopes by the utter destruction of their adversaries.'[26] On the one hand, there is anger and desperation; on the other, that is exactly what the situation called for. The men were suffering evil, pitiless and inhuman; and so the men sought a remedy of evil, which was also pitiless and inhuman. Utter persecution called for utter destruction.

Precisely because the situation was genuinely hopeless, in other words, the situation itself had to be destroyed, according to the terrorists, as Tesimond understands the matter. Catesby, according to Tesimond, 'decided after much reflection to gather together all the enemies of the Catholic religion in England and be rid of them with one blow. Liberty and religion would then be restored to Catholics with no resistance.' Parliament had been preparing to pass even more oppressive laws:

> the king, councillors, puritans and bishops...were all of them determined that in that time and place they would give the final death blow to the Catholic cause, as we have said. In that same moment of time, the plotters hoped to bring upon their heads the evil they had designed for others. They would blow them up with a mine, and the Parliament-house along with them. In this way, the authors of those most cruel laws would be removed along with the memory of the very place where they had been made.[27]

Gerard to some extent and Tesimond entirely add to the story of the Plot the idea that the choice of the House of Lords as a target was not only symbolic and 'fit', but also a preventive measure. I do not know if Gerard and Tesimond are right. I do know that Gerard and Tesimond place the personal and political motives of the conspirators into a ratio with the scene, and use that scene to accomplish two important goals: first, almost to excuse the conspirators, since the scene had not only become intolerable but was about to become even more so; and second, to explain the form of the 'remedy' the conspirators were seeking, a remedy of massacre that would destroy the very scene (as well as the very people) responsible for the oppression of Catholics.

Scenic motivations can thus become definitive in a story of terrorism, explaining both how the story originates and why it results in such deadly and destructive intentions. If tyranny could be associated with a single tyrant, as we saw in Chapter 3, then it could be imagined that tyranny could be ended with a single

---

[26] Tesimond, *The Gunpowder Plot*: 53.   [27] Tesimond: 54–5.

murder. But if tyranny was a group affair, and if it was such a group affair that it amounted not just to a collection of individuals but to the constitution of a scene, then massive violence against the scene itself might be required. The demands of justice could go so far as to exceed the mere taking of life; obliterating the possibility of a whole way of life would be required. Although the idea never seems to come up in the context of the Gunpowder Plot, we are back in the territory of the 'ban'. But we are also in the territory of something new. On the one hand, a very primitive form of destruction is returned to, where armed conflict means the utter elimination of the enemy. On the other, a new symbolic value is attributed to this elimination. For it is not only a covenant that has to be renewed through violence and destruction, but also an ancient constitution.

6. SAINT BARTHOLOMEW

This worst of all massacres in the early modern period was not without its supporters and apologists. But one of the most remarkable things about the event was that in the back-and-forth of justification and condemnation, a major point of dispute came in the question of what actually happened, and why. That a large number of what were called the *huguenots de guerre* and other prominent Huguenots were left dead after several days of massacre, having been attacked by royal guardsmen and other soldiers under the command of the Duke of Guise, that many less prominent civilians, men, women, and children, were slaughtered and their lodgings looted, having been attacked by a collective force of Parisians, that the River Seine ran red with the blood of the dead bodies heaved into the water, that in spite of royal decrees issued against it (though the seriousness of those decrees has been questioned) the violence went on for many days and was then copied in the provinces—of this there was no dispute. But how and why? On whose orders? According to many pro-Catholic accounts, after the failed assassination of Coligny the royal family had its back to the wall; it had to take pre-emptive measures against the leading Huguenots to prevent an uprising in the capital. But this pre-emptive measure, undertaken on the order of the royal council under the command of Guise, was to be distinguished from the popular violence that followed. The *Ornatissimi cujusdam viri de rebus gallicis, ad Stanislaum Elvidium epistola* (*Lettre à Elvide*) by Guy du Faur Pibrac (1572–3), a leading adviser to the royal family and a *politique* like his friend Robert Garnier, argued in a work intended for an international audience that though the pre-emptive measure had been necessary, the popular violence had been unnecessary and was much to be regretted. Most of what happened was 'reprehensible and vehemently deplored by our king'.[28]

Pibrac made a hard and fast distinction between mob violence and targeted military action; he defended only the latter, and in that respect his argument was consistent with humanist thought about war and peace and the always-to-be-deplored phenomenon of spontaneous riot. But Pibrac's distinction was not

[28] Pibrac, 'Lettre à Elvide': 24.

universally accepted. One apologist for Saint Bartholomew, the Italian Camille Capilupi, whose work was promptly published in Paris, both in the original Italian and in French translation, suggested not only that both forms of violence were ordered by the king and coordinated by his councillors, but also that such a coordinated attack had been planned in advance. The royal wedding between Henry of Navarre and Margaret of Valois, the reason for the visit to Paris by so many Huguenot military leaders, was actually a pretext, a snare, an invitation to a slaughter. After three civil wars, according to Capilupi, the king had found that it was 'impossible to exterminate' the Huguenots and restore order to his kingdom, and so 'he resolved to obtain by art and deftness what he has tried in vain by force of arms'.[29] The Huguenots were trapped as a minority in the very city that had invited them to celebrate a new peace. As soon as Coligny and his men were killed in Coligny's chambers, 'immediately all the people having taken up arms, following the command that had been given, every Catholic having put a small piece of white fabric around his left arm in order to be identifiable, and having been given leave to kill the Huguenots and sack and pillage their houses, the people began a very cruel killing, and horribly slaughtered the poor wretches'.[30] So according to Capilupi, although there was a difference between the action taken against Coligny and other *huguenots de guerre* and mass murder, both forms of violence were ordered and coordinated by the central government. The attack was 'cruel', 'horrible', and all that; but that is what it was supposed to be. 'The king in Paris', he wrote without irony, 'seeing the whole city turned upside down, dyed and bathed in blood, and full of horrible spectacles of death ... went to church to give thanks to God'.[31]

More nuanced is the account given in the anonymous *Discours sur les causes de l'execution faict ès personnes de ceux qui avoient conjuré contre le roy et son estat* (1572), which distinguishes between the two types of violence, applauds the first and excuses the latter.

> The people of Paris, who are Catholic and very fond of their prince, reminding themselves of the evils they had suffered during the civil wars started by the violence and rebellion of the Huguenots, partisans of the Admiral, and hearing about the cruel and detestable conspiracy organised by the Admiral and his adherents, could not keep themselves from rushing upon (*ne se peut tenir qu'il ne se ruast*) the Huguenots of the city, who, being of the same religion as the conspirators, would have been quite pleased if the conspiracy had succeeded. The people killed some of them, sacking and pillaging their houses. Now, this will of the people to sustain and defend their prince, to adopt his quarrel and to hate those who were not of his religion, was commendable; and if in the execution there were several pillages, one must nevertheless pardon the fury of a people urged by such good zeal, which is difficult to contain or restrain once it has been stirred up.[32]

It is noteworthy that the author of the tract tries to minimize the violence through the use of ambiguous modifiers ('some of them', 'several': the author likes the word *plusieurs*), even while he acknowledges its scope. Even more noteworthy are his

[29] Capilupi, *Stratagême*: 411.
[30] Capilupi, *Stratagême*: 435.
[31] Capilupi, *Stratagême*: 440.
[32] *Discours sur les causes*: 248–9.

paired negatives: *ne peut se tenir qu'il ne se ruast.* Unlike Capilupi's tract, this document claims that the perpetrators of the massacre acted not because they were ordered to do something, or because they had deliberated on a course of action in advance, but because they, or rather their 'zeal', was 'urged' or 'moved' (the author uses the words *poussée* and *esmeue*), and because they could not restrain themselves, given the circumstances. But most noteworthy of all may simply be the locution, the collective noun, 'the people of Paris'. The author writes as if the people were one, as if all the people were of the same mind, and collectively involved in the violence. The surgical precision of the royal council and its soldiers in their attack on Coligny and the *huguenots de guerre* is mirrored in reverse by the zealous unanimity of 'the people' in their attack on every Protestant they could get their hands on—even though it was well known that 'the people' were not unanimous, that many people stayed shut in their homes, waiting for the violence to end, that some intervened on behalf of Huguenots… and that not all victims of the violence were actually Huguenots.

Something happened during the Saint Bartholomew Massacre that even supporters could acknowledge to have been cruel and barbarous. A good deal of thought was given, and continues to be given, as to who ordered what and when, and how the attack on Coligny became a general slaughter. The Queen Mother, Catherine de' Medici, has been a favourite villainess of the piece, and at least one careful study has argued that Charles IX, the king and her son, was entirely out of the loop when the massacre began.[33] Meanwhile, a contemporary account that was published in both France and England, written by François Hotman, puts the blame squarely on the king, at the prompting of his mother, and not just for the military attack, but also for the slaughter of civilians. According to Hotman, a decision was made on the Queen Mother's advice, 'that within the space of one hour all the enemies may be slain, and the whole name and race of those wicked men be utterly rooted out'.[34] Then, after Coligny was attacked and killed, and his body thrown out of the window, a waiting Duke of Guise took charge of the situation as follows:

> Going out at the gate with the rest of the lords, he cried out to the multitude in armour, saying, My companions, we have had a good lucky beginning: now let us go forward to the rest, for it is the king's commandment: which words he did oft repeat aloud, saying, Thus the king commandeth. This is the kings will, this is his pleasure. And then he commanded the token to be given by ringing tocsin with the great bell of the palace, and alarm to be raised, and he caused it to be published, that the conspirators were in armour and about to kill the king.[35]

Even here, in Hotman's account, however, something is missing. How did the action of killing get transferred from Guise's soldiers to a general citizenry? How did a warning about 'conspirators' turn into an attack on several thousand civilians?

---

[33] Bourgeon, *L'assassinat de Coligny*. Many though not all of Bourgeon's findings have been disputed in Venard, 'Arretez le massacre!'.

[34] Hotman, *A True and Plaine Report*: 50.

[35] Hotman, *A True and Plaine Report*: 56–7.

The omission is repeated in Marlowe's *The Massacre at Paris*, evidently based on Hotman's account, where a diabolic Guise leads the way to the slaughter of civilians, as if Guise had been everywhere at once.

What gets lost in most of the accounts of Saint Bartholomew is the scale of the violence, and an appreciation of the ill will, the paranoia and the brutality that the violence expressed. What gets lost is at one and the same time what really happened—the murder of 2–5,000 citizens and visitors, most of them unarmed, in the space of a few days—and what the violence actually meant. For many of the apologists the general massacre was not really terrorism before the letter, because the violence was only incidental, not essential; it was only 'unfortunate', a 'fury' of 'the mob'. Moreover, because the planned and essential violence was only tactical and surgical, the violence was not supposed to mean anything; it was only supposed to remove turbulent rivals to the power of the central government. Even apologists who took the measure of the fury were inclined to identify it with the tactical political will of the government.

The fact is, Catholics and Protestants alike had trouble coming to terms with the riot of death and destruction. Protestants like Hotman, Nicolas Barnaud, Jean de Serres, and the anonymous author of *Le Tocsain contre les massacreurs et auteurs des confusions en France* (1579), along with Catholics like Jacques-Auguste de Thou and (in his later years) Pierre Matthieu, could see in the events a scenic catastrophe. And they could frame this catastrophe by way of a narrative of national and international struggle, factions, confessions, and states all one against the other. But there were no accounts among those that have survived which were able to tell the whole story. There was no entirely satisfactory chronology of events. As historian Nicola Sutherland once observed, we cannot even be sure that the murder of Gaspard de Coligny was the incident that 'inaugurated' the Massacre. Most contemporary chronicles begin with that event, and with a tocsin that was sounded in the early hours of the morning signalling the fact that Coligny had been killed, or was under attack, and more fighting was anticipated...but we actually do not know that that was the case.[36] All we know is that the rhetoric of the massacre, on all sides, seemed to require an inaugural event, the sacrifice of a scapegoat and a general call to arms. As an English Protestant, the poet Anne Dowriche would put it, referring to the Duke of Guise, after his triumph over the corpse of Coligny:

> ... he bade in haste the tocsin for to ring,
> Which sounding bell appointed was the fatal news to bring
> Whenas this raging rout, this murder should begin:
> Which they performed, as though they no men but monsters been.[37]

That moment when Coligny's residence was stormed and Coligny was sacrificed under the command of his arch-enemy, Henry Lorraine the third Duke of Guise, the body of Coligny being thrown into the street and abused, decapitated, and otherwise mutilated, the head of Coligny being paraded through the streets and

---

[36] Sutherland, 'The Role of Coligny': 110.
[37] Dowriche, *French Historie*: 28. On Dowriche's ideological position, see Martin, 'Anne Dowriche's *The French History*'.

perhaps secretly sent on toward Rome as a trophy for the Pope—that moment served the purposes of a narrative of the night of Saint Bartholomew which people were perhaps already telling themselves, and certainly were telling themselves within a matter of days, to provide a palpable and symbolically resonant beginning to a group of events that was probably much more diffuse, complicated, and inglorious. The sounding of the tocsin at just the moment when Coligny was killed, leading to the instantaneous fury of either a zealous 'people' or bloodthirsty 'monsters', was probably too good to have been true. At the very same moment there were no doubt other initiatives underway led by royal guards and the urban militia, as other *huguenots de guerre* found themselves trapped in other parts of the city, including the Louvre, and either summarily executed or viciously attacked and killed and despoiled. And there were other bells ringing that night. About the outbreak of what historians persist in calling 'popular violence' or 'collective violence' we know nothing except that by dawn it was already taking place, some of its first victims having been prominent Parisian Protestants who had long been the targets of resentment among members of the populace, and who were also, like Coligny, suitable subjects for inaugurating a chain of violent attacks, and for playing the role of scapegoats.[38]

Yet of this 'popular' or 'collective' violence and the massive killing on the streets of Paris we know little. There is not a single extant written record explaining exactly what went on in the streets of Paris, telling us the history of the riot from day to day. All we have is an accounting of what happened, briefly, to some of the victims, especially those who had been most prominent among them, like Pierre Ramus, the philosopher, whose death is highlighted in Marlowe's *Massacre at Paris*, and those few who left behind memoirs of how they escaped from the massacre, like Jacques Nompar de Caumont, the future Duke de la Force. Caumont was saved by a neighbour after playing dead under a heap of dead bodies.[39] We do not have a satisfactory understanding of who led the massacres (if anyone), of who perpetrated them, or of how the massacres developed from hour to hour and day to day. We do not have much of a record at all of those whom sociologist Jacques Sémelin suggests are absolutely essential to any story of a massacre, but who are almost always left out: the bystanders, the thousands of Parisians who were neither perpetrators nor victims, but who were there on the scene, and witnessed the whole thing, and were no doubt terrified as well.[40] Perhaps most scandalously of all, we know almost nothing about a fact repeated in memoir after memoir, but without any details or explanations: along with the murders and the pillage, everyone agrees, there were also rapes. How frequent were the rapes we do not know; but storyteller after storyteller (on the Protestant side) finds it necessary to remind us that rapes occurred. And if they were common, if rapes were a normal step in a sequence of assault and murder, we would have another important qualification of the position that the perpetrators were engaged in a kind of holy violence, acting

---

[38] Somewhat aware of this problem are two recent full-length treatments of the Massacre, Diefendorf, *Beneath the Cross*, and Jouanna, *La Saint-Barthélemy*. Also see Sutherland, 'Le Massacre de la Saint-Barthélemy'.

[39] La Force, *Mémoires authentiques*: 1.1–37.   [40] Sémelin, 'Analyser le massacre'.

out as if in a trance a cleansing vengeance against heretics.[41] If a holy trance can lead to rape and pillage, then we are talking about a trance that is entirely outside the framework of Christian theology and practice. In any case, I have seen no document of the period which suggests that anything like a 'trance' was experienced by the killers, the pillagers, and the rapists.

What we have, apart from stories of escape and a handful of murderous attacks against the likes of Ramus, are tableaus. Instead of narratives, we have discrete verbal pictures. On the first night we have pictures of the warm weather, the darkness, the bells ringing, the storming of houses by gangs of armed soldiers, militia men and thugs, and then daylight, and more violence under clear blue skies. The images of events at the lodgings of the Admiral, on the Rue de Béthisy, are vividly painted in many accounts, since there were eyewitnesses who survived. The soldiers storm up the stairs to the chamber of the Admiral, who stands up to them, dignified and fearless, and then is struck by uncounted blows of the sword, until his body, possibly still breathing, is hurled headfirst out the window, to be inspected by the Duke of Guise, waiting in the street (or else the courtyard) below. And then there are images of events at the Louvre: the one where the newly married Marguerite de Valois hides a wounded Huguenot soldier in her bed; the one where the guards attending upon the King of Navarre and the Prince of Condé are set upon and slaughtered in the courtyard of the Louvre; the one where the young king, Charles IX—though this image is very likely apocryphal—stood the next day at a window in a tower of the Louvre, overlooking the scene of carnage along the banks of the river, and aimed a hunting rifle against the Huguenots below: in d'Aubigné's memorable words,

> Ce Roi, non juste Roi, mais juste arquebusier,
> Giboyait aux passants trop tardifs à noyer!

> [This king, an unjust king, but a fair marksman,
> Was game-shooting the passers-by taking too long to drown.][42]

The essential settings of the scene are two. In the first place, there was the historical context. Memoirists and historians on all sides, writing within a few years after the event, can be impressively thorough in their appreciation of the many lead-ups to the massacre: the hostility between France and Spain; the pressing of Gaspard de Coligny to unite France against Spain in a war in the Protestant Low Countries; the pressing of the Guise faction for the opposite policy of a closer alliance with Spain; the wedding of the Prince of Navarre and Marguerite de Valois; the hatred of the Guises for Coligny, stoked by the belief that Coligny was responsible for the assassination nine years earlier of the second Duke of Guise; and even, too, local resentments and class rivalries among the Parisian citizenry, especially against wealthy merchants and jurists who had managed to curry favour with the crown, and practise their religion (officially banned inside the walls of Paris) with impunity. In the second place, there was the immediate, spatiotemporal context: whether by

---

[41] The subtext of rape is brought into the foreground, however, in a painting by Cornelis Van Haarlem of the Massacre of the Innocents dated 1590, and now hanging in the Rijksmuseum.
[42] D'Aubigné, *Les Tragiques*: 5.951–2.

design, as many on both sides alleged, or as it were indifferently, as others alleged, the city of Paris, in the waning summer of 1572, was a uniquely dangerous venue for so momentous an occasion as a royal wedding between a Protestant prince and a Catholic princess. The walls and gates of the city, vigorously guarded by a citizen militia at all times, the narrow streets of the crowded city, the intellectual ferment of the place, its role as the centre of (Catholic) theological learning, the preponderantly Catholic populace, often enough riled up at church by zealous priests preaching intolerance and resistance, and, not to be forgotten, since it would play so large a role in what happened, the deep and wide river that divided the city into islands and banks, left and right: all this too is vividly rendered by the redactors of the event.[43]

Nor was the symbolic significance of the historical moment or the geography of the city lost on commentators. In retrospect, according to the majority of writers, the summer of 1572 was a summer of crisis, demanding a release of some sort, a discharge of blocked-up energies, or even some sort of payback, a balancing out of credits and debits. And the city itself, in retrospect, was either a kind of domicile or a kind of snare. As a domicile it could let strangers in, showing them hospitality, and it could force strangers out, showing them the door. But as a snare, the city was a place that could draw Huguenots in and then lock them in, whether in the courtyards of palaces or in the walled confines of the city as a whole, so that they could be set upon at will.

The tableaux of riot and destruction left behind by the chroniclers only rarely rise to the occasion. But when they do, powerful and disturbing images intrude upon the consciousness, as the chroniclers intended they should. The fury of the rioters, the blood that flowed and ran down the streets and into the river, the bodies that were thrown onto the banks of the river or into the river itself, and the visible reddening of the river itself form predominant images in the account. So too—a detail otherwise easily overlooked—do the sounds of the massacre. From historian de Thou (who was not an eyewitness) in a seventeenth-century translation, we get this:

> The people, incited by the sheriffs, wardsmen and tything men that ran about, did furiously rage with all manner of licentiousness and excess against their fellow-citizens, and a sad and horrid face of things did everywhere appear. For the streets and ways did redound with the noise of those that flocked to the slaughter and plunder and the complaints and doleful outcries of dying men, and those that were nigh to danger were everywhere heard. The carcasses of the slain were thrown down from the windows, the courts and chambers of the houses were full of dead men, their bodies rolled in dirt were dragged through the streets, blood did flow in such abundance through the channels of the streets, that full streams of blood did run down into the river.[44]

Perhaps even more powerful is a passage from Protestant historian Simon Goulart (also not an eyewitness) in a three-volume collection devoted to the reign of Charles IX and the Saint Bartholomew Massacre:

---

[43] On the preaching, see Diefendorf, 'Simon Vigor'. The venomous sermons themselves can be found in Vigor, *Sermons Catholiques*.

[44] De Thou, *History of the Bloody Massacres*: 39.

The paper would cry if I recited the horrible blasphemies which were pronounced by those wild monsters and devils during the fury of all those massacres. The tempestuousness, the continual sound of arquebuses and pistols, the lamentable and frightening cries of those who were being executed, the screams of the murderers, the bodies thrown out of the windows, dragged through the muck, with strange hoots and whistles, the breaking of doors and windows, the stones they threw against them, and the pillages of more than six hundred houses, continuing for a long time, can only present to the eyes of the reader a perpetual image of extreme misfortune of all kinds.[45]

Tableaux like these may seem to require no further comment. They seem to say everything that needs to be said. And that is how historian Janine Garrisson leaves it, calling the general massacre a 'pogrom'.[46] But many problems remain—problems of which both de Thou and Goulart were aware. On the one hand, an 'extreme misfortune' had occurred at the level of the scene of Paris, a general and uncontrollable riot, a chaos of murder, rape, and pillage. On the other, there was the political intent of court figures and other leaders, which was more a function of character and deliberation, and which included attempts by the royal council not to foment but to moderate and limit the violence. Or to cite another difficulty: although along with the chaos there was paranoia and resentment, sublimated into a carnival of holy terror, enjoyed for the sake of the Church, there were few writers on either side who could see anything holy or joyous in the event. There were many writers at the time who were capable of admitting that Coligny and some number of others were being suitably punished for their militancy over the past decade, that certain individuals had to be sacrificed for the good of the state and Church, that the Massacre had 'broken the head' of the rebellious Huguenot party, that it was worthwhile singing thanks for 'the ruin and the defeat' of a 'proud and foul troop' riddled with 'error and sedition' seeking only to 'overthrow us'; but few, if any—I have in fact found none—made the claim that the Massacre had removed a divine curse on the French people, or religiously purified the people through redemptive violence.[47] Nor did any writer attempt really to address the popular violence, the mass killings, rapes, and pillages.

Lacking in the scene of the carnage was, precisely, redemption. It was one thing to rid the nation of a menace; it was another to find salvation through the ridding, especially given the scope of the action, and the way in which, from the gruesome assassination of the Admiral to the torturing and pillaging of citizens in their homes, the action was conducted, in violation of every code of either war or peace. There were no Judiths in this story; there weren't even any Ehuds, Samsons, Davids, or Maccabees. And if, from the Catholic side, there were no Judiths, from the Protestant side there were so many victims, so indiscriminately slaughtered, that it was

---

[45] Goulart, *Mémoires de l'Estat de France*: 1.226.   [46] Garrisson: *1572*: 112–19.

[47] *Cantique général des catholiques*, stanzas 2–3. According to Christian Biet, the Catholic polemical pamphlets of the time 'concerned themselves exclusively with the figure of Gaspard de Coligny'. Biet, ed., *Théâtre de la cruauté*: 831. The silence on the mass murder corresponds with the phenomenon Crouzet calls 'the massacre without massacrers'. Crouzet, *La nuit de Saint-Barthélemy*: 100.

difficult to dignify them with the name of martyrs.[48] This much suffering could
not pass an occasion for pious thanksgiving; only as a rallying cry for outrage, complaint, and resistance. 'Be sure therefore of this', says a Huguenot in Dowriche's
Historie, addressing himself to the Catholic enemy, '... / That this our blood by
shedding of thy blood shall be repaid'.[49] In the scene itself, Paris, the great city of
France, the centre of religious learning, industry, government, and trade, there was
nothing to be found that was redeeming; the city had become a bloodbath, its
waters polluted with the corpses of men, women, and children. (Even worse to
come would be the copycat bloodbath in Orléans.[50])

For the Catholics there was one notable exception, the famous 'miracle' of the
hawthorn in bloom, at the end of summer rather than at the beginning of spring,
in the midst of all the violence. The story of the miracle reports that underneath
the gruesome catastrophe there was in fact, among Catholics, an urge toward transcendence, a palpable transcendence within the body of the city. As a Protestant
writer tells it in the *Reveille-matin des Francois* (1574), without failing to mention
that the whole affair was a hoax,

> Around noon on Monday (well beyond the season for such things) a hawthorn was
> seen in bloom at the cemetery of Saint Innocent: as soon as word about it spread
> through the city, the people came running from all sides, crying 'Miracle, Miracle,'
> and the town bells rang with joy. It came to be necessary to hold back the crowd, so
> that the miracle (which was what it was known as, though actually it was a trick rigged
> by a good old Cordelier) would not be found out and impugned. It became necessary,
> I say, to plant guards all around the hawthorn, to prevent the people from getting too
> close. There was no small number of people who interpreted the miracle to mean
> nothing else but that France had recovered its lost splendour and flower. The people
> coming around again to see the hawthorn, happy and satisfied, thinking that God had
> sent a sign to show his approval for all they had done, went straight to the lodging of
> the dead admiral, where, having found the dead corpse, they took it and dragged it
> through the streets up to the banks of the river.[51]

This miracle was celebrated without irony by any number of Catholics. Historian
Arlette Jouanna quotes a letter written by a priest:

> At this time, at the cemetery of the Holy Innocents, a hawthorn which for the last four
> years seemed to be withered was covered with flowers: I saw it with my own eyes. It
> was a certain sign that religion was going to be restored, and everyone embraced this
> presage with ardour. I piously took up my rosary and touched the hawthorn with it.[52]

A similar lack of irony permeates the account of Claude Haton, another priest,
who was not an eyewitness, and who is not even sure what kind of plant was involved, but who seems certain about what the miracle was supposed to mean, even

---

[48] Roll-calls of some of the most prominent victims are nevertheless a feature of many Huguenot
accounts of the event.

[49] Dowriche, *Historie*: 32.

[50] Botzheim, 'Le massacre fait à Orléans'. And see the reports compiled in *Archives Curieuses*, 1ere
7: 261–342.

[51] Barnaud, *Le reveille-matin des Francois*: 70–1.   [52] Jouanne, *La Saint-Barthélemy*: 170.

as he also pulls no punches as to what the collective violence amounted to, a *sac-cagement* and a *sédition*: 'It seemed that God, by this miracle, approved and found pleasant the Catholic sedition and the death of His great enemy the Admiral and his men, who over the past fifteen years had so greatly and audaciously rented the fabric of His great Church and spouse.'[53]

So there was an exception on the Catholic side, an appalling exception where crimes against humanity were seen to have been blessed by God, and where the city itself gave birth to a palpable sign of its own forthcoming salvation.[54] But it is noteworthy that few apologists for Saint Bartholomew, writing for public consumption, put any stock in the miracle. When, nearly two decades later, Jacques Clément assassinated Henry III, Parisians are reported to have gone into ecstasies over the 'miracle' that had just delivered them from tyranny, and pamphlet writers themselves went into ecstasies over it anew as they told their stories about it. There are no such reports of ecstasy before, during, or after the popular violence of Saint Bartholomew, and apologists seldom even mention either the hawthorn or the general massacre it was supposed to have endorsed. Ecstasy—or at least triumphal pride—came with the defeat of Coligny and other *huguenots de guerre*. Apologists were beside themselves in celebrating the blessed deliverance of the French people from the horrible ambition of dangerous men like Coligny. And they were capable of thanking God for the conduct and success of the affair. But the blossoming hawthorn had little rhetorical force. For if the miracle of the hawthorn expressed a desperate impulse among many Catholic Parisians to see a sign of divinity in the terror about them, and even of necessity to find that sign within the material structure of the scene of Paris, the purported miracle was useless as a motive for mass violence against unarmed citizens and visitors, or as a justification for it, either during or after the fact. Although Denis Crouzet argues, based on the report of the indignant author of the *Reveille-matin*, that the miracle, almost by itself, incited the 'collective violence' of the general massacre,[55] there is no direct evidence for so implausible a claim. And there is no evidence that any thinker capable of assessing the causes, reasons, and consequences for the violence, including the author of the *Reveille-matin*, ascribed any such power to the miracle.

When Pope Pius V heard about the Massacre he is said to have been well pleased at this victory of Catholicism over heresy and led prayers in thanksgiving for it. He immediately commissioned a triptych from the painter Giorgio Vasari to commemorate the event.[56] The central panel of the work shows a dying Admiral de Coligny being defenestrated by his assassins, and below him in the foreground armed soldiers attacking Huguenots with swords. As depicted, the soldiers put us in mind of Ancient Roman troops; the Huguenots meanwhile are rendered as

[53] Haton, *Mémoires*: 2.682.
[54] One thing that I haven't noted in any of the literature, though I suspect it must be there all the same, is a recognition of the irony of the miracle taking place in the churchyard of the 'Holy Innocents' or Saints-Innocents. The 'innocents' are the children who are said, after 1560, to have been 'massacred' by Herod, in an attempt to forestall the maturity of Christ.
[55] Crouzet, *La nuit de la Saint-Barthélemy*: 525–7.
[56] Kingdon, 'Reactions to the St. Bartholomew Massacres in Geneva and Rome'; Herz, 'Vasari's "Massacre" Series in the Sala Regia Howe'; 'Architecture in Vasari's "Massacre of the Huguenots"'.

demons. The scene cannot help but remind us of images of the Last Judgement, where the wicked (led, as it were, by Coligny) are cast down into hell, though it may also remind us of scenes of Roman military history and, in Coligny's fall, the swooping dive through the air of Perseus in Titian's *Perseus and Andromeda*. There is not a blooming hawthorn in sight.

7. D'AUBIGNÉ'S *TRAGIQUES*

'We enter into a story', says Simon Goulart, in a chapter he added to Jean Crespin's *Histoire des martyrs*, 'of cruelties so strange, proceeding from hearts so execrable, that it is impossible to think about it, and even less to express it in words.' In his *Mémoires de l'Estat de France, sous Charles neufiesme*, Goulart had adopted a view akin to those of monarchomachs like François Hotman, or even by the monarchomach-inspired playwright, Christopher Marlowe.[57] Saint Bartholomew was a *civil* disaster, proceeding from a failure of civility and law, motivated from above by Machiavellian calculation and the sheer malice of the ruling Catholic faction in government. The proper response to it was therefore resistance. But in taking the longer view of a 'history of the martyrs', a view of prophetic history where disaster is supposed to be, paradoxically, evidence of progress, Goulart is literally at a loss for words. 'We will simply tell the story as things happened', he says, knowing that an account of things as they happened is not enough.[58] Like apologists for the event on the other side of the ideological divide, Goulart is at a loss to find in the event what he ought to require from it, divine immanence.

The great exception to this loss of immanence and loss of words is in the work of the nobleman Agrippa d'Aubigné. *Les Tragiques* is a tragedy that is also an epic, written in heroic verse, and as Frank Lestringant, its modern editor, puts it, it is 'a book that burns'.[59] It is a riposte to Ronsard and the *Discours des misères de ce temps*, which Ronsard wrote in parts and published between 1562 and 1567. Ronsard's first impetus was to say something about the Massacre at Vassy. Then he went on to discuss other aspects of the troubles, always laying the blame at the door of the Protestants. And *Les Tragiques* will have none of this. It will not tolerate French poetry being made into a mouthpiece for anti-Protestant ideology. But *Les Tragiques* is also a Protestant criticism of Protestantism, a work which, addressing the subject of 'Another fire, in which France consumes itself', says that Protestantism has suffered too much because Protestantism has not gone far enough in its fight for God.[60] If d'Aubigné's appeal to the Protestant struggle is in the first instance ethical, since it calls on Protestants to renew the struggle and go farther with it, the appeal is also scenic, since it subordinates action to scene. For what d'Aubigné calls upon Protestants to do is to change the scene of their lives.

[57] See Kocher, 'François Hotman'; and Briggs, 'Marlowe's *Massacre at Paris*'.
[58] Crespin and Goulart, *Histoire des martyrs*: 10.703.
[59] Lestringant, Préface, in d'Aubigné, *Les Tragiques*: 7.
[60] D'Aubigné, *Les Tragiques*: 1.58.

I have mentioned Ronsard, France's most respected writer of the sixteenth century. In his *Discours* Ronsard had repeated many of the *topoi* we saw in the case of *Gorboduc*. France was massacring itself. France was a scene, a political nation, which was undermining itself through division, in this case the division caused by religious dissent. Religious dissent, he writes,

> arms the son against his own father,
> And the factious brother arms himself against brother,
> The sister against sister, and cousin germans
> Want to soak their hands in the blood of cousins:
> The uncle hates his nephew, the servant his master,
> The wife won't acknowledge her husband,
> Unreasoning children argue about faith,
> And everything is chaos, without order or law.[61]

And Ronsard can place a lot of the blame on Protestant preachers, like Théodore de Bèze, who had done so much to stir up the populace. But Ronsard focuses attention especially on the nation as the suffering body of violence. When he writes in the *Continuation du discours à la Royne* (the second part of the *Discours*) of 'These new Christians who have plundered, robbed, assassinated and stripped France, taking her by force, and beating her stomach with a hundred thousand blows', though he is blaming the Calvinists, he is also putting the body of *la France* forward as both scenic condition and scenic victim. Just like the rioting royalty and masses of England in Gorboduc, the rebellious evangelists and their followers are the offspring of the nation they are attacking:

> You resemble too those young vipers,
> Who split open the bodies of their mothers when born:
> Thus being aborted you have caused the death
> Of France your mother, instead of nourishing her.[62]

The France of Ronsard's imagination, the France out of which and against which the Troubles have erupted, becomes a figure of multiple agonies. At the end of the *Continuation* France appears impersonated as 'une idole', a shadow of herself, 'a poor woman at the point of death', her clothes torn and her hair 'hideous', her eyes 'dull and hollow'. And Ronsard has her complain:

> Now my mutinous, arrogant and lying people
> Have broken my right hand by expelling my Senators...
> They have torn my dress by tearing apart my cities,
> Turning my citizens against me in spite:
> They have ruined my hair in ruining my Churches,
> My Churches, alas! which they have taken by force,
> Reducing the statues and altars to rubble,
> Venerable abodes of our immortal saints...[63]

---

[61] Ronsard, Discours à la Royne. In *Oeuvres complètes*: 2.995, lines 159–64.
[62] Ronsard, Continuation, in *Oeuvres complètes*: 2.999, lines 91–4.
[63] Ronsard, *Continuation*: lines 357–66.

Ronsard, however, conveniently ignores Catholic provocations and retaliations. He says nothing about the actual results of the Massacre at Vassy, or other massacres where Catholics were the attackers. And that is where d'Aubigné steps in. He accepts the premise that a scene of life is at stake, that the container of the life-action is being ruined in the course of the troubles. As a Protestant he cannot accept Ronsard's version of events, of course. In d'Aubigné's eyes, the Protestants are the victims. Yet where Ronsard sees ruin at the hands of mutinous dissenters, d'Aubigné sees a scene of terrifying progress. All kinds of suffering have been experienced on the part of the faithful. But the scene is and shall be redemptive. What Ronsard sees as a backward, pointless reversion to chaos, d'Aubigné sees as a purifying immanent drive toward transcendence.

There have been martyrs galore, in this story of progress toward transcendence; Book IV, '*Les Feux*', is a serial account of the martyrdoms of Protestants in France similar to Crespin's *Histoire des martyrs* (1554–70). Part of the story might then be seen to be motivated primarily by characterological factors: brave and holy people, volunteering to die for the faith. But Book V, '*Les Fers*', is concerned with the time when the 'fires' of martyrdom turned to the 'arms' of the Troubles, and especially with incidents like the Saint Bartholomew Massacre, and the model of martyrdom is inadequate. From character and the suffering of individuals there is a move into scene and the coming of redemption.

The context is a visionary allegory adopted in part from the Book of Job and in part from epic tradition. It is a compensatory fable; the story as things happened—for example, Saint Bartholomew is placed in another story, which gives meaning and value to the first. But it is not merely compensatory, because d'Aubigné sees in it an ethical and spiritual challenge; the allegory is a prophetic protest; it is meant to engage its spokesman and its readers in the present with an eye toward the future of the Church. Moreover, the allegory provides the author, paradoxically, with a means for keeping to the scene of the massacre and related incidents faithfully. Allegorical contextualization allows d'Aubigné to do two things at once: on the one hand, to bear witness, to see the massacre and related incidents for what they were, a catastrophe, a 'holocaust' even, a violence of and against the scene of national life in France and the evangelical Church that was rising within it; on the other, to comprehend the catastrophe as an expression of a prophetic history that is still incomplete, though all the while supervised by the eternal eye of God and still perceivable by the remnant of His people.[64]

'God withdrew his eyes from the enemy earth', Book Five, 'Les Fers', begins. 'Justice and faith, light and life / Flew off to Heaven' (lines 1–3). The notion of a *deus absconditus* is part of the narrative scaffolding of the whole of the *Tragiques*. Sometimes God concerns himself directly with affairs on earth, sometimes he turns his back on it. It is all part of God's plan, and it is all part of the ultimate redemption God has in store for His chosen people. But the idea seems to be unique to d'Aubigné

---

[64] See Tournon, 'Poétique du témoinage dans *Les Tragiques*', and Conacher, '*Les Tragiques* d'Agrippa d'Aubigné'. And for general commentary, Forsyth, *La Justice de Dieu*; Lestringant, *La cause des martyrs*; and Rigolot, 'Trois "Mises en scène"'.

that the faithful would have to live through times when the eye of God was withdrawn from them and their world, especially given the fact that the result would be the catastrophe of the Troubles, punctuated by Saint Bartholomew. What permits the idea is the double-sourced allegory. From the Book of Job, d'Aubigné brings Satan into the heavens, a Satan who challenges God to make a trial of 'the souls' of his people, first by making them prosper, then by making them suffer under the *ongles de massacreurs*, the fingernails of massacrers. Satan maintains that under such agony, the faithful will come to 'blaspheme you, the Eternal, in your face'.[65] As in Job, God permits this. But the allegory has its second dimension. From epic tradition, as from d'Aubigné's own inspiration when he first thought of writing *Les Tragiques*, a 'swoon' while injured in battle, when he had a vision of heaven, the tribulations of the faithful are revealed as paintings on the walls of the vaults of heaven. God has withdrawn himself, but angels bear witness. As if in reaction to the frescoes in the Vatican,[66] the 'perfect' angels tell the true story of the troubles, and the divine history of which they play one of the 'worst' parts.

The Massacre at Paris is by no means the only incident rendered on the vaults of heaven; all of the Troubles are of interest, including the Tumult of Amboise, the Massacre at Vassy, the assassination of the second Duke of Guise by Jean de Poltrot ('celui qui prodigua sa vie / Pour tuer Holoferne assiégeant Béthulie'), and the Battle of Dreux, which had been a huge loss for the Protestant army.[67]

The Saint Bartholomew Massacre, however, is 'the tragedy which effaces all the others', the poet declares—and by that he means not the assassination of Coligny, but the general killing. In a moment, an 'armed populace tramples on justice, defaming it under their feet'. The language itself comes to mimic the disorder it is describing.

> The brutal unbridled bristling heaps
> Of manual labourers amassed in squads
> Willy-nilly disgrace three thousand dear lives,
> Witnesses, judges, and kings, both executioners and adversaries.[68]

Though a massacre can be imagined to be completely asymmetrical, an attack of the powerful against the weak, it can also be imagined as a general confusion. Here the powerful are 'manual labourers', *ouvriers mécanics*; the very order of armed violence has been subverted; instead of military troops honourably dispatching an enemy, the squads of labourers 'disgrace' their victims, attack them 'willy-nilly'; and in a deliberately disconcerting line, seem to act at once as witnesses, judges, and kings, as lawful executioners and embattled enemies.

> The victims, for their part,
> Die abandoned of strength but not of heart,
> Having beds for shackles, restraining their limbs,
> For jailers their hosts, and for prison their bedrooms.[69]

---

[65] D'Aubigné, *Les Tragiques*: 5.148, 5.154.
[66] D'Aubigné, *Les Tragiques*: 479, note to 5:274.
[67] D'Aubigné, *Les Tragiques*: 5.383–4.   [68] D'Aubigné, *Les Tragiques*: 5.797–802.
[69] D'Aubigné, *Les Tragiques*: 5.812–14.

This world turned upside down and inside out is not just an attack by Catholics against heretics, according to d'Aubigné. It is, as Lestringant puts it, the expression of a social revolution before the letter. For it is a form of apparently spontaneous collective action on behalf of a political idea. Or it is rather, as d'Aubigné imagines it, with the blame lying not only on the labourers but also the leaders who encouraged them and authorized their behaviour, the expression of a social cataclysm.

> The rogue, in possession of royal power,
> Dragged the senators of France through the muck.[70]

Private feuds and envy were given free play during the riots, in the name of acting on behalf of the king and a war against the Huguenots. The words come back from Ronsard, and from Lucan's *Pharsalia*:

> The daughter takes from her mother the day and the life,
> There the brother feels the hand of his brother,
> The cousin knows his cousin as an executioner...[71]

Instead of a simple massacre of the innocents, where the good are as different from the bad as children from adults or women from men, the massacre of Saint Bartholomew is so violent a confusion that the distinctions themselves have been ruined. One sees:

> The water covered with humans, and the detestable Seine,
> Its two banks noisy with the half-drowned wounded,
> Factories supplying the poison of the time,
> Is more blood than water.[72]

The image of bodies hurled into the 'detestable' river, dead or alive, and left to bleed and float downstream, is particularly resonant for d'Aubigné. The horror of individual atrocities is inescapable, and so, again, is the horror of what has happened to the social coherence of the capital city, of Paris once renowned for dispensing law and life, honouring justice, nurturing the arts, 'the mother of our kings'. Its very structures, symbolic and real, have been subverted.

> The bridge, once built for the bread of the city,
> Became a sad scaffold of the civil fury...[73]

Bridges that are meant to conjoin and nourish the city are used to tear things apart, people from people, life from life, as wounded living creatures are thrown off the bridges to their death. The life-giving waters of the Seine become a sepulchre. And as d'Aubigné moves from the scene of Paris to the copycat massacres in the provincial cities, his conceit has the narrative following the flow of the river, upstream and downstream, and blood and bodies of the dead, to be joined by blood and bodies of the other dead, in the other riverside cities, with other bridges turned to scaffolds, and other rivers polluted with the carrion of innocent victims.

---

[70] D'Aubigné, *Les Tragiques*: 5.821–2. [71] D'Aubigné, *Les Tragiques*: 5.828–30.
[72] D'Aubigné, *Les Tragiques*: 5.868–71. [73] D'Aubigné, *Les Tragiques*: 5.795–6.

The most striking moment may come in a single line: 'L'homme ne fut plus homme.' Man was no longer man. The line does not, however, refer to the cruelty of men toward other men. It refers to the condition of suffering in such a way that one's humanity has been effaced:

> Man was no longer man, but the greatest sign
> Of an immeasurable excess appeared again and again:
> For the forced eyes of the father were not allowed
> To cry over his son; without a word, the mother
> Saw the fruit of her womb and her heart dragged on the ground;
> Her complaint was without voice, mute with sorrow.
> …
> It became a crime above all to bury the dead
> Who surfaced from the water and drifted ashore.[74]

In the scene, at the time of the massacre, there was no transcendence because the means of transcendence were under attack and being destroyed; man was no longer man and man was no longer able to perform the rites of respecting the dead.

The only hope and the only transcendence would have to come by way of surviving this extreme trial, set upon the faithful by Satan, with the blessing of God.

> He who wants to escape from infidel Egypt,
> Conquer Canaan and live in her,
> O tribes of Israel, must march in rows
> In the red gulf and the sea of blood.[75]

It is all part of 'God's harvest', the 'harvest of great hope':

> As in a trampled field, the grounds of it scattered,
> Its rich ears of grain ripe and yellowing
> Sorrowing under the crashing hooves of the horses,
> Or torn into pieces by the wind and the thunder
> And the hail, the straw and the seed every which way:
> None can escape from the middle of the furrows
> But several ears lifted by the whirlwinds
> And landing in the stronger shrubs, whom the living war
> Having blown against them has fixed into the earth.
> Those who, under the arbour of the thick bushes,
> Take life in death, and peace in war,
> And keep themselves for the spring …[76]

8. THE MEANING OF MASSACRE

A massacre need not be represented scenically, in the sense that the scene is made into the dominant motive of the terror. And scenic representation need not be

[74] D'Aubigné, *Les Tragiques*: 5.1031–51.   [75] D'Aubigné, *Les Tragiques*: 5.521–4.
[76] D'Aubigné, *Les Tragiques*: 5.721–33.

limited to massacres. The massacre is obviously an extreme case of terrorist violence: a mass murder, usually committed by a rather smaller mass of murderers. But what is true for scenic representations of the massacre may well be true for representations of other kinds of terror. Violence in a scene is also violence of the scene and against the scene. To the extent that terrorist violence is *internal* to the scene in which it occurs, terror is self-violation, a destructive confusion of structure emerging out of the forms and materials of structure. And when the violence takes place in early modern Britain or France, it inevitably engages with the sacred and the profane, with transcendence and desecration.

One of the most terrifying aspects of terrorist violence, in any period, is just this relation it may have to the scene in which it arises. When terrorism violates the rules of civil society, it may well do so by attacking the scenic structure of civil society. We do not really have a good way of talking about these things. The language of criminal justice is weighted toward the responsibility of persons in their violation of the rights of other persons. The destruction of property, from vandalism to sabotage and arson, may be criminal too, but violence against property, objectionable though it may be, just doesn't have the same moral force, in our eyes, as violence against persons. In criminal law, the injured parties in cases of violence against property are first of all the owners of the properties—more persons. And yet in terrorist acts it may well be that this 'property'—though 'property' is an inadequate term for what is in question here—is what is most at issue. Or, to be more precise, what may be most at issue is the connection between persons and the arrangement of the things that make up their material world. In the iconoclastic violence arising at Saint Médard—or from another point of view, the acoustic violence of Catholics against Protestant worshippers—the scenes of material life were under attack, scenes that were holy, but no less material for all that. (I think of this 'holiness' as a structure of demarcation, the sacred from the profane, following Durkheim.[77]) The holiness of a house of worship is just such a combination of the material and the meaningful as any logic of a scene must imply. Scenes can be fragile, first of all because things are fragile, but second of all because the connection between people and the meaning of their material world is fragile. Attack that material world—not just the commodities in it, but the structures of material life—with or without actually attacking the people attached to it, and you attack both security and certainty.

In the attack primarily against persons that came to be called the 'massacre', the victimization of innocents was of course the most heinous of the consequences. And yet the barbarous indifference to rules of proportion exemplified in most attacks called massacres, and the numerically massive character of most massacres worthy of the name, had this second, supplementary significance. Not just persons, but social order was under attack. Not just the right to live, but the right to live in a time and space of civility, security, opportunity, and significance was subject to destruction.

---

[77] Durkheim, *The Elementary Forms.*

In fantasias like *Gorboduc* an imaginary of just such a destruction is let loose. A massacre to come threatens the scene of 'Britain land' if division is not overcome. In the fantasia of Ronsard's *Discours*, that massacre has already come, although Ronsard diverts attention from the actual victims of religious violence to the motherland, France. The apologetic memoirs by Gerard and Tesimond explicate the logic behind massacres anticipated or experienced, a scenic nihilism, where everything must be destroyed so that something else might live. But responses to Saint Bartholomew show how difficult it really is to see an actual massacre, to narrate its events and come to terms with its ghastliness. All of early modern society was in principle governed by moral, political, and religious structures which were immanent in the time and space of material life. The Massacre was too great a violation for most writers for any recovery to be made from the Massacre's effects. A trauma without meaning, an attack not just on persons but on the structure of civil life, the Massacre could only with great difficulty be spoken about, narrated, and explained. Usually what was really traumatic about the event was left unspoken. Among accomplished literary figures perhaps only d'Aubigné succeeded in looking the holocaust in the eye and getting a meaning out of it, but only at the cost of accepting the deaths of thousands as the will of God, and only, by the same token, at the cost of changing the scene, subordinating what was known about the past to what was hoped for from the future.

5

Agency

1. THE SEMIOTIC CIRCUIT

In 1554 Matteo Bandello published his first edition of the *Novelle*, including in it a story called 'Maometto imperador de' Turchi crudelmente ammazza una sua donna'. This was then translated, with some liberty, and without a title, by Pierre Boistaurau for the first edition of his and Belleforest's *Histoires Tragiques* (1559); it was then translated anew, more faithfully to the Italian, in William Painter's first edition of *The Palace of Pleasure* (1566), as 'Mahomet one of the Turkish Emperours, executeth curssed crueltie upon a Greeke maiden, whom he tooke prisoner, at the wynning of Constantinople.'[1] Mehmed II (1432–81) reigned from 1444 to 1446 and then again from 1451 to 1481, and the conquest of Constantinople, at the age of 21, was his most famous exploit. Legends about this ruler circulated throughout both France and Britain in the sixteenth and seventeenth centuries, many of them about his cruelty, and many of them also, at the same time, about his weakness for women. *Othello* has been said to owe something to legends about the Turkish leader.[2] The story, which I will discuss here in Painter's translation, was especially stark in its political logic: it was a pointed parable of power, and a brutal illustration of the agency of terrorism before the letter.

The woman in this story is a Greek slave named Irene. As soon as he acquires her, the young emperor Mahomet is love struck. 'He conceived none other delight, but to play and dally with her, in such sort, that his spirits being in love's full possession, love dealt him so cruelly that he could take no rest day nor night.' Three years go by with Mahomet possessed by 'this amorous passion'. But as a result, the narrator asserts, Mahomet neglects his public duties. A 'confusion and disorder' comes, an 'ill government', and the people begin to 'grudge'. The Janissaries begin to express dismay, 'complaining how he consumed his life, like an effeminate person, without inferring or doing any profit to the Empire'. In fact, something of what the narrator calls a 'sedition' brews. 'Every man in particular, and all in general, conspired against him, with one determinate mind, to yield no more

---

[1] Bandello, Novella X, in *Tutto le opera*: 1.128–36; Boaistuau, Histoire seconde ('Mahomet'), in *Histoire tragiques*, ed. Carr: 49–60; Painter, 'The Fortyeth Novell', in *Palace of Pleasure*: 3.190–7. Some important observations about the Boistauau translation are made in Carr, *Pierre Boaistuau's 'Histoires Tragiques'*: 49–58. This story was later included, almost unchanged from Painter's version, in Richard Knolle's *General Historie of the Turkes* (1603): 350–3. The story was also made into a short epic or epyllion by William Barksted, *Hiren: Or the Faire Greek* (1611), and possibly a play performed in London in 1594, possibly written by George Peele (www.lostplays.org/index.php/Mahomet [19 December 2011]).

[2] See Chew, *The Crescent and the Rose*; and Vitkus, *Turning Turk*.

obedience unto him in time to come, and purposed to choose some Emperor that were more martial and warlike…'

I dwell on some of the details here, and the precise language of the story, because it renders the picture of a political structure which, though ascribed to the Ottoman Empire, is really a common backdrop to Europe's own terrorism before the letter. A monarch minding his own business instead of the state's—his privacy rendered here in terms of an 'effeminate' devotion to the pleasures of love—is considered a threat to the body politic. He is no self-assured and vicious Holofernes or Fengon, this Mahomet, but rather a picture of distracted passivity; his very lack of energy and forcefulness comes to be considered something of a danger, and even something like tyranny, warranting 'sedition'. In fact, Mahomet's weakness at this point in his life anticipates what would be thought and said by detractors about a succession of monarchs to come—Francis II, Charles IX, and Henry III in France, Elizabeth in England, Mary in Scotland. Not their strength but their apparent weakness would make people discontented. In the face of that discontent we know that Charles IX, Henry III, Elizabeth, and Mary would all at one time or another resort to desperate measures—the state terror of assassinations, judicial executions, and even (with Charles IX) a massacre.

In the case of Mahomet, the discontent gets reported to him by his most trusted adviser, who adds to the report a lecture on governance. 'Not only your soldiers, and the rest of your popular people, but the most faithful lords of your empire so murmur, conspire, and conjure against you', the adviser says. 'Your own self hath given over your self, to be a spoil and prey to a simple woman.' The adviser reminds Mahomet of the military glory of his ancestors, and cautions him about the vigilance needed to preserve a state. Among Mahomet's worries, the adviser says, is the danger posed by the Christians of western Europe, who are looking for a chance to capitalize on disarray among the Ottomans and 'despoil' the Turkish Empire. So the adviser exhorts the emperor to leave aside his effeminate ways, and go back into battle to conquer more lands, even if he must take his Greek slave woman Irene along with him. Above all, he says, 'Be now then a conqueror of yourself.' Mahomet thinks about it, and tells his adviser that in a day he 'will let it be known to thee and to other, what puissance and power I have over myself'.

Mahomet orders a banquet, for which he has Irene dress up in her finest clothes, and calls all his nobles into his and her presence. After the meal he rises and leads his mistress and the nobles into a great hall, and, with his mistress by his side, addresses the assembly. He shows them what a prize this woman is. He says he knows that people have spoken mutinously because of his devotion to her, but asks who among them would do differently than he and give her up. The nobles are 'rapt with an incredible admiration, to see so fair a thing', and concede the emperor his point. 'Well, now then', the emperor says, 'I will make you to understand, that there is no earthly thing that can bind up, or captivate my senses so much, but that from hence forth I will follow mine ancestors…' At that, Mahomet grabs Irene by the hair. Drawing his scimitar, he strikes a blow and cuts off her head, 'to the great terror of them all'. 'Now you know', says Mahomet, 'whether your emperor is able to repress and bridle his affections or not.'

LIVERPOOL JOHN MOORES UNIVERSITY LEARNING SERVICES

This anecdote represents the workings of the message of terror at its purest. There is a sender, Mahomet; there is a receiver, the nobility of Turkey, all gathered together in one hall; and there is a message, the beheading of Irene. That the killing of Irene has a symbolic resonance over and above the primary message of Mahomet to his elite, since 'Irene' after all means 'peace', is worth keeping in mind. There is more than one kind of meaning in this story, and more than one line of communication. But first of all, there is a sender, a receiver, and a message. Mahomet says something to the nobility by brutally killing his mistress. The message received, the nobility is terrorized. It is made to understand something it had not been made to understand before, and made to recognize it by a perfectly expressive and unequivocal gesture, which at once kills, horrifies, and articulates, answering a question that is on everybody's mind. 'Now you know', says Mahomet, in a supplementary comment. The nobles of the empire afterwards rallied to Mahomet's side, and went on to conquer fresh territories.

In other cases of terrorism before the letter the business of sending a message was not so facile. The question to which Mahomet's statement of violence came as an answer was not always so plainly understood. The sender of the message was not always a single individual, or the individual so uniquely and publicly in a position to act. The message itself could be ambiguously addressed or received. Messages commonly required a process of disambiguation after being sent, and even then things were not always so clear. The audience for the message was not often so homogenous, or otherwise so uniquely entitled to receive what was being said. Nor was it usually so uniquely gathered, all in one place, everyone seeing the same thing, at the same time, in the same circumstances. The story of Mahomet and Irene, which does not seem to have had much factual basis, apart from Mehmed's having married a Greek woman, involves a fantasy of the power of terror. It involves what Burke calls a 'mysticism of means', an action where means are revered as if they were ends in themselves, and getting the method right is esteemed as if it were the same thing as accomplishing one's objectives.[3] This killing in itself, in its methodology, accomplishes a kind of sacrificial transcendence. Moreover, the story involves the achievement of transcendence in a closed circuit of semiosis, with its agent rightly motivated and privileged, its message full and clear, and its audience already complete and ready to receive the message—all eyes and ears—at the precise moment of the message's being sent. The letter has found its addressee, and the addressee has recognized at once what the letter symbolically, and hence really, conveys.

The fantasy of the power of terror—often shared both by advocates of terror and its detractors in the early modern period—is the fantasy, in the face of all the obvious shortcomings and ambiguities of violence, of just such a closed circuit of communication. It is a fantasy according to which violence speaks, and speaks clearly and unmistakably to the recipients for whom it is intended, and in which the recipients of the message of violence know, immediately, exactly what it says. In other words, a demand for recognition is repaid—by recognition. Advocates of

---

[3] Burke, *Grammar of Motives*: 309–11.

tyrannicide and iconoclasm alike were commonly devoted to such a fantasy. Whether it was a priest defending Jacques Clément's deadly adventure at Saint Cloud, a monarchomach advocating the right of the people to violently depose a tyrant, a poetaster celebrating the murder of the Duke of Buckingham, or a messenger praising Samson's destruction of a temple, the ruling fantasy was the same: the letter of violence always finds its recipient, and the recipient always recognizes what it has to say.

And yet even the most important legends of terror, though they too imagined terror operating in a closed semiotic circuit, often spoke of a more complex situation. The Judith story involved a series of messages: first, the message sent to the Assyrian soldiers, when they discovered the beheaded body of Holofernes; second, the message sent to the Bethulians, when Judith showed them the head of Holofernes; then, a speech by Judith to the Bethulians, a supplementary message explaining the significance of what she had done; and finally, the message sent a second time to the Assyrian soldiers, when the head of Holofernes is nailed to the parapet, and they are terrorized again and routed. Four messages are involved. They seem to work together seamlessly: that is another fantasy. But they are four messages, not one. And as at least Du Bartas goes on to show, those four messages then get supplemented by a fifth, the disambiguating message of the abuse of the corpse of Holofernes by civilians. So one message unfolds into another. Renaissance paintings of the story of Judith usually concentrated on the decisive moment of the beheading, and as we have seen again and again, in paradigmatic dramas of terror like this one, it is the act itself—the passage into violence—that is meant to convey, in itself and by itself, the momentous message of terror. It is almost a tautology: the act is momentous, and the momentousness of the meaning of the act, its terror, is fixed into the violence of the act. Yet the meaning also unfolds; the act sets in motion a chain of meanings. So there is both complexity and simplicity. On the one hand, the Judith story imagines the message of terror as a chain of signifiers and significations. On the other, it imagines all of the meanings to unfold in a single chain, contained within a single frame of semiotic circuitry, where the end result of the violence is perpetual peace: 'No one ever again spread terror among the Israelites during the lifetime of Judith, or for a long time after her death.'[4]

The story of Amleth is similarly contained in a closed circuit, but its situation is more complex. In fact, it threatens to get out of hand, and the supplement of what Belleforest calls the 'Harangue d'Amleth aux Danois' is necessary to finish the message. There are at least six steps in the process: first, the killing of the Danish grandees and the destruction of the palace by arson; second, the killing of Fengon; third, the speech of Amleth to the corpse and departing spirit of Fengon; fourth, the gathering of the Danish people at the site of the holocaust; fifth, Amleth's 'Harangue' to the Danish people, where he explains what he has done and why; and sixth, the dismembering and burning of Fengon's corpse. Amleth's speech is initially greeted with scepticism, but eventually Amleth prevails. An incident of somewhat ambiguous circumstances, brought about by a breech in social order

---

[4] *Judith*: 16.25.

and its law of meaning, is clarified by a double act of terror, of mass destruction coupled with a pointed assassination, and then clarified anew through speech and ceremony. So disambiguated is the speech that the very nobility whom Amleth has apparently destroyed overnight reappear in their guise as civic leaders to ratify Amleth's behaviour and elect him as the next king. The very fragmentation of the kingdom that Fengon's reign seems to have signified is entirely repaired.

2. INSTRUMENTALITY

Agency refers to the instrumentality of actions, and must inevitably refer to instruments as well: scimitars, daggers, pikes, swords, arquebuses, gunpowder kegs, or even, as for Amleth when he burns down the palace at Elsinore, carpets and torches. The full story of terrorism before the letter would have to include an account of the technology of violence available to the violent. It would also have to include therefore technologies of social formation, through which violence can either be prevented or exploited. But these technologies were not unique to the agency of terrorism; they were essential to plain murder, to honour killing, to insurrection and war. Unique to this agency was instead the way certain kinds of violence were understood to signify, and the way signification was supposed to be communicated through the society and its political system. The blow of the scimitar had to be exacted in a specific communicative situation, where the blow did not just harm a victim but also *meant*, where a symbolic exchange was transacted and a suitable audience was present to witness, understand, and consent to what was meant. A woman was brutally killed; but a man was restored, immediately, without question or objection, to absolute authority.

Looking to the 'semiotic circuit', we call attention to the difference between fantasy and reality—and see that in many cases of terrorism before the letter, the fantasy prevails. Violence will signify utterly. Such is the case in Bandello's story of Mahomet and Irene. But in many cases it is recognized that violence is only one signification in a sequence of significations, many of which follow paths of their own. Shakespeare's assassins not only parade through the streets with hands smeared with Caesar's blood; and not only declare 'liberty' to the people of the city. They also have to have their leader Brutus give a speech. And the speech fails. It fails because, although the violence has apparently succeeded in accomplishing the goals that had been set for it, and said what it had to say, the speech through which it was to be re-communicated was spoken in a public forum, where counter-voices could be heard, and Brutus's cold logic was no match for Antony's crowd-pleasing passion.

Here is another complicated case, the murder of David Riccio in 1566.[5] Riccio was an Italian musician and courtier who had won the Scottish Queen Mary's favour, and was acting as her secretary and *valet de chambre*. In the wider scheme of

[5] Some of the material from the next few pages on Riccio and message-sending reappears in Appelbaum, 'Shakespeare and Terrorism'.

things he was not a terribly important figure, but the queen's consort Henry Stewart Lord Darnley and his allies Patrick Ruthven Lord Ruthven and James Stewart Earl of Moray were vexed by his rise to power and stymied in some of their own political ambitions, and so they decided to make a scapegoat of the Italian. On a winter's night, as a pregnant Mary sat at dinner with her intimates, including Riccio and a serving lady, rushing into the room came the Lords Darnley and Ruthven, followed by armed soldiers sent by Moray. They threatened Riccio and then killed him with over fifty stab wounds, throwing his body out of the room and down the stairs. Narrating the incident, George Buchanan then has Lord Ruthven deliver a speech to the queen, as she tries to flee the scene in fright:

> That in managing the affairs of the kingdom, she [sh]ould rather consult the nobility, who had a concern in the public, than vagrant rascals, who could give no pledge for their faithfulness, and who had nothing to lose, either in estate or credit; neither was the fact, then committed, without a precedent: That Scotland was a kingdom bounded by laws, and was never wont to be governed by the will and pleasure of one man, but by the rule of the law, and the consent of the nobility; and if any former king had done otherwise, he had smarted severely for it: Neither were the Scots at present so far degenerated from their ancestors, as to bear not only the government, but even the servitude of a stranger, who was scarce worthy to be their slave.[6]

Buchanan reports this speech approvingly. It is an expression of resistance theory, as Buchanan had developed it in *De juris regne apud scotus*. If a head of state should rule the country without the consent of the nobility or other magistrates in parliament, and violate the rule of law, he ought to 'smart' for it, and at a minimum be deposed and replaced. This is the meta-theory of law, the law of laws, where violence is exceptional, foundational, and expressive; and where to boot—this being an important part of Buchanan's development of the theory—it is also *traditional*, or in other words *constitutional*: 'neither was the fact, then committed, without precedent'.

But though the murder of Riccio, as Buchanan represents it, is all the things it is supposed to be—an exceptional act which is politically foundational, expressive, and constitutional—it is also appallingly inadequate, on each and every count. That the act was horrifying, there is no doubt; the act was a complete violation of the rule of law and was possibly unprecedented, an innocent foreign courtier being murdered in cold blood in the presence of the sovereign, inside the sovereign's private chambers, without the sovereign's consent. This too was a case of violence against the scene, the very scene of sovereignty, and the result is terror, a destruction of life, law, and custom in the name of a rule of fear. But still, Ruthven had to explain himself. And his explanation simply does not add up; as for one thing, and Buchanan himself is aware of this, though Riccio may have acquired a measure of

---

[6] Buchanan, *History of Scotland*: 2. 181–3. This material is also included, in a modern translation with textual commentary and background information, in Buchanan, *The Tyrannous Reign*. Buchanan's version, the only one that makes Ruthven deliver a theoretical disquisition to the queen, may be compared to the versions of Ruthven's words to the queen in Ruthven, *A Relation of the Death*; and Mary Stuart, *Letters* 1: 345. A rather different version of the story is given in Fraser, *Mary Queen of Scots*: 301–20.

power and influence at court due to Mary's patronage, he was by no means either a head of state or a tyrant, and was not in a position to promote himself as either one or the other.

Nor does the speech about constitutional precedent seal the deal. After communicating the meaning of the murder to the terrified queen, according to Buchanan, Ruthven and his men, with the participation of Darnley, tried to manage the situation. In the immediate aftermath of the violence, the town of Edinburgh rose in alarm, armed militia men and grandees and their retainers taking to the streets. Buchanan shows Darnley the uncrowned king trying to pacify the populace by reassuring language, which included his taking responsibility for the murder:

> In the meantime, the news was carried all over the town, and as every one's disposition was, right or wrong, they took arms, and went to the palace. There the king showed himself to them out of a window, and told the multitude, that he and the queen were safe, and there was no cause for their tumultuous assembly; what was done was by his command, and what that was, they should know in time, and therefore, at present, every one should go to his own house...

The message went on; the 'news' went on, percolating through an armed populace; and Darnley tried to contain it, tried to keep it in its circuit by supplementing it with the announcement of his sovereign command.

But neither Ruthven nor Darnley succeeded. The queen had her own supporters, and her own gestures of resistance to make. Her followers (rivals to the Stewart-Ruthven faction) took control of the situation in the following days. Ruthven and others were charged with treason and were forced to flee; some of the lower-ranked conspirators, under arrest, were condemned and executed; and the rest of the conspirators were either banished or condemned in absentia. The circuit broke and no one was able to repair it.

And in the breaking of the circuit we see both the hopefulness and the hollowness of the fantasy of the power that could be invested in terrorist violence. Failure in this particular instance was tactical; the conspirators overestimated their support in the city and the nation. But the failure was more than tactical. If the conspirators overestimated their support, they also overestimated the power of the message they were sending. We cannot know exactly what the Scottish conspirators were thinking. Historians are generally of the opinion that Moray and Ruthven were acting out of self-interest, and Darnley out of confusion and resentment; that they were attempting to disrupt the political system to protect themselves against parliamentary procedures and exert influence over the queen.[7] Historians do not agree with Buchanan that the conspirators were acting out of scruple for the sanctity of the Scottish constitution. But Buchanan was writing a parable about the murder of Riccio. In this parable there was a message to send, however faulty, however many detours the message had to take, and however poorly it was ultimately received. This message, beginning with its signal act of violence, was supposed to change the balance of power in Scotland; that was to be the end of it. And perhaps

---

[7] See 'David Riccio': *Oxford Dictionary of National Biography*.

in real life Moray, Ruthven, and Darnley also believed in the premises of the parable that would be told about them, thinking that whatever was troubling about the government of the nation would be put paid by murder, and that a single act of violence would send so powerful and clear a message that the queen and the rest of the nation would be intimidated into bending to their wills.

Let us then think, with regard to this and all the other cases of terrorism before the letter, about the nature and power of this kind of message and the agency it was supposed to involve. And let us focus on the two most essential features of these messages and their agencies: first, that they were violent and, second, that they were political; or, to be more precise, first, that they involved a resort to a violence of symbolic exchange, and second, that they were intended to alter the balance of power in their society.

3. SYMBOLIC EXCHANGE

Violence is the sine qua non of terrorism before the letter; if there is no violence, or no earnest threat of violence, there is no terrorism. By violence in this context we must mean physical force, applied in the course of an act of aggression. And we must also mean that the use of physical force may result in injury, captivity, or death. One can conceive of a terrorist incident where injury, captivity, or death is not an outcome, or not an intended outcome, or where even the use of physical force is avoided as much as possible; but the possibility of wound or destruction must always lie within the horizon of the recourse to force in cases of terrorism before the letter. When the Huguenots at Amboise conspired against the Guises and the king, during the infamous 'Tumult of Amboise' of 1560, their intent was to abduct or in their own minds to 'free' the king, and to kill anyone who tried to prevent them. Homicide was to be a means to an end rather than the end itself. The main *objective* of the action, taking the young king captive (or liberating him from the Guises), was not the *target* of homicidal violence. And yet homicide was not *incidental* to the achievement of their ends, as far as most surviving reports are concerned. The possibility, the threat, and even the likelihood of homicide was essential. There could be no kidnapping and, subsequent to the kidnapping, no extortion or liberation without an earnest and plausible threat of homicide.[8] The case was nearly identical in the incident of the assassination of David Riccio, undertaken so that the Darnley and his allies could take repossession of the queen and extort the parliament to bend to their will—or rather to 'free' the heads of state from foreign influence and parliamentary troublemakers. Some of the targeting of James VI and I, when he was still in Scotland and still only James VI, may have been of this nature, from his kidnapping during the Ruthven Raid of 1583 to the abortive Gowrie Conspiracy, orchestrated by the sons of William Ruthven, in 1600.[9]

---

[8] The documents pertinent to the conspiracy are collected in *Archives Curieuses*: 1er série, 4. Also see Chapter 2, section 4 of this volume.

[9] See the much disputed document, published with James's approval and attributed to him as author: James I, King of England, *The Earle of Gowries Conspiracy*. What really happened will probably

Violence in this sense, then, is the essential agency of terrorism before the letter. It is what is required for terrorism to take place. Violence is itself, to that extent, the terror. But the violence must also be an act of symbolic exchange. The real violence of terrorism is always also symbolic violence. The concept may, like a few other phenomena related to terrorism, seem to violate common sense, but such is the agency of terrorism before the letter: an act of violence marks a change in the condition of the agent, the victim, and one or more publics by forcing upon the victim an act of symbolic exchange. I harm the victim, or assert the power to do so, and in exchange for this harm or threat of harm, I (and the people on behalf of whom I act) receive a symbolic return. Terrorism isn't terrible unless it involves a genuine threat to life and limb; but terrorism isn't terrorism, at least terrorism before the letter is not so, unless the violence is intended as a sacrifice or some other form of symbolic exchange.

The concept of symbolic exchange immediately brings to mind the work of Jean Baudrillard, who devoted a monograph to the subject, but it has roots in the anthropology of Marcel Mauss, Claude Lévi-Strauss, and the economic thought of George Bataille, and a variation of it may be found in the performativity studies of Victor Turner and Richard Shechner.[10] The idea develops as a working backward from capitalism and Marx's notion of 'exchange value' and 'use value' to earlier and more widespread forms of exchange where economic value is subordinated to other forms of value: power and prestige, for example. Social transactions, whether between equals or unequals, or between friends or strangers, may be undertaken where giving and receiving, or taking and relinquishing, are involved, and expenditure outweighs economic utility. The giving of an engagement ring is a form of symbolic exchange, not because the gold band does not have a use value or an exchange value, but because the real value of the ring is not economic. It signifies a pledge. And as the giving or receiving of a ring can have an important symbolic value, so can the taking or the relinquishing of something, including a life, or an icon in a temple. We may believe—and certainly in the case of terrorist violence we have seen—that symbolic exchanges are not always self-sufficient. If they may take place within a closed circuit of semiosis, the circuit can be broken at any time, and meanings invalidated. They may need to be endlessly supplemented with additional messages, and perhaps even additional symbolic exchanges. But the primary act, the foundational resort to violence, will need already to have contained a specific and commonly recognized meaning, where one thing has been accomplished to accomplish something else, whose benefits are supposed to redound upon the accomplisher. Or to put it more precisely, when the primary act comes, and makes its way into what I have called the dialectic of recognition, it will have done so because it is believed by at least one party to the act that a symbolic exchange has

never be known, but this official narrative depicts the conspiracy as an attempt either to kidnap James or to kill him. It leaves unclear whether the Ruthvens's motives were political, personal, or some combination of the two. Another interesting contemporary account is included in Univoccatholicus, *Lucta Jacobi*.

[10] Baudrillard, *Symbolic Exchange and Death*; Schechner, *Performance Theory*; Turner, *The Anthropology of Performance*. Additional references follow below.

occurred. At least one party, I say, for not all symbolic exchanges are effective—gifts can be refused, and the meaning of gifts go unacknowledged. On the one hand, the symbolic exchange is the decisive signal: something has happened; 'now you know'. On the other, the symbolic exchange may in itself be controversial or inadequate: you think that something has happened, but it hasn't, and we don't really 'know' what you think we ought to know: you thought you were exchanging one thing for another, but all you did was expend an energy whose power we cannot accept and whose effects we cannot respect.

The best known of the forms of symbolically valuable violence, and probably the best understood, is the sacrifice, where a being is killed or injured as an offering to a higher power. Early moderns were fascinated by the idea of sacrifice: pagan, Hebrew, Christian, and secular.[11] A word search in the database Early English Books Online, out of a partial sample of texts published between 1473 and 1700, yields nearly 10,000 results for the word 'sacrifice'. Three of Shakespeare's plays feature sacrifice as a central issue—*Julius Caesar*, as have seen, as well as *Titus Andronicus* and *The Merchant of Venice*. Sacrifices do not often end well in Shakespeare, but they signify a logic of action where violence is meant to adjudicate a conflict, and restore the rule of law or even, as in *Titus*, 'appease' the shadows of the dead.[12] Early moderns would read about sacrifices in both ancient texts—Plutarch's *Parallel Lives*, for example, mentions sacrifices and sacrificing about 300 times—and in the Old Testament, where sacrifice is discussed as early as the stories of Cain and Abel and of Abraham and Isaac and where Leviticus spells out four different kinds of sacrifice to God: the gift offering (also known as the 'whole burnt of-fering', in Greek the *holókaustos*); the peace offering, including the offering of a 'thanksgiving'; the sin offering; and the guilt offering.[13] In the New Testament they would have read about the sacrifice of Christ and the concept of self-sacrifice. They would have read too, in Romans 12.1, about the 'living sacrifice': 'present your bodies', wrote Paul, 'a living sacrifice, holy, acceptable unto God, which is your reasonable service'. In *The Golden Legend*, Saint Paul is praised for having himself been a living sacrifice, and for having accomplished the salvation of the human world as a result. 'Paul sacrificed himself every day', says the legend, 'and offered double sacrifice in heart and in body, which he mortified. He offered not sheep ne meat, but he sacrificed himself in double wise, and yet that sufficed him not, but he studied to offer to God, all the world.'[14]

In the literature of terrorism before the letter, the concept of the sacrifice fre-quently appears in an overt form, but in a double guise, for the word could have both positive and negative connotations, and could be used to designate both legitimate and illegitimate violence. Moreover, it could indicate either that a sacrifice

---

[11] For general background, see Shuger, *The Renaissance Bible*.

[12] Shakespeare, *Titus* 1.1.

[13] Kraus, *Worship in Israel*: 112–24; Douglas, *Leviticus as Literature: passim*. A complication of the anthropological reading of sacrifice in ancient Judaism comes in Levenson, *Death and Resurrection*, who believes that literal child sacrifice was an ancient practice.

[14] 'Life of S. Paul the Apostle and Doctor', in Voragine, *The Golden Legend*: <http://www.fordham.edu/halsall/basis/goldenlegend/GoldenLegend-Volume4.asp#Paul%20the%20Apostle>. The idea of 'sacrifice' is repeated many times, both in pagan and Christian contexts, in *The Golden Legend*.

has taken place *in spite* of the intentions of the perpetrators or else that a sacrifice has been attempted in circumstances where such a symbolic exchange was neither called for nor ever really possible to achieve. In one set of cases, when someone has been martyred, or has martyred himself or herself in a political cause, then a sacrifice is said to have taken place. Sacrifice is then either a wrongful yet valuable victimization (a good person has been harmed by the bad, on behalf of the good) or a rightful self-victimization (a good person has harmed himself or herself for the sake of the good). Thus Henry the third Duke of Guise, having been assassinated at Blois on the orders of the king, is said by a supporter to have gone to his death as to 'la sacrifice de son sang qu'il voue à dieu pour la liberté du peuple' (the sacrifice of his blood which he devotes to God for the liberty of the people).[15] A victim of terrorist violence, Guise has sacrificed himself—for the cause *against which* the terrorist act was committed. Meanwhile, Jacques Clément, who would go on a few months later to kill Guise's killer, Henry III, is said by a supporter to have been willing to 'exposer sa vie librement à la mort, pour l'honneur de Dieu et conservation de la foy Catholique' (to freely expose his life to death, for the honour of God and the conservation of the Catholic faith). In fact, the monk was 'instantly martyred' after stabbing the king.[16] So when a terrorist act involves a martyrdom, it involves either the wrongful killing of man who was willing to die for a righteous cause or a rightful 'sacrifice' in the sense of a 'self-sacrifice' performed on behalf of a righteous cause. We have already seen a Protestant, John Felton, make a claim exemplifying this idea. A note was sewn into Felton's hat which said, 'That man is cowardly and base and deserveth not the name of a gentleman or Soldier that is not willing to sacrifice his life for the honour of his God his King and his Country.'[17]

In the first set of cases, then, a sacrifice is said to have taken place when a good cause has been expressed, witnessed, or confirmed by the loss of a good person's life. There is a grievous loss, but the loss ratifies something good. In second set of cases, however, a sacrifice is said not so much to have taken place as to have been *attempted* when a terrorist's plan has meant to achieve a symbolically valuable work of violence but did so under false pretences, such that innocent people have been targeted for death and nothing of value could ever have come of it. This alternative use of the word 'sacrifice' is either partly or completely pejorative. In 1598, Maurice of Nassau, the son of the late William of Orange, was like his father targeted for assassination. The attempt failed, but the culprit, one Pierre Panne d'Ypre, then testified (according to one angry account) that he was put up to it by the Jesuits at Douai, who told him that it would be a 'pious and worthy work, indeed a great sacrifice before God, and meriting paradise, to put to death such a man' as Nassau, a 'devourer of thousands of souls'.[18] Here the word 'sacrifice' is ambiguous, partly praiseworthy and partly blameworthy, because the offering involved could be either Panne d'Ypre the culprit or Maurice of Nassau the victim. The author, putting words into Panne d'Ypre's mouth, seems to have deliberately confused the

---

[15] Matthieu, *La Guisiade*: 153.
[16] *Portrait et histoire au vrai*, in L'Estoile, *Les Belles figures*, n.p.
[17] *Poems and Songs*: xxi.   [18] Nassau, *La conspiration*: 719.

issue; but in either case, as far as the author is concerned, simply to think of this murder as some sort of sacrifice is wrong. The author assumes that he and the reader agree that to kill a man is wrong, and to kill for the sake of going to heaven is a sacrilegious outrage.[19] An unambiguous example is given in Dekker's *Whore of Babylon*. The figure based on William Parry states that he is planning to kill Queen Elizabeth in Saint James Park, which he maliciously calls Saint Iago Park. A 'rare, rare altar!', he calls it, 'The fitt'st to sacrifice her blood upon.'[20] In this case, the fate of the killer is a matter of indifference; but the killing of the monarch is openly a sacrifice after the Roman or Hebraic fashion, and obviously objectionable. In Ben Jonson's *Catiline*, the malicious conspirators make plans for a mass murder:

CATILINE.   It must be fire or nothing.
LONGINUS.   What else should fright or terrify 'em?
VARGUNTEIUS.   True.
In that confusion must be the chief slaughter.
CURIUS.   Then we shall kill 'em bravest.
CEPARIUS.   And in heaps.
AUTRONIUS.   Strew sacrifices.
CURIUS.   Make the earth an altar.[21]

A similar comparison of a conspiracy to murder with a sacrifice is made in Corneille's *Cinna*. The title character recounts what he said to a gathering of conspirators:

> The moment is propitious. Let us strike.
> Tomorrow on the Capitol he makes
> A sacrifice. Let that be *him*, and there
> Let us before the gods see justice done.[22]

The essential difference between pre-Christian and Christian notions of sacrifice was well known.[23] Pre-Christian, a victim was chosen and slaughtered or otherwise harmed on an altar, which might then be an 'offering' entirely to God or an offering to the community, which shared in the consumption or other uses of the victim. With Christ came 'self-sacrifice'. Communion among Catholics and the Lord's Supper among Protestants reiterated the exploitation of the victim by the community in front of God, but the victim in this case was the self-sacrificed Christ. For all those who followed Christ in this, to sacrifice a victim was wrong, but to sacrifice oneself might be right. In praising the would-be assassin Jean Chastel, who tried to kill the 'heretic' King Henry IV in 1595, the priest Jean Boucher

[19] Among many similar statements about outrages of this kind, I have found a statement by Sir Francis Bacon in a letter on colonization in the New World to be particularly interesting. Bacon advises his correspondent, 'To make no extirpation of the natives under pretence of planting religion: God surely will no way be pleased with such sacrifices.' Bacon, *Advice to Sir George Villiers*: 386.
[20] Dekker, *Whore of Babylon*: 5.1.65–6.   [21] Jonson, *Catiline*: 3.3.131–5.
[22] Corneille, *Cinna*, trans. Cairncross: 1.3.229–32.
[23] Strenski, *Contesting Sacrifice*.

approvingly quoted from John 15.14 the words of Christ: 'No one has greater love than this, to lay down one's life for one's friends.'[24]

So if one sacrificed oneself, as when an assassin exposed his or her life to mortal danger, one might be a praiseworthy terrorist. (This was an underhanded displacement of the issue, of course: the victimizer announces himself as the victim.) But if one sacrificed another person, if one deliberately killed without a notion of self-sacrifice attached to it, the practice was archaic and very likely misguided and wrong. Yet there were plenty of instances, both in fiction and in real life, where violent people have thought that in killing another person they were making something like a valid sacrifice before God or country. Mahomet kills Irene. Henry III kills the Duke of Guise. In the first case, something valuable to Mahomet is given up; a sacrifice in the common sense of relinquishing something held dear is accomplished, brutally, and 'now you know'. In the second case, an impediment to Henry III is given up, but apparently given up in the same spirit. The Duke of Guise, Henry's companion since childhood, is killed collectively, openly. And all accounts have Henry saying something afterwards to the effect that now he is really the king since he has eliminated his lifelong counterpart. Not just an inconvenience but a genuine victim, and offering, has been given up, although in this case not to God but to the people of France.

Sacrifice was not the only form of violent symbolic exchange that terrorism before the letter performed. Similar to sacrifice was scapegoating, where a victim bore away the guilt of others, and was condemned to violent punishment as its reward.[25] And there are perhaps a few other forms of symbolic exchange which played a part in terrorism before the letter, which may or may not be subsumable under the categories of the sacrifice or scapegoating:

Liberation.
Hostage-taking.
Retribution.
Eradication.
Purification.
Exemplification.

These forms of symbolically valuable violence are perhaps merely variations or subcategories of sacrificing and scapegoating; in any case, they are not mutually exclusive. The killing of David Riccio, I have claimed, was a scapegoating (having an individual take the blame for a corporate misdeed by being harmed), but it also had features of purification and exemplification. Killing Riccio put a form of blame on Riccio, and banished the evil with him, but it also served as a step toward

---

[24] Boucher, *Apologie pour Jehan Chastel*: 61.

[25] In Leviticus, especially chapter 16, scapegoating is both differentiated from the sacrificial offering and coupled with it, as a complementary rite; and it is made clear that the scapegoat is not only being sent away with the sins of the people on its head but also being driven, like a sacrificial victim, to a gruesome death. In *The Scapegoat*, Girard continuously assimilates the scapegoat to the sacrificial victim, but this misses, in my opinion, an important nuance. This omission helps confirm Girard's own theory of sacrifice and scapegoating, however, where the sacrifice of Christ becomes a semiotic solution to a perennial problem of human history.

purifying the court of foreign, Catholic influence and of setting an example to the queen and the people of Scotland. The killing of Gaspard de Coligny was predominantly a sacrifice (an offering of a victim for a higher good) but all the other elements listed above probably formed a part of the meaning of the killing as well, including liberation (freeing Paris from the clutches of the Huguenots) and vengeful retribution. Even prisoner-taking was involved. Part of the myth of the killing of Coligny was that he was beheaded and that his head made the rounds of Paris, ultimately to become a trophy exhibited in Rome. The hostage who cannot be returned, who has been taken forever, who has been made into a trophy for his enemies to crow over, is a theme of literature going back to both the Greek epic and the Bible. As for the killing of Henry III, though his murder was apparently sacrificial, it was also a purification, ridding Paris and the nation of what his detractors considered an abominable pollution.

What all of these acts of symbolically valuable violence have in common is that by way of victimization they are supposed to accomplish an act that transcends mere utility. It may be very useful to murder a valet, an admiral or a king. What that person might have accomplished will no longer be accomplished—at least by that person. What that person possessed in terms of wealth, dignity, trust, or power that person will no longer possess, and may be seized by others more deserving of them. Taking a person hostage may be useful in a similar way. So may destroying a building or an icon. It may be strategically advantageous to eliminate them. In fact, by the logic of terrorist action it may be thought necessary to do so, lest a social order collapse and a people die. But the concept of symbolic exchange suggests that what looks like a taking away of something is actually an expenditure, that what is removed is actually given away. Because that which is taken away is also given away, a criminal and unholy act is also legal and holy.

There was no discourse on 'symbolic exchange' as such in the early modern period; but there were a great many cases where the logic of symbolic exchange was exemplified. When, for example, members of the aristocracy vied with each other to put on masques and other entertainments at tremendous expense, they were engaging in symbolic exchange. Or to give an example where violence was involved, when two men challenged one another in a duel, they were engaging in symbolic exchange. The expenditure, whether of material wealth or of a person's life in exchange not for something useful but for something of symbolic value—prestige or honour—was equally a case of symbolic exchange, and was as common in early modern Europe as it may have been in any other time or place. As for punishment and retribution in the early modern period, the subject of a great deal of commentary today, there too an exchange is accomplished. A crime is committed, and then the crime, through punishment, is in some sense paid for: a retribution is a restitution, a life, or other penalty in return for a trespass. The criminal gives up his life or his freedom and comfort… and in return there is something called 'justice'.

There was and is a great difference, to be sure, between peaceful exchange and violent exchange. If I put on a masque, I sacrifice *my wealth* for the sake of *my prestige*. But if I win a duel to the death, I sacrifice *your life* in exchange for *my honour*.

A different kind of circuit is involved. And when legitimate punishment comes, one subject gives up his life, freedom, or comfort in exchange for an abstract principle: the criminal's welfare is exchanged for society's welfare, or for the sake of a principle of sovereignty, law, and order.

As for terrorist violence, there too early moderns were aware of essential distinctions, not only between violent and non-violent means of exchange, but between lawful and sur-criminal transactions, whose power and authority might well exceed lawful violence. There was a very clear difference, as we have seen, between the sacrifice of another and the sacrifice of oneself; or between legally killing an enemy of the state and illegally killing an adversary; or between giving up one's life for the sake of one's country and giving it up for the sake of an anti-state cause for which one has nominated oneself a champion. And there were other essential distinctions: between legally arresting a suspect and extra-legally taking a hostage; between executing a criminal and undertaking an act of murderous vengeance; between legally prohibiting a form of worship and eradicating the form of worship by massacring a gathering at church; between pre-emptively attacking a faction suspected of seditious conspiracy and eradicating a population on behalf of whom a faction may have been conspiring to act; between eliminating a dangerous man and making a political example of his being eliminated.

It could be argued, of course, that what seems so easy to distinguish for us was not so easy for early moderns, that our modern notions of legality and violence were not yet so disentangled from pre-modern notions of vengeance and right. It had not been so long ago when, as a matter of course, murders were repaid by murders, and hostage-taking was repaid by hostage-taking; family loyalties outweighed loyalties not only to state officials but to officials of the Church as well; and even 'freedom' was a concept having as much to do with generosity to others and membership in a group as with political and social autonomy. A lot of what I want to call terrorist violence here can be explained at least in part as a residual form of justice, established well before the onset of the 'judicial revolution' and the cementing of the institution of the nation-state under the powerful monarchs of the late fifteenth and early sixteenth centuries.[26] But so far as terrorist acts were undertaken with the semiotic circuit of a public in mind; so far as these old rituals of justice were now explicit violations of the law; so far as early moderns themselves could see the difference between an archaic ritual and an act of state-sanctioned legitimate violence; and so far, finally, as modern anthropological thought enables us to see especially well the ritualistic, magical thinking involved in violent exchange, we are justified in seeing something new as well as old in these acts of symbolic exchange.

Modern anthropological thought has expanded the notions of symbolic exchange, sacrifice, and scapegoating well beyond their ancient and early modern boundaries. There are often societies where symbolic exchange seems especially notable, like the Northwest Americans with their potlatch, as originally described by Marcel Mauss, and the gift-giving Kabre people of northern Togo more recently

---

[26] See Chapter 1, section 2.

discussed by Charles Piot.[27] But it was a short step from examining pre-capitalist economies as 'symbolic exchange' economies to seeing, along with Baudrillard, how symbolic exchange is a function of many societies, including the most advanced. We give and receive, we take and relinquish on a great many levels. In the work of Pierre Bourdieu, 'linguistic exchange' is always already a transaction of power relations, and hence not only of 'symbolic exchange' but even of 'symbolic violence'.[28] But when real, physical violence is the medium of exchange, the expenditures of social energy are exceptional: symbolically significant assets, bodily harm, freedom of movement, comfort, life itself. When violence is the medium of exchange the principle of reciprocity, fundamental to most non-violent exchange, is often denied. That is why René Girard says that sacrificing and scapegoating are primarily acts of 'violence without risk of vengeance'.[29] In that other, lesser form of violent exchange, revenge-killing, one homicide leads to another, one death is endlessly exchanged for another death, and the cycle of violence is indefinite. In sacrificing and scapegoating, however, a cycle is meant to be broken. An exchange has been made which bespeaks finality. Something has been destroyed and it cannot be brought back.

Hubert and Mauss, in the first major anthropological text on the subject, imagine sacrifice to be primarily a form of 'consecration'. Either the victim or the perpetrator (or perhaps both) is consecrated by the violence—made sacred, set apart—and therefore functionally effective in a world structured by the divide between the sacred and the profane. The parties involved have had their 'condition' modified, so that either a form of allegiance is renewed or a kind of curse is removed.[30] Covenant-making, propitiation, atonement—these are all effective acts that stem from the symbolic exchange of the sacrifice, and the transformation of both the sacrificer and the sacrificed that results, a transformation from which in principle there is no return. George Bataille provides a still more generalized understanding of how sacrifice works. 'The victim dies', Bataille writes, 'and the spectators share in what his death reveals.... This sacramental element is the revelation of continuity through the death of a discontinuous being to those who watch it as a solemn rite.'[31] Jean Baudrillard similarly marks the uniqueness of an exchange where the result is a finality beyond exchange: 'That is the essence and function of sacrifice: to extinguish what threatens to fall out of the group's symbolic control and to bury it under the weight of the dead.'[32]

Hostage-taking, retribution, purification, eradication, and exemplification all share features of the violent exchanges of sacrificing and scapegoating, though by themselves some of them—liberating, hostage-taking, retribution, and exemplification—may lack finality, and the others—purification and eradication—may lack consecration. The first three may end up summoning more of the same, or counter-instances of the same. A person can be freed, and then recaptured.

[27] Mauss, *The Gift*; Piot, *Remotely Global*.
[28] Bourdieu, *Language and Symbolic Power*.   [29] Girard, *Violence and the Sacred*: 13.
[30] Hubert and Mauss, *Sacrifice*: 13. Also see Beattie, 'On Understanding Sacrifice'; Eagleton, *Holy Terror*: 128–40; and Nancy, 'L'insacrifiable'.
[31] Bataille, *Eroticism*: 82.   [32] Baudrillard, *Symbolic Exchange*: 138–9.

A hostage can be taken, and then in retaliation another hostage can be taken. A punishment may be exacted, but another act of wrongdoing of the same sort can be committed again. An example may be made of a victim or a hero, but other examples, even counter-examples, can be provided. There is no guarantee of finality, only a hope of deterrence. As for the latter two, purification and eradication, they are metaphors of elimination we sometimes see attributed to massacres and executions: the enemy has been purged from the body politic, or the enemy has been pulled out by the roots from the body politic. Purification and eradication may remind us, again, of the Judaic ban, the *hērem*. The general logic of agency in purification and eradication seems to be the same as in the sacrifice or scapegoating, but early moderns sometimes expressed sensitivity to distinctions. The enemy was purged or eradicated, not 'offered' to God. Victims underwent a similar fate as that which was meted out, by a court of law, to witches and heretics, where they were meant to be eliminated from the community. And yet the *holókaustos* amounted to much the same thing, as did the *hērem*. Disputes over what to call an act of violence were one thing; what we, from a distance, might wish to call the general logic of the agency involved may be another. After the incident at Vassy, according to Pierre Matthieu, after which at least 30 people died out of a total of over 100 dead or injured', 'The City of Paris praised as a sacrifice that which the ministers decried as a massacre.'[33] But Matthieu says this as a condemnation of the City of Paris. It appears that no one in print praised the massacre as a 'sacrifice'; but some people seemed to admire the massacre *as if* it were one, and are reported as having said so.

4. POLITICS AND RELIGION

The mind reels. An apparently religious concept enters the terrain of what have been characterized as political disputes. The religious concept itself is a subject of dispute, however, and accusations going back and forth appear to be built on an unstable linguistic foundation. In Shakespeare's *Othello*, we hear the dispute enter into the inner life of the main character, as he contemplates killing his wife and adjures her to confess her sins.

> O perjured woman! thou dost stone my heart,
> And makest me call what I intend to do
> A murder, which I thought a sacrifice:
> I saw the handkerchief.[34]

Even Othello wants to do something with the religious concept in a situation which most of us, and probably most contemporary viewers of the play as well, would consider non-religious. But how does feeling less about his victim make his murder a murder, and not a sacrifice? The idea behind Othello's thought seems to

---

[33] Matthieu, *Histoire*: 255.   [34] Shakespeare, Othello: 5.2.67–71.

be Abraham's sacrifice of Isaac, but it was just that kind of sacrifice that most Christian-inspired thought seemed to abjure.

According to the anthropology of symbolic exchange, a sacrifice or a similarly symbolic act of violence need not adhere to any specific religious credo, or perhaps any at all. What matters is the function. Early moderns disputed over the religious ideas that could be applied to certain acts of violence, believing that some uses of those ideas were right and some were wrong; but that was part of a deeper dispute over the violence itself, which, whatever one wanted to call it, was undertaken in a spirit not only of what we now call terrorism, but also, by the same token, of what we now call symbolic exchange. The recourse to violence itself played a role in exciting the disputes, imposing them on the population. Denis Crouzet has called attention to the role violence played in 'naming' its victims. Crouzet is concerned almost entirely with the ideas of pollution and purification, and with violence that he conceives of as 'religious' rather than political. It would appear that his idea of 'religious violence' is sometimes inadequate for the situations he describes, because in many cases what he calls 'religious'—for example, the Massacre at Vassy—may be more accurately conceived rather as a religiously motivated incident undertaken on the level of political struggle.[35] But in any case, Crouzet's insight into religious violence is also an insight into the symbolic value of political violence. It names. It nominates its victim as a victim, its self-sacrificing hero as a hero. Or at least, that is what it *tries* to do.[36]

The symbolic exchange that came with violence, whatever its religious associations, was first of all, to repeat, an exchange in the realm of the political. According to Pierre Bourdieu, since all symbolic exchange involves the assertion and acceptance of power relations, all symbolic exchange is inherently political, and it is ideology that makes it seem otherwise.[37] But here the question is about an explicitly political gesture, with an explicit articulation of power relations, expressed through victimization. On many occasions, it is violence that politicizes the scene. But as a political gesture, the violence is also inherently controversial. It is a gesture that begs not only for victory but also for resistance.

A recognizable form of 'the political', I have suggested, was already in place, if not fully consolidated, organized, or understood, by the late sixteenth century. The political is action undertaken within or with reference to a frame of social organization where the state has achieved a monopoly on the legitimate use of violence, and therefore holds sway over crime, law enforcement, and civil defence.[38]

[35] Cavanagh, *Myth of Religious Violence*, makes a convincing case that most so-called religious violence is indistinguishable from secular violence.

[36] The 'exercise of violence against the body', says Crouzet, 'conforms to a conscious plan for pronouncing that the pollution needs not only to be brought down, like an idol, and vanquished, but also contemplated and named …' Crouzet, *Guerriers de Dieu*: 1.254. Also see Carroll, *Blood and Violence*: 170–81; and van Dülmen, *Theatre of Horror*: 88–106.

[37] Bourdieu, *Symbolic Power*.

[38] It will be seen here that I am defining 'the political' not in the terms of Carl Schmitt, whose proto-National Socialist ideas have been surprisingly current in discussions about political theory in recent years, where 'the political' is born with the notion of 'the enemy', but in the terms of Max Weber and classical political theory generally, where the political means the rise of a state and the

Terrorism before the letter *violates* this frame, for terrorism challenges the state's monopoly on legitimate violence; in other words, it challenges the *sovereignty* of the state. But terrorism before the letter usually also works *on behalf* of the frame of the state, for it tries, as it were, to reinstate the state, to re-legitimize it on the basis of a higher law of political value. Terrorism before the letter entails a *political crime* that is meant to bring about a *political restitution.* On the one hand, it operates against the state and its normative political condition; on the other, it operates on behalf of higher political principles to which its adherents believe the society ought to be allied—even perhaps principles to which the society is already and originally allied, an ancient liberty, though in a degenerate or contested condition.[39]

Terrorism before the letter is in the business of sending messages, of making declarations, attempting to force their way, through criminal violence, into the field of legitimate politics. As I have said from the outset, these declarations are at once constative and performative. They say something *about* the political condition of the state; they *express* an idea, even if only in gesture, or only by way of trope, or for that matter only by way of fatal negation. But they also *perform* a kind of rite; by way of a signal act of violence, imposing a symbolic exchange upon the public, they attempt to *change* the political condition of the state; they attempt to *enforce* the coming of a new political idea. And so this combination of the constative and the performative expresses a deadly, hopefully transformative exchange. Even such disasters as the Saint Bartholomew Massacre need to be read in this light: the violence was constative and performative, it said something and it did something, and so it was sacrificial or else a kind of ban. But since the act is meant to operate in the domain of the political, the audience for the sacrificial message is multiple and mixed rather than singular and simple, and the efficacy of the message is never absolutely certain. The message *takes time*, even if a myth of a single momentous and transformative act governs the resort to terrorist violence. And the message may well follows paths of resistance and deviation, even if a myth of a semiotic circuit governs the idea of the sacrificial act. On the one hand, a form of violence is resorted to which is supposed to be empowered with a magic-like ritualistic power; on the other, this ritualism takes place in a political and historical context which resists the magic, and undermines the ritualistic nature of the act which magical-thinking would attribute to it.

5. THE PUBLIC SPHERE

Since the publication of Hannah Arendt's *The Human Condition* in 1958 and Jürgen Habermas's *Strukturwandel der Öffentlichkeit* (*The Structural Transformation of the Public Sphere*) in 1962 there has been much discussion about the nature of the 'public sphere' at various moments in Western history, and the relation of this

state's assuming a monopoly of the legitimate use of violence. See Schmitt, *The Idea of the Political* and Weber, *Politics as a Vocation*: esp. 245–52.

[39] See Kooistra, 'What is Political Crime?'; and Ross, *The Dynamics of Political Crime.*

sphere to political democracy. Many writers have followed Habermas in examining the public sphere as a characteristically modern institution, coming into its own in the eighteenth century, especially in Georgian England, and going through stages of development, corruption, and dilution in the nineteenth and twentieth centuries. But as Arendt would lead us to expect (and as Habermas was well aware), there were 'publics' and 'public spheres' well before the eighteenth century; and some historians and literary critics have begun to discuss the nature of publics and public spheres in the sixteenth and seventeenth centuries.

Terrorism before the letter brings to light a number of 'publics' in at least two different senses. First, there are the publics involved in terrorist action, the publics to whom or on behalf of whom terrorist violence communicates its message. Second, there are the publics to whom texts *about* terrorist violence are addressed, and among whom the texts will circulate. A case in point, once again, is the assassination of the Duke of Guise in 1588. The murder was undertaken in private, in the antechambers of the king at the royal palace at Blois; but it was by its nature a public act through and through.[40] The act was public since it was an expression of royal policy with a view to the welfare of the monarchy and the kingdom. The agents were public, since the king and his guards were acting as leaders and representatives of the French people. The scene was public, because even if the act was undertaken out of the public view, it was nevertheless accomplished in a royal palace, at the time of a convening of the Estates General in the same facility: all of France was in principle represented at this meeting, and the king's antechamber adjoined one of the meeting rooms. The agency of the assassination was public too. For this murder was also a sacrifice, and if the sacrifice was to work it was to do so through the public effects of the sacrifice, the reception of the public of the terrorist message. Henry's stratagem did not work as planned, but it aroused activity in the public sphere all the same. In the wake of the murder, which the majority of the French people seem to have resented, the king oversaw a massive campaign of letter-writing and mass publication to get the government's message across; some Protestant supporters of the king weighed in with their own publications in favour of the assassination and what it meant for the French people; and the members of the Catholic League and its sympathizers responded with an even greater campaign of polemical response. Public meetings, sermons in the churches, even religious processions in public streets were a part of this response.[41] As for published texts, as historian Andrew Wilkinson puts it, 'By a significant margin, 1589 witnessed the largest outpouring of publications in sixteenth-century French history.'[42] Among those publications was Pierre Matthieu's tragedy, *La Guisiade*, which may also have been performed in parts of the kingdom (the theatre being another medium of public discourse), and which in any case went through three editions over

---

[40] Somewhat more public in spirit was the follow-up execution of the Duke's brother, the Cardinal of Lorraine, by royal order the next day.

[41] An account of the scale of the response appears in Wilkinson, 'Homicides Royaux', where the difference of importance between the Duke's and the Cardinal's death is explained as well.

[42] Wilkinson, 'Homicides Royaux': 131. Also see Bell, 'Unmasking a King'; Racaut, *Hatred in Print*; and for a general overview, Pallier, *Recherches sur l'imprimerie*.

the course of the year.[43] In Matthieu's play, there is both *represented*, within the play, a Chorus which stands for part of the French public, and *invoked*, through the rhetoric of the play, a national public, whose indignation is called upon, and to whom, in the end, a curse on the head of Henry III is delivered. This invoked public is both the actual readership (or audience) of the play and the larger general public of which the readership or audience is only a part.

Early modern France was not a democracy, and yet clearly something on the order of 'public opinion' was frequently appealed to, and appealed to both in public spaces and in the medium of publication. The public is an audience for terrorist acts, and the public is enjoined to act in response to both terrorist acts themselves and to all the messages that are circulated about them. Habermas mentions how, before the emergence of the 'bourgeois public sphere', public acts were performed by representatives of the public, for example a monarch, performing the rites of monarchy in a palace; the monarch performs his own public-ness before an audience which can only assent to it. And certainly there is an element of this representativeness in the performance that sixteenth and seventeenth-century terrorists enact in the literature that describes them. The sultan performs his public-ness at the banquet where he kills and makes an example of Irene. Henry III performs his public-ness in his palace as he has the Duke of Guise killed. Ravaillac, attacking Henry IV on a narrow, blocked Parisian street, also performs a kind of public-ness. The violence in all these cases moves outward from an agent who enacts his own public-ness. But the violence is also meant to *persuade*. It may seem that the violence is only a performance, to which assent must be granted; but the violence must also makes its appeal to a public that in one way or another needs to be convinced of what the violence is trying to say. The sultan, the king, and even the king-killer—all are both performing a public-ness which is self-instantiating and yet appealing to a public for assent.

The actual *composition* of this public, or these groups of publics, is a subject that would require separate study, and which in any case demands a variety of important qualifications. For example, if 100 per cent of French adults (the sane and healthy ones at least) were capable of receiving oral or visual information about terrorist acts and legends, according to Wilkinson only about 30 per cent could read; or again, if 30 per cent were literate, only a small number of those could afford to purchase a substantial number of publications, and only a small number, again, played a role in governing the nation, or influencing those who governed. So this public could participate in a public sphere in only a limited number of ways, and was divided into a variety of sub-publics, and even into competing publics: citizens against landed aristocrats, or Protestants against Catholics. Similar observations could be made about Scotland and England. But public opinion mattered; public opinion was appealed to; and the public sphere was the medium in which both terrorist violence and written accounts of terrorist violence circulated. *Recognition* to terrorist acts and messages could only come if a public sphere existed

[43] See Richard Hillman, Introduction, in Matthieu, *The Guisiade*, trans. Richard Hillman, for a thorough discussion of the background to the work and its revisions.

in which recognition could be actualized or withheld. In fact, both terrorist acts themselves and publications on the subject of terrorist acts could be seen, in the context of the early modern period, to be involved in constructing a public capable of recognizing or denying recognition to the messages of terrorist violence.

Peter Lake and Steven Pincus emphasize that the public to whom rhetorical appeals are made is an 'adjudicating' public.[44] The public is not only the recipient of a message, but also its judge. It is because a public can be thought to play an adjudicating role that political agents will appeal to it. But in the sixteenth and seventeenth century, in the face of terrorist violence, 'adjudication' is too limited a term. I have been appealing instead to the idea of 'recognition', that the public is called upon to 'recognize' a political constituency and its appeals, and I have tried to emphasize how this recognition could come not only in judgement but also in other forms of assent and dissent, including political behaviour, ritual performance, and even panic. The act of assassinating Gaspard de Coligny on the eve of Saint Bartholomew precipitates, according to many people who recount the story, assent by 'the people' of Paris in the form of a riot of mass murder. The act of assassinating Concino Concini on the streets of Paris in 1616 precipitates, according to all accounts, an orgy of scapegoating ceremonies. The Gunpowder Plot, observers testify, precipitates a kind of mass panic. On 20 March 1606, as the investigation into the Gunpowder Plot continued, the British government had to release a royal proclamation denying rumours that the king had been attacked and killed by unidentified assailants, and that the nation was called to arms in defence: the rumours themselves were 'seditious', according to the document. Yet for a while it was said that 'for certain news the King was slain at Woking. . . . Some said the treason was performed by English Jesuits, some by Scots in women's attire, others by Spaniards and French, most reports agreeing that the King was stabbed with an envenomed knife'.[45] 'Some' said this; 'some' said that. And, in the post-Plot atmosphere of the time, a characteristic response to the terrorist conspiracy was, in a word, terror. The public was on edge, afraid for the safety of their king, their state, and themselves.

Terrorist violence creates a public for itself, but this is not only a deliberative public, adjudicating social issues. It is also a public that is meant to be roused or intimidated, coerced into taking sides and demonstrating assent or dissent, registering a degree of recognition or refusal. Many texts about terrorist violence make an effort to *show* this public formation and the passions and actions that result from it. Yet what is most important about it may not be the actual public to which events and texts appeal but the *fantasy* of the public that events and texts imply. Amleth's harangue to 'the people' of Denmark in Belleforest's story and Marcus Brutus's speech to 'the people' of Rome in Shakespeare's play involve fantasies of public-hood. A 'people' as a whole can be represented as gathered by the ruins of Elsinore castle, or at the steps of the forum in Rome, functioning not as a crowd composed of diverse individuals so much as a unit responding, deliberating, and taking action, on the scene of a performance of public-ness. And this 'people' can

---

[44] Lake and Pincus, 'Rethinking the Public Sphere'.   [45] Harrison, *Jacobean Journal*: 286.

be imagined to operate within a closed semiotic circuit, although, as subsequent events show, the circuit is an illusion; communication is open rather than closed, and messages and counter-messages propagate indeterminately. The supposition of a public operating in response to acts of public-ness within a semiotic circuit is one of the great motives of terrorist violence. With the beheading of Irene, the sultan's work is done. With his *coup d'état*, Henry III seems to have supposed, the menace of the Catholic League will have been defeated. The French public will get the message; the sacrifice will have been effected, and the menace that the Guises embody will have been eliminated from the body politic. Sultanship over the Ottoman Empire or kingship over France can resume anew.

Two related social developments lay behind the emergence of terrorism before the letter and its supposed public, no doubt: the rise of printing and the outbreak of the Reformation. The importance of printing speaks for itself. A 'public' is created as a product of publication, and this public grows in size, influence, and complexity, forming a body of adjudication and emotional response in all spheres of life, well beyond the confines of immediate locations.[46] The French public, the English public, the Scottish public—these are entities that exist nowhere in particular, but are understood to pervade the commonwealths. As for the Reformation, it must be remarked that all agitation for or against the Reformation involved calls for people to decide which and what kind of religious community they were to belong to. With or without overt *political* choice, people were asked, encouraged, cajoled, or coerced into making a *religious* choice which had political implications. And so the 'public sphere' that historians are beginning to see as having emerged in the sixteenth century has to be placed in the context of religious controversy, which inevitably brought in its wake political controversy as well. In other words, along with the rise of printing, religious controversy helped generate a general public whose adjudications and recognitions were necessary to both religious worship and statecraft. If terrorist violence and its stories are involved in a dialectic of recognition, that is largely because religious controversy creates a public in waiting, a public being asked at various points to make important decisions about its own life world, and a public therefore upon which a faction might think it practical to make *demands*: such demands that could be sometimes be enforced by law (the Pope excommunicating a monarch, a monarch declaring the rules under which religious worship may be undertaken) and that at other times could be imposed by force (a monarch unleashing a massacre, an assassin taking down a monarch).

But we should be wary of making too many assumptions about the nature of the public sphere in this period. Much of what was understood about the public and its role in political and religious life in this period was largely, again, a fantasy. The 'people' of Denmark could not actually have been gathered en masse in front

[46] The standard accounts of the effect of print in this sense are Eisenstein, *The Printing Press as an Agent of Change* and Eisenstein, *The Printing Revolution*. Eisenstein's ideas are modified but not seriously challenged in Chartier, *The Cultural Uses of Print* and Zaret, *Origins of Democratic Culture*. A revisionist account appears in Johns, *The Nature of the Book*. Also see Bell, 'Unmasking a King' and Racaut, *Hatred in Print*.

of the ruined castle. The 'people' of Paris did not, working as a whole, with unanimity, actually rise up against the Huguenots in their midst. Nor did all the 'people' of Paris approve of the mayhem and murder. Actual facts on the ground depend upon the myths in which the makers of the facts believe, and the actual consequences of violent acts depend upon not only violence itself but also the myths that are spread about them. So a distinction has to be made between the actual composition of identifiable publics in the early modern period and the myths of the public sphere.

A distinction also has to be made between actual agents of message-sending and receiving and the subjectivities that are imagined to be involved. Jacques Clément apparently imagined himself to be another Ehud or Judith, and a representative of the French people, or all good French Catholics, when he assassinated Henry III. Clément was not simply *himself* when he acted. Moreover, he was not simply acting *alone*. He may have had collaborators. The stories that circulated about him for and against made a point of determining whether he acted alone or in concert with others; clearly the *meaning* of what he did depended upon it.[47] Even more important, for his supporters and no doubt for Clément himself, Clément was not acting simply through his own human agency. He was also acting by the power of God and for the sake of the glory of God.

It is a flaw in Lake and Pincus's theory of the early modern public sphere that they occlude any talk about God. For in early modernity, God was not in fact excluded from the public realm; He was immanent in it. Or at least, He was always supposed to be immanent in it, and if not, or if His immanence seemed to have been withdrawn, measures from public prayer to public violence to recall His immanence, to bring Him back by bringing the people back to Him. The presence of God was always either assumed or else in dispute. A striking example came in the discourse of the Gunpowder Plot. We have already seen how the conspirators' Jesuit friends imagined the affair, always keeping their eyes on the wishes of God and the scene of His church. In the discourse counter to the Catholic version of events, there appeared a rhetorical plea by the jurist Edward Coke, in his prosecution of the surviving conspirators:

> Lord, what a Wind, what a Fire, what a motion and Commotion of Earth and Air would there have been! But as it is in the book of Kings, when Elias was in the Cave of Mount Horeb, and that he was called forth to stand before the Lord, behold a mighty strong Wind rent the Mountains, and brake the Rocks, *sed non in vento Dominus*, but the Lord was not in the wind. And after the wind came a Commotion of the

[47] Especially important in this regard is Fonteny, *Cleophon*, a clever comedy which portrays Clément as entirely the dupe of religious fanatics and Machiavellian members of the Guise faction. Says one character:
> If he knew what he was doing and undertaking
> Believe it, he would not be so courageous.
> He doesn't think of the future, the poor idiot thinks
> That the coup is a game, or some gay dance.
> He has his eyes blinded, his head conducts him,
> And the fool does not know that it is we who have seduced him (Act 4, page 36).

Earth and Air: *Et non in igne Dominus*, the Lord was not in the fire: So neither was GOD in any part of this monstrous action.[48]

In this case, the issue is whether the Gunpowder Plot was to have been a wholly religious sacrifice, with God in its wind and its fire, as the conspirators had hoped. The answer is no. Coke acknowledges that the conspirators were looking for God, but he insists that like Elias they were looking for Him in the wrong way, in the wrong place. Here, in the byplay of the dialectic of recognition, a master of juridical rhetoric attacks the terrorists in view of the agency of their behaviour, and shows that agency to be symbolically, but also in reality, hollow.

The 'public' is always a construct, a fiction. But the public is nevertheless central to political life. And the fiction of the public in early modernity included not only people but, hopefully, the eye of God. In the Christian world—not the world of Brutus and Mahomet, but the world of Charles IX and James I—terrorist violence could therefore be undertaken on behalf of God, and also before the eye of God. Whatever God desired—a difficult matter to establish, more a matter of faith, usually, than a matter of knowledge—when one engaged in terrorist violence, killing a tyrant or massacring a people, one called upon God as a witness and a guarantor of the legitimacy of what one had done. Hence, again, if political violence could be undertaken as an act of symbolic exchange, and come to have a great effect on social life, it was in part because within the semiotic circuit of the act there was not only a human public but also a divine one, which in principle could testify to its transcendent lawfulness, in spite of the fact that the act was intended to lead to harm, and very possibly violate several of God's Ten Commandments.

6. THE CIRCUIT OF JUSTICE

Consider a final example of how the semiotic circuit was assumed to operate, which combines an impulse toward allegory with an impulse toward historical reconstruction. It comes from an incident in Book Five of Spenser's *The Faerie Queene*, which I have mentioned before. Book Five as a whole is dedicated to the virtue of Justice, as embodied in the form of its main character, Sir Artegall. Following upon earlier books devoted to the virtues of Faith, Temperance, and Chastity and published six years later (1596) along with books devoted to Friendship and Courtesy, Book Five seems to signify a change in Spenser's attitude toward allegory and the main task of epic poetry.[49] In Book Five, allegory gets settled into a rigid framework of representation. Events in the epic directly refer to actual events in Spenser's lifetime. Where before, Book One on the virtue of Faith, for example, the epic might exemplify a general struggle, spiritual as well as physical, between forces of faith and forces of falsehood and doubt, this Book on the virtue of Justice amounts to an allegory about specific struggles encountered by the English nation in its dealings with foreign and domestic enemies, especially its enemies

---

[48] Coke, *A True and Perfect Relation*: Hv.   [49] Anderson, 'Spenser's *Fairie Queene*'.

in the Ireland where Spenser worked as a colonial secretary and on the Continent its nemesis the Spanish Empire. Book Five is also probably the least liked of all the *Fairie Queene*'s six parts. It is in Book Five that the morality of the tale seems coarsest—and oddly so, it would seem, since this is book devoted to the principle of Justice. Of course, from a critical perspective it may not seem odd at all: the justice upon which the nation-state was built in an era of perpetual war was commonly a justice of uncompromising aggression, and international warfare could not obey the same principles of equity by which internal conflict in a nations-state was adjudicated. Still, there is a brazenness in Spenser's adoption of the principle which is unsettling. 'Who so upon him self will take the skill / True Justice unto people to divide', says the poet, 'Had need have mighty hands...Power is the right hand of Justice truly hight.'[50]

'Retribution', I have said, was one of the main forms of symbolic exchange in which terrorism before the letter was involved. There are a number of cognate terms for retribution, however: vengeance, punishment, compensation, redemption, and of course justice, each with its own measure of connotative and denotative associations, but each belonging to the same class of symbolic exchanges, where a wrong is supposed to be righted, and where the righting of the wrong comes with the physical harm or penalty exacted against the wrongdoer. The wrongdoer may well rise, as we have seen, to the condition of a sacrificial victim or a scapegoat. But what, then, is 'justice'?, asks Book Five of *The Fairie Queene*. The Book does not provide an ultimate answer. The story with which it opens, Artegall's double quest for justice and for the woman he loves, Britomart, is never completed. But along the way a second main character is introduced, Prince Arthure, Britain's great leader-to-be, who has been in other episodes before, and who will perform an act of violence that shows, with particular clarity, how the semiotic circuit works. It acts as a necessary fiction in the performance of politically significant symbolic exchange.

Writing about justice, but writing about justice from the point of view of international and colonialist affairs, Spenser develops themes that have been encountered elsewhere in this study: tyranny and resistance, treason and terror. He also alludes to some of the main historic events this study has been preoccupied with: assassination attempts against Elizabeth, the machinations of the Guise, the execution of Mary Queen of Scots, religious warfare on the Continent, the career of Henry IV and the iconoclastic resistance against the Catholic Church and Spanish rule waged among Protestant militants. And then, in one episode, where Prince Arthure is the lone hero, Spenser provides an allegorical treatment of an Elizabethan campaign in Belgium, on behalf of the Protestants there.

In this story a feminine *Belge*, in character much like the feminine France encountered in the verse of Ronsard, is oppressed by a 'Tyrant', which is to say Spain and the Spanish King, 'who invaded has/Her land, and slain her children ruefully alas'.[51] The claim is that the Tyrant has 'devoured' twelve of Belgium's children,

---

[50] Spenser, *Fairie Queene*: 5.11.33.   [51] Spenser, *Fairie Queene*: 5.10.6.

which is to say twelve of her provinces, and 'to his Idols sacrifice their blood'.[52] But Prince Arthure is to be her 'Champion'.

Belge's problem is in fact threefold. A foreign tyrant holds her in thrall. He has held her in thrall by having 'pulled down' her main city and castle, and set up an oppressive guard there led by a 'Seneschal' who seems to be a stand-in for the notorious Duke of Alba. But the first problem, the tyrant, and the second problem, the Seneschal, are compounded by a third, the Idol itself. It is to this Idol that the children of Belge are sacrificed; and, once sacrificed, the children are literally devoured by a 'hideous Monster', which otherwise stands guard over the Idol. What this refers to probably is the idea that when Belgian provinces were reconquered by Spain and more or less forced to reconvert to Catholicism, the souls of the converts were forfeited, devoured by the Church, and damned to hell. Prince Arthure takes care of both the first and second problems, killing the Seneschal and the Tyrant, or at least a stand-in for the Tyrant, a giant named Gerioneo, but before he can claim victory he still has to take care of the problem of the Idol and its guardian monster.

The pairing of the Idol and the monster seems to indicate Spenser's own understanding of the act of symbolic exchange he himself calls Justice. On the one hand, a symbol is at stake, a symbol to which individuals may be attracted in spite of its falsity, or even because of its falsity. On the other, physical force is also at hand. Without the physical force, the power of the Idol is nominal only.

What this means, too, is that opposition to the Idol and the power it exerts may take the form of a violent exploit. Prince Arthure's attack on the Idol and the monster is not a good example of terrorism before the letter; Arthure is literally a knight, obeying a code of chivalry, and he does not attack enemies who are unworthy of his rank and dignity. And yet, though transposed into the terms of archaic chivalry, the battle signifies that the way to counter a symbolic enemy is precisely to engage it in an act of violent symbolic exchange: sacrifice the Idol, and annihilate the force that protects it.

We may be reminded of the incident at Saint Médard, or other riots of iconoclastic violence. The aim is to kill an idol. But killing the idol actually involves killing the people, like priests, who harbour it. Spenser's Arthure engages in the usual fierce battle of a knight against a huge monster, reckoned as at once female and repulsive, over the course of several stanzas struggling to withstand the blows of a mighty foe and finally to find the vulnerable part, where his weapon can do its job:

> Under her womb his fatal sword he thrust,
> And for her entrails made an open way,
> To issue forth.

The monster reminds us some of the images often attached, by Spenser as by other poets of the time, to the Whore of Babylon, and Spenser twice puns on the word 'mass' to describe her volume and weight. One of the puns develops as follows:

---

[52] Spenser, *Fairie Queene*: 5.10.6; 5.10.8.

> Then down to ground fell that deformed Mass,
> Breathing out clouds of sulphur fowl and black,
> In which a puddle of contagion was...[53]

Killing the monster means killing the Catholic mass, and relieving it of its 'contagion'. And once the monster is killed, sacrificing the Idol, though it is made of 'massy gold', is easily accomplished. Arthur 'did all to pieces break and foil' the Idol, 'In filthy dirt, and left so in loathly soil'.

This may seem to be the opposite of the 'consecration' of the victim that Huber and Mauss might lead us to expect, but it is a consecration-in-reverse that fulfils a similar function, a desecration such as those that often came in the aftermath of terrorist violence. No hostage-taking happens: in iconoclastic violence, the idol must not be made into a trophy, but rather left in 'loathly soil'; it must not be marked out as an object of contempt but rather reduced to nothingness. But still, a symbolic exchange has taken place. An object of value has been reduced to nothing, its value annihilated, its remembrance reduced to nastiness. The Idol had previously been named as a supernatural power; it has now been un-named in an act of Justice. A cause of pernicious 'sacrifices' has been eradicated, according to the fiction.

A fiction it is, let us remember, not only in that the incident is a fictional story, but also in that the story relies on an enabling myth, according to which demolishing an idol is actually an effective way of destroying a religion. It was not always so effective. Iconoclasm in France and Belgium provoked resistance to Protestantism; it helped radicalize members of the Catholic faith, and led to the formation of such anti-Protestant, militant organizations as the Catholic League. If in the mind of iconoclasts and their supporters attacking idols of the Church really had a powerful impact on the practices of religion, in reality that impact was often just the opposite of what the iconoclasts intended.

But in Spenser's fantasy, the killing of the monster and the destruction of the idol are part of a closed semiotic circuit, and communicate vibrantly within it. They watch the battle. They see the monster defeated.

> Then all the people which beheld that day,
> Gan shout aloud, that unto heaven it rung;
> And all the damsels of that town in ray,
> Came dancing forth, and joyous carols sung.[54]

So the violence succeeds, utterly. Now you know. And yet the great victory over the Idol of the Low Countries is a poetic hallucination. The expedition that Spenser models his story on, the incursion into the Netherlands by Elizabeth's favourite, Leicester, ended in disaster. The monster of Spain and the idol of the Catholic Church continued to hold the upper hand in most of the Low Countries, and Leicester returned to England in disgrace. Spenser imagined Leicester as a heroic terrorist, defeating the guilty world of Spanish rule once and for all, with a sword

---

[53] Spenser, *Fairie Queene*. 5.11.31–2.   [54] Spenser, *Fairie Queene*. 5.11.33.

of justice in his hand, striking against an abomination; but Leicester was only, at best, an ineffective governor and a mediocre military leader.[55]

Stories of terrorism before the letter not only depend upon enabling fictions like the idea of a closed semiotic circuit, or the efficacy of violent symbolic exchange, but also promote the enabling fictions, communicating the idea that violence works and maybe only violence works in politically troubled situations, even if the evidence of real life suggests that violence often doesn't work at all. The myth is more powerful than the reality, and reality must suffer for it.

[55] See Gregory, 'Shadowing Intervention'; and Kaske, 'The Audiences of *The Faerie Queene*'.

6

Purpose

1. THE ENDS OF ALL THINGS

What is the purpose of terrorism before the letter? As we have seen time and again, there are always at least two kinds of purposes or ends involved: first, the purpose for which agents undertake to commit violence; second, the purpose for which writers compose and publish texts about the violence. The difference between the two kinds of purposes is very stark in cases like that of the first example of the previous chapter, the story of Mahomet and Irene. The fictionalized Mahomet murdered Irene to re-establish his authority over his empire. Bandello, Boaistuau, and Painter retold the story for reasons of their own: it was a good story, arousing pity and fear; it warned European readers about the fierceness of the Ottoman enemy; it said something about how the world operates, and how brutal power and politics can be; it argued (perhaps) that European countries would have to be equally fierce if they were to resist the Ottomans; at the same time it made a plea on behalf of love and peace. The violence within the story meant one thing; the story itself, as a parable, meant something different.

The contrast between the two orders of purpose is not always so blatant, however. Nor is it always enough to imagine that only two orders of ends are involved. Sometimes there are many. And latently there are always many purposes, as there are always many kinds of answers to the question 'why?' Terrorism before the letter is overdetermined, though it is not always overdetermined in the same way.

A merging of purposes, so that the written word and acts of violence come to amount to the same thing, often appears in texts produced in support of violence. A case in point is Jean Boucher's *Apologie pour Jehan Chastel* (1595), written to defend the attempted assassination of Henry IV, which was thwarted when the young Chastel's knife missed its mark, and the blade struck the king in the teeth. (Chastel was apprehended as he tried to flee the scene, brought to trial, and executed as a traitor.[1]) We have encountered this text before. Boucher praises Chastel for his heroism, when the young man attempted to kill 'a heretic, a recidivist, a profaner of sacred things, a declared public enemy, an oppressor of religion, and as such excluded from any right to achieve the crown, and playing the part of a tyrant instead of king, a usurper instead of a natural lord, a criminal instead of a legitimate Prince'. Chastel's shining model, according to Boucher, was Jacques Clément, the

---

[1] See Sutto, 'Quelques consequences politiques'.

killer of Henry III. According to Boucher, the assassination of Henry III had been 'praiseworthy, as against a public enemy, condemned by the courts, towards whom all obligations of respect and duty had been lifted'. In fact, in neither case, Clément's or Chastel's, had the 'intention' been to 'kill a king', for their targets were no such thing; at best they were kings 'so-called'.[2] Boucher, a Paris priest and a leader of the Catholic League, who would soon be forced to flee the kingdom, but who would live to a ripe old age overseeing a diocese in Belgium,[3] is as it were trying to kill Henry III a second time: having been killed in reality, Henry III has to continue being killed in parable. As for Henry IV, according to Boucher the attempt to kill the man was little more than an expression in reality of what Boucher and others were keen to argue in words. Boucher's language is already violent. It condemns Henry to death, basing its argument on the idea that Henry has already condemned himself to death. Language can never be violent in the same way that physical force can be violent. But as Boucher represents it, the violence of men like Clément and Chastel is a completion of something that has already been determined in language; it is the fulfilment of a condemnation.

So words and deeds can merge in the literary space of words. And no doubt the act itself, the dagger in the belly or the neck, can represent a merging of words and deeds in the scene of deeds. It is worth remembering that for a faithful Christian, killing a condemned and unrepentant man means sending him to hell.

But there are cases, again, where words and deeds split apart, and purposes multiply. A good example is Thomas Middleton's *The Revenger's Tragedy* (1606). This revenge story, as it were, slides into terror: private revenge seems to be what the play is about, but revenge itself, to be completed, needs to slip into the public territory of terrorist activity. And so the purposes of violence multiply, both in themselves, as revenge turns partway into terror, and in the realm of parable, as the purposes of the text multiply too.

The main story of this play, it will be recalled, is adapted from the legend of Lorenzino de' Medici and the assassination of Alessandro de' Medici, Duke of Florence—in a bedroom, and under the pretext that Lorenzino had arranged an assignation there between the duke and a young woman, possibly Lorenzino's own sister.[4] *The Revenger's Tragedy* repeats the story, but has the assignation arranged instead with the main revenger's beloved. And the play adds several gruesome complications. For the beloved, named Gloriana, is already dead. She committed suicide by poisoning herself years ago to avoid being raped by the Duke. Vindice, the main revenger (his brother Hippolito gets into the act as well), has dressed up the skeleton of Gloriana, making it look like an unknown, shy, sleeping woman, waiting to be kissed into wakefulness. And instead of attacking the duke directly, the revenger spikes the skull's lips with a deadly poison, which the duke duly kisses, only to find that they are not real lips at all, and that the poison on them is hurting

---

[2] Boucher, *Apologie*: 11–17. A journalistic account of Chastel's adventures appears in *Procedures faicte contre Jean Chastel*.

[3] See Cameron, Introduction, in Boucher, *La vie et faits notables de Henry de Valois*.

[4] For background see Bawcutt, 'The Assassination'; and Mullaney, 'Mourning and Misogyny'. For a general look at the role of the assassin on the English stage, see Wiggins, *Journeymen In Murder*.

and killing him. As the duke is dying, Vindice forces him to look at evidence that his wife has been cheating on him, with his own bastard son. Finally, as the duke rages with pain and humiliation, Vindice finishes him off with a dagger.

Revenge merges with political violence here because, as the play makes clear, no merely private redress will do; judicial recourse against the duke is impossible, and private revenge is coloured by the public position of the person who is to be revenged upon. The duke is an absolute ruler and a tyrant; he can do what he wants. The sign of his being able to do what he wants, in fact, apart from his manipulation of the courts and administration of the law, is his sexual misconduct. So to avenge the duke is not only to exact blood for blood; it is also to tackle the tyranny he represents. But along with his brother Hippolito, Vindice discovers that killing the duke will not be enough, for the duke has a legitimate son, a wife, stepsons, and an illegitimate son, any of whom would stand to inherit the duke's power and with it the duke's tyranny. The brothers have been given direct evidence of the systematic nature of the tyranny when one of the stepsons rapes a nobleman's wife without being punished to the full extent of the law, and when the duke's legitimate son proves himself to be just as corrupt as his father, conspiring to extort sex from a poor young woman of the town—who happens this time to be Vindice and Hippolito's own sister.

There is no escape from tyranny and corruption, signified above all by sexual crime, apart from the annihilation of the ducal family. The play makes this very clear. And so a second plot develops, which concludes with a mass murder, where all the rest of the ducal family are killed, the first of them a victim in another perversion of justice, engineered this time by the brothers, the rest of the victims in the midst of a banquet, at the scene of a counterfeit masque. The first plot climaxes with the poisoning, humiliation, and stabbing of the duke; the second climaxes with the massacre of everyone else. And both climaxes involve not just killing but the sending of messages, messages of revenge, humiliation, and symbolic catastrophe. The victims are made to learn who their persecutors are, and why they are being executed, and they are caused to be executed by way of ironic and catastrophic reversals of their own systems of meaning: the Duke dies with an illicit kiss, the bastard son dies through a judicial trick, and the rest of the family die by way of a murderous masque which was supposed to celebrate their authority. The symbolic acts of the ducal family are turned against them. Yet Vindice and Hippolito get nothing out of the massacres except the satisfaction of a job well done. To a surviving nobleman, one Antonio, the nobleman whose wife was raped by the bastard, Hippolito turns and says, 'Now the hope / Of Italy lies in your reverend years.' And Vindice says, 'Your hair will make the silver age again, / When there were fewer but more honest men.'[5]

It ends badly for Vindice and Hippolito; Antonio accepts the power graciously and seems to promise that he will use it justly. 'May I so rule that heaven may keep the crown.'[6] But then Vindice and Hippolito betray themselves, bragging that they were the ones who assassinated the former duke, and Antonio immediately uses his

---

[5] Middleton, *Revenger's Tragedy*: 5.3.88–9.   [6] Middleton, *Revenger's Tragedy*: 5.3.91.

power to condemn the two for murder. It turns out that restoring ancient liberty also requires executing the men who restored it, since their recourse to violence cannot be condoned; their crimes will not be an exception that proves the rule. They have to be eliminated from the state no less than their ducal oppressors. But if that is the case, then, as Middleton represents it, the purpose of terrorism is the ending of terrorism. Terrorism wins in this play by eliminating both tyrants and terrorists, erasing both tyranny and itself.

What we are to make of Middleton's revision of the story of Lorenzino is a big question.

Vindice and Hippolito are struggling to make their case. They have got to have their revenge and they have got to make their revenge speak to the world. But that's Vindice and Hippolito. We readers or playgoers, like Antonio once he has been elevated to power, are caused to adopt a different perspective. Though we might sympathize with the revengers and take some pleasure in their violence, by the end of the play we may well find ourselves equally glad of their stupidly betraying themselves, and getting punished for their impertinence. This is a logic familiar in a great many crime dramas, where the audience is caused both to sympathize with criminals and to enjoy it when they are punished. It is not the criminal act in itself that gives us pleasure. It is the criminal act accomplished, accompanied by the criminal act penalized. Early modern revenge plays express this pattern repeatedly. And when, as in the case of *The Revenger's Tragedy*, the revenge slides into an act of terrorist violence, aiming to make a general political statement, the pleasure is double too: we are gratified by the terror, which has eliminated a corrupt and odious regime, but we are also gratified by the punishment of the terror, which is a dangerous way to respond to oppression, and which law-abiding citizens eschew.

Terrorism does not come plain. We have already seen two kinds of purposes embedded in any representation of terrorism before the letter. Two kinds of ends are embedded in any representation:

(1)   The ends of a terroristic *action*, so far as the terrorists have established their political and tactical objectives.

(2)   The ends of *representing* a terrorist action, which may of course be completely different from anything the represented terrorists want to accomplish.

Vindice and Hippolito have their goals. They come to include terror. But Middleton has a different goal. He is constructing a parable out of an episode of violence, which explains, admires, enjoys, and condemns the violence, and is really saying something altogether different.

Unfortunately, trying to explain what Middleton's parable actually means may lead one into a critical aporia. It is possible, as Jonathan Dollimore once argued, that Middleton's play is an example of 'radical tragedy', undermining authority with campy humour, the thrills of the macabre, and an exposure of the absurdities of power.[7] But Dollimore does not address the ending of the play, and so avoids having to address the inevitable crux, the inevitable containment-subversion controversy that arises in critical discussions of plays like this. This kind of controversy originated among critics with Stephen Greenblatt's essay on *1 Henry IV*, 'Invisible Bullets', where subversion is everywhere a critic wants to look for it, but only so far as the evidence also suggests the security of subversion contained.[8] In so many of the English plays of this period, authority is both flouted and restored, and if *The Revenger's Tragedy* flouts authority in the way Dollimore suggests it does, it also restores it. There is subversion through much of the play, but there is also containment, and Greenblatt's model suggests that the subversion may well perform a kind of work on behalf of authority: after subversive release (Vindice flouting conventional morality, or Prince Hal doing much the same thing) comes a gratifying restoration of order. Moreover, since the drama takes place in an always already corrupt Italy, showing that Vindice and Florence solved their problems by violence does not make a clear and direct comment on social relations in England. Jacobean England was capable of delighting in the spectacle of the villainy of foreigners without worrying too much that the same villainy was prevalent among the English.

But although the play raises the familiar subversion-containment problem, it does so while openly adopting its material from the mythography of terrorism before the letter. Knowing this does not make it easier to solve the crux of the meaning of the drama, but it does add important qualifying information. One of the main sources for Middleton was probably the twelfth tale in Marguerite of Navarre's *Heptaméron*, first published in 1558 though it had been written some years earlier. The tale is told from the point of view of the real-life assassin, Lorenzino, who himself had written for posterity, as we have seen before, that he had 'liberated Florence, having left her free of tyrants'.[9] For several years Lorenzino was sheltered in Marguerite's court. In the version of his story included in the *Heptaméron*, where the story is told by a (fictional) member of the court on Lorenzino's behalf, the assassination plot is triggered by Alessandro's demand that Lorenzino provide him Lorenzino's own sister as a bedfellow (as in the last but not the most important part of *The Revenger's Tragedy*). Lorenzino then pretends that his sister lay in a bedroom waiting for the duke, and, trapping the duke there, with an accomplice stabs the duke to death. After the story is told, the meaning of the story is debated among those who have listened to it. 'Opinion', we are informed, is divided. 'For some maintained that the gentleman [i.e. Lorenzino] had done his duty, having saved the life and honour of his sister, together with having delivered his country from such a tyrant. The others said no, but that it was too great an expression of ingratitude to put to death someone who had done the gentleman so much good and honour.'[10] The debate does not develop much. Competing notions of honour and obligation are

---

[7] Dollimore, *Radical Tragedy*: 139–50.   [8] Greenblatt, *Shakespearean Negotiations*: 21–65.
[9] Lorenzini de' Medici, *Apology for a Murder*: 18.
[10] Marguerite de Navarre, *Heptaméron*: 137.

understood to be at stake, and the question of the right to tyrannicide or the obligations of the citizen to the state are passed over in favour of questions about the status of women in society, the nature of the love men may have for women, and their obligations to the 'honour' of those women. In other words, although the story raises questions about the nature of the political, it gets diverted into a discussion of love and honour. The parable of Marguerite's story, no less than the parable of *The Revenger's Tragedy*, thus becomes uncertain. What is the point of telling the story, except that it is a true story and an odd one? Perhaps no point needs to be made: Marguerite's courtiers are not disturbed about political questions; rather, they are concerned about the ethics of personal conduct, which Lorenzino either succeeded or failed to exemplify in a satisfactory way. If there is a parable in Marguerite's story, it is a parable not about terrorism but about personal conduct, and the different positions different people can take about the same course of behaviour.

Middleton changes Marguerite's story by making the violence against the Duke of Florence not an act based on the pretext of protecting the innocent, a woman about to be raped (that violence would be saved for violence against the Duke's son), but on avenging a wrong, a woman having been pressured into killing herself. Not just personal conduct and codes of love and honour are at stake then, but also revenge. And in the exacting of this wild justice, as Sir Francis Bacon once called revenge, the audience sees a pulling of energies between two extremes: on the one hand, the purely psychological, even pathological demand for retribution in the face of an outrage against a member of one's family; on the other, the more reasonable but also dangerous demand for political transcendence.

I have said that in looking at any discourse about terrorist violence, one can divide purposes between the ends of the action represented and the ends of representing it. But within the first category there is usually another distinction to be made, between

(1a)   The *ends* of a terroristic action, so far as the terrorists have established their political objectives

and

(1b)   The *personal motives* or *private ends* of a terrorist action, which may work in tandem with, in support of, or even against the public objectives of the terrorists.

This distinction between the two types of motives, as we have seen in the chapter on character, could be very important to writers. More often than not, writing that supported a terrorist act would fit personal motives inside public motives; it was important to stress that the terrorist acted, as we say today, 'selflessly', or in early modern terms, either 'honourably' or in a spirit of 'self-sacrifice'. It was hoped that character would supplement or confirm the ideology on behalf of which the agent acted. The classic case of the division between such motives, and the way it could either confirm or deny ideology, was a common distinction between the honourable Brutus and the cagy Cassius, most famously put into the mouth of Marc Antony by Shakespeare, as a eulogy to Brutus:

> This was the noblest Roman of them all:
> All the conspirators save only he
> Did that they did in envy of great Caesar;
> He only, in a general honest thought
> And common good to all...[11]

It is therefore extremely significant that *The Revenger's Tragedy* shows a pair of figures based on Lorenzino de' Medici and his partner acting morbidly out of private interest, apparently taking delight in insulting and killing their victims. The political meaning of what they do is not necessarily erased by that, but certainly it is modulated: selfless goals have been accomplished by crude and selfish means, through the agency of a pair of perverts. Of course, the private grievances on behalf of which the revengers have acted had public causes; the revengers' family was aggrieved because of the doubly public nature of tyranny under which they suffered, first in that it abused power, and second in that it sustained the power to abuse. But *The Revenger's Tragedy* thus makes the problem of tyranny into a pathologization of the victim of tyranny, a pathology expressed through the joyfully reckless, obsessive, and subversive behaviour of the revengers.

The play also calls attention, however, to yet another split in motivations, between

(1a)   the *ends* of a terroristic action, so far as the terrorists have established their political objectives

and

(1c)   the end *result* of a terrorist action, which may be very different from what the terrorists intended.

Showing the end result of a terrorist action, and showing it in one way or another, is also a function of (2) the representation of terrorism for the sake of making a parable out of it. But it is an important modification in the representation of the objectives of action in itself. Lorenzino escaped at first with his life; an assassin sent by the de' Medici family made him pay for his crime only eleven years later. In the meantime, Cosimo de' Medici, who achieved the dukedom upon the death of his cousin, Alessandro, proved to be as autocratic (if not as lecherous) a ruler as his predecessor had been. Ancient liberty was never restored. The real-life story of Lorenzino is thus a story of a possibly heroic action which was politically ineffectual. But although Middleton has the revengers engage in behaviour that is grotesque rather than heroic, the end result of their action is effective. They get the man they have chosen to take over the dukedom, apparently a good man who knows what it means to suffer under tyranny. Terrorism worked. But it only worked halfway, for they get themselves condemned to death. Or rather, terrorism worked entirely but with a self-consuming qualification, not only by forcing a regime change but also by exposing the heinous criminality of forcing such a change.

---

[11] Shakespeare, *Julius Caesar*. 5.5.69–73.

This itself, Vindice declares to his brother, is a good thing. Demanding not just a public recognition of the meaning of the deaths they have engineered but also personal recognition for their adventure, as if they deserved commendation, the brothers have brought a just destruction upon themselves:

> May not we set as well as the duke's son?
> Thou hast no conscience: are we not reveng'd?
> Is there one enemy left alive amongst those?
> 'Tis time to die when we are ourselves our foes.
> When murders shut deeds close, this curse does seal 'em:
> If none disclose 'em they themselves reveal 'em![12]

So we see in the context of a representation of terrorist violence that there can be a distinction between the ends of action and the end result of action. Just as the motives of the terrorists can be divided between the public and the private, so can the action of terrorist violence be divided between objectives and consequences. And a representation of terrorist violence therefore can very well construct a parable where the exposure of these distinctions can be just as important as the joining of them in a coherent tale with a beginning, a middle, and an end. It is not only important in *The Revenger's Tragedy* that the brothers succeed; it is also important that they fail.

The subversion-containment aporia, however, suggests still another complication. For one can ask why Middleton, in 1606, in the aftermath of the Gunpowder Plot, thought it a good idea to show a pair of obsessive rebels massacring a ruling family and causing a regime change. Middleton is sometimes grouped among writers who were less enthralled by power than Shakespeare evidently was; Middleton's later play, *A Game of Chess*, was once suggested to be paradigmatic of 'opposition' theatre, theatre that was brave enough to oppose royal policy.[13] But *The Revenger's Tragedy* is not political propaganda; it is macabre or comic tragedy. It raises no questions about what should be done, now, in Jacobean England. But it does raise general questions about the nature of action. It draws a picture of a historically situated social world, where agents aspire to achieve attractive and unattractive goals, by attractive and unattractive means, in circumstances where outcomes are uncertain but some sort of justice is always being either served or stymied. I would not go so far as to agree with Dollimore that *The Revenger's Tragedy* is in this respect 'anti-Providentialist' and therefore 'radical'. But I would say that the play reminds us that in examining the purposes of representations of terrorist violence one has to consider not just the ends of action and the ends of representation, but also

(3)   The ends of historical action in general.

What does it mean to act, to take revenge, to enter the arena of public affairs, to strive for private and public justice? It may be that *The Revenger's Tragedy* is actually a cautionary tale. In answer to the general question of the dialectics of recognition, 'of what shall we be conscious in the realm of the political', it says, we should beware tyranny and rebellion alike. But then it may also be saying something like history is

---

[12] Middleton, *Revenger's Tragedy*: 5.3.109–14.
[13] Heinneman, *Puritanism and Theatre*; Yachnin, 'A Game at Chess'.

tragic; at one time or another tyranny and rebellion will come, and bring disaster along with them. And maybe even Providence has something to do with this.

2. THE DEMANDS OF VIOLENCE

Violence and politics and the connection between the two need to be thought about very carefully. It is easy to take a detached point of view about literature of the past. But that is seldom what the authors of terrorism texts want their readers to do. Unless their goal is to change the subject and divert our attention, they want either our enthusiasm, our outrage, or our grief. Or, if they are a writer like Middleton, they want it all; they want writing to excite a great range of emotions and ideas in us, and leave us somewhere in the middle of them, perhaps in the end both satisfied and puzzled, as well as entertained. What they do not want is indifference. And they want what they want not just because that is something that stage plays can do, but because that is what the representation of terrorism calls for. Terrorism makes demands. How should we respond to those demands? From whom are those demands being made, and from whom is something being demanded? What is the nature of those demands? How should they be satisfied, resisted, or ignored? Who are we in relation to those demands? Do they come from within us, or only from without? What if anything shall be *exchanged* in return of the demand, and the damages that have been inflicted to make them? And in what kind of world, finally, do we live, that such demands keep recurring? What is the purpose of living in such a world? How is it that violence seems to be so pressing upon us? What is the power it holds over us? What is the power of the death and destruction it threatens? Why is it there?

I have called attention several times to the *histoires tragiques* and the falls of princes. Whatever the meaning of such stories to the medieval imagination in which they originated, in the hands of the major humanists and playwrights of the sixteenth and seventeenth centuries these stories of violent catastrophe seem generally to leave the scene of trauma in a condition of irresolution. One time after another, faced with terror, individuals are called upon to assert their independence from it, their stoical resistance to the call of violence, and yet also to succumb to its power. Cases in point include a pair of nearly contemporary Jacobean plays, Chapman's *The Revenge of Bussy d'Ambois* and Webster's *The Duchess of Malfi*. Like *The Revenger's Tragedy*, these two plays, among the most read of non-Shakespearean early modern plays, operate on a number of levels; but throughout they adopt materials from the mythography of terrorism before the letter, and they inquire into what should be recognized by them. And they say: the demands of political violence, the objectives they serve, are to be resisted; but the results of political violence cannot be resisted. They can only be experienced, regretted, and mourned.

Chapman's play was published in 1613 but was probably first performed a year or two earlier.[14] It tells the story of one fictional Clermont d'Ambois and the

---

[14] For background see Kirk, *The Mirror of Confusion*: 155–210.

relation of this character to such genuine historical figures as his supposed brother, Bussy d'Ambois, Henry III of France, and Henry the third Duke of Guise, whose close companion and client Clermont is. Clermont has begrudgingly revenged his brother's death, and his future seems secure.[15] But then comes the assassination of Guise, and Chapman provides a unique, fictionalized, ideologically compromised version of it. 'Let [the king] appear to justify his deed', Guise cries out while dying,

> In spite of my betrayed wounds; ere my soul
> Take her flight through them, and my tongue hath strength
> To urge his tyranny.[16]

The king appears, and claims he has acted in defence against Guise's 'ambitious mad idolatry'. The familiar charges of tyranny, ambition, betrayal, and idolatry are hurled back and forth. 'This blood I shed', says the king, 'is to save the blood / Of many thousands.' But Guise replies,

> That's your white pretext;
> But you will find one drop of blood shed lawless
> Will be the fountain to a purple sea.
> The present lust and shift made for kings' lives,
> Against the pure form and just power of law.[17]

The by-now decades-old debate is renewed, with the twist that Guise, usually a villain in English literature, is made into something of a hero, asking just the right questions.[18] Is it permissible to break a law to protect the law, or break the peace to preserve the peace? Can terrorism before the letter, here in the form of a *coup d'état*, be permitted? Can it even work?

Surprisingly, in spite of Guise's eloquent 'no', terrorism does work, but not in a way that could have been expected. Clermont, having just avenged the death of his brother, asserts that he cannot and will not avenge the death of Guise. 'There's no disputing with the acts of kings', he says. 'Revenge is impious on their sacred persons.' Unlike so many of Guise's supporters in real life, this fictional one will not allow himself to be outraged. Instead, cut off from his patron and best friend, Clermont determines to kill himself.

> Shall I live, and he
> Dead, that alone gave means of life to me?
> …
> Shall I here survive,
> Not cast me after him into the sea,
> Rather than here live, ready every hour
> To feed thieves, beasts, and be the slave of power?
> I come, my lord! Clermont, thy creature, comes.[19]

---

[15] Actually, in an interesting turn of dramatic irony, Chapman has both killings take place simultaneously, but Clermont finds out about Guise's death only after he has felled his brother's killer.

[16] Chapman, *Revenge*: 5.4.38–41.   [17] Chapman, *Revenge*: 5.4.51–5.

[18] See Mcintosh, 'The Massacre of St Bartholomew on the English Stage'.

[19] Chapman, *Revenge*: 5.4.149–93.

He kills himself on stage.

A good deal has been written on Chapman and stoicism and the apparently contradictory demands that stoicism places on Chapman's characters.[20] For stoicism seems to demand both participation in political struggle and indifference to it. It trumpets the exercise of virtue and thereby resistance to evil; but it also counsels non-resistance when evil has the upper hand. Clermont would seem to exemplify these contradictions, which he escapes by the usual stoic route of escape: suicide. But in the context of terrorism before the letter, this customary embrace and escape from political trouble has something additional to say. Whatever the ends of terrorism may be in view of the *objectives* of the violence and the *personal motives* of those who commit it, the *end result* is commonly defeat. The objectives and motives may be suspect. If King Henry thinks that the Guise must be killed to preserve the kingdom, the Guise of *The Revenge of Bussy d'Ambois* is nevertheless a good man, not the monster of Protestant propaganda, and the play suggests that Henry's fears for his kingdom were false. Even Guise's part in the Saint Bartholomew Massacre is by his friend Clermont excused. Hearing Guise accused of the 'heinous' crime of leading the Massacre, Clermont asks, 'Who was first / Head of that Massacre?' And when his interlocutor answers, 'The Guise', Clermont says,

> 'Tis nothing so.
> Who was in fault for all the slaughters made
> In Ilion, and about it? Were the Greeks?
> Was it not Paris ravishing the Queen
> Of Lacædemon; breach of shame and faith,
> And all the laws of hospitality?[21]

Like many apologists before him, Clermont apparently blames the Massacre on the victims, whom he accuses of violating a taboo. The *end result* may have been terrible, just as the destruction of Troy was terrible. But the Huguenots, or maybe at least one Huguenot, Coligny, started the quarrel, first coming to the French capital to celebrate a wedding and then making threats.

Afterwards, Guise being assassinated on the orders of Henry III, Clermont seems to imply that the *end result* is terrible, but that the motive in this case, whether good or bad, is irrelevant. For what has happened has happened, and nothing can be done about it without violating a sacred trust. Instead, out of good motives, Clermont shall kill himself, rewarding one tragic end result with another. Here is still another violation of common sense, which begins with denying the most fundamental of instincts, self-preservation. In response to a tragic event, I will engineer another tragic event and kill myself. In *Hamlet*, a play that Chapman clearly has on his mind, the good Horatio offers to do the same thing, on behalf of a dying Hamlet; but Horatio is stopped. Someone needs to survive and tell the tale. In *The Revenge of Bussy d'Ambois*, Guise is already dead, and instead of living to tell the tale Clermont adds to the tale through suicide, joining another unfortunate

---

[20] See for example Hillman, 'The Tragic-Channel Crossing'; Ide, 'Exploiting the Tradition'; Leggatt, 'The Tragedy of Clermont'; and Rowe, 'Memory and Revision'.
[21] Chapman, *Revenge*: 2.1.208–15.

end result to the story. It is against common sense; but it makes sense to the stoic as well as to the tragedian making a drama about a stoic.[22]

If we try to think about the purposes of terrorism in an Aristotelian sense, as an action with a final cause, and then try to generalize the final cause of terrorism in view of the final cause of historical action, we may well confront such doubly tragic outcomes as *The Revenge of Bussy d'Ambois* presents us with. The case is similar in Webster's *The Duchess of Malfi* (1612–14) where in the end nearly everyone dies, and largely for the sake of nothing.[23] The campaign of terror waged by the brothers against the duchess has very little meaning, as Webster represents it. In the source for the play, Bandello's novella, which was faithfully translated by both Belleforest into French and Painter into English, legitimate concerns about family honour and public governance are raised. In the play, if such concerns are involved, they go unexpressed, and the terror seems to have no motives but personal urges, including greed and jealousy, as well what appears to be a delight in the exercise of tyranny for its own sake. That is one reason why the assassin Bosola makes his well-known Lear-like remark about tennis balls: 'We are merely the stars' tennis-balls, struck and banded / Which way please them.'[24] And yet there is no question that the targets of the brothers' wrath, the Duchess, Antonio, and their children, stand for a kind of stoical virtue. Everyone except one son dies, but the Duchess and her family have died in resistance to systematic tyranny, a plan of dominance and destruction for the sake of dominance and destruction. The end result of the tyranny in the play is tragic death; resistance has been futile. But tragic death is also an assertion. That is a main reason why Bosola dies saying something different: 'Let worthy minds ne'er stagger in distrust / To suffer death or shame for what is just.'[25] On the one hand, in view of the end results of the objectives of terror, the *coup d'état* waged by the brothers against their own sister, resistance is futile. On the other, in view of the aims of historical action and the stoic code of virtue, resistance is necessary. Even if the objectives are tainted and mute, resistance speaks; and futile resistance speaks all the more loudly. 'I am the Duchess of Malfi still' says the Duchess moments before her death.

But we don't need to look only at fictionalized accounts of events well in the past to find expressions of futile virtue in the face of historical pressures. For shortly before the production of plays like *The Revenge* and *The Duchess*, Henry IV was murdered, and reaction to his death was similar in thought and tone to the two English plays. Whether either playwright was thinking about the murder of Henry IV is a matter of speculation. But certainly, reactions to Henry's death, like the bleak plays by Chapman and Webster, draw upon the mythography of terrorism before the letter, at once reiterating a number of commonplaces and inventing

---

[22] Clermont's stoicism may all the same be imperfect, contaminated by private motives. See Bertheau, 'Passion et néo-stoïcisme'.

[23] Much of the best recent criticism on the play is included in two volumes, Callaghan, ed., *The Duchess of Malfi*; and Luckyj, ed., *The Duchess of Malfi*. There has been a noticeable absence, however, of criticism that deals with the play as a drama of political violence. The notable exceptions are Griffin, *John Webster*, and Coddon, '*Duchess of Malfi*'.

[24] Webster, *Duchess*: 5.53–4.   [25] Webster, *Duchess*: 5.5.102–3.

ideas, tropes, and dramatic energies of their own. And like those plays, reactions to Henry's death express what seems to be a new willingness to dwell upon the *tragique* of a current event as a space of mourning, where futility in the face of the end result of violence dominates the scene.

We have already taken a long look at texts concentrating on the life and death of François Ravaillac.[26] But just as what could be discovered about the character of Ravaillac was unsatisfactory, so what could be discovered about the event itself and its consequences was wanting too. On the one hand, it was impossible to circulate any document that expressed any sort of support for what Ravaillac had done; and in fact the only possible responses were ones that magnified the stature of the man whom Ravaillac had killed and that demonized the killer himself. 'Wicked villain', writes an anonymous author, in an apostrophe to Ravaillac, 'thou hast bereaved us of this great Prince, whom we lament with tears, and whose loss we shall ever feel.'[27] But according to historian Roland Mousnier, unhappiness with Henry IV had been widespread, and Ravaillac's mischief was not committed in an ideological vacuum. Yet once Henry had been killed, he was remade, and had to be remade, into Henry the Great, in whom no flaw was ever perceived, even as Ravaillac had to be made into a pathology, an 'abortion' of nature, possessed by the devil.[28] Henry had been great. He was now to be remembered as Henry the Great. But his death, not his legacy but his death, the incident that brought his reign to an end, was tragic, and there was nothing much to be done about it but grieve.

Two volumes of collected writings edited by the courtier Guillaume du Peyrat, an anthology of poems on his death, *Recueil de diverses poésies sur le trepas de Henry le Grand*, and an anthology of funeral obsequies, *Les Oraisons et discours funebres de divers autheurs, sur le trespas de Henry le grand*, along with a long poem published separately by Claude Billard, *Larmes sur la tombe de très grand, très victorieux, très chrestien roy de France et de Navarre Henry IIII*, testify to the mixture of moral exaggeration with a sense of unredeemable tragic loss that came with Henry's murder.[29] The death of Henry IV could be made into a parable of high moral value so far as it scapegoated Ravaillac and celebrated the greatness of Henry—even if the scapegoating of Ravaillac was never completely satisfactorily accomplished, and even if the magnification of the reputation of Henry came, as many knew, at the expense of recognizing the dissent and dissatisfaction he had always attracted. But there was little if anything that could be made out of the event itself. Henry was dead and that was all there was to it. Apart from narrations and dramatizations of that one dramatic day in May, there was no *story* to tell about the life and death of Henry IV; or rather there was no story that was permissible to tell that could make sense of the event and find redeeming or for that matter Providential value in it.

[26] See Chapter 3, section 5.
[27] *Lamentable Discourse Upon the Parricide and Bloody Assassination*: 3.
[28] Mousnier, *The Assassination of Henry IV.*
[29] Du Peyrat, *Recueil des diverses poésies*; Du Peyrat, *Oraison funèbres*; Billard, *Larmes.* A shorter version of Billard's poem is included in Du Peyrat's *Receuil.* And see Hennequin, *Henri IV dans ses oraisons funèbres.*

The literal martyrization of Henry was off-limits. For the one thing it was impermissible to express in public was that Henry had been killed for religious reasons.[30] That Henry had died for the sake of 'France' or for the sake of 'peace' was perfectly admissible; so then too was the placing of Henry in what I have called the 'actantial role' of the martyr, the role of agent who suffers and bears witness. But it was impossible to say that Henry had died for the sake of his professed religion, Catholicism, or for the sake of his formerly professed Protestantism, or for the welfare of either one sect or the other. He had died for all, for France—but not literally, then, as a martyr on the religious model. Moreover, it was impossible to point out any kind of weakness or vulnerability in the person of Henry the Great. Henry had to go down as a military hero, the great pacifier of France and the great champion of the country in international affairs. He was of course preparing to go to war before he was killed.[31] And the legend that was already being spread about him insisted on comparing him to military figures like Hercules or even Mars—not to mention Julius Caesar. But if Henry had not been killed for religious reasons, and if he was a great warrior who always fought and won on behalf of the prosperity of the French people, why had he been killed? Why, that is, apart from the fact that Ravaillac was crazy, *insensé*, a 'furious rage in his breast / Smouldering night and day' as one poet put it?[32] As I mentioned earlier, the people who inherited power from Henry, his widow Marie de' Medici and the circle of counsellors she gathered around her (to the exclusion of many old stalwarts of Henry's staff, including the staunch Protestant, the Duke of Sully), had an interest in de-politicizing the murder.[33] Henry could not be represented as having been killed because of opposition to his politics. And yet he was murdered in his political greatness, and it was as a political community that France most felt itself wounded. As Jacques Hennequin has written, the death of Henry was experienced as 'the rupture of a unity'. Indeed, as Hennequin suggests, it was not as a 'catastrophe' that it was experienced—the coming of an event that reversed a historical trajectory—but precisely as a 'rupture'. So, on the one hand, to respond in a public fashion to the death of Henry meant dismissing or marginalizing any religious or political motives that might have been attached to it. On the other, it also meant responding to the experience of rupture. Among religious officials, Hennequin adds, and he could have said that same thing about secular spokesmen, the task then was to discountenance the threat of political and religious 'diversity' that came with Henry's death, and 'to try to reconstitute the lost unity'.[34] So martyrization was not only off-limits for ideological purposes; it was also off-limits as a form of discourse-making, of myth-making.

Hennequin's observations call attention to ideas that we are almost mechanically aware of in the early twenty-first century when a terrorist episode occurs: that to the victims, terrorist episodes are traumatic; that they are traumatic insofar as they

---

[30] Here I argue precisely against the position taken by Biet in his introduction to Billard's *Henry le Grand*.

[31] See Babelon, *Henri IV*: 967–79.

[32] Borbonius 'Le Furies Contre Le Parricide', in Du Peyrat, *Receuil*: 54.

[33] See Chapter 3, section 5.   [34] Hennequin, *Henri IV dans des oraisons*: 75.

rupture 'the fabric of everydayness';[35] that they bring a populace from compla-
cency to mourning; and that they frighten a populace by sending a message that
undermines its security. The death of a king or a similarly symbolically potent
figure, in this way, unexpectedly, and even perhaps irrationally, is the death of a
symbolic unity which may potentially have real as well as symbolic effects. The
diarist Pierre de l'Estoile gives several examples of panic in the countryside at the
news of the death of the king, although in fact no security-threatening incidents
seem ever to have come to fruition. He also describes the deep state of grief that
almost everyone he knew and saw had been thrown into.[36] There was hysteria, too,
even hysteria that came in retrospect to be seen as prognostication of the assassination: 'During this month, and even before the death of the king, a number of
maladies overtook Paris, frenetic illnesses, mental alienations, melancholic humours, hypochondrias, very strange and distressing, more than the doctors had
ever seen before.'[37]

Public responses to the assassination came, then, in reaction to a rupture rather
than a catastrophe. The result could take the form of a 'tragédie en cinq actes', as it
does in the case of Billard's stage play, *La mort d'Henry le Grand*, but it could not
come in the form of a tragic tale about 'the fall of Henry IV'. For Henry did not
fall. He was felled—in fact, the image of a felled tree was not out of the question,
as we will see—and the difference was crucial. The parable that could be constructed about this death could not therefore follow the path of catharsis and the
histoire tragique; nor for that matter could it follow the paths of faith or war. It
could only follow the path of grief. 'We die in his death', writes Billard at the end
of his poem published at about the same time as his stage play was written, *Larmes
sur la tombe*: 'this grand monarch dying; / 'Arms and valour have been ravished by
Fate...'[38] The poem refuses to find solace in anything that could be said or thought
about Henry and his assassination.

The same goes for the stage play, where Billard places similar sentiments in the
mouths of Henry's surviving friends. The Protestant Duke of Sully, Henry IV's
right-hand man in the management of the state, is given the last word. 'I am im-
mobile like a pillar of salt', the Duke had already complained in the play.[39] And
now this 'blow of fortune'—the language in Billard on this subject always attributes it to 'fortune' and 'fate', those arbitrary forces of good and evil—leaves the
Duke, in tortured syntax and an unresolved conceit, to observe

> That I do no more, with neither strength nor virtue,
> But with a dying soul and a broken heart,
> —So cold, so dead, so covered with ashes—,
> Than do those tree trunks struck by lightning,
> Between life and death, ready to be finished off with one more blow,
> Teeter over life and straddle over death.[40]

[35] Houen, *Terrorism and the Modern Novel*: 199–201.
[36] L'Estoile, *Journal d'Henry IV*: 3.75–110.
[37] L'Estoile, *Journal d'Henry IV*: 3.109–10.
[38] Billard, *Larmes sur la tombe*: 13. [39] Billard, *Mort*: 1768.
[40] Billard, *Mort*: 1794–9.

The very image leaves the subject incomplete. It keeps it within a frame of grief, and prevents the subject from being moved outside that frame, into acceptance. If Billard is aiming toward the 'unity' that Hennequin appeals to, it is a unity of grief. Everyone together on Billard's stage will mourn, and be unable to move past the state of grief.

Looking at a deadly act of terrorist violence from the point of view of the survivors, as we do in the case of the plays by Chapman and Webster and the real-life responses to the death of Henry IV, we are confronted with a spectacle of futility. Whether or not the culprit can be punished for what he has done, the end result cannot be undone, and there can be no compensation for it. Nothing can make it right. And yet, from a stoic point of view, in the negation comes an assertion. Guise, Clermont, the Duchess, and the King of France have in their deaths asserted something good. Futile resistance is all the same resistance. D'Aubigné thought that such resistance could serve as a winnowing that would eventually bring forth the prosperity of the righteous. Such a teleological hope is absent from the thought of most writers responding to terrorist violence from a tragic point of view. End results trump the ends of history. But that is the tragic point of view, in the context of which victims are heroes, heroes are victims, and the reader or audience member is caused to sympathize with them as victims and heroes alike.

3. SAMSON TRANSCENDENT

The findings so far should be summarized. In the construction of terrorism before the letter, at least five different kinds of ends are pertinent.

(1a)   The ends of a terroristic *action*, so far as the terrorists have established their political and tactical objectives.

(1b)   The *personal motives* or *private ends* of a terrorist action, which may work in tandem with, in support of, or even against the public objectives of the terrorists.

(1c)   The end *result* of a terrorist action, which may be very different from what the terrorists intended.

(2)   The ends of *representing* a terrorist action, which may of course be completely different from anything the represented terrorists want to accomplish.

(3)   The ends of *historical action* in general.

All of these purposes have purely formal functions, establishing ends-oriented structures for elaborations of language and action. But they are also historically bounded and binding. Just to speak of a terrorist action, as we have seen again and again, is to speak of a certain kind of scene and a certain kind of disposition of agents, both of which require the formation of a certain kind of culture of politics and resistance, of sovereignty and citizenship.

The last of the purposes, the ends of historical action, may be the most salient of purposes, a final cause among final causes, even in cases like *The Revenge of Bussy d'Ambois*, *The Duchess of Malfi*, or the literature surrounding the death of Henry IV, where the issue of action is a tragic rupture, a felling rather than a fall. But that is because when writers attempt to think through the motives involved in major terrorist events, including the motives for writing about them, they arrive at an underlying drive for historical transcendence, which terrorist action either fuels or thwarts. In the early twenty-first century we may imagine ourselves beyond that. We may belong in the economistic or otherwise statistical societies of social scientists, which 'trend' and 'cycle' rather than 'progress', lacking a teleological underpinning; or we may belong to that condition of being 'after the future', which is to say after belief in historical transcendence, discussed by such Continental thinkers as Franco Berardi Bifo.[41] But in early modern France and Britain, thinking itself was founded in the possibility, if not the inevitability, of historical transcendence: narrative thinking no less than theoretical speculation was founded in it. That is not to say that most early moderns believed, precociously, in a form of the idea of progress, or of progress before the letter; but they were bound to the teleological assumptions of Christianity, in which history has a literal endpoint which will involve a final judgement, and they were bound as well to the supposition of an afterlife. For every event there was the context of an ultimate Event, and for every life there also came an aftermath of eternity.

Terrorist violence, in such a case, violence that was intended to rupture and restore, to destroy and recreate, was a special challenge to the imagination as well as to moral sensibilities. The political assassinations in Florence, Malfi, Blois, and Paris—to what purposes could the mind assign them, and to what purposes could the mind's own preoccupation with such events be assigned? Even when events ended triumphantly for all concerned, as in the mythical cases of Ehud and Judith, doubts might linger not only about proximate motives but also about final consequences and causes. Although the allegorical qualities of these stories gave them a kind of eternal relevance—at any moment, when actual affairs matched with one of the biblical models—their historical quality placed them in a past which had long since suffered reversals, more trials and tribulations, more moments when 'The Israelites again did what was evil in the sight of the Lord' (Judges 3.12), or when, after Judith's death after a long and happy (but celibate and therefore barren) life, Judea would again be challenged by its enemies, and the Jews would face destruction and dispersal. When the mind tried to consider the most deplorable of events, the massacres in France, or the near-massacre at Whitehall anticipated for the Gunpowder Plot, the outcome was often nothing less than bad faith: the triumphalist scapegoating of enemies, many of whom, in the form they were scapegoated, being entirely imaginary. The alternative response, looking at disaster, as D'Aubigné did, as an example of mass martyrdom, a massive defeat for the sake of a triumph to come, may have been more plausible from a religious point of view, but it was not much comfort—it wasn't meant to be—and it did not make much sense. It required the survivors to 'Take life in death, and peace in war', as D'Aubigné put it.[42] It required the embrace of self-contradiction. But that seemed to be D'Aubigné's meaning.

---

[41] This is not the place to rehearse the 'end of history' debate, but Bifo, *After the Future*, at least provides an example of an effort to recover history and the future after the purported end of both.
[42] See Chapter 4, section 7.

A key example of the difficulty of accounting for the ends of terrorism before the letter—similar in this respect to texts like *The Revenger's Tragedy*—comes in the story of Samson, whose adventures in homicide bring the main narrative pattern of the Book of Judges to an end.[43] For the Samson story illustrated what was perhaps the most extreme case known of the intersection of religion, politics, violence, and the drive toward historical transcendence. What ends of action, of personal motivation, of historical results, of representation, or of teleology could such a case be meant to serve? As already noted, the example of Samson would be taken up in the years of the English Revolution, where Samson became a figure for the English people, and find an artistic climax in Milton's *Samson Agonistes*, where Samson is also perhaps a figure of the blind, defeated poet of revolution. But before this shift in allegorical value, the story was more problematic.

Samson, as also mentioned, was all but ignored in the context of terrorism in the sixteenth century, and only made a comeback as a figure of political and religious heroism in the seventeenth. He had been lurking in the background, perhaps, the culmination of a national-liberation-by-heroic-violence myth that was central to political thought in the period, especially in its monarchomach version. But the culmination had come at a cost, it was well known: the death of the hero as well as the victims, and instead of the festival of liberation that marks the end of the stories of Ehud and Judith, a massive ruination, a ban, followed by a family funeral, not a public one. All we hear at the end of Judges 16 is this: 'Then his brothers and all his family came down and took him and brought him up and buried him between Zorah and Eshtaol in the tomb of his father Manoah. He had judged Israel for twenty years.' The last chapters of Judges shift gears, and tell unrelated tales, almost as if the story of Samson had never happened. Perhaps, as Boccaccio and Lydgate suggested, Samson's victory was no victory at all, but rather a defeat that Samson brought down upon himself (along with the collateral victimization of thousands of Philistines), in return for allowing himself to be fooled by a woman.[44] But other mythographic possibilities eventually emerged, where Samson could be celebrated as a warrior of faith, even if the allegorical value of that celebration was uncertain.

I have found four such treatments in the early seventeenth century in Francophone and Anglophone territories: *Simson, Tragoedia Sacra* (1600–4), written in Latin by the Calvinist minister, Marcus Andreas Wunstius, who resided in the Franco-German Protestant stronghold of Strasberg; a fifty-page section in the 900-page-long *Commentary on the Whole Book of Judges* (1612) by the English Puritan minister Richard Rogers; the stage play *Tragédie nouvelle de Samson le fort* (1620) by an otherwise unknown Sieur de Ville-Toustain; and *The History of Samson* (1631) by the popular English religious poet Francis Quarles.

The French play, *Tragédie nouvelle de Samson le fort*, is especially ambivalent. It belongs to the tradition started by Grévin and his *César*, where the passions of the characters are key to the drama and yet often, in the end, are left unresolved.

---

[43] For background see Brettler, *The Book of Judges* and Mayes, *Judges*.
[44] See Chapter 1, section 1.

Actions are suited to passions, and just as Grévin's Cassius 'burns' with desire to plunge his knife into Caesar, Ville-Toustain's Samson aches for revenge against the Philistines for their having taken away his first wife. An important additional feature of his revenge is that he wants to destroy the Philistine economy as well as the lives of those particulars who have offended him. This is anti-scenic violence:

> I would rather have the earth enshroud me in its breast
> Than let anyone soil my bed, or ravish my wife.
> No, no, I want to spoil by a pitiless fire
> The vines, wheat fields, and green olive trees
> That honour them with fruits in the spring.
> …
> I want totally to undo the Philistines
> By fire, by blood, by homicidal arms,
> And burn their wheat fields and vines.[45]

It becomes possible in this play to see Samson as something of a monster, or at least a nihilist before the letter. 'Alas!' says a Jewish prince. 'All this for a woman, Samson, / To put all of Israel in extreme peril?'[46] And it can seem that Ville-Toustain is using the Samson story to condemn religious violence. Certainly, at the end of the play Ville-Toustain pulls no punches, as a messenger comes to report Samson's destruction of the Philistine temple:

> All fell confusedly by the fury of a single captive
> Who was supposed to lose his life that day.
> O the monstrousness, o the wickedness, o the sinister misfortune,
> O the hideous spectacle, o the scandal, o the sorrow!
> What eyes could bear to see these fatal ruins?

But there is perhaps an element here of that delight in horror that we saw in Capilupi's discussion of Saint Bartholomew, where the king is said to have been appalled by the terrible spectacle before him, and then to have gone to thank God for having delivered him from his enemies.[47] For the messenger goes on to praise Samson for his 'power, heart, audacity and courage', after which the play abruptly comes to an end.[48]

Those who have or would have committed massacres in the past, from the incident at Vassy to the Gunpowder Plot, were usually portrayed as men who planned on surviving their attacks. They were warriors, and maybe willing to die if necessary, but losing their lives was not their goal. Here with the Samson story, writers were confronted not only by the surreal scale of Samson's violence, but also by either unwonted recklessness or suicidal impulses. 'Let me die with the Philistines', Samson calls out to God, as he stands at the pillars he is about to bring down (Judges 16.30). One could argue against the idea that Samson was reckless or suicidal—in 1612 Richard Rogers would make an extensive case against both ideas—

[45] Ville-Toustain, *Samson le fort*: 8–10.   [46] Ville-Toustain, *Samson le fort*: 14.
[47] See Chapter 4, section 6.   [48] Ville-Toustain, *Samson le fort*: 32.

but still, one had to deal with the issue.[49] In any case, unlike the stories of Ehud and Judith, or even the story of Brutus, the Samson story forced the reader to think about what it means to destroy without exultation.

To the post-teleological mind this impulse toward destruction without exultation may seem like an expression of the Freudian death drive, in both a characterological and a historical sense. From a characterological point of view, it is easy to see Samson as a figure bent on self-destruction for the sake of self-destruction. His rages against the Philistines are tempers he had brought upon himself by insisting on trying to intermarry with them, or to play dangerous word games with them, or to hook up with a prominent 'harlot', in the middle of a Philistine town. Samson goes looking for trouble. But in looking for trouble Samson is not only flirting with death, in an expression of what may be taken to be a personality disorder, or else an inevitable development of character given his birth right; he is also infiltrating the Philistine people to complete a project, the divine project called 'judging'. That may seem a rational or supernaturally rational plan of action. Samson's strategy is to infiltrate, cohabit, and betray. But such a mode of action also means acting in accordance with a Freudian death drive, in keeping with what is perhaps the most profound of Freud's elaborations of the idea, for it means going looking for death to fulfil the ends of life.

The historical plan of action and the metaphysical drive toward death operate together. Samson's historical plan is to save by destruction; and his personal plan is to save by destruction too, though what is saved in either case is left unspoken and may remain unfathomable unless one thinks (as Freud did) about how aggression may work against both the victim aggressed upon and the self doing the aggression. On the one hand, in 'judging', Samson's behaviour is squarely within the productive precincts of religious eschatology, driving forward the historical project of the Jewish people. If there is something odd in that, still, many of the heroes of Judges, as I have suggested, are odd—left-handed, feminine, orphaned, longhaired. If there is something monstrous about Samson's violence, moreover, it nevertheless accords with the Old Testament project of the ban, of total destruction of the enemy. The chief difference from other examples of the ban in the Bible is that a situation of utter non-equivalence has been established for the violence, literally one man against thousands, so that the ban itself requires new technologies of murder—mass murder with a jawbone, even more massive murder with demolition. Samson judges, and judges oddly, mischievously, and cruelly; but still, he judges, on behalf of Israel and God. And yet, on the other hand, in judging by way of homicide and suicide, Samson also fulfils a personal project of preserving an ideal, an ideal which is at once a nationalistic imperative and a model of the very self who would obey and satisfy the nationalistic imperative. In killing himself and others, Samson saves both himself and the nation.

American psychoanalyst John Rosenberger, thinking about the modern suicide bomber, has argued that such a the terrorist is involved in 'depressive equivalent'

---

[49] Apparently, Israelis today deal with the same figure of Samson as a model Jew who is at once a champion of his people and despairing. See Grossman, *Lion's Honey*; and Harris, 'Samson's Suicide'.

behaviour, where, in effect, 'I kill you because I want to kill me', or even, in the case of suicide missions, 'I kill you-and-me because I want to kill me': and 'killing me' is in fact a way of preserving 'me', putting an end to the 'me' who interferes with the survival of the 'ideal me'.[50] This is an idea that Freud develops in his 'Mourning and Melancholy', with reference to Hamlet; that he develops in several works in reference to sado-masochism—the harming of another to displace a harming of oneself, and vice versa; and that Freud finally develops in his ideas about the death drive.[51] To survive is to die; in order that the ideal ego may live, other egos, even perhaps the real ego of the subject, will have to be sacrificed. As Albert Camus would say of 'the rebel', bent on what Camus calls 'metaphysical rebellion', 'The rebel has only one way of reconciling himself with his act of murder if he allows himself to be led into performing it: to accept his own death and sacrifice. He kills and dies so that it shall be clear that murder is impossible.'[52] The terrorist of this type, in short, wants to live, as the person he would be if he could; that is why the terrorist chooses the way of sacrificial death, while denying the idea that killing is murder.

To take a dialectical step beyond Rosenberger's analysis, one could even say that Samson's behaviour expresses a depressive *non-equivalence*. Samson is one, the Philistines are many. Samson is sacred, a Nazarite, and the Philistines are profane, an alien tribe who worship the wrong god. In return for trickery on a bet, thirty men are killed, and spoils taken from them too. In return for the loss of a wife, largely as the result of his own actions, crops and fields are devastated. 'This time', Samson says, as if earlier he had truly been guilty of malfeasance, 'when I do mischief to the Philistines, I will be without blame' (Judges 15.3). And when it is all over: 'As they did to me, so I have done to them' (Judges 15.11). In return for his having been arrested for arson and murder, 1,000 men are slaughtered. At the end of the story, Samson is blind, captive, and a butt of derision, whereas the Philistines appear to be in the fullness of their powers. And still, Samson speaks of violence in terms of non-equivalence: he calls upon the Lord to strengthen him 'that with this one act of revenge I may pay back the Philistines for my two eyes'. Three thousand lives are exchanged for a pair of eyes, in the course of a single act. Three thousand equals one and also equals two. According to the law of depressive equivalence, or perhaps rather depressive non-equivalence, in killing the Philistines and himself alike, Samson restores to life his ideal ego, the one who has never been shackled and ridiculed, who has never had his eyes plucked out, and maybe who has never been forced to compromise himself by sleeping with the enemy.

A peculiar coincidence thus informs the many purposes behind Samson's destruction of the temple: the strategic purpose of killing Philistines and subverting their rule over the Jews; the personal purpose of revenging his two eyes and

---

[50] Rosenberger, 'Discerning the Behaviour'. For a contrasting point of view, see Gambetta, 'Can We Make Sense of Suicide Missions?'

[51] Freud, *Beyond the Pleasure Principle*: esp. 38–40; *The Ego and the Id*: esp. 40–6; *Civilisation and Its Discontents*: esp. 118–22. For discussion of the relation between the death drive and the 'vicissitudes' of the ego's subject positions, see Laplanche, *Life and Death in Psychoanalysis*: 85–124. And on the relevance of the death drive to the problematic of terrorism, see Eagleton, *Holy Terror*: 5–11, 31–41; and Zulaika, *Terrorism*: 90–107.

[52] Camus, *The Rebel*: 246.

restoring his ideal ego to life; the result of bringing to an end the project of judging, making as it were a final if unsatisfactory judgement (unsatisfactory because there is no follow-through) on the Jews and their relation to the Philistines who ruled over them; the teleological purpose of confirming God's covenant with the Jewish people. Even with all these purposes tied together in a story of massive violence, the reader or adapter of the story at any time and place may still have cause for moral, intellectual, and religious reservation. Subversion, revenge, devastation, an end to 'judging' through a self-destructive judgement, a marking of a covenant through the loss of so many lives—these are not the ingredients of a happy story, a comedy. It is, as Wunstius and Ville-Toustain saw, a 'tragedy'.

The suggestion may nevertheless lurk, as Wunstius and Ville-Toustain knew, that the Samson story prefigured the story of Christ, that Samson was either in a positive or negative sense a forerunner of Christ: maybe positive because Samson saved a people by sacrificing himself, maybe negative because Samson's sacrifice was murderous and ineffective, bringing a political peace between two peoples, perhaps, but doing nothing for the achievement of eternal life.[53] But in either case Samson's story was a tragedy, not a comedy: it was the story of the fall (and perhaps also the felling) of a prince.

And so, one may ask, what was its message? What did the death of Samson and the Philistines *say*? What was its message from God? And what, given the difficulty of understanding these matters, was the point of reading the story, interpreting it, or adapting it? What was the *parable* of Samson all about?

4. SAMSON THE PARABLE

In the versions of the Samson story by Wunstius and Quarles, the first a closet drama in verse, the second a narrative poem with meditative asides, conditions of non-equivalence are exaggerated to the limit. They even expand into what for these writers is the crucial point, that Samson is not only sacred, marked out by God for special treatment, but a living, mortal expression of the Godhead. Says Wunstius's Samson, after he has been shorn of his hair and taken prisoner by the Philistines,

> My deep despair at my calamities now moves me less,
> O Father, than the fact Thy sacred name
> Is scorned and mocked at by these impious dogs.[54]

Or again:

> Here I must stand, a theme of jest and laughter
> To men and women; but the dreadful thing
> Is that, with me, Thy power will be mocked.[55]

---

[53] On the controversial subject of the idea of Samson as a forerunner of Christ, much beloved by Miltonists until recently, see Shawcross, '*The Uncertain World*'; Wittreich, *Interpreting*; and Wittreich, *Shifting Contexts*.

[54] Wunstius, *Simson*: 2:28.   [55] Wunstius, *Simson*: 4: 44–6.

I am not only me, according to this development of the dialectic of equivalence and non-equivalence; I am also You, and if I am harmed, You are harmed. But here I am, actually harmed, and harmed through humiliation. So You are harmed and humiliated. As Quarles has Samson put it:

> I am thy Champion, Lord. It is not me
> They strike at. Through my sides they strike at thee.
> Against thy Glory 'tis, their Malice lies.
> They aim'd at that when they put out these eyes.[56]

The essential thing, both from the point of view of Samson's psychology and from the point of view of the parable that his life expresses, is Samson's identification of himself as the Lord's 'champion', as if this made Samson a metonymic equivalent of God, a part or a contiguous aspect of a whole. Such a notion may help along the suggestion that Samson prefigures Christ. But apart from potential identifications between Samson, God, and Christ, something still more important seems to be happening: the identification of Samson with each and every Protestant believer of the seventeenth century in the struggle against heresy, persecution, and invasion: Samson, in other words, as the figure of Everyman, the true-believing Christian in the age of the Wars of Religion.

Wunstius and Quarles alike make the claim. Wunstius assures his readers that the story of Samson is an allegory of religious hope. The drama concludes:

> God himself, in that last victory
> Poured out on Samson's frame a power divine
> More notable than all he knew before.
> This victory shall later generations
> Hand down with loftiest praise...
> Of this stupendous work, this matchless gift,
> God gives His promise in the death of Samson,
> As by a metaphor.[57]

Samson's story is a legendary, metaphorical reminder of God's 'promise' to bring about the victory of his chosen people over their enemies, in this case the victory of Protestants over Catholics.

Quarles seems to think the same thing. But he also takes that promise literally, if also twistedly, turning the story into what appears to be propaganda in favour of English intervention in the Thirty Years War. As he puts it in an aside to his readers,

> Know leaden Magistrates, and know again,
> Your Sword was given to draw, and to be dyed
> In guilty blood; not to be laid aside...

And again,

> ...where the ground's religion, to defend
> Abused faith; let princes, there, contend,
> With dauntless courage: May their acts be glorious,
> Let them go, prosperous, and return, victorious.[58]

[56] Quarles, *Samson*: 139.   [57] Wunstius, *Simson*: 5: 53–4.
[58] Quarles, *History of Samson*: 68; 103.

If for Wunstius Samson's violence seems to indicate a 'promise' that might be construed as an eventual victory of the saints over their enemies, for Quarles the violence is a call for more violence, though not in the form that Samson's took, since princes are called upon to wage war by raising and leading armies, not by getting killed alone in battle while avenging their eyes. (They 'return, victorious.') Samson's struggle and terrible triumph is a pretext for holy war, but not for suicide and mass destruction.[59]

If the true believer is identified with Samson, and if Samson is identified with God, if one body is identified with another body and all with the Godhead, then the relation between the individual and violence, including political violence, has been significantly, and dangerously, modified. Calvin famously argued for obedience to secular authority, even when that authority was religiously oppressive. Let persecution serve as a humiliation and chastisement, Calvin argued. Let it serve as a reminder of the *distance* between the believer and the almighty God, and let it therefore accentuate the meaning of faith.[60] But Wunstius, Quarles, and perhaps Ville-Toustain argue for the opposite. Violence against individuals, so far as they are true believers, is violence against God; and therefore violence in defence of true believers, against their enemies, is violence *on behalf* of God. It may even be violence *by* and *in* God.

Wunstius at least appeals in this regard to a monarchomach idea, which provides a modern legal premise for violence. He has his Samson claim, 'Against our public enemies all things / Are still permissible.'[61] 'The public' is not an ancient Jewish idea; appeals to such a notion appear nowhere in Judges, although seeds of the idea may appear in the notion of 'Israel' and its 'Israelites'. But for Wunstius a 'public' exists in ancient Palestine no less than one exists for the author of *Vindiciae contra tyrannos* in France. And the legal argument is clear: while it is forbidden to injure someone because of a private grievance, such injuries being the province of the sovereignty and code of civil law, in modern Europe it is legally allowed and perhaps even encouraged, given the right conditions, to injure an enemy of 'the public'. Thus in Wunstius's eyes, too, the hegemony of the Philistines over the Jews is conceived of as a kind of tyranny, to which a legal response may well be an otherwise illegal resort to violence.

Yet in the will to destruction we hear openly expressed in Wunstius's and Quarles's text, with or without an underpinning in monarchomach or just-war theory, we also hear a supercharged vindictiveness. This vindictiveness is familiar from neither the minimalist narration of Judges 13–16 nor the cautious language of political theorists, though it is reminiscent of what we have seen in texts like Du Bartas's *Judit* and real-life accounts of massacres and executions in the period. Cries out Wunstius's Samson to God:

> Punish through me the sinful mockeries
> Heaped on Thy godhead by this impious crew!
> Breathe back my former strength in these my limbs;
> So may the glad, exulting celebrations,

[59] Tollington, 'The Ethics of Warfare'.
[60] Calvin, *Institutes*: Book 4, Section 20. <http://www.spurgeon.org/~phil/calvin/>.
[61] Wunstius, *Simson*: 1; 28.

Prepared to scorn thy deity and honour
An evil idol, end in sad lamenting.[62]

It is not enough for my enemies to be defeated, Samson says; my enemies must *suffer*. And it is not so much in revenge of Samson's two eyes that the Philistines must suffer; it is rather in exchange for their blasphemy, for their gloating over the true God. In dramatizing Samson's story, Wunstius has introduced emotions and motives for action that were not in the original, and that may well be in violation of its spirit. Samson becomes the vehicle not only for the end of a certain historical struggle between the Jews and their neighbours (brought on, according to Judges, again, by the Jews' own wrongdoing in the eyes of the Lord), but of a vindication of God and his godly people, and a punishment of their hapless, blasphemous enemies.

Something similar happens in Quarles's text, where the 'exulting celebrations' of the Philistines are exaggerated over the space of about one hundred lines. The Philistines are not only, as the Bible says, 'merry'. They order a great feast. They get drunk. They taunt and laugh at Samson. They spit in his face. They call for him to be lashed anew. Samson responds by continuing to think of himself as a stand-in for God, at once the means through which God has been flouted and the means through which God will 'rescue' his 'Glory':

> Revenge thy wrongs, great God, o let thy hand
> Redeem thy suffering honour, and this land:
> Lend me thy power; Renew my wasted strength,
> That I may fight thy battles; and, at length,
> Rescue thy Glory, that my hands may do
> That faithful service, they were born unto:
> Lend me thy power, that I may restore
> Thy loss, and I will never urge thee more.[63]

The language of justice, vengeance, and punishment is coupled with a language of 'honour' (another concept, like 'the public', alien to Judges). God's honour needs to be redeemed, and it can only be redeemed by way of an excess of justice, vengeance, and punishment. The violence, as Quarles especially emphasizes, is indiscriminate, and even leads to desecration, the humiliation of the corpse:

> [The pillars] cracked, and, with their fall,
> Down fell the Battlements, and Roof, and all;
> And, with their ruins, slaughtr'd at a blow,
> The whole Assembly. They that were below,
> Receiv'd their sudden deaths from those that fell
> From off the top; whilst none was left, to tell
> The horrid shrieks, that filled the spacious Hall,
> Whose ruins were impartial, and slew all:
> They fell; and, with an unexpected blow,
> Gave every one his death, and Burial too.[64]

[62] Wunstius, *Simson*: 4; 46.   [63] Quarles, 139.
[64] Quarles, *History of Samson*: 140.

So in both Wunstius and Quarles we find similar departures from the biblical story, echoing similar departures into vindictiveness and cruelty in other texts of terrorism before the letter. Samson's sacredness is exaggerated, to the point where his own welfare is identified with the welfare of the Lord. The wickedness of the Philistines is exaggerated, to the point where they show themselves to be not just the worshippers of Dagon, a rival god, but blasphemers and sadists. Both Wunstius and Quarles make the final massacre itself into a spectacle, where the reader is encouraged to take a kind of delight in the exhibition of death and destruction. And yet the question arises: why? Apart from wanting colourfully to dramatize the story, that is, why do the writers shift the story toward the pleasures of religious vindictiveness?

The answer may lie, paradoxically, not in a surcharge of bloodthirstiness and fundamentalist passion, but rather the opposite. If the story of Samson has found new allegorical associations—the Wars of Religion in France, the Thirty Years War in Germany—these associations are primarily formalistic, emotive, figurative, literary. They belong to parable rather than to life. They express abstract wishes rather than concrete objectives. And in this they illustrate one of the most significant developments of the discourse of terrorism before the letter, that up until the 1640s, where the language of political violence would acquire a new revolutionary power, the discourse became more and more self-referential, associated less and less with the mythic power of action in life and more and more with the mythic power of myth itself. The story of Samson, for all its violence, is homiletic. It sustains the soul. It makes the figure of self-destruction into a figure of survival. It makes the ritual ban, the elimination of the gentile enemy, into a figure of modern warfare, waged by armies of true believers against heretical princes.

5. RICHARD ROGERS AND THE END OF THE WICKED

In other words—and this phenomenon is not unfamiliar in the literature of other times and places—Wunstius and Quarles have written about violence vehemently, spectacularly, viciously, and gloriously, but only in parable, only in detachment from real-life violence. Violence has become a sign of a certain attitude, a faith, a vigilance, a wish; but it is not a sign of violence itself. The language of terrorist violence has been hijacked to serve purposes related but not identical to terrorist violence. Even the language of violence may have been appropriated for alien purposes. For one may ask, how serious are Wunstius and Quarles really are in their glorification of violence? How seriously have they thought about the idea of what violence is, what happens when it is undertaken, what results when armies clash, or when lone individuals nominate themselves champions of holy war? Quarles spent most of his life at home, writing devotional poems, many of them arguing on behalf of Christian patience. When the civil wars came, he sided with Charles I.[65]

---

[65] 'Francis Quarles' in *Oxford Dictionary of National Biography*.

In Richard Rogers's *Commentary*, which provides a careful chapter-by-chapter reading of the whole of Judges, the *license* of heroes like Ehud, Jael, and Samson to engage in holy war is sharply distinguished from the *prohibition* against recourse to violence that obtains in modern English society. Rogers accepts the idea of an identification between a biblical hero and God, but he is cautious about it. Discussing Ehud, he says, 'here must be a caveat observed, that is, that no man presume by these examples to enterprise such like matters without warrant from God'. Above all, he thinks, it is dangerous to lie to one's self, to reason that one's cause is good and then pretend that one has God's warrant to take justice into one's own hands. When Jael kills Canaanite general Sisera in her tent, having deceived him with hospitality, Rogers says that she did what she did to an enemy, 'not hers, but God's', and was therefore to be commended. But it is not like that for believers in the present day, he adds. 'For us who have not the like commandment (except the civil magistrate, and the lawful executioner) we have in no wise liberty to follow her example, but to stick fast to the rule that teacheth us to walk toward all men in uprightness and all good simplicity and innocency, giving unto the worst their due.'[66] It is almost as if Rogers were producing a variation on the theme of the death of the age of miracles: in the old days, the age of miracles, God gave his champions direct commandments to do His work, including His violence, along with the power to succeed; nowadays, there are no direct commandments to pass into violence, and God's champions must do their work by peaceful means.

Yet the violent stories continue, coming to a climax with Samson. Samson had a 'calling', Rogers says, 'to plague the Philistines, God's enemies'. Moreover, having turned to sin on many occasions—Rogers does not hesitate to accuse Samson of misdeeds and character flaws—Samson, having been captured and tortured by the Philistines, is now repentant. He has begged God's forgiveness. 'And as he had his strength restored to him again, as we see, so had he also his inward grace...'[67] Rogers does not read Samson as a man set apart from birth and therefore always holy, but rather as a man who had a special calling from birth who nevertheless had to earn his religious credentials. Samson's calling as a hero of faith was not unlike the callings of any one of the godly in contemporary England who considered themselves among the elect but who had to earn the privilege by entering the condition that Puritans called 'sanctification', or 'inward grace'. Earn a sanctification Samson does, in Rogers's eyes, on several occasions. Every time Samson returns to God's favour, and hence to his calling, he expresses his dignity at once through conviction and massive violence. Yet the violence itself, again, is not something for any Christian of the early seventeenth century to emulate. It belonged to then, not to now.

Here comes the twist. Now that violence in the Bible has been detached from the conduct of life in the present day, now that it no longer urges or ought to urge anyone into similar action, now, in short, that terrorism is no longer warranted or sanctified, the signs of violence may nevertheless serve as vehicles for the expression and displacement of violent wishes. The death drive returns, though only in a wistful form.

[66] Rogers, *Commentary*: 222.   [67] Rogers, *Commentary*: 784.

Rogers himself, it is worth noticing, was not a stranger to persecution. A Puritan divine among a clergy dominated by anti-Puritan moderates, he was several times in trouble with the Church establishment for unorthodox preaching and suspended from his duties. At the end of a diary for 1590, for example, we find Rogers worrying about 'this likelihood of losing my liberty and breaking up of family', his 'liberty' in this instance meaning his liberty to preach, and his 'family' having to do with the possibility of having part of his estate confiscated.[68] But Rogers was socially well connected and popular and he gradually became part of the Church establishment, though inclined toward a Presbyterian rather than an Anglican order.[69] He was not a sectarian or a separatist. He believed in what was at once a radical vision of Protestant faith and an establishment vision of Protestant worship. And so the Samson story comes to serve an unexpected purpose, where what Samson does, destroy thousands of people in what might be called a theatre, signifies a wish and a presentiment about what the Puritan establishmentarian would like to see done to the real enemies of Puritan faith and worship—the enthusiasts for modern secular English theatre.

Like Wunstius and Quarles, Rogers capitalizes on what he takes to be the festivities of the Philistines as they meet to celebrate Samson's captivity. The Philistines actually have a pretty good case, according to the Bible, for they meet to perform a sacrifice to their god in thanksgiving, and their logic is impeccable: 'Our god has given our enemy into our hand, the ravager of our country, who has killed many of us' (Judges 16.24). But for Rogers the spectacle is what counts, as the Philistines gather to 'behold' their captive and 'please themselves therein'. And this reflects poorly on the Philistines. For the scene 'clearly layeth out the folly, yea the deceitful folly of the ignorant and irreligious, who have been, and still are so ready to flock together by hundreds and thousands to satisfy their eye, and to behold that which may provoke foolish laughter'. The target on which Rogers has displaced a signifier of aggression is laid bare: 'the ignorant and the irreligious'. And he means not just those benighted Philistines of the past, but the Philistines of today, 'who now long after, as also in years past and yet still in the light of the Gospel, have invented other manner of spectacles to delude the simple withal; even shameless shows, and most dangerous stage plays, omitting none to play a part in them, that they may increase sin'.[70] There follows a standard Puritan complaint against playing, with an emphasis on the corruptness of the visual and the counterfeit, in the spirit of Stephen Gosson's *School of Abuse* (1579) and Philip Stubbes's *Anatomie of Abuse* (1583).[71] And then comes a chilling statement: referring to the playgoers, he says, 'if God should show some such strange judgement upon [them], as upon these here (as we have heard that some of them have had lately fair warnings in that kind, while they have been in the midst of their pastimes) I deny not but it were lamentable; but doubtless not less (what do I say? nay by far more) deserved than this'.[72] On the one hand, a commitment to non-violence is asserted, and a humaneness

[68] Knappen, ed., *Two Elizabethan*: 101.
[69] See 'Richard Rogers', *Oxford Dictionary of National Biography*.
[70] Rogers, *Commentary*: 779. Rogers refers among other things to an earthquake in 1580.
[71] See Barish, *The Anti-theatrical Prejudice*.   [72] Rogers, *Commentary*: 780.

toward all men is insisted upon; on the other, a judgement and a wish are expressed—against actors and their fans—both of which are murderous.

The importance of thinking about the relation between objectives, passions, end results, and the ends of historical action is no more evident than here, in the text of a non-violent man at once rejecting and wishing for violence. Rogers is no more Providentialist than a tragedian like Chapman, in the sense that he will claim no original foresight about the end of history, and admit to the fact that history has been a story of many bad things, many of which are beyond human understanding. A Puritan like Rogers is similar to a stoic like Chapman in that they both seem to believe that resistance should be its own reward. But in Rogers there is also the wish, transposed to the field of history. Noting that the Bible concludes Samson's story by saying that 'his brothers and all his family came down and took him and brought him up and buried him' (Judges 16.31), Rogers infers that there were Philistine survivors who allowed Samson's family to take Samson's body away. And he infers from this the general effect of the slaughter, which was not just death and destruction but also a message of terror:

> By this verse it appeareth, that at this strange spectacle of the casting down the house upon the Philistines and their princes, the rest of them were so amazed that they suffered the kinsmen of Samson to come thither and carry him back again unto their land and inheritance, and to bury him there. Which, if they had considered advisedly, they would have taken them and the rest, being under their power, and have put them to most cruel death.

By Philistine law, by the rules of the Philistine right to self-preservation and the administration of justice, Samson's kinsmen were fit to be arrested and executed, even put to 'a most cruel death'. But something else has happened here: the Philistines have been incapacitated; their ability to exercise their own justice has been frightened off. And there is a lesson to be drawn from this: 'Thus we see God sometimes appals the wicked, so his people may fare the better by it.' Or, as he goes on to say:

> Thus by the death of some that are maliciously minded against the faithful, other of their company are so astonished and appalled that they desist from their wicked attempts, and are in such fear that for a time they cannot tell what they may do.[73]

For Rogers, the slaughter of 3,000 Philistines was divine terrorization. It intimidated a whole people into quiescence. But it was not only a terrorist act of the past. 'Thus we see God sometimes...', he says. From the example of Samson comes a 'thus' and a 'sometimes', spread across the field of history, as something we 'see'. And with that too comes the expression of a wish. 'Sometimes' it happens. We have nothing to do with it. It is up to God. But sometimes it happens, as it ought to happen, and would happen if all our wishes came true. Yet it is 'not always expedient' that God should act this way, 'for then he should make a riddance of the wicked from the earth, and so the innocent and righteous should not have their

[73] Rogers, *Commentary*: 789.

faith and patience tried by them, as he hath appointed them to be'.[74] We shall wish to make a riddance of the wicked, but we shall not have it yet. We don't deserve it, and in any case we need them.

The objective in the Samson story for Rogers is the liberation of the Jewish people. The personal motivation is sanctification. The end result is the terrorization of the Philistines. And in view of the ends of historical action, as well as the ends of parable, Samson and the mass murders he commits are the confirmation of a mysterious hope. It is anticipated that in the course of history the wicked will perish, and Samson confirms the divine warrant for the expectation; but it is not hoped for so much—not today—because otherwise life would not be an ordeal, and we would not have to earn our own redemption. The myth of terrorism before the letter, by way of Samson, is our myth: for it shows us who we want to be or used to be, and who unfortunately we are now. We are (we suppose) a chosen people, a political people who want to keep choosing themselves, trapped in our death drives, but looking for life.

---

[74] Rogers, *Commentary*: 789.

A Brief Conclusion

Always, it would seem, the literature of terrorism before the letter was a literature in combat. It tried to pronounce on the meaning of historical action. Sometimes it encouraged violent intervention in the affairs of nations. Sometimes it celebrated profound and delirious triumphs over the nations and individuals its authors took to be their enemies. But just as often it raised doubts about violence and the uses of violence in history. What shall we be conscious of in the realm of the political? The answer to that question was always controversial, having to do with such questions as the extent to which religious problems ought to be settled politically, by negotiation or by force, or how private individuals ought to respond to tyranny and martyrdom, or to armed heroism and the victimization of innocents. Many times the significance of an expression of the mythography of terrorism before the letter was conclusive as a parable but inconclusive in life—as in the case of a play like *The Revenge of Bussy d'Ambois*. But sometimes a discourse was conclusive in life but inconclusive as a parable—as in the account of the execution of Ravaillac.

The stories of terrorism before the letter come from a variety of rhetorical and mimetic angles, arguing for or against the violence or somewhere in between. Some of the texts, like *The Revenger's Tragedy*, seem overtly secular and irreverent, even though we know that the author Thomas Middleton had strong reformist Protestant sympathies.[1] Some of the texts, like Quarles's *History of Samson*, seem specifically religious in character, even in extolling a form of holy war; and yet Quarles openly uses the story as a pretext for urging princes to make what would be very nasty wars on one another, although the only result he can imagine is a glorious victory. In some cases the language of texts seems continuous with the language of violence. In others the two languages split off from one another, purposes multiply, and the result are allegories whose referents are unclear.

In the case of Rogers's *Commentary*, however, some clarity on the issue arises, indicative of a general though not universal trend in the seventeenth century. Life is one thing: the parable is another. In life, in his life, Samson was killed and was a hero. In our life there are no Samsons. But in parable, Samson kills and we kill along with him; we kill in the realm of wishes. So on the one hand, there can be no satisfaction of our wishes. All of this is up to God, not to us. We are committed to non-violence, and life, as Kafka's narrator would say, is incomprehensible. But on the other hand, we nevertheless wish, and sometimes the wish becomes reality, if only for a temporary period, and if only for reasons beyond our control.

---

[1] Rist and others have argued, however, that reformist impulses play a big role in the tragedy. See Rist, *Revenge Tragedy*: 98–106.

The language of terrorist violence becomes disjoined from the practice of ter-rorist violence, even if, in this disjunction, we find one of the best understandings of how terrorism works among writers of the period, and even if this language has become *internalized*, made into a project of piety. But such was the destiny of the mythography of terrorism before the letter. Whether terrorist acts came or did not come, the language for them was operating in the imagination. And the language spoke not only to fears but also to wishes. An arché-terror had been made empir-ical on the level of the imagination. Let me repeat those words by Rogers, which express a very full understanding of the power of what we now call terrorism. 'Thus by the death of some that are maliciously minded against the faithful, other of their company are so astonished and appalled that they desist from their wicked at-tempts, and are in such fear that for a time they cannot tell what they may do.' When Westerners indulged their imaginations in this way, they could find many things about themselves with which it was otherwise difficult to cope. Politics meant both security and danger. Action could lead both to liberty and catastrophe. History gave evidence that violence could at once appal and sanctify. Though there was therefore much to fear, there was also much to hope. For if political violence was on the side of irreversible destruction, it was also on the side of transcendence. If the violence destroyed, it also judged. If it judged, it disposed of the wrongdoing of the past, bringing about ancient liberty, peace, and justice in the present.

Much of the violence of the period, in real life as in fiction, was understood to express a ritualistic force. Violence wasn't only violence. It was also symbolic. It involved a provocation of exchange. But violence was also irreversible, or meant to be irreversible. It was not a circulation of commodities and moneys, or even an ongoing trade in honour and influence or status. It had a symbolic power which demanded both an inequality and an irreversibility. Although it is in the nature of rituals that they establish equivalencies (this ring for that pledge, this life for that blessing) and may be repeated indefinitely, the ritual of terrorism before the letter was undertaken in a situation where the perpetrators aimed to achieve unequal and irreversible effects, such that a repeated ritual would be both unnecessary and unthinkable.

Of course, the terrorists, whether fictional or real, could not succeed. Terrorist violence never can. It cannot control its own aftermath. But certainly it could dra-matically change the course of history, and sometimes it could seem that it changed the course of history in just the way intended, with just the consequences previ-ously envisaged, in keeping with the model of historical action with which it was designed. Even if it could not quite measure up to the expectations it aroused, sometimes terrorist violence was apparently necessary. After all, a crisis of meaning was being experienced, and the crisis was existential too. How would Protestantism survive the war the Catholics were so successfully waging against it in 1563? How would Catholicism survive the reign of the arch-Protestant James I? How would the English constitution survive the depredations and the encroaching tyranny of the Duke of Buckingham? It was to take the measure of these perceived crises and responses that poetasters circulated their encomiums, that playwrights like Garnier and Marlowe produced their plays—tragedies of defeat like *Cornélie* or comedies of atrocity and triumph like *The Massacre at Paris*—that populations staged their festivals of scapegoating and thanksgiving, and that divines like Richard Rogers in effect changed the subject, holding onto aggressive wishes but bottling them up in the name of Christian patience and resentment.

In the 1640s England, Scotland, and France alike would experience a resurgence of political violence, fought in part over issues familiar from the 1560s, in part over issues entirely new. The language of terrorism before the letter would continue to be useful on many occasions, even with respect to events that bore little in common with the events that inspired the earlier discourse. But it was a language with a history now, and so bore sedimentary and self-referential as well as emergent and exogenous referential meanings. It had been included in a great many texts that by now were national classics—works by Ronsard, Montaigne, Spenser, Shakespeare, Jonson, Corneille. It was saturated with the recent memory of scandalous domestic events, above all the Saint Bartholomew Massacre and the Gunpowder Plot. What was once an application of ancient concepts and tropes to the disturbing new conditions of the Reformation was now a body of literature stemming from national genius coupled with the memory of national traumas and triumphs. Meanwhile, though many of the terms of the old conflicts would resurface in the 1640s, it became clear almost at once that new sorts of discourse were needed as well. In fact, new sorts of discourse were now being produced, again and again. For the conflicts of the 1640s—the civil wars in England, the battles over autonomy and hegemony between England, Ireland, and Scotland, the Fronde in France—turned out to be very different from those of earlier years. The General Crisis was also a new sort of crisis, requiring a vaster scale of warfare for resolution than had been imagined before.

Beginning in the 1640s, and periodically through to the twentieth century, political and religious conflict of the type that roused expressions of terrorism before the letter may increasingly have been made into causes for collective action: the Roundheads as an expression of the English people against the crown, or 130 years later the French Sans-Culottes against the royalist government in France. The lone hero was eschewed for the heroism of the collective will. After all, a lot of lone acts of terrorism had not worked out that well, and it was known that collective action was more likely to prosper. The most decisive act of terrorism in the period in question, the Saint Bartholomew Massacre, was undertaken not by an individual or two but, apart from a squad of appointed royalist soldiers, a faceless cooperative, about whom almost nothing is known apart from the fact that its members acted cooperatively, in a kind of social revolution before the letter, waged against a population of scapegoats. One of the second most decisive acts of the period, the assassination of Henry III, though undertaken by a lone assassin, was accomplished by a man who was clearly supported by a mass, perhaps the majority of Parisians, who had already chased Henry III outside their gates and who were engaged in continuing to resist—and scapegoat—him in the name of the liberty of the French people.[2] So even past experience could speak on behalf of collective as opposed to

---

[2] See Weber, 'La journée des Barricades'.

individual initiative, and toward something like revolution as opposed to terrorist sedition. The discovery of a collective political will—even of a will that needed no scapegoats—was one of the great achievements of modern political thought, beginning in the 1640s. The recruitment of a collective will into the raising of revolution was one of the great moves forward in the history of the West. But still, acts of terrorism, rogue terrorism, seditious terrorism, and state terrorism, against all kinds of symbolic targets, continued across the centuries, as did atrocity in warfare.

There were probably many more such acts than historians have accounted for yet. Even if the long eighteenth century was, up to 1789, much more pacific within the boundaries of Western Europe than the seventeenth or sixteenth centuries,[3] European colonialism in the Americas, Africa, and Asia was a pretext for all sorts of terrorist crimes, for and against European incursion. Meanwhile, writers from Racine and Dryden to Addison and Voltaire could adopt the literary legacy of terrorism before the letter: they could appropriate the material to express their own artistic and ideological visions, responding to their own historical situations. Dryden, for example, responding to the Popish Plot, collaborated with fellow playwright Nathaniel Lee in producing *The Duke of Guise* (1683), a play that owes a good deal to Marlowe and Chapman as well as to contemporary French accounts of the assassination, including perhaps Matthieu's *Guisiade*. Voltaire in the next century had one of his greatest successes with *La Henriade* (1723), an epic poem about Henry IV, which could not fail to reflect on Henry's eventual assassination and all the literature that had previously been written about it, even if its subtext was anti-clerical feeling in the 1720s. Ten years later he would collaborate with the great composer Jean-Phillipe Rameau in an opera called *Samson: Tragédie en musique*, which was first produced, controversially, in 1734. Voltaire's Samson is much like the Samson of the seventeenth century, except that his main enemy is sensuality, along with a king (though the biblical Philistines did not have a king) who incarcerates and tortures him. Nine years later, in 1743, George Frideric Handel would premiere his own oratorio *Samson*, based on Milton's *Samson Agonistes*, which concludes not with Miltonic ambivalence but rather epic certainty over what Samson has accomplished and why. 'Oh, lastly overstrong against thyself!' says Manoa in Handel's version. 'A dreadful way thou took'st to thy revenge: / Glorious, yet dearly bought!'[4] The present of terrorism before the letter between 1559 and 1642 became part of the past of modern European society and its literary tradition. The more pacific eighteenth century was not above taking seventeenth-century discourse and making it simpler rather than more complicated, less nuanced about violence, and also more enthusiastic about it.

The afterlife of terrorism before the letter, along with subsequent developments in the histories of terrorist violence and the enabling fictions that surrounded it, would be material for another book, or maybe several books. How extensive this material is has yet to be explored. But it is there, and we shall never completely

---

[3] So we hear from most of the historians of violence, cited in Chapter 1, section 2.
[4] Handel and Hamilton, *Samson*: 78.

understand the history of terrorism in the West until scholars take the trouble to find and explain it.

Meanwhile, I hope that in the realm of terrorism studies, including critical terrorism studies, it will now be seen that a long history precedes present-day preoccupations with terrorist violence, and that this long history includes a complex discourse, a mythography, that operates from within the deepest interiors of Western thought, and speaks to some of the most significant horizons of hope and fear toward which Western, not to mention many non-Western, experiments in self-governance have inclined. To have a *public* to whom political questions may be addressed, in a hope of recognition—even so little a public as an Israel ruled by Philistines, or a Florence lorded over by a corrupt ducal family—is to be vulnerable to that form of political violence we call terrorism. There is no escaping that vulnerability without escaping the phenomenon of the public and the dialectics of recognition. So, though experts on terrorism may well often preoccupy themselves with how to prevent terrorist incidents, or how to respond to them after they have happened, they need to bear in mind that even if terrorists are sometimes our enemies, they are enemies on our terms, responding to questions that we have formulated. And they need to bear in mind that sometimes they are not even our enemies. Sometimes they are us, or people purportedly acting on our behalf. If the supreme law is the safety of the people, it might be that anything is possible, and almost anything is allowed.

Because 'terrorism' has become such a term of abuse, some people are disinclined to use the word even when it fits, and even when fitting the word to the deed can help clarify how history works, or how it may come to work in the future. But there it is, working on behalf of causes good and bad, progressive and retrograde, emancipatory and repressive. And there it is too in our imaginations, in an endless series of television programmes, some of them stupid, some of them quite brilliant as works of televisual art, and most of them altogether ignorant—perhaps deliberately so—about what terrorism is, or what its significance may be.[5] There it is as well in the cinema, in literature high and low, in media reports and opinion pieces. We need to understand this spectral life of terrorism in modern-day culture better than we do, just as we need to better understand terrorism itself. If nothing else, this volume should have shown that what we talk about when we talk about terrorism is a multi-faceted thing. Bringing terrorism into discourse means bringing in a long tradition of enabling fictions, as well as of historical facts on the ground; and that to think about the phenomenon, if it is not to be reduced to a parody of itself, may mean thinking about how its discourse is structured according to the principles of human action and the grammar used to express it. For in every action there is an act, an agent, a scene, an agency, and a purpose. In fact, there are usually a great many of them.

---

[5] See Appelbaum, 'Fantasias of Terrorism'.

Bibliography

1. PRIMARY TEXTS

Admirable et prodigieuse mort de Henry de Valois. Paris, 1589.

Advertissement envoyé à la Noblesse de France, tant du party du Roy, que des Rebelles & Conjurez. Paris, 1574.

Advertissement particulier et veritable, de tout ce qui s'est passé en la ville de Tholose, depuis le massacre & assassinat commis en la personne des Princes Catholiques, touchant l'emprisonnement & mort du premier President & Advocat du Roy d'icelle. Paris, 1589.

Allen, William [Edward Sexby]. *Killing noe Murder. Briefly discourst in three quæstions.* Holland: 1657.

Amboise, Adrien d'. *Holoferne. Tragedie sacrée extraite de l'histoire de Judith.* (1580) In *La tragédie à l'époque d'Henry III: Théâtre français de la Renaissance.* Deuxième Série Vol. 2. 1579–1582. Florence: Olschki, 2000.

Andrewes, Lancelot. *Works.* 10 Volumes. Oxford: Parker, 1854.

Archives curieuses de l'histoire de France depuis Louis XI jusqu'à Louis XVIII. 27 volumes. Ed. Louis Cimber and Charles Danjou. Paris: Beauvais, 1834–48.

Aristotle. *Poetics.* In *The Basic Works of Aristotle.* Ed. Richard McKeon. New York: Random House, 1941.

Arrest de la cour de Parlement contre le Mareschal d'Ancre et sa femme. Paris, 1617.

Artus, Desiré. *La Singerie des Huguenots.* Paris, 1574.

Augustine of Hippo. *The City of God.* Trans. Henry Bettenson. Revised Edition. Harmondsworth: Penguin, 2003.

Augustine of Hippo. *Reply to Faustus the Manichaean.* Gnostic Society Library. <http://gnosis.org/library/contf1.htm>.

Aultruy, Jean d'. *Larmes sur la mémoire de Henry Le Grand.* Paris, 1610.

Bacon, Francis. *Advice to Sir George Villiers.* In The *Works of Francis Bacon.* 3 Volumes. Ed. Basil Montagu. Philadelphia: Carey & Hart, 1841. 2: 375–88.

Bacon, Francis. *A True Report of the Detestable Treason Intended by Dr Roderigo Lopez, a Physician Attending Upon the Person of the Queen's Majesty.* In *The Works of Francis Bacon.* Ed. R. L. Ellis, J. Spedding, and D. D. Heath. London, 1861. 8: 274–87.

Bandello, Matteo. *Histoires tragiques.* Trans. Pierre Boaistuau and Françoise de Belleforest. Ed. Richard A. Carr. Paris: Champion, 1977.

Bandello, Matteo. *Tutte le opere.* Ed. Francesco Flora. Milano: Mondadori, 1966–72.

Bandole, Antoine de. *Parallèles de César et d'Henri IV … avec les commentaires de César et les notes de Blaise de Vigenère.* Paris, 1609.

Barlow, William. *Sermon Preached at Paules Crosse, the Tenth Day of Nouember Being the Next Sunday After the Discouerie of this Late Horrible Treason.* London, 1606.

Barnaud, Nicolas. *Le reveille-matin des Francois, et de leurs voisins.* Edimbourg, 1574.

Bartas, Guillaume du. *Bethulians Rescue.* In *All the Small Workes of That Famous Poet.* Trans. Joshua Sylvester. London, 1616: 44–204.

Bartas, Guillaume du. *La Judit.* Ed. André Baiche. Toulouse: Faculté de Lettres, 1970.

Bartas, Guillaume du. *The Historie of Judith.* Trans. Thomas Hudson. Edinburgh, 1584.

Belleforest, François de. *Advertissement sur les rébellions, auquel est contenu qy' elle est la misère qui accompaigne les traistres, séditieux et rebelles et les récompenses qui les suivent selon leurs mérites.* N.p., 1586.

Belleforest, François de. *Amleth: Avec quelle ruse Amleth, qui depuis fut roy de Dannemach, vengea la mort de son pere Horevendille, occis par Fengon son frere, et autre occurence de son histoire.* In Belleforest, *Le cinquiesme tome des Histoires tragiques.* Paris, 1572: 149–66.

Belleforest, François de. *The Hystorie of Hamblet* (1608), in *Narrative and Dramatic Sources of Shakespeare.* Trans. Anon. Ed. Geoffrey Bullough. 8 Volumes. London: Routledge, 1973: 7: 81–124.

Belleforest, François de. 'L'infortuné marriage de Seigneur Antoine Bouloigne, avec la Duchesse de Malfi, er la mort piteuse de tout les deux'. In Belleforest, *Le second tome des Histoires tragiques, extraites de l'italien de Bandel.* Paris, 1566: 11–51.

Belyard Simon. *Le Guysien, ou Perfidie tyrannique commise par Henry de Valois.* Troyes, 1592.

Bertheau, Gilles. 'Passion et néo-stoïcisme dans *The Revenge of Bussy d'Ambois* (1613) de Chapman (1559?-1634)'. *Études Épistémè,* 1 (2002): 63–84.

Béthune, Maximillian de, duc de Sully. *Memoires des sages et royales.* In *Nouvelle collection des Memoires pour servir à l'Histoire de France.* Ed. Joseph-François Michaud and Jean-Joseph-François Poujoulat. Paris: Guyot. 33 Volumes 1839–54. Volume 11. Paris, 1850.

Bèze, Theodore de. *Du droit des magistrats.* Ed. Robert M. Kingdon. Genève: Droz, 1970.

Bèze, Theodore de. *Histoire ecclésiastique des églises reforme'es au royaume de France, depuis l'an 1521, jusques en l'année 1563.* Ed. T. Marzial. 3 Volumes. Lille, 1841–2.

Biet, Christian. Ed. *Théâtre de la cruauté et récits sanglants en France (XVIe–XVIIe siècle).* Paris: Robert Laffont, 1996.

Billard, Claude. *Larmes sur la tombe de très grand, très victorieux, très chrestien roy de France et de Navarre Henry IIII.* Paris: Rolin Thierry, 1610.

Billard, Claude. *La mort d'Henry IV: Tragédie en cinq actes et en vers.* Paris: L. Collin, 1806.

Boaistuau, Pierre. 'Mahomet and Irene.' In *The Palace of Pleasure.* Trans. William Painter. Ed. Joseph Jacobs. 3 Volumes. Honolulu: University Press of the Pacific, 2002: 1:190–7.

Boaistuau, Pierre and Francois de Belleforest. *Histoires Tragiques, extraictres des oeuvres Italiennes de Bandel, et mises en langue Françoise Les six premieres, par Pierre Boisteau, Les douzes suivans, par Franc. De Belle Forest, Comingeois.* Turin, 1582.

Bodin, Jean. *On Sovereignty.* Trans. Julian Frank. Cambridge: Cambridge University Press, 1992.

Boétie, Estienne de La. *The Politics of Obedience: The Discourse of Voluntary Servitude.* Trans. Harry Kurz. Montreal: Black Rose Books, 1975.

Bordier, Henri-Léonard. Ed. *Le chansonnier huguenot du 16e siècle.* Paris, 1870.

Bordier, Henri-Léonard. *La Saint-Barthélemy et la critique moderne.* Genève: H. Georg, 1879.

Bordier, Henri-Léonard. Ed. *Peinture de la Saint-Barthélemy par un artiste contemporain comparée avec les documents historiques.* Genève: J. Jullien, 1878.

Botero, Giovanni. *The Reason of State and the Greatness of Cities.* Trans. P. J. Waley, D. P. Waley, and Robert Peterson. London: Routledge, 1956.

Botzheim, Johann Wilhelm von. 'Le massacre fait à Orléans au mois d'août 1572.' *Bulletin de la Société de l'histoire du protestantisme français.* 21 (1872): 346–92.

Boucher, Jean. *Oraisons colligees pour les princes catholiques & pour obtenir la victoire encontre les ennemys.* Paris, 1589.

Boucher, Jean. *Apologie pour Jehan Chastel,…et pour les pères et escholliers de la Société de Jésus* [1595]. In *Mémoires de Condé.* Paris, 1743. Volume 6.

Boucher, Jean. *La vie et faits notables de Henry de Valois* [1589]. Ed. Keith Cameron. Paris: Champion, 2003.

Brantôme, Pierre de. *Oeuvres Complètes*. 5 Volumes. Paris: 1858–1895.

Braunmuller, A. R. Ed. William Shakespeare, *Macbeth*. Cambridge: Cambridge University Press, 1997.

Bref receuil de l'assassinat commis en la personne du très illustre prince, Monseigneur le Prince d'Orange, Conte de Nassau, Marquis de la Vere, etc. par Jean Jauregui, Espaignole. Anvers, 1582.

Brief discours et histoire d'un voyage de quelques Français en la Floride et du massacre qui en a été fait par les Espagnols en 1565, par Urbain Chauveton, avec une requête présentée au Roi Charles IX. N.p. 1579.

Buchanan, George. *Ane Detectiovn of the duinges of Marie Quene of Scottes, touchand the murder of hir husband, and hir conspiracie, adulterie, and pretensed mariage with the Erle Bothwell: And ane defence of the trew Lordis, mainteinenis of the Kingis graces actioun and authoritie*. London, 1572.

Buchanan, George. *A Dialogue on the Law of Kingship*. Trans. Roger A. Mason and Martin S. Smith. Edinburgh: Saltire Society, 2006.

Buchanan, George. *The History of Scotland...Faithfully Rendered into English*. London, 1690.

Buchanan, George. *The Tyrannous Reign of Mary Stuart: George Buchanan's Account*. Trans. W. A. Gatherer. Edinburgh: Edinburgh University Press, 1958.

Bullough, Geoffrey. Ed. *Narrative and Dramatic Sources of Shakespeare*. Volume 7. London: Routledge, 1973.

Burghley, William Cecil. *A True Report of the Sundry Horrible Conspiracies of Late Times Detected to Have (By Barbarous Murders) Taken the Life Away of the Queenes Most Excellent Majestie, Whom Almighty God Hath Miraculously Conserved against the Treachery of Her Rebelles and the Violences of Her Most Puissant Enemies*. London, 1594.

Burin, Pierre. *Response* à *une epistre commenceant, Seigneur Elvide, ou est traitté des Massacres faits en France, en l'an M. D. LXXII*. Basle: 1574.

Burton, Robert. *Anatomy of Melancholy*. New York. New York Review Books, 2001.

Calvin, John, *Institutes of Christian Religion*. Trans. Henry Beveridge (1845). <http://www.spurgeon.org/~phil/calvin>.

Campion, Thomas. *De Puluerea Coniuratione (On the Gunpowder Plot)*. Ed. David Lindley. Trans. Robin Sowerby. Leeds: Leeds Texts and Monographs, 1987.

Cantique general des catholiques sur la mort de Gaspard de Coligny. Paris, n.d.

Capilupi, Camille. *Le Stratageme, ou la ruse de Charles IX, Roy de France, contre les Huguenots rebelles à Dieu et à luy*. 1573. In *Archive Curieuses*. 1re série, 4.

Carmichael, James. *Newes from Scotland, declaring the damnable life and death of Doctor Fian a notable sorcerer, who was burned at Edenbrough in Ianuary last. 1591*. London, 1592.

Cayet, Pierre Victor Palma. *Chronologie novenaire, contenant l'histoire de la guerre, sous le règne du très-chrestien Roy de France et de Navarre, Henry IIII*. Paris, 1608.

Chapman, George. *The Revenge of Bussy d'Ambois*. In *Four Revenge Tragedies*. Ed. Katharine Eisaman Maus. Oxford: Oxford University Press, 1995.

Chantelouve, François de. *La Tragedie de feu Gaspar de Colligni* (1575). Ed. Keith Cameron. Exeter: University of Exeter, 1971.

Chantelouve, François, de. *The Tragedy of the Late Gaspard De Coligny*. Trans. Richard Hillman. Ottawa: Dovehouse Editions, 2005.

Chaulmer, Charles. *La mort de Pompee*. Paris, 1638.

Chef du procez fait à la memoire de Conchino Conchini n'agueres mereschal de France, & a` Leonora Galigaj sa veufue & complices. N.p: n.d.

Chrétien Des Croix, Nicolas. *Les Royalles Ombres, où Henry le Grand, Alexandre et César, racontent succintement leur vie au poète Orphée, qui adjuge le prix au plus digne, pour l'annuel du très-chrestien et incomparable monarque Henry le Grand IIII, roy de France et de Navarre, de l'invention de N. Chrestien, sieur Des Croix*: Paris: J. Jesselin, 1611.

Coignard, Gabrielle de. *Imitation de la victoire de Judich*. In *Oeuvres chrétiennes*. Ed. Colette H. Winn. Genève: Droz, 1995: 368–460.

Coligny, Gaspard de. *An Answer to the Examination Said to Have Been Made of One Named John de Poltrot*. London, 1563.

Coligny, Gaspard de. *Response à l'interrogatoire, qu'on dit avoir esté fait à un nommé Jehan de Poltrot soy disant seigneur de Merey, sur la mort du feu duc de Guyse*. Orléans, 1562.

Complainte du gibet de Mont-faucon sur la mort du Marquis d'Ancre, La. N.p., 1617.

Concini, Concino Marquis d'Ancre. *Confession generale du Seigneur Conchine, Marquis d'Ancre, Trouvee apres sa mort en son cabinet*. Paris, 1617.

Concini, Concino Marquis d'Ancre. *The Last Will and Testament of the Marquis d'Ancre. Together with his Araignment. His Obsequies. His Wifes teares on his death. The Re-union of the King with his men of Warre. The rousing of the Soldat François*: London, 1617.

Considérations sur le meudre commis en la personne de feu Monsieur le Duc de Guyse. Paris, 1589.

Constant, Pierre. *Invective contre l'abominable parricide attenté sur la personne du Roy Très-Chrestien Henry IV*. Paris, 1595.

Coppée, Denis. *L'Exécrable assassinat perpetré par les Janissaires en la personne du Sultan Osman, Empereur de Constantinople*. Rouen, 1623.

Corneille, Pierre. *Cinna*. In Corneille, *Theatre II*. Ed. Jacques Morens. Paris: Flammarion, 2006.

Corneill, Pierre. *Cinna*. In Corneille, *The Cid/Cinna/The Theatrical Illusion*. Trans. John Cairncross. Harmondsworth: Penguin, 1975.

Crashaw, Richard. *Steps to the Temple…and Other Poems*. Ed. A. R. Waller. Cambridge: Cambridge University Press, 1904.

Crespin, Jean. *Histoire des martyrs: persecutez et mis a mort pour la verite de l'Evangile, depuis le temps des apostres jusques a present*. (1619). Ed. Daniel Benoit and Mathieu Lelievre. Toulouse: Société des Livres Religieux, 1885–9.

D'Aubigné, Agrippa. *Les Tragiques*. Ed. Frank Lestringant. Paris: Gallimard, 2003.

Davila, Arrigo Caterino. *Histoire des guerres civiles de France: François II—Henri IV*. Trans. M. L'Abbé M. [Mallet]. Paris, 1757.

De Lillo, Don. *Libra*. New York: Viking, 1988.

De Lillo, Don. *Mao II*. New York: Viking, 1991.

Debofle, Pierre. 'L'engagement politico-religieux de François de Belleforest à l'époque des guerres de religion'. *Bulletin de la Société archéologique du Gers*. 1995, 407–39.

Declaration, et Protestation du Tres-illustre Prince Wolfgang, Comte Palatin, du Rhin…des causes qui l'ont meu à venir en France au secours de ceux de la Religion reformee, enuoyee au Roy. Auec une lettre par luy escrite, sur l'inhumain et cruel massacre commis en la personne de feu Monseigneur le Prince de Condé. N.p., 1569.

Defense of Liberty Against Tyrants, A. Trans. Junius Brutus [1589]. Ed. Harold J. Laski. Gloucester, MA: Peter Smith, 1963.

Dekker, Thomas. *The Double PP*. London, 1607.

Dekker, Thomas. *If This Be Not a Good Play, the Devil Is In It*. London, 1611.

Dekker, Thomas. *Newes from Hell*. London, 1606.

Dekker, Thomas. *The Whore of Babylon*. Ed. Marianne Gateson Riely. New York: Garland, 1980.

Destruction du saccagement exercé cruellement par le duc de Guise et sa cohorte en la ville de Vassy (1562). In *Archives curieuses*: 1re série, 4.

Detestation des cruautez sanguinaires et abominables de Henry Devalé, en forme de regrets sur la mort et cruel assassinat par luy commis et perpétré en la personne de tres-haut et puissant Prince Henry de Lorraine, Duc de Guyse. N.p., 1589.

Devise du grand Henry IV où il est comparé à César, et les guerres de la Ligue avec celle de César et de Pompée. Utrecht, 1598.

Dialogue sur les nouvelles de la mort de monsieur de Guyse, et de son frère Cardinal, massacrez à Blois le Vendredy XXIII et samedy XXIII de Decembre, lors des Estats. Paris, 1589.

Discours au vrai, sur la mort et le trépas de Henry de Valois, Le. In *Théâtre de la cruauté et récits sanglants.* Ed. Biet, 1589: 869–73.

Discours au vray et en Abbrege de ce qui est dernierement aduenu à Vassi, y passant Monseigneur le Duc de Guise. Paris, 1561. In *Archives Curieuses*, 1re série, 4.

Discours deplorable du meurtre et assassinat, traditoirement et inhumainement commis et perpetré en la ville de Blois, les Estatz tenant. De treshaut, trespuissant, et tres-Catholicque, feu Henry de Lorraine Duc de Guyse, Per et grand Maistre de France, le vendredy vingt-quatriesme iour de Decembre mil cinq cens quatrevingts huict. N.p: n.d.

Discours du Roy Henry III. In *Mémoires d'Estat, recueillis de divers manuscrits, en suite de ceux de Monsieur de Villeroy.* Paris, 1623.

Discours du Roy Henry Troisieme à un personnage d'honneur et de qualité estant près de sa Majesté, des causes et motifs de la St-Berthelemy. In Bordier, *La Saint-Barthélemy et la critique moderne*: 53–61.

Discours entier de la persécution et cruauté excercée en la ville de Vaissy, par le duc de Guise. N.p. 1563.

Discours et procédures faites dans le parlement de Paris au sujet des tumultes arrivées a Saint Médard. In *Archives curieuses*, 1ere: 4.

Discours sur la mort de Gaspart de Coligny qui fit Admiral de France et de ses complices le jour saint Berthelemy. Paris, 1572.

Discours sur la mort de Monsieur le Président Brisson. Ensemble les arrests donnez à l'encontre des assassinateurs. Paris, 1595.

Discours sur les occurences des guerres intestine de ce royaume et de la justice de Dieu contre les rebelles. Paris, 1572.

Discours sur les causes de l'execution faicte ès personnes qui avoyent conjurés contre le Roy et son Estat. In *Archive Curieuses*, 1ere série, 7.

Discours sur les rébellions, auquel est contenu qu'elle est la misère qui accompagne les trahistres, sédicieux et rebelles, et les récompenses qui les suivent selon leurs rébellions. Paris, 1572.

Discours véritable de l'étrange et subite mort de Henri de Valois, advenuë par permission divine, lui étant à Saint Cloud, ayan assiégé le Ville de Paris, le Mardy premier jour d'Août 1589. Par un Religieux de l'Orde des Jacobins. In L'Estoile, *Journal de Henry III.* 3: 453–60.

Discours veritable sur la mort de François Ravaillat, executé à Paris le 27 mai. Lyon, 1610.

Donne, John. *Ignatius His Conclave.* London, 1611.

Dowriche, Anne. *The Frenche Historie.* London, 1589.

Dryden, John and Nathaniel Lee. *The Duke of Guise: A Tragedy.* London, 1683.

Du Bourg, Anne. *Oraison au senat de Paris pour la cause des Chrestiens, á la consolation d'iceux.* Paris, 1560.

Du Coignet, Pierre. *Anti-Coton, or a Refutation of Cottons Letter Declaratorie: lately directed to the Queene Regent, for the Apologizing of the Iesuites Doctrine, touching the killing of Kings.* Trans. G. H. London, 1611.

Du Peyrat, Guillaume. *Les Oraisons et discours funebres de divers autheurs, sur le trespas de Henry le grand.* Paris, 1611.

Du Peyrat, Guillaume. *Recueil de diverses poesies sur le trespas de Henry le Grand... et sur le Sacre et couronnement de Louis XIII son successeur.* Paris, 1611.

Duplessis, Mornay. *Memoires.* N.p.: 1624.

E.G.C. *Pastorelle pour le bout de l'an Henry le Grand.* Paris, 1611.

Effects espouvantables de l'excommunication de Henry de Valois et de Henry de Navarre. Paris 1589.

Eglisham, George. *The Forerunner of Reuenge Vpon the Duke of Buckingham, for the Poysoning of the Most Potent King Iames of Happy Memory King of Great Britan, and the Lord Marquis of Hamilton and Others of the Nobilitie Discouered.* Frankfurt, 1626.

Extraict du procès criminel facit à Pierre Barrière dict la Barre, natif d'Orleans. Melun, 1593.

Felton, John. *The Prayer and Confession of Mr Felton, Word for Word as Hee Spake it Immediately Before His Execution.* London, 1628.

Fletcher, Phineas. *The Locusts, or Apollyonists* (1627). In Giles and Phineas Fletcher, *The Poetical Works.* 2 Volumes. Ed. Frederick S. Boas. Cambridge: Cambridge University Press, 1908. 1:124–86.

Fonteny, Jacques de. *Cleophon.* Paris, 1600.

Fonteny-Mareuil, François, de. *Mémoires.* In *Nouvelle collection des memoires pour server à l'histoire de France.* Ed. Joseph-François Michaud and Jean-Joseph-François Poujoulat. Paris: Guyot. 33 Volumes 1836–54. 2eme série. 5. 1–292.

Frégeville, Jean de. *The Reformed Politicke: That Is, An Apologie For The Generall cause of Reformation, written against the sclaunders of the Pope and the League. With most profitable aduises for the appeasing of schisme, by abolishing superstition, and preseruing the state of the Clergie. Whereto is adioyned a discourse vpon the death of the Duke of Guise, prosecuting the argument of the booke.* London, 1589.

Garnier, Robert. *Pompey the Great His Cornelia's Tragedie.* Trans. Thomas Kyd [1595]. In *The Works of Thomas Kyd.* Ed. Frederick Boas. Oxford: Clarendon Press, 1954: 101–60.

Garnier, Robert. *Porcie. Cornélie.* Ed. Raymond Lebègue. Paris: Belles Lettres, 1973.

Garnier, Robert. *Porcie: Tragédie.* Ed. Silvan Turzio. In *La tragédie à l'époque d'Henri II et d Charles IX.* Première Série. Volume 4 (1568–73). Florence: Olschki, 1994: 3–85.

Gascoigne, George. *The Spoyle of Antwerpe. Faithfully Reported, by A True Englishman, Who Was Present At the Same.* London, 1576.

Gentillet, Innocent. *Anti-Machiavel.* Ed. C. Edward Rathé. Genève: Droz, 1968.

Gerard, John. *The Autobiography of an Elizabethan.* Trans. Philip Caraman. London: Longmans, 1951.

Gerard, John. *The Condition of Catholics under James I: Father Gerard's Narrative of the Gunpowder Plot.* Ed. John Morris. London: Longmans, Green, & Co., 1871.

Goulart, Simon. *Mémoires de l'Estat de France, sous Charles neufiesme... Édition Seconde.* Heidelbourg, 1578–9.

Goulart, Simon. *Mémoires de la Ligue: contenant les évenemens les plus remarquables depuis 1576, jusqu'à la paix accordée entre le roi de France & le roi d'Espagne, en 1598.* Paris, 1758.

Graces et Louanges dues à Dieu pour la justice faites de cruel tyran et enemy capital de la France. Paris, 1589.

Grévin, Jacques. *César.* Ed. Ellen S. Ginsberg. Genève: Droz, 1971.

Guérin de Bouscal, Guyon. *La mort de Brute et de Porcie, ou La vengeance de la mort de César. Tragédie.* Paris, 1637.

Guise, François de Lorraine. *Discours faits dans le parlement de Paris... sur l'enregistrement de la déclaration du 11 d'Avril 1562 sur le tumulte de Vassy.* In *Archives Curieuses*: 1re série, 4.

Hakewill, George. *A Comparison Betweene the Dayes of Purim and that of the Powder Treason for the better continuance of the memory of it, and the stirring up of mens affections to a more zealous observation thereof.* Oxford, 1626.

Handel, Georg Friedrich, and Newburgh Hamilton. *Samson; An Oratorio* (1743). <http://opera.stanford.edu/iu/libretti/samson.htm>.

Harrison, G. B. Ed. *A Jacobean Journal, Being a Record of Those Things Most Talked of During the Years 1603–06.* London: Routledge, 1941.

Haton, Claude. *Memoires.* 2 Volumes. Paris, 1857.

Hawes, Edward. *Trayterous Percies & Catesbys Prosopopoeia.* London, 1606.

Herring, Francis. *Pietas Pontificia, Seu, Conjurationis Illius Prodigiosae, Et Post Natos Homines Maximè Execrandae, in Iacobum Primu[M] Magnae Britanniae Rege[M], Augustam.* London, 1606.

Herring, Francis. *Popish Pietie, or the First Part of the Historie of That Horrible and Barbarous Conspiracie, Commonly Called the Powder-Treason Nefariously Plotted against Iames King of Great Britaine, Prince Henrie, and the Whole State of That Realme Assembled in Parliament; and Happily Disc[Ou]Ered, Disappointed, and Frustrated by the Powerfull and Sole Arme of the Almightie, the Fifth of Nouember, Anno 1605. Written First in Latin Verse by F. H. in Physicke: And Translated into [En]Glish by A.P.* London, 1610.

Heyns, Pieter. *Les comédies et tragédies du Laurier. La Jokebed, Susanne, Judith. Miroir des mères, mesnagères, vefves, représentans l'estat des femmes, tant mariées, qu'à marier. Fort utiles et propres pour le sexe feminin.* Amsterdam: Z. Heyns, 1596.

His Maiesties Speach in this Last Session of Parliament as Neere His Very Words as Could Be Gathered at the Instant. Together with a Discourse of the Maner of the Discouery of this Late Intended Treason, Ioyned with the Examination of Some of the Prisoners [The King's Book']. London, 1605.

Histoire abregée du procés criminel de Jean Chastel, avec l'arrest donné contry luy et contre les Jesuistes. In *Mémoires de Condé.* Paris, 1743. Volume 6: 147–55.

Histoire du tumulte d'Amboise. 1560. In *Archives Curieuses*: 1er série, 4.

Histoire generale des larrons contenant les vols, massacres, assassinats, finesses & subtilitez qui se sont par eux faictes en France, & principalement en la ville de Paris. Paris, 1623.

Histoire nouvelle du nouveau monde par U. Chauveton, Ensemble, une petite histoire d'un massacre commis par les Hespagnoles sur quelques françois en la Floride. Vignon, 1579.

Histoire prodigieuse du détestable parricide attenté contre le Roy Henry quatriesme de ce nom, très-Chrsetien, Roy de France et de Navarre, par Pierre Barriere, à la suscitation des Jesuites. In *Memoires de Condé.* Paris, 1743. Volume 6: 142145.

Histoire véritable de la cruelle et outrageuse blesseure de monsieur le Prince d'Orange, faicte par un jeune homme biscain... au mois de février dernier 1582. N.p., 1582.

Histoire veritable de la mutinerie, tumult et sedition faites par les Pretres Saint Medard contres les Fideles. In *Archives curieuses*: 1re série, 4.

Hobbes, Thomas. 'The Answer of Mr. Hobbes to Sir Will. Davenant's Preface to *Gondibert*.' In D'Avenant, William, *Gondibert: An Heroick Poem.* London, 1651: 51–4.

Hobbes, Thomas. *Human Nature and De Corpore Politico.* Ed. J.C.A. Gaskin. Oxford: Oxford University Press, 1994.

Hobbes, Thomas. *Leviathan.* Ed. C. MacPherson. Harmondsworth: Penguin, 1981.

Horrible Murther of a Young Boy of Three Yeres of Age, Whose Sister Had Her Tongue Cut Out, The. London: 1606.

Hotman, François. *Francogallia* [1573]. In *Constitutionalism and Resistance in the Sixteenth Century.* Trans. and Ed. Julian H. Franklin. New York: Pegasus, 1969: 47–96.

Hotman, François. *Le Tigre de 1560*. Facsimile. Ed. M. Charles Read. Genève: Slatkine, 1970.

Hotman, François. *A True and Plaine Report of the Furious Outrages of Fraunce*. London, 1573.

Hotman, François. *La Vie de Messire Gaspar de Colligny Admiral de France* (1577). Facsimile of 1643 edition. Ed. Emile-V. Telle. Geneva: Droz, 1987.

Hurault de L'Hospital, Michel. *Anti-Sixtus. An Oration of Pope Sixtus the Fift, Upon the Death of the Late French King Henry III, With a Confutation Upon the Same Oration*. London, 1590.

Hurault de L'Hospital, Michel. *Excellent Discourse Upon the Now Present State of France*. London, 1592.

James I, King of England. *Political Works*. Ed. Charles Howard McIlwain. New York: Russell and Russell, 1965.

James I, King of England. *The Earle of Gowries Conspiracy Against the Kings Majestie of Scotland*. London, 1600.

Jonson, Ben. *Catiline* [1611]. Ed. W. F. Bolton and Jane F. Gardner. London: Edward Arnold, 1973.

Knappen, M. M. Ed. *Two Elizabethan Puritan Diaries*. Chicago: American Society for Church History, 1933.

L'Estoile, Pierre de. *Journal de Henry III. Ou Memoires pour sevir à l'histoire de france*. The Hague, 1754.

L'Estoile, Pierre de. *Journal du règne de Henri IV, roi de France et de Navarre: Avec des remarques historiques et politiques et plusieurs pièces historiques du même tems*. 4 Volumes. The Hague, 1741.

L'Estoile, Pierre de. *Les Belles figures et drolleries de la Ligue, 1589–1600*. Paris: P. Daffis, 1877.

La Force, Jacques Nompar de Caumont. *Mémoires authentiques de Jacques Nompar de Caumont duc de la Force maréchal de France et de ses deux fils*. Ed. Marquis de La Grange. Paris, 1843.

La Taille, Jacques de. *Daire*. Ed. Maria Giulia Longhi, in *La tragédie à l'époque d'Henri II et de Charles IX*. Première Série. Vol. 4. Florence: Olschki, 1992.

Lally-Tolendal Trophime-Gérard, marquis de. *Défense des émigrés français: Adressée au peuple français*. London, 1797.

Lamentable Discourse Upon the Parricide and Bloody Assassination Committed on the Person of Henry the Fourth, A. Trans. Peter Courant. London, 1610.

Last Will and Testament of the Marquis d'Ancre, Together with His Arraignment. His Obsequies. His Wifes Tears on His Death, The Re-union of the King with His Men of Warre. The Rousing of the Soldat François. All Declaring the Divine Judgement of God on the Death of the Said Marshall d'Ancre. London, 1617.

Leigh, William. *Great Britaines Great Deliuerance, from the Great Danger of Popish Powder by Way of Meditation, Vpon the Late Intended Treason*. London, 1606.

Letter Written Out of England to an English Gentleman remaining at Padua, containing a true report of a strange conspiracie contriv'd betweene Edward Squire . . . and Richard Walpole London, 1599.

Liberté vangée ou César poignardé. Rouen, 1606.

Lipsius, Justus. *Six Bookes of Politickes or Ciuil Doctrine*. Trans. William Jones. London, 1594.

Lodge, Thomas. *The Wounds of Civil War*. [1586]. Ed. J. Dover Wilson. Oxford: Malone Society, 1964. London: Heinemann, 1928.

Lucanus, Marcus Annaeus. *Lucan: The Civil War. Books 1–10. (Pharsalia)*. Trans. J. D. Duff.

Lydgate, John. *The Fall of Princes.* Ed. Henry Bergen, London: Early English Text Society, 1924.

Lydgate, John. *The Serpent of Division.* London, 1590.

Maistre, Joseph Marie, Comte de. *Considérations sur la France.* London, 1797.

Marguerite de Valois. *Memoires et autres ecrits de Marguerite de Valois: la Reine Margot.* Ed. Yves Cazaux. Paris: Mercure de France, 1971.

Marillac, Michel de. *Assassinat du maréchal d'Ancre, relation anonyme attribuée au Garde des sceaux Marillac.* In *NC*: 5. 447–84. Paris: Hachette, 1853.

Marlowe, Christopher. *The Massacre at Paris.* In *The Complete Plays.* Ed. Frank Romany and Robert Lindsey. London: Penguin, 2003.

Martine Mar-Sixtus. *A second replie against the defensory and apology of Sixtus the fift late Pope of Rome, defending the execrable fact of the Iacobine frier, vpon the person of Henry the third, late King of France, to be both commendable, admirable, and meritorious.* London, 1591.

Matthieu, Pierre. *La Conjuration de Conchine.* Paris, 1618.

Matthieu, Pierre. *La Guisiade.* Ed. Louis Lobbes. Genève: Droz, 1990.

Matthieu, Pierre. *The Guisiade.* Trans. Richard Hillman. Ottawa: Dovehouse Editions, 2005.

Matthieu, Pierre. *Histoire de France sous les règnes de François I., etc. [to Louis XIII].* Paris, 1631.

Matthieu, Pierre. *Histoire de la mort déplorable du Roi Henri le Grand.* Paris, 1612.

Matthieu, Pierre. *The Heroic Lyfe and Deplorable Death of the most Christian King Henry the Fourth.* London, 1612. 1618 *Histoire d'Ælius Sejanus,* Paris, 1617.

May, Thomas. *A Continuation of Lucan's Historicall Poem Till the Death of Julius Caesar.* London, 1630.

Medici, Lorenzino de. *Apology for a Murder.* Trans. Andrew Brown. London: Hesperus, 2004.

Medici, Lorenzino de. 'Apologia.' In *Lorenzaccio: Lorenzino de Medici: un ribelle in familigia.* Ed. Marcello Vannucci. Rome: Newton Compton, 1984.

Melville, James. *The Diary of Mr James Melville, 1556–1601.* Edinburgh: Ballantyne, 1829.

Middleton, Thomas. *The Revenger's Tragedy.* Ed. Brian Gibbons. London: A & C Black, 1991.

Milton, John. *Areopagitica.* London, 1644.

Milton, John. *In quintum novembris.* In *John Milton (Oxford Authors).* Ed. Stephen Orgel and Jonathan Goldberg. Oxford and New York: Oxford University Press, 1991.

Miron, François. *Relation de la mort des messieurs les duc et cardinal de Guise.* In *Archives Curieuses,* 1 ere série: 12.

Mirror for Magistrates, The. Ed. Lily B. Campbell. Cambridge: Cambridge University Press, 1938.

Montaigne, Michel de. *The Complete Works.* Trans. Donald Frame. London: Everyman, 2003.

Montchrestien, Antoine de. *La Reine d'Escosse.* In *Two Tragedies.* Ed. C. N. Smith. London: Athlone, 1972.

Moore, Carey A. *Judith: A New Translation with Introduction and Commentary.* New Haven: Yale University Press, 1985.

Morison, Richard, Sir. *A Remedy for Sedition Wherin Are Conteyned Many Thynges, Concernyng the True and Loyall Obeysance, That Comme[n]s Owe Vnto Their Prince and Soueraygne Lorde the Kynge.* London, 1536.

Mort du prince d'Orange, tue en raison d'un coup de pistolle, ensemble la deploration de la Princesse d'Orange. Lyon, Paris, 1584.

Mort prodigieuses de Gaspart de Coligny. Paris, 1572.

Morton, Thomas. *An Exact Discoverie of Romish Doctrine in the Case of Conspiracie and Rebellion.* London, 1605.

Mounchy, Antoine de. *Response à quelque apologie que les heretiques ces jours passés ont mis en avant.* Paris, 1560.

Muret, Marc Antoine. *La tragédie de Iulius Caesar.* Ed. and Trans. Pierre Blanchard. Thonon-les-Bains: Alidades, 1995.

Nassau, Maurice de. *La conspiration faicte par les peres Jesuites de Douay pour assassiner le prince Maurice d'Orenge.* Leiden, 1598. In Goulart, *Memoires de la Ligue.* 6: 717–23.

Gabriel Naudé. *Considérations politiques sur les coups d'É tat.* Ed. Frédérique Marin and Marie Odille. Perulli Paris: Éditions de Paris, 1988.

Navarre, Marguerite de. *Heptaméron.* Ed. Simone de Reyff. Paris: Flammarion, 1982.

Néré, Richard Jean. *Le Triomphe de la ligue, tragoedie nouvelle.* Leyden, 1607.

Norton, Thomas, and Thomas Sackville. *Gorboduc.* In *The Minor Elizabeth Drama.* London: J. M. Dent, 1958. 1: 1–54.

Oration Made unto the French King, By the Deputies of the National Synod of the Reformed Churches, Upon the Death of the Marquise d'Ancre. London, 1617.

Owen, Thomas. *A Letter of a Catholike Man Beyond the Seas, Written to His Friend in England Including Another of Peter Coton Priest, of The Society of Iesus, to the Queene Regent Of France/Translated out of French Into English; Touching The Imputation of the Death Of Henry The Iiii, Late K. of France, to Priests, Iesuites, or Catholicke Doctrine.* London, 1610.

Painter, William. 'The infortunate marriage of a Gentleman, called Antonio Bologna, wyth the Duchesse of Malfi, and the pitiful death of them both'. In Painter, *The Palace of Pleasure.* 2 Volumes. London: 1567: 2: 360–411.

Parry, William. *A True and Plaine Declaration of the Horrible Treasons, Practised By William Parry the Traitor, Against the Queenes Maiestie the Maner of His Arraignment, Conuiction and Execution, Together with the Copies of Sundry Letters of His and Others, Tending to Diuers Purposes, for the Proofes of His Treasons.* London, 1585.

Paschal, Pierre de. *Journal de ce qui s'est passé en France durant l'année 1562.* Ed. Michel François. Paris: H. Didier, 1950.

Pasquier, Étienne. *L'Antimartyr de Frere Jacques Clément, de l'ordre de Jacobins.* Paris, 1590.

Pelletier. *De l'Inviolable et sacree personne des Rois. Contre tous Assassins et Parricides qui ozent attenter sur leurs Majestez.* Paris, 1610.

Perrissin, Jean, and Jacques Tortorel. *Premier volume, contenant quarante tableaux ou Histoires diuerses qui sont memorables touchant les guerres, massacres, & troubles aduenus en France en ces dernieres annees.* Geneva, 1570.

Pibrac, Guy Du Faur. 'Lettre à Elvide.' In *L'Apologie de la Saint-Barthélemy.* Ed. A. Cabos. Paris and Auch, 1922.

Pinselet, Charles. *Le Martire des deux freres contenant au vray toutes les particularitez les plus notables des massacres, & assainats.* N.p., 1589.

Pinselet, Charles. *Le Martyre de frere Jacques Clement… contenant au vray toutes les particularitez plus remarquables de sa saincte resolution & tresheureuse entreprise à l'encontre de Henry de Valois.* Paris, 1589.

Poems and Songs Relating to George Villiers, Duke of Buckingham, and His Assassination by John Felton, August 23, 1628. Ed. F. W. Fairholt. London: Percy Society, 1850.

Poésies protestantes sur Jean Poltrot, Sr de Meré, 1563. Ed. Edouard Tricotel. Paris: A. Claudin, 1878.

Pollen, John Hungerford. *Mary Queen of Scots and the Babington Plot.* Edinburgh: Scottish History Society, 1922.

Pompée. Tragédie nouvelle appellée Pompée. In *La tragédie à l'époque d'Henri III.* Deuxième Série. Vol. 2 (1579–82): Florence: Olschki, 2001: 1–60.

Pontchartrain, P. Phelypeaux de. *Mémoires concernant les affaires de France sous la régence de Marie de Medicis.* In *Nouvelle collection des mémoires pour servir l'histoire de France.* Ed. Joseph-François Michaud and Jean-Joseph-François Poujoulat. 33 Volumes. Paris, 1836–54. 2eme. 5: 292–484.

Pricket, Robert. *The Jesuit's Miracle; or New Popish Wonders.* London, 1607.

Procedures faicte contre Jean Chastel, in *Mémoires de Condé.* 6: 126–46.

Quarles, Francis. *The Historie of Samson.* London, 1631.

Quintus, Curtius Rufus. *History of Alexander.* Trans. John C. Rolfe. London: Heinemann, 1946.

Relation de la blessure et de la mort du duc de Guise. In *Archives curieuses*: 1ere série 5.

Relation du massacre de la Saint-Barthelemy. In *Archives curieuses*: 1ere série, 7.

Rencontre de M. D'Epernon et de François Ravaillac. In Pierre de l'Estoile, *Journal du Regne du Henry IV. 4 Volumes.* La Haye, 1741. 4: 266–71.

Reuss, R. Ed. 'Un nouveau récit de la Saint-Barthelémy par un bourgeois de Strasbourg'. *Bulletin historique et littéraire [Bulletin de la Société de l'histoire du protestantisme français].* 22 (1873) 534–40.

Richelieu, Cardinal. *Mémoires.* Paris: H. Laurens, 1907.

Rogers, Richard. *A Commentary upon the Whole Booke of Judges.* London, 1615.

Ronsard, Pierre. *Oeuvres complètes.* Ed. Jean Ceard, Danie Menager, and Michel Simonin. 2 Volumes. Paris: Gallimard, 1993–4.

Rushworth, John. *Historical collections of private passages of state, weighty matters in law, remarkable proceedings... beginning the 16th year of King James, anno 1618 and ending... [with the death of King Charles the first, 1648].* 8 Volumes. London: D. Browne, 1721–2.

Ruthven, Patrick, Lord. *A Relation of the Death of David Rizzi.* London, 1699.

Sainct et pitoyable discours comme ce bon prince Françoys de Lorraine, duc de Guise, Le. In *Archives curieuses*: 1ere série, 5.

Sainctes, Claude de. *Discours sur le saccagement des églises catholiques par les hérétiques anciens et nouveaux calvinistes, en l'an 1562.* In *Archives curieuses*: 1ere série, 4.

Satyre ménippée de la vertu du Catholicon d'Espagne et de la tenue des estats de Paris. Ed. Martial Martin. Paris: Champion, 2007.

Saulx-Tavannes, Gaspard de. *Mémoires.* In *Collection complète des mémoires relatifs à l'histoire de France.* Ed. M. Pettitot. Paris, 1822. Volumes 27–8.

Scudéry, Georges de. *Discours politiques des rois.* Paris, 1647.

Scudéry, Georges de. *Le Prince déguisé. La Mort de Caesar.* Ed. Eveline Dutertre and Dominique Montand'Huy. Paris: Société des Textes Français Modernes, 1992.

Serres, Jean de. *A General Historie of France .../Contynued by Peter Mathew to the Death of King Henry the Fourth in the Yeare 1610; and Againe Continued unto the Peace Concluded Before Montpellier in the Yeare 1622.* Trans. Edward Grimston. London, 1624.

Serres, Jean de. *An Historical Collection of the Most Memorable Accidents, and Tragicall Massacres of France, under the Raignes of Henry 2, Francis 2, Charles 9, Henry 3, Henry 4, Now Living: Containing All the Troubles Therein Happened, During the Said Kings Times, until this Present Yeare, 1598.* London, 1598.

Serres, Jean de. *Recueil des choses memorables avenues en France sous le regne de Henry II, François II, Charles IX, Henry III, et Henry IV.* Paris, 1603.

Shakespeare, William. *The Norton Shakespeare.* Ed. Stephen Greenblatt. New York: Norton, 1996.

Shirley, James. *The Traitor* [1635]. Ed. John Stewart Carter. London: Edward Arnold, 1965.

Sixte, V. *Harangue prononcee par N. S. Pere en plein Consistoire et assemblee des Cardinaux, XI de septembre.* Lyon, 1589.

Song, or Story, For the Remembrance of divers famous works, which God had done in our time, A. With an addition of certaine other Verses (both Latine and Englishe) to the same purpose. London, 1626.

Speed, John. *The Historie of Great Britaine.* Second Edition. London, 1623.

Spenser, Edmund. *The Fairie Queene.* Ed. Thomas P. Roche. Harmondsworth: Penguin, 1987.

Stirling, William Alexander, Earl of. *The Monarchicke Tragedies: Croesus, Darius, The Alexandraean, Iulius Caesar. Newly enlarged by William Alexander, Gentleman of the Princes priuie chamber.* London, 1607.

Stowe, John. *Annales, or, A Generall Chronicle of the England, Begun by John Stow. Continued by Edward Howes.* London, 1631.

Stuart, Mary Queen of Scots. *Letters of Mary Stuart.* Ed. Alexandre Labanoff. 4 Volumes. London, 1845.

Stubbes, John. *The Intended Treason of Doctor Parrie and His Complices Against the Queen's Most Excellent Majestie.* London, 1585.

Sully, Maximilien de Béthune, duc de. *Memoires de Maximilien de Bethune, Duc de Sully.* Edinburgh: A. Donaldson, 1760. 5 Volumes.

Supplice, mort, et fin ignominieuse du parricide inhumain, & desnaturé François Ravallat (sic) executé à Paris le 27 may 1610. Lyon, 1610.

Tesimond, Oswald. *The Gunpowder Plot. The Narrative of Oswald Tesimond alias Greenway.* Trans. Francis Edwards. London: Folio Society, 1973.

Thou Jacques-Auguste de. *Histoire universelle depuis 1543. jusqu'en 1607.* Traduite sur l'edition latine de Londres. 16 Volumes. London, 1734.

Thou Jacques-Auguste de. *The History of the Bloody Massacres of the Protestants in France... 1572.* London, 1674.

Thou Jacques-Auguste de. *Abrégé de l'Histoire universelle.* 10 Volumes. Trans. M. Rémond de Sainte-Albine. Paris, 1759.

Titcheborne, Chidiock. *Verses of Praise Written Upon Her Maiesties Preservation.* London, 1586.

Tocsain contre les massacreurs et auteurs des confusions en France. In *Archives curieuses*: 1ere série, 7.

Touchard, Jean. *Allegresse chrestienne de l'heureux succes des guerres de ce royaume et de la justice de Dieu contre les rebelles au Roy.* Paris, 1572.

Tragédie de Blois: quatre siècles de polémique autour de l'assassinat du duc de Guise. Exposition. Château de Blois, 17 décembre 1988–19 février 1989. Blois: Conservation du château et des musées, 1988.

Tragedie of Caesar and Pompey or Caesars Revenge. London, 1607.

True and Perfect Relation of the Whole Proceedings Against the Last Most Barbarous Traitors, Garnet a Jesuit, and His Confederates. London, 1606.

True and Plaine Declaration of the Horrible Treasons Practised by William Parrie Against the Queens Majestie, and of His Conviction and Execution for the Same, The Second of March 1584, According to the Account of England. In *Holinshed's Chronicles of England, Scotland, and Ireland*, 6 Volumes [1808]. New York: AMS Press, 1965. 4: 561–88.

True Discourse of the Assault Committed on the Person of the Most Noble Prince, William Prince of Orange, Countie of Nassau, Marques de la Vere, etc., by John Jauregui Spaniarde. Trans. Christopher Plantin. London, 1582.

True Report of Sundry Horrible Conspiracies of late time detected to have (by Barbarous murders) taken away the life of the Queen's Most Excellent Majestie; whom Almighty God hath miraculously conserved against the treacheries of her Rebelles, and the violences of her most puissant Enemies. London, 1594.

True Report of the Lamentable Death of William of Nassau, Prince of Orange, who was trayterously slayne with a dagge in his own courte. Middleborowgh, 1584.

True Report of the most execrable Murder committed vppon the late French King Henrie the 4 ... Written in a Letter from good place, & much differing from the uncertaine relations thereof heretofore published. London, 1610.

Univoccatholicus. *Lucta Jacobi; Or, A Bonefire for His Majesties Double Deliverie*. London, 1607.

Vaissière, Pierre de. *Récits du Temps des troubles (XVIe siècle)*. Paris: Emile-Paul, 1912.

Vestegan, Richard. *Le théâtre des cruautés des hérétiques de notre temps* [1587]. Ed. Frank Lestringant. Paris: Chandeigne, 1995.

Vicars, John, and Francis Herring. *Mischeefe's Mysterie: Or Treason's Master-Peece, the Powder-Plot*. London, 1617.

Vigor, Simon. *Sermons Catholiques pour tous les jours de Careseme et Féries de Paques*. Paris, 1577.

Ville-Toustain, Sieur de la. *Tragédie nouvelle de Samson le fort*. Rouen, 1620.

Voltaire, 'Fanaticisme', in *Dictionnaire Philosophique*: <http://fr.wikisource.org/wiki/Page:Voltaire_-_%C5%92uvres_compl%C3%A8tes_Garnier_tome19.djvu/83>. Accessed 26 May, 2015.

Webster, John. *The Duchess of Malfi*. Ed. Elizabeth M. Brennan. London: A & C Black, 1993.

Whetstone, George. *The Censure of a Loyall Subject Upon Certaine Noted Speach and Behaviours of those fourteene notable Traitors*. London, 1587.

Wilson, John. *A Song or, Story, for the Lasting Remembrance of Diuers Famous Works, Which God Hath Done in Our Time with an Addition of Certaine Other Verses (Both Latine and English) to the Same Purpose*. London, 1626.

Wotton, Henry, Sir. *A Parallel Betweene Robert Late Earle of Essex, and George Late Duke of Buckingham*. London, 1641.

Wotton, Henry, Sir. *A Short View of the Life and Death of George Villers, Duke of Buckingham*. London, 1642.

Wunstius, Marcus Andreas. *Simson, Tragoedia Sacra* (1600–4). Trans. Watson Kirkconnell. In Watson Kirkconnell, *That Invincible Samson. The Theme of 'Samson Agonistes' in World Literature, with Translations of the Major Analogues*. Toronto: University of Toronto Press, 1964: 12–59.

2. SECONDARY TEXTS

Agamben, Giorgio. *State of Exception*. Chicago: University of Chicago Press, 2005.

Anderson, Judith H. 'Spenser's *Fairie Queene*, Book V: Poetry, Politics, Justice'. In *A Companion to English Renaissance Literature and Culture*. Ed. Michael Hattaway. Oxford: Wiley-Blackwell, 2000: 195–205.

Appelbaum, Robert, and Alexis Paknadel. 'Terrorism and the Novel, 1970–2001'. *Poetics Today* 29.3 (2008): 387–436.

Appelbaum, Robert. 'Flowing or Pumping? The Blood of the Body Politic in Burton, Harvey, and Hobbes.' *Blood: A Cultural History*. Ed. Kimberley Anne Coles et al. New York: Palgrave Macmillan, 2015.

Appelbaum, Robert. 'Judith Dines Alone: From the Bible to Du Bartas'. *Modern Philology* 111.4 (2014): 683–710.

Appelbaum, Robert. 'The Gunpowder Plot (1605)'. *Oxford Bibliographies*: British and Irish Literature (2014): <http://www.oxfordbibliographies.com/view/document/obo-9780199846719/obo-9780199846719-0112.xml>.

Appelbaum, Robert. 'Milton, the Gunpowder Plot, and the Mythography of Terror'. *Modern Language Quarterly* 68.4 (2007): 461–93.

Appelbaum, Robert. *Literature and Utopian Politics in Seventeenth-Century England*. Cambridge: Cambridge University Press, 2002.

Appelbaum, Robert. 'Shakespeare and Terrorism'. *Criticism*. (forthcoming).

Appriou, Daniel. *Les destins tragiques de l'histoire de France*. Paris: Pré aux Clercs, 2001.

Arendt, Hannah. *The Human Condition*. Chicago: University of Chicago Press, 1958.

Arendt, Hannah. *The Origins of Totalitarianism*. New York: Shocken, 2004.

Arendt, Hannah. *On Violence*. San Diego: Harcourt Brace, 1970.

Arnade, Peter. *Beggars, Iconoclasts, and Civic Patriots: The Political Culture of the Dutch Revolt*. Ithaca: Cornell University Press, 2008.

Ashton, Harry. *Du Bartas en Angleterre*. Genève: Slatkine, 1969.

Aston, Trevor. Ed. *Crisis in Europe 1560–1660: Essays from 'Past and Present'*. London: Routledge and Kegan Paul, 1965.

Austin, J. L. *How to Do Things with Words*. Oxford: Clarendon, 1962.

Axton, Marie. *The Queen's Two Bodies: Drama and the Elizabethan Succession*. London: Royal Historical Society, 1977.

Babelon, Jean-Pierre. *Henri IV*. Paris: Fayard, 1982.

Bailbé, J. 'La Saint-Barthelemy dans la littérature française'. *Revue d' Histoire littéraire de la France* 73.5 (1975).

Baker, Nicholas Scot. 'Writing the Wrongs of the Past: Vengeance, Humanism, and the Assassination of Alessandro de' Medici'. *Sixteenth Century Journal: Journal of Early Modern Studies* 38.2 (2007): 307–27.

Bakhtin, Mikhail. *Problems of Dostoevsky's Poetics*. Trans. Caryl Emerson. Minneapolis: University of Minnesota Press, 1984.

Bal, Mieke. *Death and Dissymmetry: The Politics of Coherence in The Book of Judges*. Chicago: University of Chicago Press, 1988.

Ball, Patrick, Paul Kobrak and Herbert F. Spirer. *State Violence in Guatemala, 1960–1996: A Quantitative Reflection*. Washington, DC American Association for the Advancement of Science. 1999. <http://www.aaas.org/sites/default/files/migrate/uploads/Guatemala_en.pdf>.

Barish, Jonas. *The Anti-theatrical Prejudice*. Berkeley: University of California Press, 1981.

Barnavi, Élie and Robert Descimon. *La Sainte Ligue, le juge, et la potence: l'assassinat du président Brisson (15 novembre 1591)*. Paris: Hachette, 1985.

Barthes, Roland. *S/Z*. Trans. Richard Miller. New York: Farrar, Straus & Giroux, 1991.

Bataille, George. *Eroticism*. Trans. Mary Dalwood. London: Marion Boyars, 2006.

Baudrillard, Jean. *Symbolic Exchange and Death*. Trans. Ian Hamilton Grant. London: Sage, 1993.

Baudrillard, Jean. *The Spirit of Terrorism and Other Essays*. New York: Verso, 2003.

Bawcutt, N. W. 'The Assassination of Alessandro de' Medici in Early Seventeenth-Century English Drama'. *Review of English Studies* 56. 225 (2005): 412–23.

Beattie, J. H. M. 'On Understanding Sacrifice'. In *Sacrifice*. Ed. M. F. C. Bourdillon and Meyer Fortes. London: Academic Press, 1980: 29–44.

Beik, William. *Urban Protest in Seventeenth-Century France: The Culture of Retribution* Cambridge: Cambridge University Press, 1997.

Beik, William. 'The Violence of the French Crowd from Charivari to Revolution'. *Past and Present* 197.1 (2007): 75–110.

Bell, David A. 'Unmasking a King: The Political Uses of Popular Literature under the French Catholic League, 1588-89'. *Sixteenth Century Journal* 20.3 (1989): 371–86.

Bellanger, Claude, Jacques Godechot, Pierre Guiral and Fernand Terrou. Eds. *Histoire générale de la presse française. 1, Des origines à 1814.* Paris: Presses Universitaires de France, 1969.

Benedict, Philip et al. Eds. *Reformation, Revolt and Civil War in France and the Netherlands 1555–1585.* Amsterdam: Academy of Arts and Sciences, 1999.

Benedict, Philip, and Myron P. Gutman. Eds. *Early Modern Europe: From Crisis to Stability.* Newark: University of Delaware Press, 2005.

Benedict, Philip, Lawrence M. Bryant, and Kristen B. Neuschel. 'Graphic History: What Readers Knew and Were Taught in the Quarante Tableaux of Perrissin and Tortorel'. *French Historical Studies* 28.2 (2005): 175–229.

Benedict, Philip. 'The Saint Bartholomew's Massacres in the Provinces'. *Historical Journal* 21 (1978), 205–25.

Benedict, Philip. *Graphic History. The Wars, Massacres and Troubles of Tortorel and Perrissin.* Genève: Droz, 2007.

Benjamin, Walter. 'Critique of Violence'. In *Reflections: Essays, Aphorisms, Autobiographical Writings.* Trans. Edmund Jephcott. New York: Schocken, 1978: 277–300.

Benjamin, Walter. *The Origin of German Tragic Drama.* Trans. John Osborne. London: Verso, 1977.

Bercé, Yves Marie. *History of Peasant Revolts: The Social Origins of Rebellion in Early Modern France.* Trans. Amanda Whitmore. Ithaca, NY: Cornell University Press, 1990.

Bercé, Yves Marie. *Revolt and Revolution in Early Modern Europe: An Essay on the History of Political Violence.* Trans. Joseph Bergin. Manchester: Manchester University Press, 1987.

Berleant, Arnold. 'Art, Terrorism and the Negative Sublime'. *Contemporary Aesthetics.* 7 (2009). <http://www.contempaesthetics.org/newvolume/pages/article.php?articleID=568>.

Biberman, Matthew, and Julia Reinhard Lupton. *Shakespeare After 9/11: How a Social Trauma Reshapes Interpretation.* Lewiston, NY: Edwin Mellen Press, 2011.

Boecker, Alexander. *A Probable Italian Source of Shakespeare's 'Julius Caesar'.* New York: AMS Press, 1971.

Boehmer, Elleke, and Stephen Morton. Eds. *Terror and the Postcolonial.* Oxford: Blackwell, 2010.

Boehrer, Bruce. 'Jonson's Catiline and Anti-Sallustian Trends in Renaissance Humanist Historiography'. *Studies in Philology* 94. 1 (1997): 85–102.

Bolzoni, Lina. 'An Epic Poem of Peace: The Paradox of the Representation of War in the Italian Chivalric Poetry of the Renaissance'. In *War in Words: Transformations of War from Antiquity to Clausewitz.* Ed. Marco Formisano, Marco and Hartmut Böhme. Berlin: De Gruyter, 2011: 271–90.

Bordier, Henri-Léonard. *Peinture de la Saint-Barthélemy par un artiste contemporain comparée avec les documents historiques.* Genève: J. Jullien, 1878.

Bordier, Henri-Léonard. *La Saint-Barthélemy et la critique moderne.* Genève: H. Georg, 1879.

Borradori, Giovanna. *Philosophy in a Time of Terror: Dialogues with Jurgen Habermas and Jacques Derrida.* Chicago: University of Chicago Press, 2003.

Boucher De Guilleville, M. J. *Concino-Concini, marquis d'Ancre, maréchal de France: récit de sa mort.* Orleans: Herluison, 1883.

Bourdieu, Pierre. *Language and Symbolic Power.* Ed. John B. Thompson. Trans. Gino Raymond and Matthew Adamson. Cambridge, MA: Harvard University Press, 1991.

Bourgeon, Jean-Louis. *L'assassinat de Coligny.* Geneva: Droz, 1992.

Boyarin, Daniel. *Dying for God: Martyrdom and the Making of Christianity and Judaism.* Stanford: Stanford University Press, 1999.

Braud, Philippe. *Violences politiques.* Paris: Éditions de Seuil, 2004.

Briggs, John et al. *Crime and Punishment in England: An Introductory History.* London: University College London, 1996.

Briggs, Julia. 'Marlowe's *Massacre at Paris*: A Reconsideration'. *Review of English Studies,* New Series, 34.135 (1983): 257–78.

Brown, Keith M. *Bloodfeud in Scotland 1573–1625: Violence, Justice and Politics in an Early Modern Society.* Edinburgh: John Donald, 1986.

Burgess, Glenn. *British Political Thought, 1500–1660. The Politics of the Post-Reformation.* Basingstoke: Palgrave, 2009.

Burke, Kenneth. 'Dramatism'. In *International Encyclopedia of the Social Sciences.* New York: Free Press, 1968: 445–52.

Burke, Kenneth. *A Grammar of Motives.* Berkeley, CA: University of California Press, 1969.

Bushnell, Rebecca W. *Tragedies of Tyrants: Political Thought and Theater in the English Renaissance.* Ithaca, NY: Cornell University Press, 1990.

Butler, Martin. *Theatre and Crisis, 1632–1642.* Cambridge: Cambridge University Press, 1984.

Callagahn, Dympna. Ed. *The Duchess of Malfi.* Basingstoke: Macmillan, 2000.

Campbell, Gordon and Tom Corns. *John Milton: Life, Work and Thought.* Oxford: Oxford University Press, 2008.

Cameron, Gavin and Joshua D. Goldstein. 'The Ontology of Modern Terrorism: Hegel, Terrorism Studies, and Dynamics of Violence'. *Cosmos and History: The Journal of Natural and Social Philosophy* 6.1 (2010): 60–90. <http://cosmosandhistory.org/index.php/journal/article/viewFile/190/273>.

Camus, Albert. *The Rebel.* Trans. Anthony Bower. London: Penguin, 2000.

Carey, John. 'A Work in Praise of Terrorism?: September 11 and Samson Agonistes'. *Times Literary Supplement.* 6 Sep. 2002: 15–16.

Carr, Richard A. *Pierre Boaistuau's Histoires Tragiques: A Study of Narrative Form and Tragic Vision.* Chapel Hill: University of North Carolina Press, 1979.

Carroll, Stuart. *Blood and Violence in Early Modern France.* Oxford: Oxford University Press, 2006.

Carroll, Stuart. *Martyrs and Murderers: The Guise Family and the Making of Europe.* Oxford: Oxford University Press, 2009.

Carroll, Stuart. 'The Rights of Violence'. *Past & Present* 214, supplement 7 (2012): 127–62.

Castelli, Elizabeth. *Martyrdom and Memory: Early Christian Church Making.* New York: Columbia University Press, 2004.

Catholic League, 1588–9. *Sixteenth Century Journal.* 20.3 (1989): 371–86.

Cavanagh, William T. *The Myth of Religious Violence: Secular Ideology and the Roots of Modern Conflict.* Oxford: Oxford University Press, 2009.

Chaliand, Gerard and Arnaud Blin. Eds. *History of Terrorism: From Antiquity to Al Qaeda.* Trans. Edward Schneider et al. Berkeley, CA: University of California Press, 2007.

Chartier, Roger. *The Cultural Uses of Print in Early Modern France.* Trans. Lydia C. Cochrane. Princeton: Princeton University Press, 1987.

Cheek, Macon. 'Milton's *In quintum novembris:* An Epic Foreshadowing'. *Studies in Philology* 54 (1957): 172–84.

Chevallier, Pierre. *Les régicides: Clément, Ravaillac, Damiens.* Paris: Fayard, 1989.

Chew, Samuel. *The Crescent and the Rose: Islam and England during the Renaissance.* New York: Octagon Books, 1974.

Chisholm, Robert B, Jr. 'Ehud: Assessing an Assassin'. *Bibliotheca Sacra* 168 (2011): 274–82.

Chomsky, Noam. *9–11.* New York: Seven Stories Press, 2001.

Chomsky, Noam. 'International Terrorism: Image and Reality'. <http://www.chomsky.info/articles/199112--02.htm>. Accessed Feb. 12, 2012.

Christin, Olivier. *Une révolution symbolique: l'iconoclasme huguenot et la reconstruction catholique.* Paris: Éditions de Minuit, 1991.

Clark, Peter. *The European Crisis of the 1590s: Essays in Comparative History.* London: Allen & Unwin, 1985.

Clarke, Arthur Melville. *Murder Under Trust: The Topical 'Macbeth' and Other Jacobean Matters.* Edinburgh: Scottish Academic Press, 1981.

Clarke, David. *Pierre Corneille: Poetics and Political Drama under Louis XIII.* Cambridge: Cambridge University Press, 1992.

Clouas, Ivan. *Henri II.* Paris: Fayard, 1985.

Coddon, Karin S. '*The Duchess of Malfi*: Tyranny and Spectacle in Jacobean Drama'. In *Madness in Drama.* Ed. James Redmond. Cambridge: Cambridge University Press: 1–19.

Coddon, Karin S. '"Unreal Mockery": Unreason and the Problem of Spectacle in *Macbeth*'. *ELH* 56 (1989), 485–501.

Coldiron, A. E. B. 'French Presences in Tudor England'. *Blackwell Companion to Tudor Literature.* Ed. K. Cartwright. Oxford: Blackwell, 2010: 246–60.

Collins, John J. 'The Zeal of Phinehas: The Bible and the Legitimation of Violence'. *Journal of Biblical Literature* 122.1 (2003): 3–21.

Collins, Randall. *Violence: A Micro-sociological Theory.* Princeton: Princeton University Press, 2008.

Comay, Rebecca. 'Dead Right: Hegel and the Terror'. *South Atlantic Quarterly* 103.2–3 (2004): 375–95.

Conacher, Agnès. '*Les Tragiques* d'Agrippa d'Aubigné: Les Qualités d'un témoignage ou écho d'une histoire qui est arrivée et d'une histoire qui aurait pu être'. *French Studies* 57.1 (2003): 11–25.

Conquest, Robert. *The Great Terror; Stalin's Purge of the Thirties.* London: Macmillan, 1968.

Craze, Jack M. 'Balls of Missive Ruin: Milton and the Gunpowder Revolution'. *Cambridge Quarterly* 26.4 (1997): 325–43.

Crenshaw, Martha and John Pimlott. Eds. *Encyclopedia of World Terrorism.* 3 Volumes. Armonk, NY: Sharpe Reference, 1997.

Crenshaw, Martha. 'The Logic of Terrorism: Terrorist Behavior as a Product of Strategic Choice'. In *Origins of Terrorism: Psychologies, Ideologies, Theologies, States of Mind.* Ed. Walter Reich. Washington DC: Woodrow Wilson Center Press, 1998: 7–24.

Crenshaw, Martha. 'Relating Terrorism to Historical Contexts'. In *Terrorism in Context.* Ed. Martha Crenshaw. University Park, PA: Pennsylvania State University Press, 1995: 4–26.

Crenshaw, Martha. *Terrorism in Context.* University Park, PA: Pennsylvania State University Press, 1995.

Cressy, David. *Bonfires and Bells: National Memory and the Protestant Calendar in Elizabethan and Stuart England.* London: Weidenfeld and Nicolson, 1989.

Crouzet, Denis. *La Nuit de la Saint-Barthélemy: un rêve perdu de la renaissance.* Paris: Fayard, 1994.

Crouzet, Denis. *Les guerriers de Dieu: La violence au temps des troubles de religion, vers 1525-vers 1610.* 2 Volumes. Seyssel: Champ Vallon, 1990.

Crum, Roger J. 'Severing the Neck of Pride: Donatello's "Judith and Holofernes" and the Recollection of Albizzi Shame in Medicean Florence'. *Artibus et Historiae* 22.44 (2001): 23–9.

Culliere, Alain. 'Le Saint-Barthélemy au théâtre: De Chantelouve à Baculard d'Arnaud'. In *L'écriture du massacre en literature entre historice et myth*. Ed. Gérard Nauroy. Bern: Peter Land, 2006: 121–52.

Cunningham, Karen. *Imaginary Betrayals: Subjectivity and the Discourses of Treason in Early Modern England*. Philadelphia: University of Pennsylvania Press, 2002.

Daly, Robert J. *The Origins of the Christian Doctrine of Sacrifice*. London: Darton, 1978.

Dassonville, Michel. Ed. *Ronsard et Montaigne: Écrivains engagés?* Lexington, KY: French Forum, 1989.

Davidson, Donald. *Essays on Actions and Events*. Oxford: Clarendon Press, 1980.

Davis, Natalie Zemon. 'The Rites of Violence: Religious Riot in Sixteenth Century France' (1973). In Natalie Zemon Davis, *Society and Culture in Early Modern France*. Stanford: Stanford University Press, 1975: 152–87.

De Grazia, Margareta. 'Anachronism'. In *Cultural Reformations: Medieval and Renaissance in Literary Theory*. Ed. Brian Cummings and James Simpson. Oxford: Oxford University Press, 2010: 13–32.

De Vries, Jan. 'The Economic Crisis of the Seventeenth Century Reconsidered'. *Journal of Interdisciplinary History* 40.2 (2009): 151–94.

Delamare, George. *Concino Concini. Un aventurier maître du royaume de France*. Paris: Société des Éditions Denoël, 1946.

Demaray, John G. 'Gunpowder and The Problem Of Theatrical Heroic Form'. *In Quintum Novembris. Milton Studies* 19 (1984): 3–19.

Derrida, Jacques. *Writing and Difference*. Trans. Alan Bass. Chicago: University of Chicago Press, 1978.

Derrida, Jacques. 'Marx and Sons'. In *Ghostly Demarcations*. Ed. Michael Sprinker. London: Verso, 1999.

Derrida, Jacques. 'Forces of Law: The "Mystical Foundation of Authority"'. In *Deconstruction and the Possibility of Justice*. Ed. Drucilla Cornell, Michael Rosenfled, and David Gray. New York: Routledge, 1992: 3–67.

Derrida, Jacques. 'Interview'. In Borradori, *Philosophy in a Time of Terror*. 85–136.

Desan, Phillipe. Ed. *Humanism in Crisis: The Decline of the French Renaissance*. Ann Arbor, MI: University of Michigan Press, 1991.

Desan, Suzanne. 'Crowds, Community, and Ritual'. In *The New Cultural History*. Ed. Lynn Hunt. Berkeley, CA: University of California Press, 1989: 47–71.

Dewald, Jonathan. 'Crisis, Chronology, and the Shape of European Social History'. *American Historical Review* 113. 4 (2008): 1031–52.

Diefendorf, Barbara B. *Beneath the Cross: Catholics and Huguenots in Sixteenth-century Paris*. New York: Oxford University Press, 1991.

Diefendorf, Barbara B. 'Simon Vigor: A Radical Preacher in Sixteenth-Century Paris'. *Sixteenth-Century Journal* 18.3 (1987): 399–410.

Diken, Bulent. *Nihilism*. London: Routledge, 2008.

Docherty, Thomas. *Reading (Absent) Character: Towards A Theory of Characterization in Fiction*. Oxford: Clarendon Press, 1983.

Dolan, Frances E. 'The Subordinate('s) Plot: Petty Treason and the Forms of Domestic Rebellion'. *Shakespeare Quarterly* 43.3 (1992): 317–40.

Doran, Susan. *Elizabeth I and Foreign Policy, 1558–1603*. London: Routledge, 2000.

Dubois, Jean, Henri Mitterand and Albert Dauzat. *Grand dictionnaire étymologique & historique du français.* Paris: Larousse, 2005.

Dubois, Jean. *Dictionnaire du francais classique: le 17e siecle.* Paris: Larousse, 1992.

Duffy, Christopher. *Siege Warfare: The Fortress in the Early Modern World 1494–1660.* London: Routledge, 1996.

Dülman, Richard van. *Theatre of Horror.* Trans. Elisabeth Neu. Cambridge: Polity Press, 1990.

Dunning, W. A. 'The Monarchomachs: Theories of Popular Sovereignty in the Sixteenth Century'. *Political Science Quarterly* 19. 2 (1904): 277–301.

Durkheim, Émile. *The Elementary Forms of Religious Life.* Trans. Karen E. Fields. New York: Free Press, 1995.

Dutertre, Eveline. *Scudéry dramaturge.* Geneva: Droz, 1988.

Dutton, Richard. *Ben Jonson, 'Volpone' and the Gunpowder Plot.* Cambridge: Cambridge University Press, 2008.

Duval, Edwin M. 'The Place of the Present: Ronsard, Aubigné, and the "Misères de ce Temps"'. *Yale French Studies* 80 (1991): 13–29.

Eagleton, Terry. *Holy Terror.* Oxford: Oxford University Press, 2005.

Edwards, David, Pardaif Leniahn and Clodagh Tait. Eds. *Age of Atrocity: Violence and Political Conflict in Early Modern Ireland.* Dublin: Four Courts Press, 2010.

Eisenstein, Elizabeth L. *The Printing Press as an Agent of Change: Communications and Cultural Transformations in Early Modern Europe.* Cambridge: Cambridge University Press, 1979.

Eisenstein, Elizabeth L. *The Printing Revolution in Early Modern Europe.* Cambridge: Cambridge University Press, 1983.

El Kenz, David. 'La civilisation des moeurs et les guerres de Religion: un seuil de tolérance aux massacres'. In *Le massacre, objet d'histoire.* Ed. David El Kenz. Paris: Gallimard, 2005: 183–97.

El Kenz, David. 'Le massacre, objet d'histoire'. In *Le massacre, objet d'histoire.* Ed. David El Kenz. Paris: Gallimard, 2005: 9–14.

Elmore, Rick. 'Revisiting Violence and Life'. *Symplokē* 20. 1–2 (2012), 35–51.

Erlanger, Philippe. *Richelieu.* 3 Volumes. Paris: Librairie Academique Pérrin, 1970.

Fabiny, Tibor and Németh, Jenö U. 'Les histoires tragiques'. *In L'Epoque de la Renaissance (1400–1600), IV: Crises et essors nouveaux (1560–1610).* Ed- Eva Kushner, Tibor Klaniczay, and Paul Chavy. Amsterdam: John Benjamins, 2000: 579–95.

Fausz, J. Frederick. 'First Act of Terrorism in English America'. *History News Network*: <http://hnn.us/article/19085> (21-10-2013).

Ferguson, Arthur B. *The Chivalric Tradition in Renaissance England.* Washington D.C.: Folger Shakespeare Library, 1986.

Ford, Franklin L. *Political Murder: From Tyrannicide to Terrorism.* Cambridge, MA: Harvard University Press, 1985.

Forsyth, Elliott. *La Justice de Dieu. 'Les Tragiques' d'Agrippa d'Aubigné et la Réforme protestante en France au XVIe siécle.* Paris: Champion, 2005.

Forsyth, Elliott. *La Tragédie française de Jodelle à Corneille (1533–1640). Le thème de la vengeance.* Paris: Champion, 1962.

Forsyth, Neil. *The Satanic Epic.* Princeton: Princeton University Press, 2003.

Foucault, Michel. *Discipline and Punish: The Birth of the Prison.* Trans. Alan Sheridan. Harmondsworth: Penguin, 1991.

Foucault, Michel. *The Archaeology of Knowledge and the Discourse on Language.* Trans. A. M. Sheridan Smith. New York: Pantheon, 1972.

Fowler, Elizabeth. *Literary Character: The Human Figure in Early English Writing.* Ithaca, NY: Cornell University Press, 2003.

Fox, A. *Oral and Literate Culture in England 1500–1700.* Oxford: Clarendon Press, 2000.

Fraser, Antonia. *The Gunpowder Plot: Terror and Faith in 1605.* London: Phoenix, 2002.

Fraser, Antonia. *Mary Queen of Scots.* London: Phoenix, 1969.

Freud, Sigmund. *Beyond the Pleasure Principle.* In *Complete Psychological Works.* Trans. James Strachey. 24 Volumes. New York, Vintage: 18.3–66.

Freud, Sigmund. *Civilisation and Its Discontents.* In *Complete Psychological Works*: 21.64–148.

Freud, Sigmund. *The Ego and the Id.* In *Complete Psychological Works.* 19.3–68.

Frisch, Andrea. 'French Tragedy and the Civil Wars'. *Modern Language Quarterly* 67.3 (2006): 287–312.

Frow, John. 'Spectacle Binding: On Character'. *Poetics Today* 7.2 (1986): 227–50.

Frow, John. 'The Uses of Terror and the Limits of Cultural Studies'. *Symploke.* 11.1–2 (2003), 69–76.

Gallagher, Catherine. 'What Would Napoleon Do?: Historical, Fictional, and Counterfactual Characters'. *New Literary History* 42.2 (2011), 315–36.

Gambetta, Diego. 'Can We Make Sense of Suicide Missions?' In *Making Sense of Suicide Missions.* Ed. Diego Gambetta. Oxford: Oxford University Press, 2005: 259–300.

Gardiner, Samuel Rawson. *History of England from the Accession of James I to the Outbreak of the Civil War, 1603–1642.* 10 Volumes. Cambridge: Cambridge University Press, 2011.

Gardiner, Samuel Rawson. *What Gunpowder Plot Was.* London: Longmans, 1897.

Garrisson, Janine. *1572, La Saint-Barthélemy.* Bruxelles: Editions Complexe, 1987.

Gaskill, Malcolm. *Crime and Mentalities in Early Modern England.* Cambridge: Cambridge University Press, 2000.

Giddens, Anthony. *A Contemporary Critique Of Historical Materialism. Vol. 2, The Nation-State and Violence.* Cambridge: Polity, 1985.

Giesey, Ralph E. 'The Monarchomach Triumvirs: Hotman, Beza And Mornay'. *Bibliothèque d'Humanisme et Renaissance* 32.1 (1970): 41–56.

Gil, Daniel Juan. '"Bare Life": Political Order and the Specter of Antisocial Being in Shakespeare's *Julius Caesar*'. *Common Knowledge* 13.1 (2007), 67–79.

Girard, René. *A Theatre of Envy: William Shakespeare.* New York: Oxford, 1991.

Girard, René. *The Scapegoat.* Trans. Yvonne Freccero. Baltimore: Johns Hopkins University Press, 1986.

Girard, René. *Violence and the Sacred.* Trans. Patrick Gregory. London: Continuum, 2005.

Gombrich, E. H. *Meditations on a Hobby Horse and Other Essays on the Theory of Art.* Oxford: Phaidon, 1985.

Gordon, D. J. 'Gianotti, Michelangelo, and the Cult of Brutus'. In *The Renaissance Imagination: Essays and Lectures.* Ed. S. Orgel, 233–45. Berkeley, CA: University of California Press, 1975.

Grady, Hugh. 'Moral Agency and Its Problems in *Julius Caesar*: Political Power, Choice, and History'. In *Shakespeare and Moral Agency.* Ed. Michael D. Bristol. London: Continuum, 2010: 15–28.

Grandsaignes D'Hauterive, Robert. *Dictionnaire d'ancien francais: Moyen Age et Renaissance.* Paris: Larousse, 1947.

Gravaili, Anne de Vaucher. 'Violence représentée, violence exorcisée: François de Rosset et la peinture de son temps'. In *Violence et fiction jusqu'à la Révolution.* Ed. Martine Debaisieux and Gabrielle Verdier. Tübingen: Narr, 1988: 63–76.

Gray, Richard J. *After the Fall: American Literature since 9/11*. Oxford: Wiley-Blackwell, 2011.

Greenblatt, Stephen. *Shakespearean Negotiations*. Berkeley, CA: University of California Press, 1988.

Greenblatt, Stephen. *Will in the World: How Shakespeare Became Shakespeare*. New York: Norton, 2005.

Greengrass, Mark. *France in the Age of Henry IV: The Struggle for Stability*. London: Longman, 1984.

Gregory, Tobias. 'The Political Messages of *Samson Agonistes*'. *Studies in English Literature, 1500–1900* 50.1 (2010): 175–203.

Gregory, Tobias. 'Shadowing Intervention: On the Politics of *The Fairie Queene* Book 5 Cantos 10-12'. *ELH* 67 (2000): 365–97.

Greimas, Algirdas Julien. 'Actants, Actors, and Figures'. In *On Meaning: Selected Writings in Semiotic Theory*. Trans. Paul J. Perron and Frank H. Collins. Minneapolis: University of Minnesota Press, 1987: 106–20.

Greimas, Algirdas Julien. *Dictionnaire du moyen français: la Renaissance*. Paris: Larousse, 1992.

Griffin, Robert P. *John Webster: Politics and Tragedy*. Salzburg: Institut für Englische Sprache und Literatur, Universität Salzburg, 1972.

Grimshaw, Mike. 'Religion, Terror and the End of the Postmodern: Rethinking the Responses'. *International Journal of Baudrillard Studies* 3. 1 (2006). <http://www.ubish-ops.ca/baudrillardstudies/vol3_1/grimshaw.htm>.

Grossman, David. *Lion's Honey: The Myth of Samson*. Trans. Stuart Schoffman. London: Canongate, 2007.

Gunning, Jeroen and Richard Jackson. 'What's So Religious About Religious Terrorism?' *Critical Studies on Terrorism* 4:3 (2011): 369–88.

Gusfield, Joseph R. 'The Bridge over Separated Lands: Kenneth Burkes's Significance for the Study of Social Action'. In *The Legacy of Kenneth Burke*. Eds. Herbert W. Simons and Trevole Melia. Madison, WI: University of Wisconsin Press, 1989: 28–54.

Haan, Bertran. *Une paix pour l'éternité: La Négociation du traité de Cateau-Cambrésis*. Madrid: Casa de Velázquez, 2010.

Habermas, Jürgen. *The Structural Transformation of the Public Sphere: An Inquiry into a Category Of Bourgeois Society*. Trans. Thomas Burger. Cambridge, MA: MIT Press, 1991.

Habermas, Jürgen. *Theory of Communicative Action*. 2 Volumes. Trans. Thomas A. McCarthy. Boston: Beacon Press, 1984–7.

Hadfield, Andrew. 'Thomas Lodge and Elizabethan Republicanism'. *NJES: Nordic Journal of English Studies* 4.2 (2005): 89–105.

Hadfield, Andrew. *Shakespeare and Republicanism*. Cambridge: Cambridge University Press, 2005, esp. 160–81.

Hall, Bert S. *Weapons and Warfare in Renaissance Europe: Gunpowder, Technology and Tactics*. Baltimore: Johns Hopkins University Press, 1997.

Halpern, Baruch. *The First Historians: The Hebrew Bible and History*. University Park, PA: Penn State University Press, 1988.

Harmer, Tanya. *Allende's Chile and the Inter-American Cold War*. Chapel Hill, NC: University of North Carolina Press, 2011.

Hamon, Philippe. *Le personnel du roman: le système des personnages dans les Rougon-Macquart d'Emile Zola*. Genève: Droz, 1983.

Hampton, Timothy. *Writing from History: The Rhetoric of Exemplarity in Renaissance*. Ithaca, NY: Cornell University Press, 1990.

Handy, Lowell K. 'Uneasy Laughter—Ehud and Eglon as Ethnic Humor'. *Scandinavian Journal of the Old Testament* 6.2 (1992): 233–46.

Hardin, Richard F. 'The Early Poetry of The Gunpowder Plot: Myth in the Making'. *English Literary Renaissance* 22.1 (1992): 62–79.

Harris, Rachel. 'Samson's Suicide: Death and the Hebrew Literary Canon'. *Israeli Studies* 17.3 (2012): 67–91.

Hassner, Ron E. and Gideon Aran. 'Religion and Violence in the Jewish Traditions'. In *The Oxford Handbook of Religion and Violence*. Ed. Mark Juergensmeyer, Margo Kitts, and Michael Jerryson. Oxford: Oxford University Press, 2013: 126–53.

Heath-Kelly, Charlotte. 'Critical Terrorism Studies, Critical Theory and the "Naturalistic Fallacy"'. *Security Dialogue* 41.3 (2010): 235–54.

Hegel, G. W. F. *Phenomenology of Spirit*. Trans. A. V. Miller. Oxford: Oxford University Press, 1977.

Heinemann, Margot. *Puritanism and Theatre: Thomas Middleton and Opposition Drama Under the Early Stuarts*. Cambridge: Cambridge University Press, 1980.

Hennequin, Jacques. *Henri IV dans ses oraisons funèbres; ou la naissance d'une légende*. Paris: Klincksieck, 1977.

Herman, Peter. '"A Deed without a Name": *Macbeth*, the Gunpowder Plot, and Terrorism'. *Journal for Cultural Research* 18.2 (2014): 114–31.

Heron, Alasdair I. C. *Table and Tradition: Towards an Ecumenical Understanding of the Eucharist*. Edinburgh: Handsel Press, 1983.

Herz, Alexandra. 'Vasari's "Massacre" Series in the Sala Regia: The Political, Juristic, and Religious Background'. *Zeitschrift für Kunstgeschichte* 49.1 (1986): 41–54.

Herzog, Annabel. 'Hobbes and Corneille on Political Representation'. *The European Legacy* 14.4 (2010): 379–89.

Hillman, Richard. *Shakespeare, Marlowe, and the Politics of France*. Basingstoke: Palgrave, 2002.

Hillman, Richard. 'The Tragic-Channel Crossing of George Chapman, Part I: *Bussy d'Ambois*, *The Conspiracy and Tragedy of Byron*'. *Cahiers Elisabethains* 65 (2004): 25–43.

Hoffman, Bruce. 'Current Research on Terrorism and Low-Intensity Conflict'. *Studies In Conflict and Terrorism* 15.1 (1992): 25–38.

Hoffman, Bruce. *Inside Terrorism*. Second Edition. New York: Columbia University Press, 2006.

Hoffmann, George. 'France's First Revolution: Hamlet and the "Unresolved Man" of 1589'. In *Civilization in French and Francophone Literature* (French Literature Series XXXIII). Ed. Buford Norman and James Day. Amsterdam: Rodopi, 2006: 1–32.

Horgan, John. 'The Search for the Terrorist Personality'. In *Terrorists, Victims and Society: Psychological Perspective on Terrorism and Its Consequence*. Chichester: Wiley, 2003: 3–28.

Horgan, John and Michael J. Boyle. 'A Case Against "Critical Terrorism Studies"'. *Critical Studies on Terrorism* 1.1 (2008): 51–64.

Holderness, Graham and Bryan Loughrey. 'Shakespeare and Terror'. In *Shakespeare After 9/11: How a Social Trauma Reshapes Interpretation*. Ed. Matthew Biberman and Julia Reinhard Lupton. Lewiston, NY: Edwin Mellen, 2011: 23–56.

Holstun, James. *Ehud's Dagger: Class Struggle in the English Revolution*. London: Verso, 2002.

Holstun, James. '"God Bless Thee, Little David!": John Felton and his Allies'. *ELH* 59. 3 (1992): 513–52.

Holt, Mack P. *The French Wars of Religion, 1562–1629*. Cambridge: Cambridge University Press, 2005.

Hogge, Alice. *God's Secret Agents*. London: HarperCollins, 2005.

Houen, Alex. *Terrorism and Modern Literature from Joseph Conrad to Ciaran Carson*. Oxford: Oxford University Press, 2002.

Howe, E. 'Architecture in Vasari's "Massacre of the Huguenots"'. *Journal of the Warburg and Courtauld Institutes* 39 (1976): 258–61.

Hubert, Henri and Marcel Mauss. *Sacrifice, Its Nature and Function*. Trans. W. D. Halls. Chicago: University of Chicago Press, 1981.

Hughes, Derek. *Culture and Sacrifice: Ritual Death in Literature and Opera*. Cambridge: Cambridge University Press, 2006.

Hurstfield, Joel. 'A Retrospect: Gunpowder Plot and the Politics of Dissent'. In Hurstfield, *Freedom, Corruption, and Government in Elizabethan England*, 1973.

Hutson, Lorna. *The Invention of Suspicion: Law and Mimesis in Shakespeare and Renaissance Drama*. Oxford: Oxford University Press, 2007.

Ide, Richard S. 'Exploiting the Tradition: The Elizabethan Revenger as Chapman's "Complete Man"'. *Medieval & Renaissance Drama in England* 1 (1984): 159–72.

Jackson, Richard. 'The Study of Terrorism after 11 September 2001: Problems, Challenges and Future Developments'. *Political Studies Review* 7 (2009): 171–84.

Jackson, Richard. *Writing the War on Terrorism: Language, Politics and Counter-terrorism*. Manchester: Manchester University Press, 2005.

Jackson, Richard, Marie Breen Smyth and Jeroen Gunning. Eds. *Critical Terrorism Studies: A New Research Agenda*. London: Routledge, 2008.

Jacobus, Laura. 'Motherhood and Massacre: The Massacre of the Innocents in Late-Medieval Art and Drama'. In *The Massacre in History*. Ed. Mark Levene and Penny Roberts. New York: Berghan Books, 1999: 39–55.

Jameson, Fredric R. 'The Symbolic Inference; Or, Kenneth Burke and Ideological Analysis'. *Critical Inquiry* 4.3 (1978): 507–23.

Jantzen, Grace M. *Foundations of Violence (Death and the Displacement of Beauty)*. London: Routledge, 2004.

Jantzen, Grace M. *Violence to Eternity*. Ed. Jeremy Carrette and Morny Joy. London: Routledge, 2009.

Javeau, Claude. *Anatomie de la trahison*. Belval: Circé, 2007.

Jenkins, Brian M. *Terrorism: A New Kind of Warfare*. Santa Monica, CA: Rand Paper Series, 1974.

Johns, Adrian. *The Nature of the Book: Print and Knowledge in the Making*. Chicago: University of Chicago Press, 1998.

Jondorf, Gillian. *Robert Garnier and the Themes of Political Tragedy in the Sixteenth Century*. Cambridge: Cambridge University Press, 1969.

Jouanna, Arlette. *La Saint-Barthélemy: Les mystères d'un crime d'État*. Paris: Gallimard, 2007.

Joutard, Philippe, Janine Estebe, Elisabeth Labrousse, and Jean Lecuir. *La Saint-Barthélemy: Ou les résonances d'un massacre*. Neuchâtel: Delachaux et Niestlé, 1976.

Juergensmeyer, Mark. *Terror in the Mind of God: The Global Rise of Religious Violence*. 3rd Edition. Berkeley, CA: University of California Press, 2003.

Kafka, Franz. 'On Parables'. In *The Complete Stories and Parables*. New York: Schocken, 1971: 459.

Kaeuper, Richard W. *Chivalry and Violence in Medieval Europe*. Oxford: Oxford University Press, 1999.

Kantorowicz, Ernst. *The King's Two Bodies: A Study in Mediaeval Political Theology*. Princeton: Princeton University Press, 1957.

Kaske, Carol V. 'The Audiences of *The Faerie Queene*: Iconoclasm and Related Issues in Books I, V, and VI'. *Literature and History* 3. 2 (1994): 15–35.

Keith, Robert. *History of the Affairs of Church and State in Scotland: From the Beginning of the Reformation to the Year 1568*. Edinburgh: Spottiswoode Society, 1844–50.

Keohane, Nannerl O. *Philosophy and the State in France: The Renaissance to the Enlightenment*. Princeton: Princeton University Press, 1980.

Kerrigan, John. *Revenge Tragedy: Aeschylus to Armageddon*. Oxford: Oxford University Press, 1996.

Kewes, Paulina. 'Julius Caesar in Jacobean England'. *The Seventeenth Century* 17.2 (2002): 155–86.

Kingdon, Robert M. 'Reactions to the St. Bartholomew Massacres in Geneva and Rome'. In *The Massacre of St. Bartholomew: Reappraisals and Documents*. Ed. Alfred Soman. The Hague: Martinus Nijhoff, 25–49.

Kingdon, Robert M. *Myths About the St. Bartholomew's Day Massacres, 1572–1576*. Cambridge, MA: Harvard University Press, 1988.

Kirk, Andrew M. *The Mirror of Confusion: The Representation of French History in English Renaissance Drama*. New York: Garland, 1996.

Kirkconnell, Watson. *That Invincible Samson. The Theme of 'Samson Agonistes' in World Literature, with Translations of the Major Analogues*. Toronto: University of Toronto Press, 1964.

Knecht, R. J. *The French Wars of Religion, 1559–1598*. London: Longman, 1996.

Knolle, Richard. *General Historie of the Turkes*. London, 1603.

Knott, John R. *Discourses of Martyrdom in English Literature, 1563–1694*. Cambridge: Cambridge University Press, 1993.

Kocher, Paul. 'Contemporary Pamphlet Backgrounds for Marlowe's *The Massacre at Paris*, Part Two'. *Modern Language Quarterly* 8 (1947): 309–18.

Kocher, Paul. 'Francois Hotman and Marlowe's *The Massacre at Paris*'. *PMLA* 56 (1941): 349–68.

Kojève, Alexander. *Introduction to the Reading of Hegel*. Trans. James H. Nichols. New York: Basic Books, 1969.

Kooistra, P. G. 'What is Political Crime?' *Criminal Justice Abstracts*. 17.1 (1985): 100–15.

Krantz, Susan E. 'Thomas Dekker's Political Commentary in *The Whore of Babylon*'. *Studies in English Literature* 35.2 (1995), 271–92.

Kraus, Hans Joachim. *Worship in Israel: A Cultic History of the Old Testament*. Trans. Geoffrey Buswell. Oxford: Blackwell, 1966.

Krueger, David. 'Christianity and Violence'. *Religion Compass* 7.7 (2013): 243–51.

Kruglanski, Arie W. and Shira Fishman. 'The Psychology of Terrorism: "Syndrome" Versus "Tool" Perspectives'. *Terrorism and Political Violence* 18.2 (2006).

Kunzle, David. *From Criminal to Courtier: The Soldier in Netherlandish Art 1550–1672*. Leiden: Brill, 2002.

Lacan, Jacques. *The Seminar. Book I. Freud's Papers on Technique, 1953–54*. Trans. John Forrester. New York: Norton, 1988.

Lake, Peter and Steve Pincus. 'Rethinking the Public Sphere in Early Modern England'. *Journal of British Studies* 45.2 (2006), 270–92.

Lancaster, Dabney. *Claude Billard: Minor French Dramatist*. Baltimore: Johns Hopkins University Press, 1932.

Langan, John. 'The Elements of St. Augustine's Just War Theory'. *Journal of Religious Ethics* 12.1 (1984): 19–38.

Laqueur, Walter. Ed. *Voices of Terror. Manifestos, Writing and Manuals of Al Qaeda, Hamas, and Other Terrorists from around the World and throughout the Ages*. New York: Reed Press, 2004.

Laqueur, Walter. *The New Terrorism: Fanaticism and the Arms of Mass Destruction.* New York: Oxford University Press, 1999.

Laqueur, Walter. *No End to War: Terrorism and in the Twenty-first Century.* New York: Continuum, 2004.

Larson, Anthony T. 'On the Uses and Abuses of Terror for Life: Terror and the Literary Clinic'. *Parallax* 9.1 (2003): 48–57.

Landry, Jean-Pierre. '*Cinna* ou le paradoxe de la clémence'. *Revue d'Histoire littéraire de la France* 102.3 (2002): 443–53.

Lazard, Madeleine. *Le théâtre en France au XVIe siecle.* Paris: P.U.F., 1980.

Le Person, Xavier. '*Practiques' et 'practiqueurs': la vie politique à la fin du règne de Henri III (1584-1589).* Genève: Droz, 2002.

Le Roux, Nicholas. *Un régicide au nom de Dieu. L'assassinat d'Henri III.* Paris: Gallimard, 2006.

Le Roy Ladurie, Emmanuel. *Carnival in Romans: A People's Uprising at Romans 1579–1580.* Trans. Mary Feeney. Harmondsworth: Penguin, 1981.

Lebègue, R. *La Tragédie religieuse en France.* Paris: H. Champion, 1929.

Lee, Peter. 'Selective Memory: Augustine and Contemporary Just War Discourse'. *Scottish Journal of Theology* 65. 3 (2012): 309–32.

Lee, Sidney. *The French Renaissance in England: An Account of the Literary Relations Of England And France In The 16th Century.* Oxford: Clarendon, 1910.

Leggatt, Alexander. 'The Tragedy of Clermont d'Ambois'. *Modern Language Review* 77. 3 (1982): 524–36.

Lemon, Rebecca. *Treason by Words: Literature, Law, and Rebellion in Shakespeare's England.* Ithaca, NY: Cornell University Press, 2006.

Lenient, Charles. *La satire en France, ou la littérature militante au XVIe siécle.* Paris: Hachette, 1877.

Lenman, Bruce, and Geoffrey Parker. 'The State, the Community and the Criminal Law in Early Modern Europe'. In *Crime and the Law: The Social History of Crime in Western Europe since 1500.* Eds. V. A. C. Gatrell, Bruce Lenman, and Geoffrey Parker. London: Europa, 1980: 11–48.

Lentricchia, Frank, and Jody Macauliffe. *Crimes of Art and Terror.* Chicago: University of Chicago Press, 2003.

Lépront, Catherine, Marc de Launay, and Laura Weigert. *Judith et Holopherne.* Paris: Desclée de Brouwer, 2003.

Lestringant, Frank. *La cause des martyrs dans 'Les Tragiques' d'Agrippa d'Aubigné.* Mont-de-Marsan: Editions Interuniversitaires, 1991.

Lestringant, Frank. *Lumière des martyrs. Essai sur le martyre au siècle des Réformes.* Paris: Honoré Champion, 2004.

Lévi-Strauss, Claude. 'The Structural Study of Myth'. In Lévi-Strauss, *Structural Anthropology.* Trans. Claire Jacobson and Brooke Grundfest Schoepf. Garden City, NY: Anchor, 1967: 202–28.

Levenson, Jon D. *The Death and Resurrection of the Beloved Son.* New Haven, CT: Yale, 1993.

Levine, Amy-Jill. 'Sacrifice and Salvation: Otherness and Domestication in the Book of Judith'. In *No One Spoke Ill of Her: Essays on Judith.* Ed. James C. VanderKam. Atlanta, GA: Scholars Press, 1992: 17–30.

Lewis, C. S. *The Allegory of Love: A Study in Medieval Tradition.* Oxford: Clarendon, 1936.

Lieb, Michael and Albert C. Labriola. *Milton in the Age of Fish: Essays On Authorship, Text, and Terrorism.* Pittsburgh, PA: Duquesne University Press, 2006.

Lucking, David. 'Brutus's Reasons: *Julius Caesar* and the Mystery of Motive'. *English Studies* 91.2 (2010): 119–32.

Luckyj, Christina. Ed. *The Duchess of Malfi: A Critical Guide*. London: Continuum, 2011.

Luna, B. N. De. *Jonson's Romish Plot: a Study of Catiline and its Historical Context*. Oxford: Oxford University Press, 1967.

Lynch, Deidre Shauna. *The Economy of Character: Novels, Market Culture, and the Business of Inner Meaning*. Chicago: University of Chicago Press, 1998.

Lyons, John D. 'The Barbarous Ancients: French Classical Poetics and the Attack on Ancient Tragedy'. *MLN* 110. 5 (1995): 1135–47.

Maffesoli, Michel. *Essais sur la violence: banale et fondatrice*. Third Edition. Paris: CNRS, 2009.

Marche, Stephen. 'John Webster and the Dead: Reading the *Duchess of Malfi's* Eschatology'. *Renaissance and Reformation* 28.2 (2004): 79–95.

Marin, Louis. *Portrait of the King*. Trans. Martha M. Houle. Minneapolis: University of Minnesota Press, 1988.

Marin, Louis. 'Pour une théorie baroque de l'action politique'. Preface to Gabriel Naudé, *Considérations sur les coups d'état*: 7–61.

Marotti, Arthur F. *Religious Ideology and Cultural Fantasy: Catholic and Anti-catholic Discourses in Early Modern England*. Notre Dame: University of Notre Dame Press, 2005.

Marsh, Jack. E. Jr. 'Of Violence: The Force and Significance of Violence in the Early Derrida'. *Philosophy and Social Criticism* 35.3 (2009): 269–86.

Martin, Randall. 'Anne Dowriche's *The French History*, Christopher Marlowe, and Machiavellian Agency'. *Studies in English Literature* 39.1 (1999): 69–87.

Marzano, Michela. Ed. *Dictionnaire de la violence*. Paris: Presses Universitaires de France, 2011.

Mattox, John Mark. *Saint Augustine and the Theory of Just War*. London: Continuum, 2006.

Matusitz, Jonathan. *Terrorism and Communication: A Critical Introduction*. Thousand Oaks, CA: Sage, 2013.

Maus, Katharine Eisaman. *Inwardness and Theater in the English Renaissance*. Chicago: University of Chicago Press, 1995.

Maxwell, Julie. 'Counter-Reformation Versions of Saxo: A New Source for *Hamlet*?' *Renaissance Quarterly* 57. 2 (2004): 518–60.

McGowan, Margaret M. *The Vision of Rome in Late Renaissance France*. New Haven, CT: Yale: 2000.

McHam, Sarah Blake. 'Donatello's Bronze "David" and "Judith" as Metaphors of Medici Rule in Florence'. *The Art Bulletin* 83. 1 (2001): 32–47.

Mcintosh, Shona. 'The Massacre of St Bartholomew on the English Stage: Chapman, Marlowe, and the Duke of Guise'. *Renaissance Studies* 26 (2012): 325–44.

McLaren, Anne. 'Rethinking Republicanism: *Vindiciae, contra tyrannos* in Context'. *Ante* 49 (2006): 23–352.

McMillin, Scott. 'Acting and Violence: *The Revenger's Tragedy* and Its Departures from Hamlet'. *Studies in English Literature, 1500–1900* 24.2. (1984): 275–91.

McPherson, C. B. *The Political Theory of Possessive Individualism*. Oxford: Oxford University Press, 1962.

Mees, Ludwig. *Nationalism, Violence and Democracy: The Basque Clash of Identities*. Basingstoke: Palgrave Macmillan, 2003.

Melchiori, Barbara Arnett. *Terrorism in the Late Victorian Novel*. London: Croom Helm, 1985.

Ménard, Jean-Louis. *La révolte des Nu-Pieds en Normandie au XVIIème siècle*. Paris: Dittmar, 2005.

Michaud, Yves. *La Violence*. Paris: Presses Universitaires de France, 2007.

Michel, Lou, and Dan Herbeck. *American Terrorist: Timothy McVeigh and the Oklahoma City Bombing*. New York: HarperCollins, 2001.

Miller, Elizabeth C. 'The Inward Revolution: Sexual Terrorism in *The Princess Casamassima*'. *Henry James Review* 24. 2 (2003): 146–67.

Miller, Elizabeth C. *Framed: The New Woman Criminal in British Culture at the Fin de Siecle*. Ann Arbor, MI: University of Michigan Press, 2009.

Miller, Martin. A. 'The Intellectual Origins of Terrorism in Europe'. In *Terrorism in Context*. Ed. Martha Crenshaw. University Park, PA: Pennsylvania State University Press, 1995: 27–62.

Miola, Robert. '*Julius Caesar* and the Tyrannicide Debate'. *Renaissance Quarterly* 39 (1985): 271–89.

Mohamed, Feisal G. *Milton and The Post-Secular Present: Ethics, Politics, Terrorism/Feisal G. Mohamed*. Stanford, CA: Stanford University Press, 2011.

Monta, Susannah Brietz. *Martyrdom and Literature in Early Modern England*. New York: Cambridge University Press, 2005.

Moote, A. Lloyd. *Louis XIII, The Just*. Berkeley, CA: University of California Press, 1989.

Mousnier, Roland. *The Assassination of Henry IV*. Trans. Joan Spencer. London: Faber and Faber, 1971.

Muchembled, Robert. *A History of Violence*. Trans. Jean Birrell. Cambridge: Polity, 2008.

Mullaney, Steven. 'Mourning and Misogyny: *Hamlet*, *The Revenger's Tragedy*, and the Final Progress of Elizabeth I, 1600–1607'. *Shakespeare Quarterly* 45.2 (1994), 139–62.

Muro, Diego. *Ethnicity and Violence: The Case of Radical Basque Nationalism*. New York: Routledge, 2007.

Nancy, Jean-Luc. 'L'insacrifiable'. In Nancy, *Une pensée finie*. Paris: Galilée, 1990: 65–106.

Nathanson, Stephen. *Terrorism and the Ethics of War*. Cambridge: Cambridge University Press, 2010.

Neal, Andrew W. *Exceptionalism and the Politics of Counter-Terrorism: Liberty, Security and the War on Terror*. London: Routledge, 2010.

Neill, Michael. 'English Revenge Tragedy'. In *A Companion to Tragedy*. Ed. Rebecca Bushnell. Oxford: Blackwell, 2005: 328–50.

Nicholls, Mark. *Investigating Gunpowder Plot*. Manchester: Manchester University Press, 1991.

Nicholls, Mark. 'Strategy and Motivation in the Gunpowder Plot'. *Historical Journal* 50. 4 (2007): 787–807.

Norbrook, David. '*Macbeth* and the Politics of Historiography'. In *Politics of Discourse: The Literature and History of Seventeenth-Century England*. Ed. Kevin Sharpe and Steven N. Zwicker. Berkeley, CA: University of California Press, 1987: 78–1.

Nowak, Thomas S. 'Propaganda and the Pulpit: Robert Cecil, William Barlow and the Essex and Gunpowder Plots'. In *The Witness of Times: Manifestations of Ideology in Seventeenth-Century England*. Ed. Katherine Z. Keller. Pittsburgh, PA: Duquesne University Press, 1993: 34–52.

O'Connor, Timothy, and Constantine Sandis. Eds. *A Companion to the Philosophy of Action*. Oxford: Wiley-Blackwell, 2009.

Okines, A. W. R. E. 'Why Was There So Little Government Reaction to Gunpowder Plot?' *Journal of Ecclesiastical History* 55.2 (2004): 275–92.

Oltean, Roxana. 'An "unnatural alliance": Realism and Revolution in Henry James's *The Princess Casamassima*'. *The Henry James Review* 30.2 (2009): 144–61.

Orgel, Stephen. *The Illusion of Power: Political Theater in the English Renaissance*. Berkeley, CA: University of California Press, 1975.

Otzen, Benedikt. *Tobit and Judith*. London: Sheffield Academic Press, 2002.

Pallier, Denis. *Recherches sur l'imprimerie à Paris pendant la Ligue, 1585–1594*. Genève: Droz, 1975.

Parker, David. 'The Social Foundation of French Absolutism 1610–1630'. *Past and Present*, 53.1 (1971): 67–89.

Parker, Geoffrey. 'Crisis and Catastrophe: The Global Crisis of the Seventeenth Century Reconsidered'. *American Historical Review* 113.4 (2008): 1053–79.

Parker, Geoffrey, and Lesley M. Smith. Eds. *The General Crisis of the Seventeenth Century*. London: Routledge, 1978.

Parker, Geoffrey. *The Dutch Revolt*. Harmondsworth: Penguin, 1979.

Parker, Geoffrey. *Europe in Crisis 1598–1648*. Second Edition. Oxford: Blackwell, 2001.

Parmalee, Lisa Ferraro. *Good Newes from Fraunce: French Anti-League Propaganda in Late Elizabethan England*. Rochester: University of Rochester Press, 1996.

Parrow, Kathleen A. 'Neither Treason nor Heresy: Use of Defense Arguments to Avoid Forfeiture during the French Wars of Religion'. *Sixteenth Century Journal* 22. 4 (1991): 705–16.

Pettegree, Andrew, Paul Nelles and Philip Conner. Eds. *The Sixteenth-century French Religious Book*. Aldershot: Ashgate, 2001.

Phelan, James. *Reading People, Reading Plots: Character, Progression, and the Interpretation of Narrative*. Chicago: University of Chicago Press, 1989.

Pillorget, René. 'Le Complot Papiste dans l'imaginaire anglais au xviie siècle'. *Storia della Storiografia* 14 (1988): 119–35.

Pincombe, Mike. 'Robert Dudley, *Gorboduc*, and "The Masque of Beauty and Desire": A Reconsideration of the Evidence for Political Intervention'. *Parergon*. 20.1 (2003): 19–44.

Piot, Charles. *Remotely Global: Village Modernity in West Africa*. Chicago: University of Chicago Press, 1999.

Pineaux, Jacques. '*César* dans la tragédie humaniste de la Renaissance française'. In *Présence de César*. Ed. Raymond Chevallier. Paris: Belles Lettres, 1985: 213–22.

Pocock, J. G. A. *The Ancient Constitution and the Feudal Law: A Study of English Historical Thought in the Seventeenth Century*. Baltimore: Johns Hopkins University Press, 1987.

Poirier, Jacques. *Judith: échos d'un mythe biblique dans la littérature française*. Rennes: Presses universitaires de Rennes, 2004.

Polachek, Dora E. 'Le Mécénat meurtrier, l'iconoclasme et les limites de l'acceptable: Anne d'Este, Catherine-Marie de Lorraine et l'anéantissement d'Henri III'. In *Patronnes et mécènes en France à la Renaissance*. Ed. Kathleen Wilson-Chevalier. Saint-Étienne: Université de Saint-Étienne, 2007: 433–54.

Pollen, John Hungerford. *Mary Queen of Scots and the Babington Plot*. Edinburgh: Scottish Historical Society, 1922.

Pouey-Mounou, Anne-Pascale. 'Des prêches, des armes et des livres: la figure de Théodore de Bèze dans la polémique des *Discours des miseres de ce temps* (1562–1563)'. In *Writers in Conflict in Sixteenth-Century France*. Ed. Elizabeth Vinestock and David Foster. Durham: University of Durham, 2008: 153–72.

Preece, Julian. *Baader-Meinhof and the Novel: Narrative of the Nation, Fantasies of the Revolution, 1970–2010*. New York: Palgrave Macmillan, 2012.

Quint, David. 'Milton, Fletcher and the Gunpowder Plot'. *Journal of the Warburg and Courtauld Institutes* 54 (1991): 261–8.

Quint, David. *Epic and Empire*. Princeton University Press, 1993.

Rabb, Theodore K. *The Struggle for Stability in Early Modern Europe*. Oxford: Oxford University Press, 1976.

Racaut, Luc. *Hatred in Print: Catholic Propaganda and Protestant Identity during the French Wars of Religion*. Aldershot: Ashgate, 2002.

Rai, Milan. *7/7: The London Bombings, Islam and the Iraq War*. London: Pluto Press, 2006.

Rancière, Jacques. *The Future of the Image*. Trans. Gregory Elliott. London: Verso, 2008.

Ranum, Orest. *The Fronde: A French Revolution, 1648–1652*. New York: W. W. Norton, 1993.

Ranum, Orest. 'The Ritual of Tyrannicide in the Late Sixteenth Century'. *Sixteenth Century Journal* 11 (1980): 63–81.

Rapoport, David. 'Fear and Trembling: Terrorism in Three Religious Traditions'. *American Political Science Review* 78.3 (1984): 658–77.

Rapoport, David. 'The Four Waves of Modern Terrorism'. In Audrey Cronin and James Ludes (Eds.) *Attacking Terrorism: Elements of a Grand Strategy*. Washington DC: Georgetown University Press, 2004: 46–73.

Redfield, Marc. *The Rhetoric of Terror: Reflections on 9/11 and the War on Terror*. New York: Fordham University Press, 2009.

Reiss, Timothy J. *The Meaning of Literature*. Ithaca, NY: Cornell, 1992.

Revard, Stella P. 'Milton's Gunpowder Poems and Satan's Conspiracy'. *Milton Studies* (1972): 63–78.

Ricoeur, Paul. 'Narrative Identity'. In *On Paul Ricoeur: Narrative and Interpretation*. Ed. David Wood. London: Routledge, 1991: 188–200.

Ricoeur, Paul. *Time and Narrative*. 3 Volumes. Trans. Kathleen McLaughlin and David Pellauer. Chicago: University of Chicago Press, 1984–8.

Rigolot, François. 'Essaying Hatred: Montaigne's Poetics of Ethical Allusiveness'. *L' Esprit Créateur* 46.1 (2006): 32–8.

Rigolot, François. 'Trois "Mises en scène" littéraires du politique: Ronsard, Aubigné, Montaigne'. In *Spielwelten. Performanx und Inszenierung in der Renaissance*. Ed. Klaus W. Hempfer and Helmut Pfeiffer. Stuttgart: Franz Steiner Verlag, 2002: 147–63.

Rist, Thomas. *Revenge Tragedy and the Drama of Commemoration in Reforming England*. Aldershot: Ashgate, 2008.

Roberts, Penny. 'Urban Conflict and Royal Authority: Popular Revolts in Sixteenth-Century Troyes'. *Urban History* 34 (2007): 190–208.

Robin, Corey. *Fear: The History of a Political Idea*. Oxford: Oxford University Press, 2004.

Roelker, Nancy Lyman. *One King, One Faith: The Parlement of Paris and the Religious Reformation of the Sixteenth Century*. Berkeley, CA: University of California Press, 1996.

Rogers, H. L. 'An English Tailor and Father Garnet's Straw'. *Review of English Studies* 16. 61 (1965): 44–9.

Roosbroeck, Gustave L. van, 'Corneille's *Cinna* and the *Conspiration des Dames*'. *Modern Philology* 20.1 (1922): 1–17.

Rosenberger, John. 'Discerning the Behaviour of the Suicide Bomber: The Role of Vengeance'. *Journal of Religion and Health* 42.1 (2003), 13–20.

Ross, Jeffrey Ian. *The Dynamics of Political Crime*. Thousand Oaks, CA: Sage, 2003.

Ross, Jeffrey Ian. *Varieties of State Crime and its Control*. Monsey, NY: Criminal Justice Press, 2000.

Rowe, Katherine. 'Memory and Revision in Chapman's Bussy Plays'. *Renaissance Drama* 31, (2002): 125–52.

Rubenstein, Richard. *Comrade Valentine: The True Story of Azef the Spy—The Most Dangerous Man in Russia at the Time of the Last Czars*. New York: Harcourt Brace, 1994.

Ruble, Alphonse, Baron de. *L'assassinat de François de Lorraine, Duc de Guise, 18 Fevrier 1563*. Paris: E. Paul et Fils, 1897.

Ruby, Charles L. 'Are Terrorists Mentally Deranged?' *Analyses of Social Issues and Public Policy* 2.1 (2002): 15–26.

Rudrum, Alan. 'Milton Scholarship and the "Agon" over *Samson Agonistes*'. *Huntington Quarterly* 65.3–4 (2002): 465–88.

Ruff, Julius R. *Violence in Early Modern Europe 1500–1800*. Cambridge: Cambridge University Press, 2001.

Rummel, Rudolph J. *Death by Government*. New Brunswick, NJ: Transaction, 1994.

Salmon, J. H. M. 'Cicero and Tacitus in Sixteenth-Century France'. *American Historical Review* 85.2 (1980): 307–31.

Salmon, J. H. M. 'Stoicism and Roman Example: Seneca and Tacitus in Jacobean England'. *Journal of the History of Ideas* 50.2 (1989): 199–225.

Salmon, J. H. M. *The French Religious Wars in English Political Thought*. Oxford: Clarendon Press, 1959.

Salmon, J. H. M. *Society in Crisis: France in the Sixteenth Century*. London: Ernest Benn, 1975.

Sanders, Julie. 'Beggars' Commonwealths and the Pre-Civil War Stage: Suckling's *The Goblins*, Brome's *A Jovial Crew*, and Shirley's *The Sisters*'. *Modern Language Review* 97.1 (2002): 1–14.

Saul, Nigel. *For Honour and Fame: Chivalry in England 1066–1500*. London: Bodley Head, 2011.

Sauzet, Robert. Ed. *Henri III et son temps, Acte du colloque international du Centre de la Renaissance de Tours, Octobre 1989*. Paris: J. Vrin, 1992.

Scanlan, Margaret. *Plotting Terror: Novelists and Terrorists in Contemporary Fiction*. Charlottesville, VA: University Press of Virginia, 2001.

Scanlan, Margaret. 'Terrorism and the Realistic Novel: Henry James and *The Princess Casamassima*'. *Texas Studies in Literature and Language* 34:3 (1992): 380–402.

Schaefer, David Lewis. 'Montaigne's Political Reformation'. *Journal of Politics* 42.3 (1980): 766–91.

Schechner, Richard. *Performance Theory*. London: Routledge, 1988.

Schmitt, Carl. *The Concept of the Political*. Expanded Edition. Trans. George Schwab. Chicago: University of Chicago Press, 2007.

Schmitt, Carl. *Political Theology: Four Chapters on the Concept of Sovereignty*. Trans. George Schwab. Chicago: University of Chicago Press, 2005.

Scott, Paul. 'Resistance Theories, Orthodoxy and Subversive Drama in Early Modern France'. *Seventeenth-Century French Studies* 21 (1999): 57–73.

Sémelin, Jacques. 'Analyser le massacre. Réflexions comparatives'. *Questions de Recherche* 7 (September 2002), 1–42. www.ceri-sciences-po.org/publica/qdr.htm

Shapiro, Barbara J. *Political Communication and Political Culture in England, 1558–1688*. Stanford, CA: Stanford University Press, cop. 2012.

Sharpe, J. A. *Crime in Early Modern England 1550–1750*. Second Edition. London: Longman, 1999.

Shawcross, John. *The Uncertain World of 'Samson Agonistes'*. Rochester, NY: D. S. Brewer, 2001.

Shimizu, J. *Conflict of Loyalties: Politics and Religion in the Career of Gaspard de Coligny, Admiral of France, 1519–1572*. Geneva: Droz, 1970.

Shuger, Debora Kuller. *The Renaissance Bible: Scholarship, Sacrifice, and Subjectivity*. Berkeley, CA: University of California Press, 1994.

Signorile, Vito. 'Ratios and Causes: The Pentad as an Etiological Scheme in Sociological Explanation'. In *The Legacy of Kenneth Burke*. Eds. Herbert W. Simons and Trevole Melia. Madison, WI: University of Wisconsin Press, 1989: 74–98.

Silberstein, Sandra. *War of Words: Language, Politics and 9/11*. London: Routledge, 2004.

Silverman, Lisa. *Tortured Subjects: Pain, Truth and the Body in Early Modern France*. Chicago: University of Chicago Press, 2001.

Simon, Jeffrey D. *The Terrorist Trap: America's Experience with Terrorism*. Second Edition. Bloomington, IN: Indiana University Press, 2001.

Simonin, Michel. *Vivre de sa plume au XVIe siècle, ou, la carrière de François de Belleforest*. Genève: Droz, 1992.

Simons, Herbert W. and Trevole Melia. Eds. *The Legacy of Kenneth Burke*. Madison, WI: University of Wisconsin Press, 1989.

Skinner, Quentin. *The Foundations of Modern Political Thought*. 2 Volumes. Cambridge: Cambridge University Press, 1978.

Sloan, Stephen. *Terrorism: The Present Threat in Context*. New York: Berg, 2006.

Smith, Lacey Baldwin. *Treason in Tudor England: Politics and Paranoia*. Princeton, NJ: Princeton University Press, 1986.

Smith, Nigel. *Literature and Revolution in England 1640–1660*. New Haven, CT: Yale, 1997.

Smither, James R. 'The St. Bartholomew's Day Massacre and Images of Kingship in France: 1572–1574'. *The Sixteenth Century Journal* 22. 1 (1991): 27–46.

Smyth, Marie Breen et al. 'Critical Terrorism Studies—An Introduction'. *Critical Studies on Terrorism* 1.1: 1–4.

Soman, Alfred. Ed. *The Massacre of St. Bartholomew*. The Hague: Martinus Nijhoff, 1974.

Sommers, Paula. 'Gendered Readings of The Book of Judith: Guillaume du Bartas and Gabrielle de Coignard'. *Romance Quarterly* 48.4 (2001): 211–20.

Sommerville, Johann. *Politics and Ideology in England 1603–1640*. London: Longman, 1986.

Spierenburg, Pieter. *A History of Murder: Personal Violence in Europe from the Middle Ages to the Present*. Cambridge: Polity Press, 2008.

Spierenburg, Pieter. *The Spectacle of Suffering: Execution and the Evolution of Repression: From a Preindustrial Metropolis to the European Experience*. Cambridge: Cambridge University Press, 1984.

Sproxton, Judith. 'Peut-on définir le genre de la *Judit* de Du Bartas d'après l'étude des temps?' *Journal of European Studies* 18.1 (1988): 9–20.

Stabler, Arthur P. 'King Hamlet's Ghost in Belleforest?' *PMLA* 77.1 (1962): 18–20.

Stabler, Arthur P. 'Melancholy, Ambition, and Revenge in Belleforest's *Hamlet*'. *PMLA* 81. 3 (1966): 207–13.

States, Bert O. *Hamlet and the Concept of Character*. Baltimore, MD: Johns Hopkins University Press, 1992.

Strenski, Ivan. *Contesting Sacrifice: Religion, Nationalism, and Social Thought in France*. Chicago: University of Chicago Press, 2002.

Stern, Jessica. *Terror in the Name of God: Why Terrorists Kill*. New York: HarperCollins, 2004.

Stocker, Margarita. *Judith, Sexual Warrior: Women and Power in Western Culture*. New Haven, CT: Yale University Press, 1998.

Stone, Lawrence. *The Crisis of the Aristocracy 1558–1641*. Oxford: Clarendon Press, 1965.

Stone, Lawrence. *An Open Elite? England 1540–1880*. Abridged Edition. Oxford: Oxford University Press, 1984.

Stone, Lawson G. 'Eglon's Belly and Ehud's Blade: A Reconsideration'. *Journal of Biblical Literature* 128.4 (2009): 649–64.

Sutherland, Nicola Mary. 'The Assassination of François Duc de Guise, February 1563'. *Historical Journal* 24 (1981): 279–95.

Sutherland, Nicola Mary. 'Le Massacre de La Saint-Barthélemy: La valeur des temoignages et leur interpretation'. *Revue d'Histoire Moderne & Contemporaine* 38 (1991): 529–54.

Sutherland, Nicola Mary. 'The Role of Coligny in the French Civil Wars'. In *Actes du colloque "l'Amiral de Coligny et son temps"*. Société de l'histoire du protestantisme français: Paris, 1974: 323–39.

Sutto, Claude. 'Quelques conséquences politiques de l'attentat de Jean Chastel'. *Renaissance & Reformation* 13. 2 (1977): 136–54.

Teague, Frances. 'Jonson and the Gunpowder Plot'. *Ben Jonson Journal* 5 (1998): 249–52.

Tennenhouse, Leonard. *Power on Display: The Politics of Shakespeare's Genres*. New York: Methuen, 1986.

Thompson, E. P. 'The Moral Economy of the English Crowd in the Eighteenth Century'. *Past and Present* 50 (1971): 76–136.

Todorov, Tzvetan. *Poétique de la prose*. Paris: Éditions du Seuil, 1980.

Tollington, Janet. 'The Ethics of Warfare and the Holy War Tradition in the Book of Judges'. In *Ethical and Unethical in the Old Testament: God and Humans in Dialogue*. Ed. Katharine Dell. London: Continuum, 2010: 71–87.

Tournon, André. 'Poétique du témoignage dans *Les Tragiques*'. In *Poétiques d'Aubigné*. Ed. Oliver Pots. Geneva: Droz, 1999: 135–46.

Trevor-Roper, Hugh. 'The General Crisis of the Seventeenth Century'. In *Crisis in Europe*. Ed. Trevor Aston. London: Routledge and Kegan Paul, 1965: 59–96.

Trotsky, Leon. 'Terrorism' (1911). <http://www.marxists.de/theory/whatis/terror2.htm> (1 February 2012).

Tuck, Richard. *Philosophy and Government 1572–1651*. Cambridge: Cambridge University Press, 1993.

Tuman, Joseph S. *Communicating Terror: The Rhetorical Dimensions of Terror*. Second Edition. Los Angeles: Sage, 2010.

Turner, Victor. *The Anthropology of Performance*. New York: PAJ, 1986.

Turner, Victor. 'Social Dramas and Stories about Them'. *Critical Inquiry* 7.1 (1980): 141–68.

Tutino, Stefania. *Law and Conscience: 1570–1625: Catholicism in Early Modern England*. Aldershot: Ashgate, 2007.

Vaissière, Pierre de. *De Quelques assassins: Jean Poltrot, seigneur de Méré, Charles de Louviers, seigneur de Maurevert, Jean Yanowitz, dit Besme, Henri III et les 'Quarante-cinq', Jacques Clément*. Paris: Émile-Paul, 1912.

VanderKam, James C. *'No one spoke ill of her': Essays on Judith*. Atlanta, GA: Scholars Press, 1992.

Vanhoutte, Jacqueline. 'Community, Authority, and the Motherland in Sackville and Norton's Gorboduc'. *SEL: Studies in English Literature, 1500–1900* 40.2 (2000): 227–39.

Venard, Marc. 'Arrêtez le massacre!' *Revue d'histoire moderne et contemporaine* 39.4 (1992): 645–61.

Venard, Marc. 'Catholicism and Resistance to the Reformation in France, 1555-1585'. In Benedict, Philip et al. Eds. Reformation, Revolt and Civil War in France, 133–48.

Vermeule, Blakey. *Why Do We Care about Literary Character?* Baltimore, MD: Johns Hopkins University Press, 2009.

Verhoeven, Claudia. *The Odd Man Karakozov: Imperial Russia, Modernity, and the Birth of Terrorism*. Ithaca, NY: Cornell University Press, 2011.

Versluys, Kristiaan. *Out of the Blue: September 11 and the Novel*. New York: Columbia University Press, 2009.

Vitkus, Daniel J. *Turning Turk: English Theater and the Multicultural Mediterranean, 1570–1630*. Basingstoke: Palgrave Macmillan, 2008.

Wagner-Pacifici, Robin Erica. *The Moro Morality Play: Terrorism as Social Drama*. Chicago: University of Chicago Press, 1986.

Walter, Christian. Ed. *Terrorism as a Challenge for National and International Law: Security versus Liberty?* Berlin: Springer, 2004.

Walter, John. *Understanding Popular Violence in the English Revolution: The Colchester Plunderers*. Cambridge: Cambridge University Press, 1999.

Waszink, Jan. Introduction. Justus Lipsius. *Six Books of Politics or Political Instruction*. Assen: Royal Van Gorcum, 2004.

Weber, Henri. 'La journée des Barricades et l'assassinat du duc et du cardinal de Guise'. *Cahiers du renaissance* 1 (2002): <http://publications.univ-montp3.fr/c.renaissance/numero1/journee-des-barricades?artsuite=0>.

Weber, Max. *From Max Weber: Essays in Sociology*. Trans. H. H. Gerth and C. Wright Mills. New York: Oxford University Press, 1946.

Weinberg Leonard, Ami Pedahzur, and Sivan Hirsch-Hoefler. 'The Challenges Of Conceptualizing Terrorism, Terrorism and Political Violence'. *Terrorism and Political Violence* 16:4 (2004): 777–94.

Weisgerber, Jean. *La mort du prince: le régicide dans la tragédie européenne du XVIIe siècle*. Bruxelles: Peter Lang, 2006.

Wess, Robert. *Kenneth Burke: Rhetoric, Subjectivity, Postmodernism*. Cambridge: Cambridge University Press, 1996.

Whelehan, Niall. *The Dynamiters: Irish Nationalism and Political Violence in the Wider World, 1867–1900*. Cambridge: Cambridge University Press, 2012.

White, Hayden. *The Content of the Form: Narrative Discourse and Historical Representation*. Baltimore, MD: Johns Hopkins University Press, 1987.

White, Hayden. *Figural Realism: Studies in the Mimesis Effect*. Baltimore, MD: Johns Hopkins University Press, 1999.

White, Hayden. *Tropics of Discourse: Essays in Cultural Criticism*. Baltimore, MD: Johns Hopkins University Press, 1990.

Wiggins, Martin. *Journeymen In Murder: The Assassin In English Renaissance Drama*. Oxford: Clarendon Press, 1991.

Wilkinson, Alexander. '"Homicides Royaux": The Assassination of the Duc and Cardinal de Guise and the Radicalization of French Public Opinion'. *French History* 18.2 (2004): 129–53.

Wills, Gary. *Rome and Rhetoric*. New Haven, CT: Yale, 2009.

Wills, Gary. *Witches and Jesuits: Shakespeare's 'Macbeth'*. New York and Oxford: Oxford University Press, 1995.

Wilson, Luke H. *Theatres of Intention: Drama and the Law in Early Modern England*. Stanford, CA: Stanford University Press, 2000.

Wilson, Richard. '"A Bleeding Head Where They Begun": Julius Caesar and the Mystical Foundations of Authority"'. In *Shakespeare in French Theory: King of Shadows*. Ed. Richard Wilson. London: Routledge, 2007: 163–201.

Wilson, Richard. '"Blood Will Have Blood": Regime Change in *Macbeth*'. *Shakespeare Jahrbuch* 143 (2007): 11–35.

Wilson, Richard. 'The Pilot's Thumb: *Macbeth* and the Martyrs'. In *Secret Shakespeare: Studies in Theatre, Religion, and Resistance*. Manchester: Manchester University Press, 2004.

Wilson, Richard. '"Worthies Away": The Scene Begins to Cloud in Shakespeare's Navarre'. In *Representing France and the French in Early Modern English Drama*. Ed. Jean-Christophe Mayer and Ton Hoenselaars. Newark, DE: University of Delaware Press, 2008: 93–109.

Winston, Jessica. 'Expanding the Political Nation: *Gorboduc* at the Inns of Court and Succession Revisited'. *Early Theatre* 8.1 (2005): 11–34.

Winston, Jessica. '*A Mirror for Magistrates* and Public Political Discourse in Elizabethan England'. *Studies in Philology* 101.4 (2004): 381–400.

Wittgenstein, Ludwig. *Philosophical Investigations*. Trans. G. E. M. Lanscombe. Oxford: Blackwell, 2001.

Wittreich, Joseph Anthony. *Interpreting Samson Agonistes*. Princeton, NJ: Princeton University Press, 1986.

Wittreich, Joseph Anthony. *Shifting Contexts: Reinterpreting Samson Agonistes*. Pittsburgh, PA: Duquesne University Press, 2002.

Wokler, Robert. 'Contextualizing Hegel's Phenomenology of the French Revolution and the Terror'. *Political Theory* 26. 1 (1998): 33–55.

Woloch, Alex. *The One vs. The Many: Minor Characters and the Space of the Protagonist in the Novel*. Princeton, NJ: Princeton University Press, 2003.

Worden, Blair. 'Politics in Catiline: Jonson and His Sources'. In *Re-Presenting Ben Jonson: Text, History, Performance*. Ed. Martin Butler. Basingstoke: Palgrave Macmillan, 1999: 152–73.

Wormald, Jenny. 'Gunpowder, Treason, and Scots'. *Journal of British Studies* 24 (1985): 141–68.

Worthington, Andy. *The Guantanomo Files: The Stories of the 774 Detainees in America's Illegal Prison*. London: Pluto Press, 2007.

Yachnin, Paul and Jessica Slights. Eds. *Shakespeare and Character: Theory, History, Performance and Theatrical Person*. Basingstoke: Palgrave Macmillan, 2009.

Yasmin, Ibrahim. 'Commodifying Terrorism: Body, Surveillance and the Everyday'. *M/C Journal* 10.3 (2007). 15 Oct. 2013: <http://journal.media-culture.org.au/0706/05-ibrahim.php>.

Zagorin, Perez. *Rebels and Rulers, 1500–1660*. 2 Volumes. Cambridge: Cambridge University Press, 1982.

Zamparelli, Thomas L. *The Theater of Claude Billard: A Study in Post-Renaissance Dramatic Esthetics*. New Orleans, LA: Tulane University, 1978.

Zaret, David. *Origins of Democratic Culture: Printing, Petitions, and the Public Sphere in Early-Modern England*. Princeton, NJ: Princeton University Press, 1999.

Zirakzadeh, Cyrus E. *A Rebellious People: Basques, Protests and Politics*. Reno, NV: University of Nevada Press, 1991.

Žižek, Slavoj. *Violence. Six Sideways Reflections*. London: Profile, 2008.

Žižek, Slavoj. *Welcome to the Desert of the Real: Five Essays on 11 September and Related Dates*. London: Verso, 2002.

Zonza, Christian. 'La Tragédie à sujet actuel: *La Mort d'Henry IV* de Claude Billard'. *Revue d'Histoire Littéraire de la France* 100. 6 (2000): 1459–79.

Zulaika, Joseba and William Douglass. *Terror and Taboo: The Follies, Fables, and Faces of Terrorism*. New York: Routledge, 1996.

Zulaika, Joseba and William Douglass. *Basque Violence. Metaphor and Sacrament*. Reno, NV: University of Nevada Press, 2000.

Zulaika, Joseba and William Douglass. *Terrorism: The Self-Fulfilling Prophecy*. Chicago: University of Chicago Press, 2009.

Index

All entries followed by an asterisk (*) are listed in the Chronology, pages 66–70.